HIKING
ROCKY MOUNTAIN
NATIONAL PARK

THE ESSENTIAL GUIDE

Erik Stensland

ROCKY TRAIL
PRESS

HIKING
ROCKY MOUNTAIN
NATIONAL PARK

Erik Stensland

Hiking Rocky Mountain National Park: The Essential Guide (1st Edition, 3rd Printing)

Published by:
Rocky Trail Press
P.O. Box 2843
Estes Park, CO 80517
USA
RockyTrailPress.com
Tel. 970-586-4352

All photos and text by Erik Stensland

Book design by Jerry Dorris, AuthorSupport.com

Edited by Janna Nysewander

Maps by Shawn Wignall

Maps created using: QGIS Geographic Information System, 2018. Open Source Geospatial Foundation Project. http://qgis.osgeo.org

Publisher's Cataloging-in-Publication Data

Names: Stensland, Erik, author.

Title: Hiking Rocky Mountain National Park : the essential guide / Erik Stensland.

Description: Includes index. | Estes Park, CO: Rocky Trail Press, 2019.

Identifiers: LCCN 2018915038 | ISBN 978-0-9969626-8-1

Subjects: LCSH Hiking--Colorado--Rocky Mountain National Park--Guidebooks. | Rocky Mountain National Park (Colo.)--Guidebooks. | Hiking. | Colorado--Rocky Mountain National Park. | BISAC TRAVEL / United States / West / Mountain (AZ, CO, ID, MT, NM, NV, UT, WY) | TRAVEL / Parks & Campgrounds | SPORTS & RECREATION / Hiking

Classification: LCC GV199.42.C62 .S74 2019 | DDC 917.8--dc23

Printed in South Korea with eco-friendly inks and paper from renewable forests.

Disclaimers

Although I have done my very best to offer the most accurate information I can, there may be inaccuracies in this book. With that in mind, you need to always use your own best judgment and hike with care and common sense. It is also possible that some of the information may have changed since this book was published. You can find a list of known changes at: www.HikingRocky.com/updates.

If you come across any errors, please let me know so I can make changes in the next printing. I can be contacted at: corrections@rockytrailpress.com. Be aware that there are many circumstances this book cannot predict, such as sudden changes in weather, a change in trail conditions, difficult people on the trail, or other unexpected circumstances. Be aware of your own limitations and stay within your comfort zone. Also realize that my recommendations are not meant to replace the advice of park rangers, medical professionals, safety and law-enforcement professionals, etc. The author and publisher are not responsible for the dangerous circumstances our readers may encounter or problems they may experience while hiking, including injuries, accidents, inconvenience, loss of life or limb, etc.

Front cover image: Longs Peak towers over the Chasm Lake Trail

CONTENTS

THE HIKES

CONTENTS

Special Sections

ENDORSEMENTS

JIM PICKERING, Rocky Mountain Conservancy–Board President:

"Every generation must write its hiking guides anew. This is particularly true for Rocky Mountain National Park whose well-worn trails to high and special places traverse a fragile ecosystem that is ever-changing. That ecosystem needs our protection and our respect; the kind of good stewardship that is predicated on knowledge and understanding. This is precisely what Erik Stensland has provided in his Hiking Rocky Mountain National Park. In over 500 pages, covering 75 hikes, Erik guides us along trails to much-visited places, destinations made fresh and new with updated topographical maps and trail distances, essential site-specific information, and his own stunning color photographs. Particularly praiseworthy is Stensland's lengthy introductory section, "First Things First," in which he carefully prepares us for our journeys and teaches us how to make them safe and enjoyable ones. He also teaches us something more: how to be responsible caretakers of the national treasure that is Rocky Mountain National Park—to be ever mindful, in the words of the 1916 charter of the National Park Service, of our responsibility to protect what we encounter along the way so as to "leave them unimpaired for the enjoyment of future generations." **The Rocky Mountain Conservancy, which since 1931 has served as the philanthropic steward of Rocky Mountain National Park, recommends Erik Stensland's book. His message is very much our own.**"

VAUGHN BAKER (Rocky Mountain National Park Superintendent 2002-2015):

"Stensland and his team have taken a fresh approach to hiking guides and compiled an easy to use guide for hikers of all levels. In addition, Erik shares the beauty of the park through his stunning photography and photographer's eye. As a former park manager, I appreciate Erik's sensitivity to protecting the park's resources and the emphasis on safety. **The guide is a must for anyone concerned with the stewardship of Rocky Mountain National Park for future generations.**"

LARRY FREDERICK (Chief of Interpretation, Rocky Mountain National Park 2001-2012):

"Erik Stensland's Hiking Rocky Mountain National Park: The Essential Guide is a must to have for the novice or avid hiker. Seventy-five of the most spectacular, official trails are featured with thorough descriptions, updated mileages, routes and maps. Trails are organized into four categories of difficulty: accessible, easy, moderate and strenuous. Each section describes trails from easiest to most challenging allowing readers to quickly select a trail suitable for their interest and hiking ability. The trail descriptions are prefaced by nearly 100 pages of background material, advice, logistics, park regulations, and information on how to get the most out of the guide and your hike. Low impact principles are emphasized which is extremely important as the park experiences increasing visitation. **Don't just think of this as a book of trail descriptions, but also as well-researched treatment on hiking safely, responsibly and respectfully.** An accompanying website—hikingrocky.com—provides additional explanations, guidance, updates and corrections as well as a conduit to the author. Depend on Stensland's book to help you get the most out of your Rocky Mountain National Park hiking adventure."

ACKNOWLEDGMENTS

Creating this book was by no means a solo effort. Dozens of people contributed many hours of their time to assist me in making this book as helpful and accurate as possible. To all of you I say, "Thank you!"

I want to give a special shout-out to my wife, Joanna. She's a gifted editor and always goes through my books. Despite having a very busy schedule she somehow found time to clean up my redundancies and poor wording to make this book more readable. I would be very reluctant to send anything to press before she's gone through it.

This book would most definitely not be what it is without the assistance of Shawn Wignall. After long days at his regular job, he spent many evenings and weekends creating the specialized maps and graphs for the book as well as helping me finalize the book's mileage and elevation.

I would also like to thank my online feedback group. These hikers from various skill levels gave me valuable input on how this book would be received and understood. Those who were regular contributors: Aaron Cooper, Aime Robicheaux, Anna, Marie, Anne Rusk, Ashli Adams, Brenda Toungate, Carol Murin, Gretchen Barclay, Jennifer Frank, John Bowen, John Hall, Anna Marie, Kelly Shaw, Kevin Fruechting, Mark Zemmin, Paige Fulton, Paul Beiser, and Scott Bacon.

Janna Nysewander, my longtime friend and editor, spent a lot of time preparing the final copy and ensuring that everything was perfect.

Last but not least, Jerry Dorris, another longtime friend and owner of AuthorSupport.com, created the attractive design of this book, including both the cover and inside pages.

I would most certainly be lost without these two gifted friends.

To others whom I met on the trail and who let me take their photo or gave me input, I thank you!

THE ROCKY PLEDGE

If you care about Rocky Mountain National Park then I encourage you to take the Rocky Pledge. This pledge was created by Rocky Mountain National Park leadership to help us all be mindful of key behaviors that have a significant impact on the park. By taking this pledge and acting in accordance with it, you are helping to preserve this national treasure for generations to come.

"To preserve unimpaired for this and future generations the beauty, history, and wildness therein, I pledge to protect Rocky Mountain National Park."

- To prevent fire scars and human-caused fires, I pledge to never build a fire outside of a campground or picnic area fire grate.

- To protect plants, meadows, and alpine tundra, I pledge to park and drive only on designated asphalt or gravel parking areas, never on vegetation.

- To respect other visitors' experiences, if I need to go but am not near a restroom, I pledge to leave no trace by stepping well away from the trail and water sources, burying my waste at least six inches deep or packing it out in a waste bag, and carrying out my toilet paper.

- To respect Rocky's wild creatures and to protect myself, I pledge to watch wildlife from a distance that doesn't disturb them in any way. I will never feed an animal—doing so causes it harm.

- To respect history, heritage, and natural processes, I pledge to remove nothing from the park except my own and others' trash—not even a flower, pinecone, or rock. I will leave no trace of my visit so that the next person can experience the same beauty as I did.

- To keep my pet, wildlife, and other visitors safe, I pledge to keep my leashed pet only on roads, in campgrounds, and in picnic and parking areas. I will never take my dog on Rocky's trails, meadows, or tundra areas.

- To preserve them for the enjoyment, education, and inspiration of this and future generations, I pledge to honor, respect, and protect all our national parks and public lands.

Name: _____

Date: _____

Within national parks is room—glorious room—room in which to find ourselves, in which to think and hope, to dream and plan, to rest and resolve.

–ENOS MILLS

PREFACE

I still remember vividly one of my first hikes in Rocky Mountain National Park. I had just moved to the area after years of living overseas and was completely unprepared for exploring the outdoors. One January morning I decided to take a hike up to a place I had heard of called Emerald Lake. A foot of fresh snow covered the trail, but I managed to follow it up to Dream Lake. Beyond Dream the snow was waist-deep with no sign of any trail. I was dressed in jeans, Moon Boots® and an old cloth jacket. I had no idea where the trail was supposed to be, so I just waded up the middle of what I now know was the stream bed. Pillows of snow were piled high on the surrounding rocks, and the trees drooped under the weight. I was exhausted, sweaty, off trail, and soaking wet yet completely captivated by the beauty of it all. The stillness and peace of the wild seemed to embrace me. Though I never made it all the way up to Emerald Lake that day, I was grinning from ear to ear. Everything about this place spoke to my soul that it was good to be here.

Over the following years I began to become much better acquainted with this beautiful national park. Every chance I had I would hike a new trail, just to see what I might find. Then after some years I realized that I had hiked most of the trails in the park, some of them many times over. So I purchased a *National Geographic* topographical map of the park and with a yellow highlighter began to mark off every trail I had hiked. During the next year I made it a priority to finish all the sections of trail I hadn't yet hiked. Since then I've hiked those trails many more times. Each year I cover between 600 and 1,200 miles in Rocky Mountain National Park as part of my job as a landscape photographer. I know almost every turn of every trail and feel as comfortable out there, even in the middle of the night, as I do in my own house. These 400 square miles of wilderness that were originally so foreign to me are now my home.

For me, this park is so much more than my place of work. It is where I become myself and connect with the things that are most important in life. Its high peaks and grassy meadows, its rivers and forests ... they all speak to us of the wonder of wilderness and stir our souls. It is a gift I am delighted to share with you. I hope you fall in love with it just as I have and that you join me in celebrating and caring for this very special place.

BIERSTADT LAKE TRAIL

INTRODUCTION

Welcome to Rocky Mountain National Park, one of America's premier hiking destinations. With over 350 miles of hiking trails winding through deep forests, alongside rushing streams, up to dramatic mountain lakes, across open tundra, and to the top of towering peaks, there is enough here to satisfy almost any hiker of any ability. Whether you want a gentle stroll or to push yourself to your limits, Rocky has it all.

This guide is designed to meet the wide range of hiking interests and abilities, from the ease of a wheelchair-accessible hike to the strenuousness of climbing Rocky's highest peak. It is unique in its format, listing the hikes in order of difficulty beginning with the easiest hike and ending with the hardest hike. This makes it very convenient to match hikes with your ability level.

This book has been written with a strong emphasis on reducing our impact on the wilderness. With the growing visitation to Rocky Mountain National Park, we need to do all we can to ensure that our visit does no harm to this amazing national treasure. Most of the damage done to our natural places is not intentional and can simply be avoided with greater awareness. I've therefore made it a point throughout this book to bring attention to ways we can be more aware of our potential impact.

At the same time, I've written this book to help ensure that you have the safest trip possible. Hiking in the mountains is certainly not without risks and every year there are many who find themselves in situations they had never anticipated. My goal is to keep you from being one of those. One of the ways I've focused on safety is by limiting this book to only official hiking trails. This not only reduces your chances of getting lost in the wilderness but also ensures that you aren't encountering dangerous terrain such as cliff ledges or steep scree slopes. I also bring attention to most of the potential dangers you might encounter on each hike and explain how to avoid them.

As a professional landscape photographer specializing in photographing Rocky Mountain National Park, I've spent the last fifteen years exploring every corner of this incredible place. I've hiked every trail and most of them more times than I can count. When I was asked by the Rocky Mountain Conservancy to create this guide, I decided that I wouldn't rely on my memory, but I would go and hike these trails again. In the last year I've re-hiked every trail in this book. You might have seen me out there with my voice recorder taking notes or with various cameras taking photos and a GPS unit hanging from my pack. As I've written this book I've tried to make sure that the trail descriptions are accurate, easy to follow and also personal, as if I were showing you around myself.

My hope is not only that you will experience great hikes and be introduced to some new territory but also that you will fall in love with this place as I have. I hope you will be moved from being merely an admirer to becoming a supporter and champion of Rocky Mountain National Park and all of our nation's wild places. Lastly, I hope you will reconnect with your deepest self and be reminded of what is truly important in life. This is where the hope for our world lies — deep within each of us.

FERN LAKE TRAIL NEAR BEAR LAKE

INTRODUCTION

TRAILS LISTED BY LOCATION

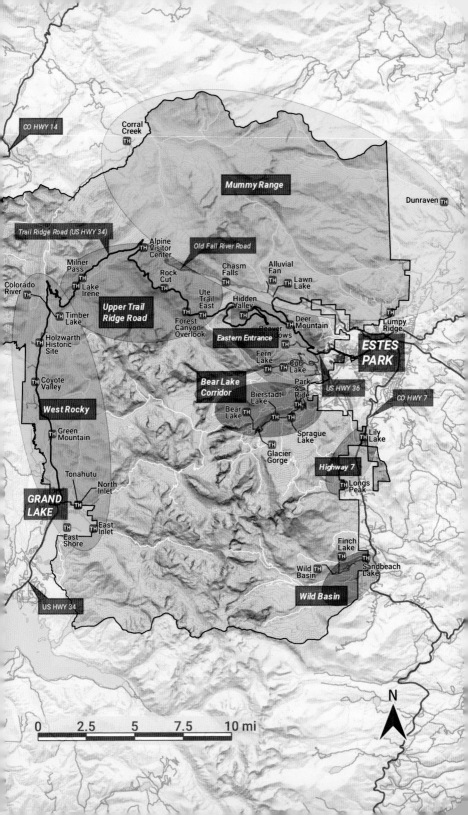

Come to the woods, for here is rest.
There is no repose like that of the green deep woods.
Here grow the wallflower and the violet.
The squirrel will come and sit upon your knee,
the logcock will wake you in the morning.
Sleep in forgetfulness of all ill.
Of all the upness accessible to mortals,
there is no upness comparable to the mountains.

–JOHN MUIR

USING THIS BOOK

APPROACH

I've taken an unconventional approach with this book and have divided the hikes by difficulty level rather than by geographical location. After the introductory pages, the hikes begin with those that are wheelchair accessible (blue), then easy (green), moderately difficult (orange), and then strenuous (red). As well as dividing the book into sections to indicate difficulty, each hike in the book is progressively more difficult. A hike at the beginning of the "Easy" section is much

SPRING IN MORAINE PARK

easier than a hike at the end of the "Easy" section. The same is true of all the other sections. This makes it easy to find the hikes that are most appropriate for your fitness level or for the group you are hiking with. However, if you would like to know which hikes are near you, visit the map on page xx to see what's in your area.

You may notice that there is a bit of page flipping to be done in this guide. The reason for this is to avoid making the book even larger by repeating information numerous times. For instance, if I listed all the trailhead information for Bear Lake with each associated hike, this information would be repeated up to eleven times. Hikes such as Thunder Lake require hiking past other destinations, in this case Calypso Cascades and Ouzel Falls. While you can just use the Thunder Lake information, if you want more details on the first part of the hike, simply flip to the Calypso Cascades hike to read about that section in more detail. If you are not a fan of flipping pages or if you find the weight of this book to be too significant, you can always purchase the Kindle version to keep on your phone or tablet; then it is just a quick click between pages.

A couple other miscellaneous notes: I rarely mention the location of campsites or intersections with campsite trails in this book. The reason for this is I've found that the NPS has moved many of them over the past years and so I didn't feel they were stable enough locations to be included in the book. I've also intentionally not mentioned everything you'll see on each hike, as some of the best things about hiking are the unexpected discoveries along the way. Pay attention as you hike so you don't miss any of those unmentioned gems. Lastly, I've only described these hikes in one direction, from the trailhead to the destination. I therefore recommend that after you pass each intersection, stop and look behind you so you know where to go on your return journey. You can find more information about my approach to creating this guide at www.HikingRocky.com.

TRAIL DISTANCES

The trail's distance listed at the beginning of each hike gives you the total distance from the starting trailhead to the ending trailhead.

TRAIL TO BLUEBIRD LAKE

SUNSET AT BEAR LAKE

This is generally the round-trip distance, except in instances where the hike is one way or is a loop trail.

When I began this project I thought calculating trail distances would be as simple as hiking the trails with my supposedly accurate GPS unit. Little did I know that calculating trail distance with accuracy is almost a fool's errand. When you use a dedicated GPS unit or your phone's internal GPS sensor, the readings can vary greatly. There are many factors that impact the accuracy of GPS, from foliage to atmospheric conditions. Also, civilian GPS varies in accuracy from about 15'–30' (feet) or more. This means that one reading could be 20' to your left and the next reading 20' to your right. When it connects the dots between the two readings, there may be an extra 40' of distance added. Multiply this by the hundreds of readings it may take on a hike and you can see how this might affect the mileage.

One of the most accurate forms of measurement is thought to be a wheel. I heard that a few years ago Rocky Mountain National Park had one of its employees push one of these measuring wheels along the trails. This is a long and laborious job, yet this also has its own accuracy issues. Anytime the wheel goes up over a rock and down the other side, it adds to the mileage, and we all know how many rocks are on the trails. I heard that at one of the national parks there is an actual retired rocket scientist hiking trails with a wheel and making complex calculations for every rock encountered. Who would have guessed that it would take a rocket scientist to accurately measure a hiking trail!

A third option for measuring trails is the use of maps or digital imagery. This avoids some of the other problems, but as I've re-hiked the trails in this park, I've found that nearly every one of these trusted maps have significant errors. Satellite imagery is helpful but often you are not able to see the actual trail and its many turns under the trees. I made numerous notes about inaccuracies in the maps in the hope that these could help correct some of the errors. While there are a couple of other options for creating highly detailed maps and measurements, the expensive equipment and long hours of labor required to do so in this mountainous terrain makes it very unlikely to happen.

In the end, I worked with GIS (geographic information system)

LAKE IRENE

professionals who were able to get their hands on a couple of different data sets showing the tracks of people who have hiked the park with various devices over the years. Finding the middle-point/most-used path between all of the tracks clarified most of the unrecorded trail changes and other inaccuracies. I also contributed my notes so that they could look more closely at those areas. They were able to reach a generally agreed-upon trail map we then used for our final measurements. These figures are not perfect but are as close as we can currently get them. We will continue to improve upon these figures as we are able to do so. Please note that if you see a slight difference between the destination mileage and the round-trip mileage, it is due to rounding the figures to the nearest tenth of a mile.

DIFFICULTY LEVEL

If several of us went on a hike together, each of us would rate the difficulty of that hike differently. For some the distance makes more of a difference; for others it is the elevation that is climbed, the roughness of the trail, or particular segments along the way that increase the sense of difficulty. The subjective nature of ratings can lead to strong differences of opinion. So I thought long and hard about how to create an impartial method for determining the **difficulty level** of each hike. I looked at several different approaches and formulas and even tried creating my own. In the end I decided to use a relatively simple formula created by Shenandoah National Park that uses a combination of elevation gain and mileage to come up with a rating. This is described in detail at: www.HikingRocky.com/ratings.

This formula is far from perfect but I found that it put the majority of hikes in an order that most people would agree wasn't too far removed from their own experience. There were, however, some hikes that clearly didn't work with this formula. For example, hikes that are one way downhill appeared easier than they are. There were also a couple of hikes where poor trail conditions or a very high starting elevation changed the difficulty level. In the end there were several hikes that I decided to manually move to better reflect their actual difficulty level. These are marked with an * next to their rating. These

TRAIL TO LONE PINE LAKE

hikes have two ratings. The first one is mine, and the formula rating is shown in brackets.

I've then divided the hikes into different categories based on their rating. The hikes with a rating of 1–49, that are not wheelchair accessible, are listed in the easy category. Hikes with a rating of 50–179 are in the moderate category, and hikes with a rating above 179 are in the strenuous category.

HIKING TIME

Determining the **hiking time** was another area presenting challenges. The speed people hike varies so widely. As I was writing this book, I had a group of about twenty hikers from all different levels who gave me feedback. Some of them hiked at nearly three miles per hour while others tended to hike at a pace of about one mile per hour, enjoying every flower and view along the way. There are various formulas for calculating hiking time, but I found that none of them really fits for everyone, so in the end I determined that the easiest option would be to simply set an average hiking time geared toward

SHIPLER CABINS   1.8 MI
LULU CITY   3.2 MI
LITTLE YELLOWSTONE   4.0 MI
DITCH CAMP #3   4.8 MI

GRAND DITCH VIA
LaPOUDRE PASS TRAIL   5.8 MI

THUNDER PASS   6.7 MI
LaPOUDRE PASS   7.0 MI

COLORADO RIVER TRAIL

those who probably don't spend much time hiking in the mountains.
After talking with numerous people and trying to find a very gener-
ous but still realistic value, I decided to base the time in this book on
a hiking speed of 1.5 miles per hour.

You may find that you hike much faster or considerably slower
than this. I recommend that you do a hike or two in this book and
figure out how your time compares. You can then create a calculation
to adjust the times for your needs. You may even want to pencil in
your completed times so you have a reference point for your next
visit. Please be aware that the listed times do not take into account
time spent on breaks or taking in the views, so be sure to figure those
into your plans.

TIME TO GO

This hiking guide lists the best time to go on each hike. You will notice
that the vast majority of hikes are listed as "morning." The reason for
this is twofold. The primary one is that strong afternoon storms are
typical during the summer months and it is dangerous to be above
tree line, in an open meadow, or at a lake during these storms. Here
in the mountains there is a lot of electrical activity, and a number
of hikers have been killed by lightning at these places. One of the
best ways to avoid danger is to complete your hike in the morning.
Second, most areas, especially on the east side of Rocky Mountain
National Park, look their very best in the morning, as the light will
illuminate the mountains rather than shine in your eyes.

SEASONS

Not every trail can be hiked year round. The winter snow moves in
starting at the higher elevations and then makes its way lower down
over a period of weeks. In the spring this process is reversed, with
the snow melting more quickly at lower elevations and the higher
elevations melting out weeks later. The suggested season to hike each
trail is based on the average time of year that trail is snow free. Every
year can be a bit different, so if you are near the limit of the suggested
season, ask a ranger about the current trail conditions.

TRAIL TO BIGHORN FLATS

ECOSYSTEMS

One of the best ways to know what to expect on the trail is to understand the three different ecosystems you will find in Rocky Mountain National Park. At the beginning of each hike, I list the primary ecosystem/s you will encounter. Below you will find some helpful information about each of these ecosystems.

Montane

The montane zone of Rocky Mountain National Park is the lowest zone in the park, beginning at about 7,000' and extending up to about 9,000'. This zone starts just below Estes Park and extends up to just below the Glacier Gorge Trailhead.

At the lower levels of this zone you'll find the large meadows where elk, mule deer, and coyotes abound. At their edges, particularly on the south-facing slopes, you'll find widely spaced pondersosa pine forests, as well as mountain juniper, mountain sagebrush, and even mountain ball cactus. On the north-facing slopes you'll find much thicker forests with Douglas fir at the lower elevations and lodgepole pine at the higher elevations. In this zone you'll find golden-mantled ground squirrels, Abert squirrels, bears, turkeys, and many other animals.

Subalpine

The subalpine zone reaches from 9,000' up to about 11,500'. The area beginning just below the Glacier Gorge Trailhead and extending up to tree line is in this zone. Here you'll find some of the most stunning areas with glacier-carved lakes and a transition from forest to rugged mountain. This is the snowiest area of the park that leads to dense forests of subalpine fir and Engelmann spruce. Here the forest floors are generally bare due to the thick trees. At the top end of this zone you'll find a transitional area where the forest gives way to tundra.

In this zone you'll find least chipmunk, pine marten, dusky grouse, snowshoe hare, Steller's jay, and gray jay. At the higher end of this zone you'll begin to find the occasional marmot and pika.

Alpine

The alpine zone begins at around 11,500' and covers the top third of the park. Here the average temperature is not warm enough to support trees. This area above tree line is often referred to as alpine tundra. It experiences below-freezing temperatures, extreme wind, and intense radiation for most of the year, leaving only forty to sixty days of growing time for plants in this harsh environment. The plant life up here is fascinating; many of the plants are miniature versions of plants you'll find elsewhere, and some of them are hundreds of years old. They have found ways to adapt to this harsh environment. Unfortunately, they are not resilient to human footsteps and so need to be treated delicately. In this zone you'll find marmot, pika, ptarmigan, bighorn sheep, and herds of elk.

WILDLIFE

At the beginning of each hike, I've listed possible wildlife that you may see on your hike. There is no guarantee you will see the animals listed or that the ones listed are the only ones you will see. Hiking early in the morning or early evening and hiking quietly will give you the best chance to see animals going about their life in the wild. Also, be sure to pay attention not only to the animals you do see but also the signs that they are present: scat, tracks, bore holes, feathers, wood shavings, scratch and bite marks, etc. When I mention forest animals, these include the following inhabitants who tend to live in the forests of Rocky: snowshoe hare, golden-mantled ground squirrel, least chipmunk, chickaree, porcupine, pine marten, gray jay, Clark's nutcracker, Steller's jay, dusky grouse, woodpecker, and many more.

TRAIL CONDITIONS

Each hike has a mention of trail conditions. Be aware that the average trail in Rocky Mountain National Park lives up to the park's name. You can expect nearly every trail, other than the accessible trails, to have numerous rocks, tree roots, and other ankle-twisting obstacles. On an average trail you may also encounter mud, snow, or fallen trees. Even if I mention that a trail is smoother than normal, you can still expect to find rough areas. The trail-conditions information listed at the beginning of each hike is primarily used to note any deviation from the average trail.

ELEVATION

At the beginning of each hike, I list not only the starting elevation and the highest elevation you'll reach but also the total elevation gain you will experience on your hike. To calculate the total elevation gain, many hiking guides simply take the highest point of the hike and subtract the starting elevation of the hike to obtain their elevation-gain numbers. This actually works quite well for hikes that have a steady incline from start to end but it does not work for

AVERAGE TRAIL - FERN LAKE TRAIL

most hikes, as they tend to both climb and descend on the way to the destination. For most hikes in this book I measured each hill along the way, taking into account the elevation lost and regained on the way to the destination as well as the elevation gained on the return journey. I chose to ignore hills with less than 25' of elevation gain. This approach gives you a more accurate sense of the energy you are likely to expend on the hike. For a more detailed explanation of my approach, visit www.HikingRocky.com/elevation.

Calculating elevations with a GPS unit is unfortunately even less accurate than GPS mileage calculations. So for this guide I've relied on recent computer models of the park, similar to what you might find with Google Earth. GIS (geographic information system) professionals helped me to determine with as much accuracy as possible the elevations listed in this book.

HIKING THE BIG MEADOWS LOOP

ELEVATION PROFILE

If you are new to hiking in the mountains, you may not be familiar with **elevation profile** graphs, which I've listed with each hike. These graphs gives you a visual picture of how much climbing you can anticipate between the trailhead and the destination. It can also give you clues about what else you can expect, such as downhills before you reach the top or longer flat stretches along the way. Knowing what is coming can help you to better pace yourself.

While maps give you a view of your hike from above, an elevation profile gives you a view of your hike from the side. It is like making a cutaway of the earth so that you can see the ups and downs of the trail. The graphs I've included only show the hike to the destination. They don't include the return trip, except on loop hikes. I've chosen not to include graphs for very short hikes.

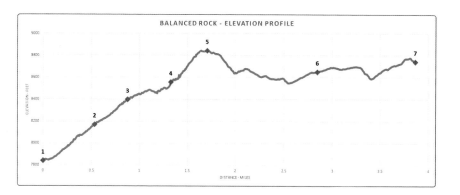

The line shows your hike. The numbers above the line correspond with the waypoints of the hike. When the line goes up or down steeply, this is where the trail goes up or down steeply. The left axis shows the elevation of the trail so you can see how much of an elevation change there is along different sections of the trail. The bottom axis of the graph lists the mileage so you can see how far along the trail each of the climbs or descents are located.

You can learn more about my graphs at: www.HikingRocky.com/graphs.

MAPS

Because of copyright restrictions, I couldn't just use any maps for this book. They had to be custom built and so I had them designed to be as helpful as possible.

These maps are topographical, meaning they accurately show the contours of the terrain. Between each of the dark lines is 200' of elevation gain and 40' between each of the light contour lines. If you are not familiar with topographical maps, visit www.HikingRocky.com/topo for a great explanation video. Once you understand topographical maps, you will almost be able to visualize the landscape before you go.

The maps I use clearly show the forested areas in green and the alpine areas in gray. They also show other trails that you may pass and identify major landmarks in the area, such as the names of lakes, mountains, streams, and glaciers.

These maps are quite reliable, even though there could be minor inaccuracies, but they do have one major limitation. They only show a very narrow area and would be of little help if you ended up off of the covered area. I therefore highly recommend that you buy a detailed topographical map of Rocky Mountain National Park and keep it in your hiking pack along with a manual compass. *National Geographic* makes a really good topographical map and I always keep one in my backpack.

TRAIL COVERAGE

This hiking guide covers a majority of the trails within Rocky Mountain National Park; however, it does not cover every single trail in the park. Some trails were deemed to be unable to support large numbers of hikers due to either the size or location of parking areas, aspects of a trail itself, or a trail heading into sensitive areas from an environmental protection standpoint. There are also some areas where the trails are not officially maintained and so those trails are not included. Other trails were not included, as they were functional but not scenic. All of the trails found in this guide are official trails that will lead you into some of Rocky Mountain National Park's most beautiful locations.

FIRST THINGS FIRST

ABOUT RMNP

Rocky Mountain National Park covers a 415-square-mile section of the lower Rocky Mountains. It was set aside for its natural beauty and abundant wildlife. Established in 1915 it became the United States' eleventh national park. Over the years, it has become one of the most visited of our nation's national parks and with good reason. There is so much packed into this area.

The park begins at an elevation of about 7,650' and climbs up to

TRAIL RIDGE ROAD

the summit of Longs Peak at a towering 14,259'. Within the park you'll find three major ecosystems: the montane, which begins just below the elevation of Estes Park (7,000') and continues up to about the elevation of Lily Lake (9,000'). Here you will find coniferous forests comprised of lodgepole pine, fir, spruce, and ponderosa as well as open meadows, streams, and lakes. From about 9,000' until tree line (about 11,500') is the subalpine zone. In this area you'll find some of the most dramatic terrain in the park, with many lakes lying just below towering peaks. Here the forests are dense, allowing little light to penetrate and limiting growth on the forest floor. At approximately 11,500' you reach tree line, the place where trees are no longer able to grow due to the consistently cold temperatures. This is the beginning of the alpine zone, which covers the park's high country. A full third of Rocky Mountain National Park is located above tree line. If you were to compare the average elevation of all national parks, Rocky would be considered the highest. Much of this alpine zone is tundra, a delicate grassy area void of trees. Most of this tundra is comprised of miniature plants that have learned to adapt in the extremely harsh environment. Within these three zones you'll find sixty peaks over 12,000', nearly 150 lakes, and hundreds of miles of clear water streams.

Rocky Mountain National Park isn't merely a place with stunning scenery, it is also home to many diverse creatures. There are close to sixty different species of mammals that live here and hundreds of species of birds that either live here or pass through. There are also eleven species of fish, nearly three hundred different types of insects, and a number of different reptiles and amphibians. This is a place where they can all live with little disturbance from humans, much as they have for hundreds of thousands of years. As visitors we get to take a little peek into their world.

Rocky Mountain National Park is a hiker's park. There are only a few roads in Rocky. To really see it you have to head out on foot. There are trails to almost every area of the park, allowing you to fully experience all that it has to offer.

History

In the late 1800s our nation began to realize the devastating impacts of unbridled logging, mining, hunting, and ranching on

CHASM LAKE

FISHING AT SPRAGUE LAKE

western lands. As a result the United States government formed the US Forest Service, which oversaw the issuing of permits for business activities on public land. This helped to reduce some of the impact but still made even the most delicate lands available for commercial use. In the little community that would become Estes Park, residents felt the protections didn't go far enough and decided that this beautiful area should be designated a national park to ensure that this fragile and inspirational place would be protected and preserved. At the time, this was a very new concept with only a small number of parks in existence.

Enos Mills, a local guide and lodge owner, was passionate about this idea and spearheaded the movement to create Rocky Mountain National Park. Years were spent battling competing interests such as mining and logging operations, settlers, ranchers, and even the US Forest Service. There were so many who wanted to extract what they could from this place.

The initial proposal for the national park stretched from the Wyoming border in the north down to near where I-70 runs today and from the town of Lyons at the edge of the Great Plains in the east across to the Never Summer Mountains in the west, an area spanning one thousand square miles. After five years of debate the size was considerably reduced and in January of 1915 President Woodrow Wilson signed the 360-square-mile park into law. Since then, the park has slowly grown to 415 square miles through property acquisitions.

Wilderness Act

In 2009 the United States Congress agreed to set aside 94 percent of Rocky Mountain National Park as designated wilderness. This act was the result of a thirty-five-year process. The National Wilderness Preservation System (NWPS), of which most of Rocky is now a part, receives much greater protection than other national lands but also has to adhere to much higher standards. In these lands mining, logging, mechanized vehicles, road building, etc., are not allowed, while noninvasive activities such as hiking, skiing, fishing, climbing, and snowshoeing are permitted. These areas operate under a Leave No Trace policy. The NWPS describes *wilderness* as "an area where the earth and its community of life are untrammeled by man, where man himself is a visitor who does not remain." It is further defined as "an area of undeveloped Federal land retaining its primeval character and influence, without permanent improvements or human habitation, which is protected and managed so as to preserve its natural conditions." The hope is that by treating these areas as true wilderness, the various ecosystems within it will be able to thrive for thousands of years to come with little damage by people.

Because of this status, the park service greatly limits its own activity in the wilderness areas. You will not find park employees driving snowmobiles or ATVs into the backcountry to patrol or conduct rescues. You will not find emergency phones or radios. You will find signage to be at a bare minimum, requiring you to be your own navigator. There are no handrails on steep trails. You will also notice that trail crews are using manual tools to do the backbreaking work of trail repair rather than noisier modern power tools, thereby keeping the forest a peaceful place so that the creatures who live there can flourish. The NPS takes great effort to keep the wilderness truly wild and not to tame it. They understand the value of having lands

LONGS PEAK WASTE REMOVAL SERVICES

where nature can thrive without the hand of humankind. Those who venture into the backcountry need to realize that it is true wilderness with all of the beauty and dangers that come with it.

National Park Service

Rocky Mountain National Park is overseen by the National Park Service (NPS), a branch of the United States Department of the Interior. They are charged with fulfilling a very challenging two-fold mission that pulls them in two opposite directions. The NPS mission is "to preserve unimpaired the natural and cultural resources and values of the National Park System for the enjoyment, education, and inspiration of this and future generations." Preserving the park while providing access is the balancing act they try to walk with every decision they make.

The National Park Service at Rocky Mountain National Park has five important divisions: Administrative, Facility Management (roads, trails, buildings, utilities, etc.), Interpretation and Education, Resource Stewardship (research on biological and cultural resources), and Resource Protection and Visitor Management (law enforcement, medical, rescue, backcountry, etc.). You'll often find rangers from the Interpretation and Education division working at the visitor centers, trailheads, and historic sites. They are tasked with helping us better understand and connect with the natural world. On the trails, you might run into rangers working with the Wilderness Office, part of the Resource Protection and Visitor Management division. They are often out there checking up on wilderness campsites, but I've found that they are more than happy to help you in any way they can. If you are driving too fast through the park or smuggling out elk antlers, you might get to know the law enforcement rangers, also part of the Resource Protection and Visitor Management division.

Those who work for the National Park Service are passionate about preserving our wild lands. They have had to jump through a lot of hoops and meet a host of requirements to become a full-time park employee. Most of those who serve with the park service have advanced degrees and have given years of volunteer service within the NPS before being hirable. They are asked to do more and more each year as visitation grows, but with fewer and fewer resources. It often looks like a very thankless and stressful job, but I'm sure they find satisfaction in knowing that their work is helping to preserve one of our most precious resources. I've heard it said that the word *ranger* comes from medieval England and originally meant "keeper of the royal lands." I imagine that this is how most park rangers view their role.

Roads and Trailheads

Rocky Mountain National Park only has a few roads running through its 415-square-mile territory. Two of these roads—Trail Ridge Road and Old Fall River Road—lead up into the alpine tundra, providing connection between the east and west sides of the park. These roads close with the first snow, which often arrives at some point in October, and remain closed through the winter, as it is impossible to keep them clear with the strong winds and blowing snow that is encountered at those elevations. Trail Ridge Road usually opens up around the end of May or sometimes early June. It is entirely weather dependent and so you are never sure when the road will open until it actually does. Old Fall River Road, the second road up to the alpine

BEAVER MEADOWS ENTRANCE

tundra, usually doesn't open until around the beginning of July. You
need to be very aware of these road closures, as travel between the east
and west side of the park, when both roads are closed, requires a long
3½-hour drive around via I-70 and Winter Park.

Over the last years we've seen a significant increase in visitation to
Rocky Mountain National Park. This means that the roads are much
busier, thereby increasing travel time. Also, the trailheads are filling up
earlier and earlier each day. It is not uncommon to find the Glacier
Gorge parking lot filled by 6 a.m. on a summer morning or the Bear
Lake parking lot filled by 7:30 a.m. or earlier. Other trailheads are
similar. Once you get to the busy period of 9 a.m. to about 3 p.m. all the
trailheads are usually filled and the roads in Rocky Mountain National
Park can be packed with bumper-to-bumper traffic. Once the Park &
Ride has been filled, additional traffic is turned away at Moraine Park.

Fortunately, the park operates a free shuttle service. While the
shuttle can't get you everywhere in the park, it can provide you with
access to the Bear Lake corridor, which is usually the busiest place
in the park. You can catch the shuttle from the Estes Park Visitor
Center in town; pick up maps and route times at the Estes Park
Visitor Center or at any of the national park visitor centers.

As an additional note, when driving through the national park,
please be aware that you should not stop in the middle of the road
and block traffic. If you see an animal or a view that you want to
enjoy, find the next designated pull-over and then walk back rather
than stopping in the road itself. Other visitors are trying to get from
one place to another and Trail Ridge Road is an actual state highway.
Imagine how you would feel at home if someone stopped in the
middle of the highway to admire the view.

Regulations

When you enter Rocky Mountain National Park you need to
remember that you are now on federal land and so federal regulations apply rather than Colorado laws. Even something as simple as
speeding is a federal offense. Rocky Mountain National Park, like all
national parks, has its own set of rules and regulations. You can find
a full list at the visitor centers, but in this section I'll highlight just a
few of them.

DOGS

Over 60 percent of families in the United States have dogs. For many families, dogs are not only wonderful companions, they are part of the family. They participate in much of our lives and if we are good to them, we take them out into the natural world for regular walks. So it can come as something of a shock to visit a place where you'll spend your time walking in the beauty of nature and yet are not allowed to take your dog with you—something you know they would absolutely love. Many find the park's restrictions on dogs to be either inconvenient or incomprehensible. So I want to take a minute to help you understand why these restrictions are in place.

It is important to remember that Rocky is a wilderness area where coyotes, mountains lions, bobcats, great horned owls, and other creatures live. Any of these could view your pet as prey. On the other side of this coin, dogs are predators. Though domesticated, they still have the instinct to chase and bark at other animals whether they are rabbits, deer, squirrels, etc. The park is meant to be a place where these animals can live at peace without disruption from the outside. Dogs also leave behind a "predator" scent that can linger, disrupting the native animals that this park protects.

The poop from domesticated dogs can transmit diseases to

Camping

Camping is only allowed in designated sites in Rocky Mountain National Park. There are five drive-in campgrounds that take reservations up to six months in advance at www.recreation.gov. There are also about 267 wilderness campsites. These are only reached by hiking and are all located more than a mile from the trailhead. All wilderness campsites require a permit from the Wilderness Office. These can be obtained online at www.nps.gov/romo/planyourvisit/wilderness-camping.htm or in person. Be warned that these wilderness sites normally book up months in advance. The park begins issuing permits on March 1 every year. (See page 70 for more details about wilderness camping.)

which wild animals are susceptible. Dogs do not eat food from this ecosystem and so they are leaving non-native bacteria and parasites. Just one gram of poop can contain twenty-three million bacteria and numerous parasites. If even some of the nearly five million visitors brought dogs onto the park trails the uncollected waste would be significant. It would get into the water systems and spread to park wildlife. If you have time I recommend an interesting article about the impact of dog waste on the environment: www.HikingRocky.com/dogs.

There is also a concern that some pets may dig or trample fragile vegetation. They might scare some who are uncomfortable with dogs and they might disturb the peace with their barking, joyful though it might be. The park has been set aside as somewhere we can see nature in its most natural and undisturbed state. Following the regulations helps to keep it that way.

Service animals that have been individually trained to perform specific tasks for the benefit of persons with disabilities are allowed in the park. Emotional support/therapy animals are not service animals under the Americans with Disabilities Act and so are not allowed on park trails.

If you have your dog with you on vacation, there are a number of trails you can take them on just outside of the national park.

Collection

It is illegal to take away any natural features including pinecones, antlers, rocks, and artifacts or to disturb soil, rocks, or vegetation (including flowers). Metal detector use is prohibited.

Dogs, Cats, and Other Pets

Rocky Mountain National Park is a designated natural area where wildlife is free to roam undisturbed. Park visitors should be able to enjoy native wildlife in their natural environment without the disruption or influence of domesticated animals. Pets may accompany you in developed areas such as campgrounds, parking areas, and picnic sites but are not permitted on trails or away from

DOG TRAILS

As dogs are not allowed on national park trails, here is a list of alternatives.

Walks Within the National Park

You are allowed to walk your dog in picnic areas, campgrounds, and on park roads. During the shoulder season—the time just before or just after peak periods—some of the roads in Rocky Mountain National Park are closed to vehicles but open to pets on leash. Check with a ranger at one of the visitor centers to find out if you are visiting during such a time.

Walks Outside the National Park

The following are suggested dog walks outside but not far from Rocky Mountain National Park:

EAST OF ROCKY MOUNTAIN NATIONAL PARK				
TRAIL	TRAILHEAD LOCATION	DISTANCE ONE-WAY (OR LOOP)	DESCRIPTION	DOG ETIQUETTE
Buchanan Pass Trail	West end of Camp Dick Campground, turnoff at Peaceful Valley, 24 miles south of Estes Park	Red Deer Lake 6.9 miles Buchanan Pass 9.1 miles	Trail parallels north side of the middle St. Vrain Creek. Many trail intersections.	Dogs must be on leash no longer than 6 feet.
Crosier Mountain	3 trailheads near Glen Haven	3.9 miles from trailhead in downtown Glen Haven	Panoramic views from the summit.	Dogs can be off leash, but leashes recommended due to wildlife.
Hermit Park	6 miles east of Estes Park on Hwy 36	2.5 miles of existing trail	Great views. Fee required.	Dogs must be on leash no longer than 6 feet.
Indian Peaks Wilderness	Brainard Lake, 30 miles south of Estes Park	Various, including Lake Isabelle (2 miles), Blue Lake (2.5 miles), Mt. Audubon (3.75 miles)	Many spectacular lakes and peaks are accessed from this beautiful area. Fee required.	Dogs must be on leash no longer than 6 feet in wilderness area.
Lake Estes Trail / Dog Park	Trail has several starting points around the lake	3.75 miles	Hard-surfaced trail encircles Lake Estes. Dog park on Community Drive by the lake.	Dogs must be on leash on the trail.

EAST OF ROCKY MOUNTAIN NATIONAL PARK

TRAIL	TRAILHEAD LOCATION	DISTANCE ONE-WAY (OR LOOP)	DESCRIPTION	DOG ETIQUETTE
Lily Mountain	Trailhead parking along Hwy 7, 6 miles south of Estes Park. This trail is not accessible from Lily Lake.	1.9 miles	Panoramic views from summit. Elevation gain is 1,006'.	Dogs may be off leash but must be under voice control and not harass wildlife or hikers.
Lion Gulch / Homestead Meadows	8 miles east of Estes Park on Hwy 36	3.4 miles	Trail accesses a historic area where eight homesteads were established 1889–1923	Dogs may be off leash but must be under voice control and not harass wildlife or hikers.

WEST OF ROCKY MOUNTAIN NATIONAL PARK

TRAIL	TRAILHEAD LOCATION	DISTANCE ONE-WAY (OR LOOP)	DESCRIPTION	DOG ETIQUETTE
Cascade Mountain, Bowen Pass, Bowen Lake Loop	US Hwy 34 to County Rd 4. Take County Rd 4 for 3 miles. Turn right at fork/FSR 120 to the North Supply Trailhead.	15-mile loop. Bowen Lake is 4 miles one way from trailhead.	Trail begins as ATV-accessible road. Several small stream crossings. Great views.	Dogs must be on leash no longer than 6 feet in wilderness area.
Grand Lake Recreation District's Colorado River Trail by the Grand Lake Golf Course/Nordic Center	US Hwy 34 to County Rd 48/ Golf Course Rd (just north of Grand Lake). Turn west and go 1 mile to parking on left at trailhead.	The Colorado River Trail (summer) is 5.2 miles round trip plus some smaller connecting trails. Winter's Way dog trail (winter) is 5.5 mi/4 km.	Summer scenic picnic area and loop by Colorado River at the end of the trail. Winter's Way dog trails are easy trails.	Dogs may be under voice control if they play well with others. In winter, dogs must stay on designated dog trails. There is a lot of wildlife in the area, including moose.
Indian Peaks Wilderness	US Hwy 34 to County Rd 6/ Forest Service Road 125/ Arapaho Bay Road. Follow this road for 10 miles east to the Monarch Lake parking area.	Access beautiful lakes and peaks, including the Monarch Lake Loop Trail (4 miles), Crater Lake (7.25 miles).	Easy loop around Monarch Lake is popular year round. The jagged and spectacular Indian Peaks predominate. Fee required.	Dogs must be on leash no longer than 6 feet in wilderness area.

This list comes directly from the Rocky Mountain National Park website:
https://www.nps.gov/romo/planyourvisit/pets.htm

roads or parking areas. Where permitted, pets must be under physical control at all times—caged, crated, or restrained by leash no longer than six feet.

It is prohibited to leave a pet unattended and tied to an object. It is also illegal to leave pets in a situation where food, water, shade, ventilation, and other basic needs are inadequate. So while it is possible for pets to remain in your vehicle while you are viewing attractions near roads and parking areas, it is strongly recommended that a party member remain behind to personally ensure your pet's well-being. (See page 28 for more details about dogs in the national park.)

Drones

Drones or any other unmanned aircraft are prohibited from use in national parks.

Firearms and Weapons

It is the responsibility of visitors to understand and comply with all applicable state, local, and federal firearm laws before entering the park. Open carry of handguns and rifles, and transport of the same in vehicles, is permitted. Concealed carry is allowed pursuant to a legal Colorado Concealed Handgun Permit and applicable state reciprocity laws. Federal law prohibits firearms in certain facilities (visitor centers, ranger stations, government offices), places that are marked with signs at all public entrances. Recreational target shooting or discharge of a firearm is not allowed. Firearms should not be considered a wildlife protection strategy. Bear spray and other safety precautions are the proven methods for preventing bear and other wildlife interactions. Possessing or carrying a weapon (bow and arrow, crossbow, slingshot, gas- or air-propelled gun, etc.) is prohibited. There are additional regulations on firearms. Stop by a visitor center and ask for the Gun Regulations brochure.

Fires

Fires are only allowed at a few designated campsites and picnic areas with provided metal rings. Very few of the wilderness camping sites allow fires. Ask the Wilderness Office for details.

Fishing

A valid Colorado fishing license is required for all persons 16 years of age or older to fish in Rocky Mountain National Park. Persons 12 years old or younger may use bait in waters open to fishing, except in designated catch-and-release areas. No other permit is necessary; however, special regulations exist. It is your responsibility to know and obey them. Pick up a brochure at any Rocky Mountain National Park visitor center for details.

Marijuana

Although the use of recreational marijuana is legal in the state of Colorado, it is not legal within Rocky Mountain National Park. If you have any, dispose of it before you visit, since both use and possession are a federal offense in the park.

Protection of Resources

Injuring, defacing, removing, digging, destroying, possessing, or disturbing natural or cultural resources or features of the park is prohibited. Leave undisturbed for others to enjoy.

Wildlife

The park has a large population of free-roaming wild animals, some of which are unpredictable and potentially dangerous. Wildlife viewing is encouraged but please do so from a safe distance. Approaching within twenty-five yards of any wild animal, including nesting birds, or within any distance that disturbs or interferes with their free movement or natural behavior is prohibited.

Contact Information

Phone Numbers:

- Visitor Information: 970-586-1206, daily 8 a.m. to 4:30 p.m. Mountain Time, recorded information after hours
- Trail Ridge Road Information: 970-586-1222, recorded information available 24 hours a day
- Phone Line for the Hearing Impaired (TTY): 970-586-1319, daily 8 a.m. to 5 p.m. Mountain Time
- Wilderness Office: 970-586-1242

- Lost & Found: 970-586-1242
- Campground Reservations: 877-444-6777

In an Emergency

- Contact the park's dispatch center at 970-586-1203

While you can call 911 it will connect you with emergency services outside the park, so it is best to first try the dispatch number above. Put this number in your phone before heading out on a hike.

Mail:

Rocky Mountain National Park
1000 Highway 36
Estes Park, CO 80517-8397

Website:

- www.nps.gov/romo

Social Networks:

- Facebook.com/RockyNPS
- Instagram.com/rockynps
- Twitter.com/RockyNPS

LOGISTICS

Travel & Transport

Rocky Mountain National Park is located seventy miles northwest of Denver, Colorado, and about an hour-and-a-half drive from Denver International Airport. If you fly in to Denver, I recommend renting a car from the airport, as there are very few car-rental options near the national park. Although there are shuttle buses that run between June and September, their service is limited to only a few trailheads. Details of the shuttle-bus system are on 86.

Lodging

Rocky Mountain National Park is bordered by two towns: Estes Park at the east entrance and Grand Lake at the west entrance. Both

of these can serve as a great base for your visit but each provides 35
access to a different set of trails. For this reason you might find it helpful to choose your trails before you choose where you want to stay. The Grand Lake side is generally quieter but the Estes Park side provides access to some of the more dramatic hikes. Either way you can't go wrong.

Both Estes Park and Grand Lake offer a wide variety of accommodation options, from beautiful hotels and lodges, to vacation rentals by owner (VRBO, Airbnb, etc.), as well as a number of campgrounds. These can all be quickly found through online searches.

If you want to stay inside the national park there are five drive-in campgrounds: Aspenglen, Longs Peak, Glacier Basin, Moraine Park, and Timber Creek. There are no hookups or electrical outlets at any of these campsites nor are there shower facilities. You'll need to go into Estes Park or Grand Lake for showers. Three of the national park campsites can be reserved well in advance and two of them operate on a first-come, first-served basis. You can find more details at: www.HikingRocky.com/camping.

Alternatively, there is the option to wilderness camp in Rocky Mountain National Park. Wilderness campsites are those you need to hike in to. They are all at least one mile from the trailhead. There are 267 wilderness campsites and most are reserved months in advance. You can find out more information about wilderness camping in the park on page 70.

Food

There is a large variety of restaurants, in Estes Park ranging from fast food to fine dining. If you stop in at the Estes Park Visitor Center they have menus on hand for most of the restaurants. Alternatively you could use a service like TripAdvisor to find the one that is right for you. For bag lunches to take on the trail, try Scratch Deli & Bakery or the Country Market & Deli, which is just across the street. There is also a deli at the local Safeway grocery store.

In Grand Lake there is also a variety of restaurants, with some great BBQ and burger places. Try Cy's Deli for lunch to take on the trail.

Timing

The main hiking season in Rocky Mountain National Park is from mid-June through mid-October. If you come earlier you are likely to encounter higher elevation trails buried in snow. If you come after this time, you are likely to be dealing with strong icy-cold winds and the arrival of the winter snow. During the main hiking season you can expect the park to be quite busy and exceptionally busy during the weekends. Early September until early October is the busiest time of all with large crowds coming to experience the wonderful autumn colors and the elk's annual rut. This is probably the best time to hike as well since there are rarely thunderstorms and most of the crowds are watching elk down in the lower meadows. However, finding accommodation in the towns or parking at the trailheads can be difficult.

Around the middle of August, as families return home to get their kids back to school, there is often a slightly slower period of about two weeks. Alternatively, you can avoid some of the crowds by coming between the end of May and early June, but plan on hiking at lower elevations.

HIKING IN ROCKY

What to Expect

Rocky Mountain National Park has about 350 miles of hiking trails, enough to keep you busy for a very long time. These many trails provide access into nearly every area of the park. They allow us to enter the wilderness with relative ease. Some of these trails will challenge us and some are great for dipping our toes in the water, with trails for every level of hiker from toddlers to backpackers.

One of the things you'll soon notice about Rocky is that the vast majority of trails climb upward from the trailhead, sometimes quite steeply. Generally you'll reach the highest point of your hike near your destination. The outbound hikes are largely uphill and the return to the trailhead is mostly downhill. This, however, doesn't necessarily mean that the return will be easy. On the way up, your lungs will work especially hard and on the way down, your feet and

TRAIL TO YPSILON LAKE NEAR WAYPOINT #5

TRAIL TO TIMBER LAKE

knees may feel the strain. It's therefore wise to take a slow-and-steady approach on your way up and have hiking poles to reduce impact on the way down.

The trails in Rocky Mountain National Park quickly lead you into official wilderness areas. This means that once you leave the trailhead, you are in a part of the park that will remain undeveloped. There are no toilets, no water stations, and no civilization after you leave the trailhead, so be sure to use the toilet before you leave the trailhead. Also, these trails are not paved, do not have handrails, benches, or any other amenity. Sorry, there are no cafés at the top, such as you might find in Europe. You must bring everything you need with you.

Although the trail crews work long, hard hours to maintain the trails, you can expect most of the trails to be quite rocky and uneven. Even if the crews were to clear a trail of rocks, the freezing earth pushes more to the surface each year, making it an impossible task to keep the trails smooth. So it is best to mentally prepare for a rough trail. Wearing boots with ankle support and using hiking poles can really help.

Most of the trails in this book will lead you to a destination. A majority of them lead to gorgeous lakes below towering peaks. Some will lead you up into the tundra to the top of a mountain, and there are a few that will lead you out to a beautiful meadow or simply through deep forest. The lakes and summit hikes tend to be the busiest, so if you're looking for a bit of solitude choose a trail that leads to a meadow or one that wanders through the forest.

Truly Experiencing the Park

In these introductory pages I talk about many things that you need to know about Rocky Mountain National Park to help make your time here safe and enjoyable, but in my opinion the following information is the most important of all. We tend to arrive on our vacation not only with full backpacks but full heads and heavy hearts as well. We come with a lot of baggage, demands from work and life that seem to follow us here. Some people try to continue to run their business or to handle a host of problems back home via phone and email. The truth is that these types of problems will be there next week, next month, and next year no matter how much time we put in on vacation trying to fix them. For the well-being of our soul, our mind, our emotions, and our families we need to consciously take time to set these things down and let ourselves be restored. Only then will we be in a healthier state and able to rightly judge and handle the incessant demands when we get back home.

So I would encourage you to leave your baggage behind. Let the office and others back home know that you will be turning off for a few days or even a week. They'll survive without you. Switch your phone off and pack it away, put an Away or Out of Office message on your email, unplug from social networks, and be fully present in this magnificent and healing wilderness.

As you hike out into the mountains practice paying attention with all your senses. Watch the dappled light touch the forest floor. Listen to the sound of the birds and try to guess what they are saying. Feel the gentle breeze on your face, on your neck, and on your arms. Smell the wafting aromas from the drying ponderosa needles. Touch its rugged bark. As you allow yourself to be immersed in the wonder of the wilderness, you will find your racing mind begin to slow down, your cares will begin to slip away, and you will begin to feel a sense of growing wholeness. We are part of the natural world and yet our society is so divorced from it. As we return to the wilderness, we start to reconnect with nature and with ourselves.

If you do this, you may discover that when you go back home, you go with a greater understanding of what's important. You may find that you've slowed down and developed a new way of looking at the world. You'll look back on this time away as one of the most meaningful of your entire life just by being fully present in nature.

Hiking With Kids

One of the best ways we can help guarantee the protection of our wild lands is to give our children and grandchildren the opportunity to fall in love with it. Exposing children to the wilderness at a very young age is one of the best ways we can instill this love in them. However, we all know that hiking with kids can either be a magical experience or a nightmare. So in this section I want to highlight some tips for parents that can help make your time with children in the natural world the best it can be.

The most important thing is to begin with realistic expectations.

LEARNING ABOUT WILDFLOWERS

As adults we tend to be goal oriented, small children are generally not that way at all. When I started hiking with my son, there were so many places I wanted to take him and things I wanted to show him, but before we even reached the trailhead he would find things that he wanted to investigate. A hike around Bear Lake was unrealistic during his younger years, not because he lacked the strength, but because he had different goals. If you are going to have a successful hike with young children, you have to set aside your goals and allow them to go at their own pace even if you never get anywhere near your destination. Let them play, explore, splash in puddles, and get dirty. If you allow yourself to let go you might even catch some of the wonder in the small things they see.

As your children get a little older, involve them in the planning process but ensure that the distances, elevation gain, and overall time you plan to spend is very conservative. You want to be sure that they get back to the trailhead before they stop enjoying it. Remember that any destination is only halfway. Some parents suggest balancing structured and unstructured times. You might balance out a bit of hiking with a bit of time for climbing rocks, exploring the forest floor, or looking at plants. Kids can get bored much more easily than adults and so need to be able to do something besides walking.

CALYPSO CASCADES TRAIL

While you are out there teach them about nature and about how they can care for it—by words and even more importantly by example. Help them understand why they can't take things from the park or pick the flowers. Help them understand the impact if the millions of visitors to Rocky each took a flower, a rock, or a pinecone. Teach them the names of the things you see and explain the signs you come across. Help them notice the little things they might not have seen and get excited about the things they point out.

Rocky Mountain National Park has a great Junior Ranger Program. This program is designed to help kids engage with nature. They have workbooks for different age groups and combine education with games like scavenger hunts and activities to be completed. These are great ways to help children understand and appreciate what they are seeing. It also gives them some activities to work on while they hike. With completion of a workbook, they can go to a visitor center and be sworn in as official Junior Rangers and receive a badge that they can proudly wear.

A few other practical things to note: Always bring more water than you need, especially when hiking with kids. Ensure that you have appropriate snacks in your bag for them as well as a change of clothes, as you never know when it will be needed. Remember to haul out all diapers and anything else you brought in with you. Did you know that it takes over four hundred years for a diaper to decompose? Keep children well away from fast-running streams and cliff edges. Don't let children run out of sight or lag behind, as they may be prey for lions—seriously! Be sure to put all electronics away when you leave the car, as they only distract from the experience. Create traditions such as visiting the same places each year, having your photo taken in the same spot, and celebrating a hike with an ice cream cone. Foster curiosity and help them to love nature as you do.

Hiking With Groups

Hiking with a group of friends or family is a special experience and is often something that will be talked about for years to come. Those shared experiences can sometimes be more meaningful and memorable than the ones we have by ourselves.

However, when hiking with others it can be easy to miss some

TRAIL TO CHASM LAKE

of the small things that are happening all around you. It's easy to get caught up in a discussion with Aunt Wilma and miss the pine marten that is watching you from just off the trail. You can miss the wafting smells of small flowers and the quiet sounds of the forest. Those conversations can also easily grow in volume without us realizing it's disturbing wildlife and other visitors. Just pay attention and talk with quiet voices. You could occasionally plan twenty minutes to hike in silence and then share your experiences of what you saw, heard, and smelled at the end of that time. It would make for a very special hike for everyone.

When you hike as a group it can be tempting to walk side by side even when the trail is fairly narrow. This can result in someone either walking off of the trail or on the edge of the trail. This kills the vegetation and causes an ever-widening trail. It is important to walk in the middle of the trails so that they don't continue to spread.

You also need to be extra aware of others when you hike as a group. It can be easy to get caught in conversation and not realize that your group is blocking the trail for others behind you. Just stay aware and be considerate and everyone will have a great time.

Over the years the opportunities for wheelchair users in Rocky Mountain National Park has slowly grown. The visitor centers and many of the restroom areas throughout the park have been made accessible. There are also accessible picnic tables located throughout the park, and the shuttle system has been converted to accessible use. Camping is now easier with four drive-in campsites designated "accessible."

There are a number of places in the park where it's possible to enjoy the wonder of nature with a wheelchair. The very first section of hikes in this book highlights the accessible trails. There is also an accessible wilderness campsite at the far end of Sprague Lake, which can be reserved at the Wilderness Office.

Under the Americans with Disabilities Act, wheelchairs are permitted on all trails (anywhere foot travel is allowed), including Wilderness, if the device is designed solely for use by a person who has mobility impairment for their locomotion, and is suitable for use in an indoor pedestrian area. This includes "mechanized" wheelchairs; e.g. battery powered, as long as it is suitable for indoor use (gasoline powered would not be suitable for indoor use).

LEAVE NO TRACE

Every year millions of people come to Rocky Mountain National Park to enjoy its incredible views and abundant wildlife. It is an escape from the world of people, a chance to experience something of relatively untouched nature. In some ways it is like a trip back in time, enabling us to glimpse something of the wilderness as it was before European settlers arrived. Here in Rocky, nature is preserved and cherished and yet it can only stay that way if we all treat it with great care and respect.

For over a hundred years people have been visiting Rocky Mountain National Park and the number of visitors has been growing. Today that number is nearing five million visitors a year. With a crowd of this size even the smallest actions can have huge implications. Over the last decade we've seen increasing damage done to the park as a result of this swelling visitation. Most of this damage isn't a result of willful destruction but it is due to a simple lack of knowledge or forethought. So in this section I want to highlight a few areas of concern that we as hikers need to be aware of if we want to preserve this place for future generations.

Mindset

The first thing we all need is a change of mindset. It was once explained to me that it's like going to our grandparents' house when we were young. We knew that the rules were different and so our manners had to be different. Rocky Mountain National Park is much the same. It is a privilege to be here but there are responsibilities that come with that privilege. Just like at our grandparents' house, we need to show good manners. Rocky Mountain National Park is sacred ground but it can only stay that way as long as we do our part.

When I find people doing something they shouldn't in the national park, most of the time they have the attitude that they are just one person and not causing any real damage. What they don't realize is that tomorrow another person will probably do the same thing, and the day after, and the day after that. No one person can see their own impact; it is only by stepping back to see it as a whole that we can perceive it. To help overcome this we all must learn to view our actions as part of the whole and not as an isolated event. As one of my close friends likes to say, "How many snowflakes does it take to cause an avalanche? Just one more."

Trash

The first and most obvious area where we need to take care is with our trash. Whatever we bring into the wilderness we must take out, every little scrap of it. Most of the trash you may find on the trail was accidently dropped or left. One of the biggest ways we can avoid contributing to this is to pay attention when getting up from a snack break. Take a look all around to see if there is anything you missed. Be sure to pick up the micro-trash, even tiny bits of food that may attract wildlife. Be sure that there is nothing left before you leave. The other time to be especially aware is when you reach into a pocket on the trail; this is often when things find their way out, especially tissues and wrappers. By using a designated garbage bag you can help stop this from

LITTER AT LAKE NOKONI

happening. You can then also use this same bag to collect any trash you find on the trail. If we all do this, it will make a big difference. I actually bring a pair of rubber gloves with me to pick up the worst trash.

Many people think that banana peels, apple cores, orange peels, sunflower seed shells, etc., are an exception to the rule of Leave No Trace. They are not. These should be packed out as well. They take a lot longer to deteriorate than you might expect. For example, a simple **banana peel can take up to two years to biodegrade** in the mountains. Such "natural waste" is not only an eyesore for other visitors but it can actually make the wildlife ill, as their bodies are not able to process it. Be respectful and take everything out with you.

Trail Care

Over the last years the increased traffic on the trails has begun to show. Some trails that were once just one or two feet wide are today over five to eight feet wide and I can only imagine how much wider they could become in future years. The best way to avoid this is to hike in the center of the trail even when it becomes wet or muddy. The temptation is to walk around the mud but it only makes the trail wider. Hopefully you are wearing waterproof hiking boots and so should not have a problem walking through a bit of mud. If it is too deep, look for rocks you can stand on rather than on any vegetation. Experienced hikers see muddy boots as a status symbol much like mud on a 4-wheel-drive vehicle.

One of the temptations when hiking down a mountain trail is to bypass a switchback by taking a shortcut down to the trail below. While this is certainly tempting, when you walk down that steep slope your feet are pulling up some of the grass and other vegetation that is holding the hillside. This then opens the hillside to erosion and with the next rain, loose dirt will come down the hill, slowly creating a new gully. As more people do this, over time it may lead to even washing away the trail below. While it may be tempting to short-cut, resist the temptation and stay on the trail.

Another growing problem in Rocky Mountain National Park is the creation of what are called "social trails." Individuals are creating these new trails that may or may not go anywhere at all. They can create confusion for other visitors and damage the surrounding environment. It only takes ten passes to create a new trail. That's just five people going out and coming back again. Be mindful to stay on the official trail and do not follow these developing social trails. They most likely only lead to a place where someone went to relieve themselves, but unfortunately enough people followed it, so a path was created. Don't be a lemming.

We also need to resist the urge to mark trails. In the winter, I often come across pink and green plastic ribbons tied to trees to help mark the way to a great spot for skiing or to help show the location of a snow-covered trail. These pollute the environment and take away from our experience of true wilderness. In the summer, people often try to help other hikers by building cairns. These are rock piles meant to guide the way. This also disturbs the environment and often where people are building them you'll find numerous ones, each built by different people who assume that their route is the best one. This leads to confusion. Building cairns is not allowed in the national park, so resist the urge.

Let It Be

Lastly—and it pains me that this even has to be mentioned—carving your name into a tree may sound like a cool thing to do but it certainly isn't. It not only damages the tree and makes it more difficult for it to get nutrients but also creates the feeling of being in the inner city marked by graffiti rather than in pristine wilderness. The same goes for scratching messages or pictures on rocks. Just don't do it!

CARVED TREE NEAR BEAR LAKE

Along a similar vein, please don't pick the flowers or damage any of the other plants, including tree branches. Let them grow and flourish. Remember that by picking a flower, you are often removing the seeds for future generations. Leave them for their own well-being and for the enjoyment of all who come after you. We want to leave the wilderness wild.

In the same spirit, give way to the animals who inhabit the park. This is their home. You are the visitor. Try not to disturb them. If you notice them changing their behavior, then you are too close. Allow them to go about life as if you were never there. Enjoy getting a glimpse into their lives from a respectful distance.

Stewards of Nature

As you spend time hiking Rocky Mountain National Park, be sure to pay attention to just how delicate this place is. Pay attention to the ways in which the world of people encroaches on the wilderness and the impact that we as humans have on the land and its natural inhabitants. Then expand your view outward to Colorado's Front Range with its rapidly growing population and the pressure this is putting on the surrounding areas of wilderness. Now think about how this is happening across our country and across this world. The ever-increasing impact of humanity is a huge threat to the natural world. Ecosystems continue to crumble; species are becoming extinct; pollution, mining, drilling, urbanization, and simple lack of regard continue to destroy some of our most precious natural places. At times it can feel almost hopeless.

Yet there are things that we can do to help preserve what is left of our wild places. We can pay attention to what is happening and act as caretakers of the wild lands near us. We can hold our politicians accountable to act on behalf of the wilderness rather than on behalf of interests that prioritize money over nature. We can also vote with our pocketbooks, refusing to support companies whose practices conflict with the preservation of our natural world. We can support organizations that work to preserve natural places, whether they be local ones like the Rocky Mountain Conservancy or national and international organizations. We can also be sure to share our knowledge and love of nature with others, particularly with our children and grandchildren, teaching them how they can become caretakers

RANGER ON HORSEBACK

of the land. If we do our part and refuse to turn a blind eye, we have a better chance of preserving what remains for generations to come.

TRAIL ETIQUETTE

When hiking anywhere in the United States, there is an unwritten code of polite behavior that most new hikers are unaware of, so in this section I'll take a minute to outline some of the main points of hiking etiquette. These are different from regulations, safety, or preservation issues and are mostly about how one is expected to act toward those with whom you share the trail. Some of these are common sense and others you may have to think about for a minute before you see its value. I encourage you to talk with others in your group about these and to teach your children to value these unwritten rules.

Greet Others

One of the things that makes hiking different from walking in the city is that there is a friendly and welcoming culture in the wilderness. Even if you head into the mountains to be alone as I do, it is important to greet other hikers as you pass them. Of the many reasons for this, it lets others know that this is a welcoming place, not reserved for "outdoors people" or those of a specific demographic, but open to all. It helps undo the sense of fear many feel in the wild. There is also a safety component to this. If a hiker goes missing, you might have been the last one to see them and your report of where and when you saw them might be very important. For this reason you should not only greet other hikers but also be aware of how many were in their party, what they were wearing, which direction they were headed, and what time you saw them. All this could be helpful in case something goes wrong. They might even be the ones who help provide crucial information on you if you end up in trouble.

HUMAN WASTE

One of the biggest problems that has arisen with increased visitation is the impact of millions of people relieving themselves in the park. It has become a major problem. People are stepping off of the trail to do their business thinking they are one of the few to do this, when the reality is far different. I have heard that trail crews working to repair sections of hiking trail are sometimes shocked to find that everywhere they go or dig for trail material, they find poop and toilet paper in abundance. It sounds like some crews have really struggled to find untouched areas where they can get dirt and rocks for their work. At one time the park maintained privies in numerous locations throughout the park, but you can only dig so many holes before there is nowhere left where one hasn't been dug.

So, what can we do about this problem? It is a natural human necessity but being the wise creatures we are, we can find ways to mitigate this problem if we use our heads. Firstly, be sure to use the toilets at the trailhead before you head out. This by itself can mitigate much of the problem. If you are on the trail and you have to pee, don't do it at the edge of the trail; instead, walk back into the woods about 70 adult steps (200') before you do so and be sure to be at least that far from any stream or lake. That will

Realize that we live in a noisy world filled with voices, music, and other sounds to mask the silence. Yet the majority of people who come to the wilderness do so to embrace the stillness and silence of the wild, to hear the wind in the trees, the sound of the birds, and the gurgle of the streams. You can help others to have this experience by talking quietly with those in your party. Don't raise your voice and definitely don't yell. It ruins the experience for others. I've also seen people hiking with music playing through a speaker. This is considered incredibly rude on the trail. Personal music should be kept personal. If you are uncomfortable or even fearful of the natural silence,

help disburse the impact somewhat and make the trails a little more hygienic. Do not bury your toilet paper. Instead, put it into a sealed plastic bag and pack it out with you. Toilet paper does not degrade as quickly as you might think and is often dug up and eaten by animals.

If you have more serious business to do, you are probably not going to like what I have to say. The Leave No Trace principles discuss finding a place 200 feet (70 adult steps) from any water source and then digging a 6-inch-deep hole in which to bury your poop while packing out your toilet paper. While this is a good practice in remote areas, it unfortunately doesn't work in high-traffic areas. You end up with woods filled with human waste. Perhaps the only way to end this problem is for us to bring human waste bags with us into the wilderness and then pack them out. These are special bags designed to carry solid waste and toilet paper. They have a powder in them that coats the poop and keeps it from smelling, enabling you to put it in your pack and deposit it in the trash when you return. These can be purchased from outdoors stores in and around Rocky Mountain National Park and from places like Amazon.com. While it may not sound appealing, it may be the only way we can get a handle on the issue of human waste along our trails. So, use the toilets before you hit the trail!

you can wear headphones so that you don't disturb others, but I encourage you to practice embracing the silence, though it may be uncomfortable at first. It is what most of us desperately need, though we might be unaware of it. Finally, either turn off your phone and pack it away or put it on mute. If you have to make a call, get away from other people and speak quietly. Don't let the sound of phone calls, from which most of us are trying to escape, break the silence. Along this same line, keep a respectful distance from other groups when you reach your destination. The ethic of Leave No Trace applies here as well. You found silence in the wilderness, so leave it as you found it. Allow everyone a chance to enjoy a taste of silence and solitude, which is so lacking in our world.

Walk Single File

The tendency we all have is to group up on trails to facilitate conversation, yet this has drawbacks for others and the environment. When we walk side by side or in a group it can block the trail for others. We need to remember that we share these trails with many others who will need to get by us. Walking single file makes it easier for other hikers to pass us. When we take a break along the trail we also need to be sure that we are not blocking the trail for others who are likely to appear when we least expect it.

Just as importantly it helps to preserve the trails themselves, keeping them from ever widening and destroying the surrounding vegetation. We should always walk in the middle of the trail and wear good waterproof boots so that even if there is a puddle or mud in the trail that we walk through it rather than continuing to expand the trail.

Know When to Yield

Just like on the highway, there are rules on the trail that you should know. One of the most important is knowing when to yield to others. You should always give way to those hiking faster than you. Don't block the trail; simply let faster hikers go by. This will make for a better experience for everyone.

When the trail is narrow and you encounter others coming toward you, always give way to the person hiking uphill. The reason

TONAHUTU TRAIL

for this is that the uphill hiker is working harder and is probably in a rhythm. It will take them more energy to stop and get started again compared to the downhill hiker. If they volunteer to stop and let you pass, that's fine, but it's their decision to make as the uphill hiker, since they by default have the right-of-way. In Rocky Mountain National Park most trails heading out from the trailhead are uphill and when returning you are generally going downhill, so as a general rule, give way to outbound hikers.

Another time you need to yield is when you encounter horses, llamas, or other stock animals on the trail. They are to be given the right-of-way. When you step aside for them, you will want to step off to the downhill side. If you stand above the animals, it can spook them; if you stand below, you are perceived as less of a threat.

Inform Before Passing

Everyone hikes at different speeds. I have one friend who can take an hour or even two to walk a mile, as he is so busy paying attention to every little detail along the trail, while I tend to hike quite quickly until I'm far from the crowds. For those of us who are passing others, be sure not to startle the people you come upon. I sometimes drag my feet a bit or make some other non-startling noise before I get close to those in front in order to give a gentle warning that I'm coming. When I get closer I let them know that I'll be passing on their left with simple words such as, "May I pass on your left?" followed by a "Thank you" once I've passed. This simple interaction can help avoid confusion and it respects the other hikers. Without this, people often get confused about who's going where and they may even forget to move aside so you can pass. If you are being passed, try to stay on the trail or stand on a rock so that you don't contribute to trail spread.

Educate Others Gently

With millions of people visiting Rocky Mountain National Park it is inevitable that you will encounter people who are breaking regulations, etiquette, or issues of preservation. Many of these folks simply don't know any better, as most of them have little experience with the outdoors and have never read a book like this. The temptation is to

PERSONAL LOCATOR BEACONS

Another safety tool that many folks use, including myself, is a personal locator beacon. These devices send signals via satellites and can be used to send distress calls with your exact coordinates. Some devices will plot your location on an online map every ten minutes or so enabling folks back home to track you. I use one of these types of tracking beacons. Even if I were unconscious and hadn't pressed the emergency button the beacon would still be transmitting my location, making it possible for me to be found. My wife likes the fact that she can see that I'm still alive and moving when I'm out on a big hike.

Some of these devices also allow for the sending and receiving of texts, which can be quite helpful if you are running late, have a twisted ankle and need assistance from friends, or have encountered some other unexpected but non-life-threatening challenge. You, however, have to be very intentional with such a device so as to not let it interfere with your time offline.

Be aware that the emergency button on these devices is similar to calling 911. It is only to be used in life-threatening situations. Once it is pushed, it initiates a large rescue operation involving dozens of people and costing many thousands of dollars.

grumble about their actions and pass on, but I would encourage you to take a moment to greet them warmly and humbly let them know not only that what they are doing is wrong but more importantly why what they are doing is inappropriate. Many will be receptive to learn why they shouldn't feed chipmunks or walk on the side of the trail. Obviously there will be some who don't want anyone to tell them anything. If you sense this is their attitude, then be wise and let it go, but take the opportunities to both encourage good behavior and to gently educate when you can.

Winter Etiquette

There are a number of additional things to mention about winter hiking etiquette but I'll just mention two of the most important here. Firstly, don't urinate on the side of the trail. No one wants to see a big yellow patch of snow while they are hiking. Be sure to hike off trail, dig a hole with your pole to pee in, and then fill it in with snow afterward so that there is no visible trace. Secondly, respect the trails you find. If you find a ski trail through the snow, leave it in good condition for other skiers. Don't walk or snowshoe on it. As for the snowshoe trails, if you don't have snowshoes and are breaking through the trail, don't continue, as you will destroy it and make it a much less pleasant journey for everyone after you. If you are determined to hike out anyway, create your own trail several feet to the side of the snowshoe or ski trail. During the winter months the snow protects the ground, making it permissible to spread out more.

PREPARATION

I know you are probably ready to get right out onto the trails, but before you rush out there, it is wise to have a plan of action, to dress appropriately, and to have packed the right things in your bag. I've run out there unprepared far too many times and am always so frustrated with myself when it happens. So take a moment to think about your trip before departing.

Planning

As you plan for your trip, one of the most important things is to be sure that you have a realistic plan. You'll want to make sure you aren't stretching yourself too far but are planning adequate time. It is much better to have a shorter, easier trip and find you have time to stop and enjoy the wonder of the wilderness than to push too hard and overreach. That can result in injury, getting stuck out in bad weather, finding yourself still hiking in the dark or simply an unpleasant time as you drag your exhausted body back to the trailhead.

Your plan should take into account the day's weather forecast. Know when storms are likely to arrive and be prepared to finish your hike by then or at least be below tree line when the storm arrives. Also keep in mind that storms are unpredictable. Know what you will do if they arrive earlier than planned.

Know your limits, as well as those of your party. It helps to have a good sense of how far you can go and how much elevation you can handle at a time, as well as how fast you typically hike. Make sure that the hike you choose can be done within the time frame you have. Also be sure to include the time it will take to get to the trailhead, consider whether you might need to take a shuttle, and remember to consider the time it will take you to get organized after you've parked your vehicle.

When to Go

Park visitation has grown significantly in the last decade, and most trailheads fill quite early in the morning, many before 8 a.m. The best way to ensure that you have a place to park is to arrive very early in the morning. Alternatively, you can arrive after 3 or 4 p.m. and find a place to park, but if you arrive later, you need to be aware of afternoon storms and the possibility that it may be dark by the time you return. Alternatively, take one of the park shuttles that provide access to the trails along Bear Lake Road. Stop by a park visitor center or the Estes Park Visitor Center for shuttle times and routes.

What to Wear

If you plan to do anything more than a very short hike, it is important to dress appropriately. Nearly every time I'm out in the mountains, I see people heading out who are completely unprepared for what they will experience. I sometimes see folks heading up Longs Peak with tank tops, shorts, and sandals and no backpack. Sometimes there are people out for a long hike wearing jeans and a cotton sweatshirt. Most of the time this results simply in discomfort but more than occasionally the lack of appropriate attire can put hikers in life-threatening situations.

Try to avoid all clothing made of cotton, such as jeans, socks, and sweatshirts. Cotton clothing tends to soak up and hold on to moisture, which then transfers cold air directly to your skin. If you sweat or are caught in the rain and then the temperature drops, you may find yourself unable to get warm. This can lead to hypothermia, which can be life-threatening. Instead, you will want to choose clothing that wicks moisture away from your body to give you a greater chance of staying warm and dry.

Most outdoor enthusiasts will encourage you to dress in layers so

NORTH INLET TRAIL

that as the weather conditions change and as you heat up or cool down, you have the option to remove or add clothing. You should begin by having a base layer made of synthetic materials or merino wool that's designed to take moisture away from the skin. The base layer includes underwear, socks, and shirt. You'll also want hiking pants that are flexible, breathable, and that expel moisture away from the body. Following this you'll want an insulating layer to keep you warm. This may be a polypropylene fleece and a compressible warm jacket that you can keep in the pack. For your outer layer you'll want what is called a shell. This is a jacket and possibly even a second set of pants that are designed to block out both the wind and rain. These will stay in your pack until you need them. (Learn more about appropriate clothing at: www.HikingRocky.com/clothing.)

As well as the primary pieces of clothing, you'll need a good pair of hiking boots. Hiking boots are designed to protect your toes as well as your ankles as you traverse the rocky terrain you'll encounter here. I recommend that you have sturdy waterproof boots. This will allow you to stay on the trail even when it is wet and muddy, thereby protecting the trail from growing ever wider. Some people prefer non-waterproof boots, as they can be a bit cooler and don't hold moisture that gets into the boot, but you'll have wet feet as soon as you walk through the first couple of puddles. You'll have to decide which works better for you. You'll also want to be sure that your boots are fully broken in before you take them on a long hike. New or rarely worn boots can often lead to blisters, which will make that wonderful hike torturous.

Additionally, take with you a pair of warm gloves or mittens and a warm windproof hat that covers your ears. You might be surprised to learn that if you have cold feet, putting a hat on your head can really help. In the summer you will be glad to have a sunproof hat to protect your head. Finally, a good pair of sunglasses will offer protection against the harsh mountain light. I recommend having all of this gear with you all year long, as you never know when you'll need it. I very often find myself putting on every piece of clothing I have even in the middle of August when the weather in the high country takes an unexpected turn.

When I first arrived in the mountains I had none of these things and I didn't have the money to buy all new hiking gear. So I did the best I could and managed to gather hand-me-downs from friends. If you are visiting and don't have the right gear, you can often rent the outdoor clothing you need from one of the outdoors stores near the park. Alternatively, you could pay a visit to one of the thrift stores. Thrift stores in mountain towns often have gear that you won't find at thrift stores back home.

What to Pack (The Essentials)

Besides dressing appropriately, it is important to bring something more with you on your hike than just your cell phone and car keys. If something were to happen while you were out on the trail, having the following essentials will enable you to better handle the situation. If you end up lost or injured and have to spend a night in the forest, you'll be very glad to have these items with you. I almost always have these in my backpack and I end up using most of them regularly.

- Navigation (maps & compass)
- Sun Protection (sunglasses, sunscreen, lip balm, sun hat)
- Extra Clothing (rain protection, warmth, extra socks, gloves, hat)
- Illumination (head lamp & batteries)
- First Aid Supplies
- Fire Starter
- Tools (knife, multi-use tools, duct tape)
- Nutrition
- Hydration (water filter & bottle)
- Signaling Devices (whistle, mirror, high-visibility clothing)
- Emergency Shelter (bivy sac, tarp)

Navigation

The first item on my list is navigation tools. The most important thing to have in your pack is an old-fashioned map and manual compass together with the knowledge of how to use them. They aren't very heavy or expensive and may save you in an emergency. I recommend the National Geographic Trails Illustrated Topographic Map. You'll also want a simple compass, which you can get for about $10–$20. If you aren't comfortable reading a topographical map and using a compass, take a few minutes to watch these two very helpful videos: www.HikingRocky.com/topo and www.HikingRocky.com/compass. I know, this is all very old school, but trust me, you want these in your pack. They may save your life.

You may be wondering why I recommend the old-school option first when there are so many newer options available. While all of these new options are wonderful and I use them all the time, they all have significant limitations. The biggest one is that they rely on battery power. You can help to compensate by bringing a battery backup but when that also runs out, it just becomes meaningless weight. In many emergency situations, people are stuck in the wilderness for days or even weeks. No battery will last that long. Additionally, these are fragile electronic devices, and if they were to be damaged by a fall, water exposure, or an electrical strike, you are again stuck. So bring a map and compass with you and know how to use them, just in case.

Once you have those in your pack, take advantage of some of the great modern options available. There are numerous apps for your phone such as Gaia GPS, AllTrails, and many others. With

LONGS PEAK FROM BEAVER MEADOWS

IF YOU'RE LOST

What do you do if you are lost in the wilderness? Remember the simple acronym STOP.

STOP: First, stop and take a deep breath. Don't take another step. Just stop right where you are and give yourself time to calm down. Don't give in to panic. Panic will not help you and is likely to make your situation worse, as it hinders your ability to think clearly. You may find it helpful to sit down right where you are while you catch your breath. Have a drink of water, eat a little bit, and wait until you begin to relax.

THINK: Once you have calmed down assess your situation very practically. Don't move anywhere until you have a well-formed plan of action. Try to remember when and where you last saw the trail. Do you remember if you were heading uphill, downhill, alongside a hill? Did it angle down to your left or down to your right? How long did you walk after you lost the trail? Try to remember as much as you can about the trail and where you last saw it.

OBSERVE: Now look around for landmarks such as peaks, streams, large outcroppings, or any other identifiable feature. Can you identify any of these on your map? Look at the slope of the hill and consider how that compares to what you last remember on the trail and how it compares to what you see on the map. Have a look at the weather and try to guess what you think it is going to do. Without going anywhere look around and see if you can identify any potential areas where you might be able to take shelter.

PLAN: Stay put until you have a clear and careful plan of action. You may want to set this location as your base. Perhaps pile up a couple of rocks to make it identifiable. You may want to use your compass and head in the most likely direction of the trail for five minutes. Time it with your watch. If you don't find the trail use your compass and watch to return back to the base before trying again in another direction. If you are with someone else, one of you can stay at the base and the other can explore while maintaining voice contact. If you have no success, you may want to start using your whistle.

Check your cell phone to see if you have a signal. If you do, you may be able to use Google Maps or another program to help you identify your location. After you have done all of the above, and if you have a signal on your phone, you can call Rocky Mountain National Park's dispatch center to let them know you are lost and what you are doing about it. You'll find their contact information on page 33. They can provide helpful advice and can send assistance if it is needed. If you can't get a signal and have a personal locator beacon, some of them have notification options other than the full-on emergency. If you are not in danger you may want to use that function to let friends and family know you could use help but that it is not life-threatening. Save the 911 feature for life-threatening situations or after you've fully exhausted your other options.

If it will be dark soon or if a storm is moving in, you may want to find shelter very nearby before it is too late, then resume your search in the morning.

Work out from your base and don't just wander off hoping that you will eventually find civilization. It is much better to stay in one place so that you can be found more easily. If you've let someone know where you've gone and when to expect your return, you can expect that they will call for help when you don't return. Patience is the name of the game.

such apps you can download detailed maps of the areas you plan to hike and they will help you know where you are even when you lose cell reception, assuming you downloaded the detailed maps before you left. These tools will not only help you find your way but can also track your trips, and many have a lot of other fun features. There are also dedicated GPS devices that are designed for this purpose. They are usually waterproof and have a long battery life. I mentioned elsewhere that there are some devices that have not only the GPS capability but can also serve as a personal locator beacon that can summon help in an emergency. Some of them even allow you to send texts via satellite when you are far from any cell connection.

Coloradans often boast that they get more sun than places like San Diego or Miami with over three hundred sunny days a year. This makes for beautiful dark blue Colorado skies and great hiking, but it also comes with some drawbacks. Because of the high elevation of Rocky Mountain National Park the rays of the sun are much more intense. At Bear Lake the UV rays are 40 percent more powerful than at sea level and they continue to increase by about 4 percent for every additional 1,000' in elevation gain. As a result it is very easy to get burned in the mountains not only in the summer but also in the winter. This harsh light can quickly burn any exposed skin; it is also very hard on the eyes and in the winter people sometimes suffer from snow blindness when their eyes become burned by the sun. It can cause you to temporarily lose your sight—something you don't want to happen out in the wilderness.

It is therefore essential that you always have sunglasses with full UV protection. Cheap sunglasses may actually cause your eyes to dilate and let in more harmful UV rays, causing even greater harm to your pupils than if you had no sunglasses at all, so get ones with

proper protection. Additionally, you'll want to lather up with sunscreen before you leave the trailhead and take additional sunscreen
with you to apply as needed. If you are heading out in the winter it is
important to also cover areas such as under your chin and nose since
light will reflect off the snow below you. You'll also want to wear
sun-protective lip balm. Some hikers wear lightweight loose clothing
that has UV protection in the fabric. You can find this at most outdoors stores such as REI or the hiking stores around Estes Park and
Grand Lake. Additionally, it is a good idea to wear a UV-protective
sun hat while out in the mountains, especially for those of us with
less hair to provide natural protection.

Extra Clothing

You never know what the weather is going to do when you are in
the mountains, no matter the time of year. The wisest thing to do is
pack your backpack with the idea of what you might need to survive
a night in the mountains if the unexpected happens. Do you have
enough clothing to stay warm at night? In particular, do you have
a warm hat, gloves or mittens, a warm sweater or jacket, as well as a
weatherproof (wind and water) shell? Some folks like to bring along
an additional pair of warm socks and two thick plastic bags about
the size of bread bags. This way if you have gotten your feet wet you
can dry them, put on a pair of dry socks and then before you put
your feet back in wet boots, put a plastic bag on each foot to serve
as a moisture barrier. This isn't a great long-term solution but for the
short term it is much more comfortable than wet, cold feet.

Illumination

Never leave a trailhead without a head lamp in your pack. If
the hike ends up taking longer than you expected, you might find
yourself out at night, which can be very disorienting. Because the
mountains block the horizon, it can get dark very quickly unlike
other places where the sky can give off light for hours. Some people
think they can rely on their phones for light. This works for only
thirty minutes to an hour. When it runs out of power, you are stuck.
It is a good idea to have some sort of light that will work for several
hours. I recommend a head lamp over a flashlight, as it allows you

to keep your hands free. I actually keep one at the top of my bag and another smaller one in my first aid kit, as well as several spare batteries. It is normally recommended that you keep the batteries separate from the device until you need it lest they discharge or the batteries corrode. Just remember to put those batteries in before it gets fully dark, as you will have some trouble changing batteries in the forest at night without another light. Without a head lamp or a full moon, you'll have to sit by the trail until the sun rises again the next day. Even in summer, this will involve some long hours out in the cold and exposed to the elements.

First Aid Supplies

I keep a rather large first aid kit in my hiking bag at all times. You don't need everything I have but you should have some essential items with you. These include antiseptic cream, bandages of various sizes, gauze pads, tape, pain reliever such as ibuprofen, tweezers, blister pads, moleskin, allergy medicine, any personal medicine you might need if you had to spend the night. You can find great little first aid kits that include most of the basics at most outdoors stores. If you plan to travel in the wilderness regularly, I highly recommend that you consider taking a Wilderness First Responder course to help you know what to do in an emergency in the backcountry. Whether or not you've taken a course, I strongly recommend that you keep either a physical or digital copy of a wilderness first aid book. It will have all sorts of helpful information to guide you if you find yourself in an emergency.

Fire Starter

While making fires in Rocky Mountain National Park is illegal in all but a few special areas, if one's life is in danger, then the wise use of fire may keep you warm and alive until help can arrive. For this reason it is good to always have what you need to start a fire in the wild. You will want to have waterproof matches, a lighter or flint, as well as perhaps fire-starter sticks or squares made of something like wood chips and wax. A candle can also be helpful to maintain a flame while getting a fire started.

Be aware that the Rocky Mountains are a high desert and so it tends to be very dry. With great ease one could burn down an entire

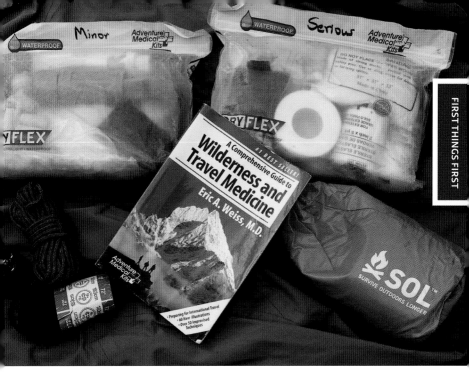

forest. So choose a location where you can completely control the fire, where the ashes are not likely to drift into the dry treetops or flammable understory. When you are done, be sure to not only extinguish the fire but also douse it completely with water and stir it well, since fire can actually continue underground. If you don't have easy access to water, use dirt and sand and a stick to really stir it in until it is no longer hot. In 2013 an illegal wildfire spread across the park and to the border of Estes Park. It cost $6 million to put it out.

Tools

No, you don't need to bring a hammer or drill, but there are a few little pieces of equipment you may find very helpful. The first is a pocketknife or better yet a multi-tool with a knife. This can be helpful for everything from creating wood shavings for a fire to making a small spear for catching fish. A multi-tool often includes things such as a small saw, pliers, a screwdriver for fixing your hiking poles, or other useful little tools that can help you fix your equipment or survive in the wild. The second item that you should certainly have with you is duct tape. There are so many uses for this in

WILDERNESS CAMPING

What can be better than not having to go back to civilization at the end of a long hike? Being able to stay in the wilderness, to watch the last light on the peaks and the first light of the morning, to listen to the sounds of the forest at night and sleep in the fresh cool air. This is something everyone should get to experience.

Most of Rocky Mountain National Park is designated wilderness where impact by humans has been greatly restricted. In this wilderness they have designated 267 wilderness campsites. You can't simply head out into the forest and set up camp; you have to stay in one of these designated sites. The main reason for this is to reduce the impact. Can you imagine if it were a free-for-all? The damage to this park would be widespread. These 267 sites are an attempt to provide us access while at the same time containing our impact.

These sites are generally reserved well in advance and they all require a permit from Rocky Mountain National Park's Wilderness Office. These permits begin being issued on March 1 of each year and most fill up shortly after that. If you arrive at the park without a permit you can always stop in at the Wilderness Office and choose from the wilderness sites that have not been reserved or see if there have been any last-minute cancelations.

the wilderness, from protecting your heels from developing blisters to patching a rain jacket or creating a splint with pieces of wood. As a side note, as soon as I start to feel a "hot spot" on my foot, a place where the boot is beginning to rub, I stop and put a large piece of duct tape on that area of my foot. It usually prevents me from developing blisters. The third item you may also want to include is a length of parachute cord. It is small, lightweight, and very strong and can come in handy for a wide variety of situations.

Nutrition

When you head out into the mountains, you'll be burning a lot of calories. To keep going you need to bring adequate food with you.

A typical campsite will be located about a quarter mile off of a main trail. You'll follow a designated path up to a clearing in the trees. Here you'll find the prepared dirt pad where you can set up camp. You should try to place your tent as near as is safely possible to the silver metal arrowhead that marks the site, ensuring first there are no dead trees that could potentially fall on you in a windstorm.

Apart from the metal stake, you'll find no other development at the campsite. Fires are allowed in very few wilderness sites and so there are usually no fire grates. Neither are there benches or stools, though there may be logs in some sites. These sites provide the true wilderness experience. You'll have to hike to the nearest stream to filter water and cook your meals over your own camping stove. All food items and garbage must be secured inside a commercially manufactured carry-in/out bear-resistant food storage canister. Other methods of food storage are not permitted in the wilderness. Food items include food, drinks, cleaning supplies, toiletries, and cosmetics. Some of the campsites have a designated privy, while some do not. Ask the Wilderness Office about this before you go, and bring human waste bags if there is no privy.

For more details about wilderness camping in Rocky Mountain National Park visit: www.HikingRocky.com/wilderness.

Candy bars and potato chips are not what your body needs. Choose foods that will last in both the heat and the cold and will provide you with proper nutrition to fuel your body. Be aware that meat and cheeses may go bad in your backpack, and chocolate may turn into a runny mess unless these types of items are properly insulated. Consider bringing things such as trail mix, granola bars, nuts, dried fruits, dried meats, and for sandwiches consider using tortillas instead of bread, as they are less compressible.

When out for a day of hiking it is best to eat a little bit often rather than eating large meals less often. One of my friends who is a mountain guide says that people tend to eat too much when they stop and then they find themselves very fatigued just a short time later, as their body has to work too hard to process all that food.

Be sure to bring an empty bag with you such as a ziplock bag where you can put all of your trash. Check all around you before you leave the place where you ate to be certain that you've picked everything up and that nothing has blown away. Pay attention to any micro-trash, those tiny pieces that might be overlooked. Take it all and leave this place pristine for the wildlife that live here and for those who will come after you.

Hydration

At these high elevations staying adequately hydrated is essential. Your body loses moisture at a much greater rate in the mountains than at sea level and surprisingly you often aren't as thirsty at higher elevations. These combine to make dehydration a real problem and often we are unaware that we are dehydrated until it is fairly advanced. At this point it can become quite serious, so the best thing we can do is to be very conscientious about our water intake. I actually have an app on my phone named Daily Water that reminds me to drink and tells

me how much I have drunk during the day. It is recommended that we
drink 48–72 ounces per day, but if you are out hiking on a hot summer
day you may need to drink as much as a liter of water per hour. Your
goal should not be to over-hydrate, just be sure you are not ignoring
your body's need for water. Also, don't substitute coffee, soda, alcohol,
or other drinks for what your body needs most, which is water.

So how do you stay hydrated while hiking? Firstly, bring water
with you. Don't go out and buy bottles of water that can be thrown
away but buy a bottle you can use over and over again while hiking,
one that won't break. The visitor centers at the park entrances have
places where you can fill them with fresh cold water. I usually bring a
couple of liters of water with me on a hike, but if I'm going to be out
for a long period, I also bring what I need to clean water that I find
along the way. Unfortunately, you won't find water at the trailheads,
so come prepared.

Water is abundant in Rocky, except at the higher elevations. If
you have a way to treat the water, this can supplement what you bring
with you. While the streams and lakes in the park come directly from
melting snow and are generally pretty clean, you'll still want to properly treat it, as elk, bighorn sheep, and other animals may have con-
taminated the water farther upstream. If you don't clean the water
you find, it could lead to giardia, which is a way to lose a lot of weight
in the most unpleasant of ways. I've tried it a few times and don't
recommend it. There are different ways to filter water. Many people
choose to bring a pump type of water filter with them, others use
special straws, and I typically use a SteriPEN (specialized UV light)
to purify the water. Each of these methods has pros and cons. A good
outdoors store can help walk you through the options. (Be aware that
if you are using one of the UV light purifiers, it only works properly
with lithium batteries even though it looks like it works with regular
batteries. They simply aren't strong enough to fully purify the water.)
Remember that without one of these purifying options, your hikes
are limited by the amount of water you can carry.

Be aware that along with water your body also needs a little salt
and electrolytes to maintain its balance. A few bites of a salty snack
and a few sips from a sports drink along with enough water can help
to keep your body chemistry in equilibrium.

BARK BEETLES

As you drive through Rocky Mountain National Park or hike some of its many trails, you are almost certain to encounter large areas where a majority of the trees have died. Many visitors wonder if this was caused by fire, disease, or some other phenomena. The cause is actually a very small beetle.

In the early 2000s Colorado and most of the western United States experienced a severe outbreak of the mountain pine beetle. In more recent years there has been a new outbreak of the spruce beetle. These bark beetles have been here almost as long as the forests, but these recent episodes are unprecedented in scope. The bark beetles—mountain pine beetle, spruce beetle, and others—burrow into the trunks of trees and lay their eggs. This doesn't necessarily hurt the trees, but what kills them is the blue stain fungus the beetles carry with them. The fungus blocks the water transport system of the trees and eventually kills them, causing them to turn brown and eventually lose their needles after a year or two.

In the past, the beetle population was controlled by the cold winters, which killed off large numbers of the eggs and larvae during the winter months. The last decades have been considerably warmer than in the past, resulting in expanding populations of bark beetle. This was exacerbated by long periods of drought, leaving the trees in a weak state and unable to fend off the beetles. Further, the lack of fire led to very uniform forests in terms of both species and age, making them even more susceptible to the beetles. It was an almost perfect storm for the forests of North America.

Although these beetle-killed forests may appear gray and lifeless, this is not the case. The needles from most of these trees have fallen, allowing sunlight to once again reach the forest floor. Now smaller trees and plants are growing at the base of the dead trees and will slowly begin to reveal themselves. Over the next couple of decades these areas will be fully renewed. In the meantime, the dead trees serve a purpose; they are becoming the homes of birds, insects, and small animals, filling the forest with life. In some instances, the dead stands may make these areas ripe for fires, but this too will only result in future life and restoration of the forest.

Signaling Devices

If you find yourself lost in the wilderness, you'll want to have some way of signaling others. The first item you absolutely must have is a whistle. You will lose your voice after about twenty minutes of yelling, but you can keep using a whistle as long as you can breathe. Another helpful thing to have with you is a small mirror. With a mirror and some sunlight, you can signal a helicopter that may be looking for you. Wearing very bright clothing also helps if you get lost, as it will make you easier to spot. Consider having a brightly colored rain jacket in your pack that you can wear if you need to be found.

Although I've already mentioned this before, it is worth repeating: Having an emergency locator beacon can be very valuable if you need to be rescued, as it will not only notify the authorities of your need for rescue but will also transmit your exact GPS coordinates. When paired with the other signaling devices listed above, this can be an invaluable tool. You can learn more about these devices on page 57.

Emergency Shelter

If you end up having to spend a night in the wilderness, you will be glad to have some sort of emergency shelter. A small tarp with string can be set up to keep the rain off of you during a cold, rainy night. An emergency bivy sac can help you hold your heat and avoid hypothermia. These are made of waterproof, windproof, reflective material that may save your life. They also can be used for signaling for help. Both the bivy and emergency tarp come in small packs that will not take up much room in your backpack.

Additional Items to Consider

Besides the essentials I've listed above, here are a few other items you might want to consider bringing with you:

Hiking Poles

I used to think that hiking poles were for older people with poor balance, but I am now a firm believer in their value for everyone and I use them myself while out on the trail. Hiking poles can absorb the impact on the knees and feet when descending, they can help you with balance on unstable terrain, and they may actually increase the speed at which you can comfortably hike. However, simply having them isn't enough; you need to know the best way to use them. There are several great YouTube videos showing the best way to use them. You can find one of them at: www.HikingRocky.com/poles.

Cell Phone and Portable Power Charger

Although the cell reception is nonexistent in many parts of Rocky, it is wise to bring a cell phone with you just in case you can get reception. Yet a cell phone by itself won't do you any good if it loses power, so bring along a portable charger. Ideally, you should keep your phone off and in a waterproof pouch inside your backpack until you need it. If you are in an emergency situation you'll want to connect with the NPS Dispatch and then set a schedule with them for ongoing communication. This way you can turn your phone off to conserve power until the scheduled check-in time.

Insect Repellent

Generally there are very few pesky insects here in Rocky Mountain National Park but on wetter years or when you are traveling near marshy areas, you may find yourself attacked by mosquitoes. For those rare situations, I keep insect repellent in my bag as well as a mesh head net that I can wear when they are at their worst. I can't tell you how glad I've been to have it on those few occasions when I've needed it.

Garbage Bag

I also recommend bringing an extra bag that you can use to haul out any trash you come across on the trail. If all of us take a little extra responsibility, we can keep this park pristine for generations to come. I also bring a pair of medical gloves to remove the worst rubbish.

Earplugs

This may sound like an odd item to carry, but often when I have to hike through the tundra there is a strong cold wind. I can develop earaches from the wind and so I keep a small pair of foam earplugs in my bag. In high winds, I simply put those in and stay pain free. Alternatively, music earbuds can serve the same purpose.

WILDFIRES

Wildfires have been a part of the natural world for as long as there have been grasses and forests. Fires are an important part of the natural cycle that brings renewal to forests, creates needed diversity, clears out old and fallen timber, and returns nutrients to the soil. Without fires our forests and grasslands would be unhealthy.

However, there is a real difference between naturally occurring fires and those started by people. According to a 2017 article titled "Wildfire Causes and Evaluations" by the National Park Service, "As many as 90 percent of wildland fires in the United States are caused by humans." That is an astonishing figure and one that should make all of us take notice.

These days as our climate continues to change we're not only seeing an increase in temperature but also more droughts. Forest fires are increasing in regularity and in intensity. These changes are stretching our local, regional, and national firefighting agencies to an almost unprecedented level, and the long-term forecast indicates that this trend will continue.

Rocky Mountain National Park is already considered a high desert area. It is dry and prone to fires, but with the changing climate this seems to be increasing. It takes very little to start a major forest fire. While we may have grown up building campfires every time we went out into the wilderness, we sadly can no longer do this here in the Rocky Mountains. Just one match, one cigarette, one candle, one careless person can destroy tens of thousands of acres and put numerous lives and structures at risk.

In October of 2012 an illegal campfire spread and set the forest alight. Firefighters from around the country battled the fire for two months and on December 1 high winds pushed the fire eastward more than three miles in thirty-five minutes, all the way across Moraine Park, prompting evacuation orders in the park and in some parts of Estes Park. In the end, after months of fighting this fire and six million dollars in expense, the illegal campfire was finally put out by a December snowstorm.

The forest's susceptibility to wildfire is likely to increase over the coming decades and so we as lovers of this special place must be extra vigilant to protect it from ourselves.

Ziplock and Human Waste Bags

If you use toilet paper in the wilderness, you need to pack it back out with you. For this purpose I recommend keeping a few ziplock bags in your pack. They don't take up any space or weight and ensure that you can leave the wilderness as you found it.

If you find that you have to do more than pee, it is recommended that you bring a human waste bag for poop and toilet paper. With the millions of visitors, burying your waste is no longer a viable option. So bring a specially designed human waste bag and pack it out. You can find more information about this on page 52.

Gaiters

A pair of gaiters can be helpful year round. They wrap around the lower part of your leg and boot. In the winter and spring they can keep snow out of your boots and during other seasons they can keep the rocks and sand out. They are handy when you encounter deep mud or if you simply want to keep the bottom of your hiking pants clean. They are also very helpful during tick season, preventing them from crawling under your pant leg.

TICK TERRAIN

If you plan to visit the park between late October and early May, you will have a much better experience on the trail if you have a set of microspikes such as those made by Kahtoola®. They stretch around your boot and provide great traction when you encounter icy trails. I use them a lot when hiking on well-traveled trails during this long cold season. While others are slipping and falling, I can hike right on by without difficulty.

SAFETY

This is the section that most people are likely to skip over, as they assume they already know what they need to know. I agree that some of what I have to say you will have heard elsewhere, but there are special considerations to take into account when visiting Rocky Mountain National Park, particularly in regard to weather patterns, wildlife, and elevation. The information in this section may end up saving your hide, so humor me and take a few minutes to read through it.

The Cardinal Rule

The first thing you should always do before you head out into the wilderness is let someone know

- exactly where you are going (destination);
- what your route will be (which trails you will travel to get there);
- when they should expect a call from you saying you've returned; and
- when they should contact the authorities.

The person you arrange this with needs to be someone you can rely on, who will remember that you are out there and will take action if they don't hear from you. The other important part of this is that you must stick to the plan you have given, even when it is inconvenient. People go missing in Rocky Mountain National Park on a regular basis, and the park has the best chance of finding them if they are informed in a timely manner and know exactly where to begin the search.

One of the most important things you can do to ensure that you have a safe and successful trip into the wilderness is to head out with the right attitude. It is not gear that will keep you out of harm's way or help you to handle an emergency; it is the important hardware that sits between your ears.

The main attitudes we need to have are humility, flexibility, and composure. These are something that you will find in all great outdoor adventurers, who know they are not as powerful as the elements they face, recognize their limitations, and then use patience and wisdom to overcome them. These folks know that when they find themselves in trouble, instead of panicking they remain calm and form a thoughtful plan of action.

One of the biggest dangers we see here in Rocky Mountain National Park is a determined insistence on reaching a particular goal, whether that be a summit or the completion of a particular hike. We often refer to this as "summit fever." This insistence can be deadly when it causes us to be so goal focused that we ignore wisdom. When that storm is building above tree line, we may feel like we should race on in order to accomplish our goal, but wisdom says to either try another day or wait below tree line until the storm has passed. Lightning has killed many who have this "summit fever" attitude. In the same way, machismo or a goal-focused determination says to push on as the headache and nausea worsen, but wisdom says to head back down to a lower elevation. The one who listens to wisdom will live; the one who ignores wisdom may encounter High Altitude Pulmonary Edema or even High Altitude Cerebral Edema, putting their life at risk. Listen to the voice of wisdom and live to conquer another day.

Elevation

Most people arrive in Rocky Mountain National Park ready to hike up into the mountains yet soon find that their bodies aren't as ready as they had thought. The very lowest trails in Rocky Mountain National Park begin at an elevation of over 7,600' and head higher from there. So be informed about the impact that elevation can have on your body. Being unprepared or uninformed can ruin your trip or worse.

LIGHTNING

One of the issues that many people don't think about when visiting Rocky Mountain National Park is lightning. No matter where you live in the United States lightning occurs, but few realize that the danger of lightning is higher in the mountains of Colorado.

Each year there are nearly half a million lightning strikes in Colorado and each year there are fatalities and injuries. Rocky Mountain National Park has had its share of these as well. They occur not only deep in the mountains but also at popular places such as Rock Cut on Trail Ridge Road, along the Ute Trail, or even at places like Mills Lake. When people are in popular areas surrounded by other people, they tend to think they are not at risk when in fact they are.

The best way to stay safe in the mountains is to be very aware of the ever-changing weather. The only truly safe place to be in an electrical storm is inside a building or inside a car. If you see storm clouds developing, it is time to get out of the high country where you are likely to be the highest object around. If you hear thunder, you are in danger. If you can't quickly make it to your car, head for the nearest forest. Stay away from lakes, marshes, and other wet places. Be aware that many of the rocks in the park may conduct electricity and so while hiding under a large rock may protect you from moisture and hail, it won't protect you from lightning.

Most lightning injuries and deaths happen during the month of July when the monsoon weather arrives, bringing almost daily afternoon thunderstorms. This can happen at other times as well, but most storms develop in the afternoon. You can therefore reduce your chances of being caught in an electrical storm by hiking early in the morning and aiming to be off of the tundra and away from lakes and meadows by noon. Nonetheless, always keep a vigilant watch on the changing weather and be prepared to change your plans when the weather moves in.

At higher elevations there is less air pressure and so the oxygen molecules are more disbursed, which results in your body struggling to take in enough oxygen. This can result in shortness of breath, especially when exerting yourself, as well as headache, fatigue, loss of appetite, and even nausea. Generally your body will adjust within a few days, but there are things you can do to help your body make that adjustment.

Before you arrive and also while you are here, increase your water intake to several quarts a day. This will keep you properly hydrated. Be aware that alcohol and caffeine may hinder your adjustment. **If you experience any of the symptoms of altitude sickness, don't head to higher elevations** until your body has adjusted, as it can lead to more serious and even life-threatening conditions. If you are hiking up a mountain and your headache keeps getting worse, don't push through it. Immediately turn around and head to a lower elevation. One way you can help your body adjust is to sleep at lower elevations. That might mean Estes Park rather than a backcountry campsite, or possibly somewhere lower, like Denver. If conditions get worse, the best thing you can do is head to an even lower elevation.

As I mentioned, hydration is a big factor when visiting the high desert. Be very deliberate in getting enough water into your body. It can be easy to overlook this while hiking or having fun. You may want to set a timer or use an app that helps track how much water you've drunk. Yet the body needs more than water. Too much water by itself can throw your body off-balance. You need salt and electrolytes to keep your system operating healthily. Some low- or no-sugar sports drinks have the proper amount of salt and electrolytes to help you maintain or regain that balance.

Another real concern is sunburn. There is less protection from the sun's rays at high elevations and so it is easy to get sunburned. Be sure to lather yourself with sunscreen and sun-protecting lip balm. This is true not only on warm summer days but also in the winter when the harsh sun reflects off of the snow and burns places you wouldn't expect such as around your nostrils or under your chin. For those of us with thin hair, a hat on the head is a wise choice. Additionally, you'll want to have a good pair of UV protective sunglasses for your eyes.

Weather

The biggest mistake anyone can make with regard to the weather is to judge it based on your own experience at home. You might look

BLOWING SNOW AND HALLETT PEAK

LONGS PEAK NEAR KEYHOLE

out the window in the morning to see blue skies and sunshine and assume that it will be a nice day. Or you might assess the weather at the trailhead when it might be warm and calm and decide to leave your jacket in the car only to later find yourself in the middle of extreme conditions.

The weather here in the mountains of Colorado is almost certainly not like the weather you have at home. Here the weather can change greatly from one part of the park to another, from one elevation to the next, and it can also transition rapidly within a very short period of time. In the mountains it is wise to be prepared for almost anything, from snow in August to sunburn in February. Even so, there are some weather trends and specific seasonal challenges to be aware of.

Summer Weather

During the busy summer months the park typically experiences intense afternoon storms. These often involve not only heavy rain and high winds but also significant drops in temperature along with dangerous lightning and sometimes a great deal of hail. It is not safe to be above the trees, beside a lake, or in open meadow when these storms move in, as you are likely to attract lightning. There have been a number of lightning-related deaths in the park. Some of these have been along Trail Ridge Road. The best way to ensure that you are not one of them is to stay below tree line or in a vehicle during the afternoon storms. If you see a storm moving in and you're up high, make your way down to the trees as quickly as you can. Because of this, if you are planning to summit a peak or planning to hike across open tundra, leave the trailhead early in the day and be back into the trees by midday. However, don't assume that the weather will always follow this pattern. Storms can creep up even in the morning or later in the evening, so always stay aware and be prepared to turn back if the weather looks threatening.

Another challenge with the weather is that while it may be mild down at the trailhead, it can be at or below freezing at higher elevations. There are days when it is about 90 degrees Fahrenheit in Denver and 35 degrees with high winds up at 13,000'. You won't want to be up there without winter gear in those conditions. Surprisingly, you can encounter a snowstorm at higher elevations during almost any month of the year.

Autumn Weather

During the autumn, especially after the second half of October, you are likely to encounter colder temperatures and very high winds. The winds can often gust upwards of 70 mph. This is enough to knock you off your feet, especially up high where there is no wind protection. If you are on cliff edges, ledges, or places where a fall could be serious, always be prepared for unexpected wind gusts. Keep your body weight low, your feet spread out a little, and keep a hand on surrounding rocks. The more points of contact you have with the ground the more stable you will be.

Such winds are also likely to blow trees down, so it's no safer in the forests. Falling trees are something you should take seriously, as they can fall on you from behind. You may not even hear them break due to the roar of the wind. You definitely don't want to be out if the winds are gusting above 40 mph and even at lesser speeds you should always stay aware of the potential for falling trees.

Winter Weather

The winter has its own unique set of challenges and must be taken seriously. The winds howl during much of the winter, scouring the

SHUTTLE BUSES

With the recent growth in visitation to Rocky Mountain National Park it has become increasingly difficult to get a parking place in the Bear Lake corridor as well as at a number of other trailheads on the east side of the park. To help alleviate this situation as well as to provide more eco-friendly alternatives for visiting the national park, the town of Estes Park and the National Park Service run a joint shuttle system. The park shuttle system actually began in the 1970s, and in 2006 a cooperative initiative was formed with the town of Estes Park. You can now take a shuttle from the visitor center in Estes Park up to the national park. This bus, which is operated by the town, runs to the Park & Ride, which serves as the main hub for buses in the park. From there you can catch one of the national park shuttles to several different locations in the park.

The shuttle buses are offered free of charge, though you still

areas above tree line and depositing the snow on the forests below. When hiking, snowshoeing, or skiing in the park during the winter months you need to be avalanche aware. Slopes between thirty and forty-five degrees are the ones that are most dangerous and should be avoided unless you know how to properly assess them. Even some popular trails cross slopes that occasionally avalanche. Check the Colorado Avalanche Information Center website (www.caic.org) to check current conditions. Another danger is that some slopes may have been turned to ice by the winds and could be dangerous to cross without the proper training and equipment. Also, it is important to be aware that the ice on the lakes and streams can be thin, particularly near inlets and outlets.

Spring Weather

In the spring (April through early June) one is likely to expect springlike conditions similar to what you may have at home, but in the mountains this is a snowy time. You can expect higher trails to still have a lot of snow cover into late May or early June. You can need to pay the park entrance fee. At the time of writing, the town-operated shuttle from Estes Park to the national park runs from late May through early September and then on weekends through early October. These buses are running from 7:30 a.m. until 8 p.m. The national park buses operate from late May through the first week of October from 7 a.m. until 7:30 p.m. The shuttle service times and locations may change from year to year and so it is worth getting a shuttle schedule from one of the park visitor centers or from the visitor center in Estes Park.

There are two main bus routes within the national park, both of which begin at the Park & Ride. The Bear Lake route makes stops at the Bierstadt Lake Trailhead, the Glacier Gorge Trailhead, and Bear Lake. The Moraine Park route stops at Glacier Creek Stables next to Sprague Lake, Hollowell Park, Tuxedo Park, the Moraine Park Campground, the Cub Lake Trailhead, and the Fern Lake bus stop. (Latest info at: www.HikingRocky.com/shuttle)

also expect large, heavy snowfalls during this time of year. While the lower meadows and surrounding towns may be snow free, the heart of the park will still be shedding its white coat. Spring is also a time to be aware of avalanches. During this time of year they occur mostly in the afternoons as the heat of the day causes the snow to melt. If you have to cross steep snowfields, you'll want to do it in the mornings and with proper equipment, as it can be quite icy at the start of the day. The spring is also a time when the rivers become dangerous. Each spring people underestimate the power of the streams and need to be rescued. It is best to keep your distance from streams and rivers at this time of year.

Wildlife

Rocky Mountain National Park is home to over sixty different species of mammals, as well as many birds, insects, and fish, so it is very likely that at some point you will encounter wildlife on your hikes through the park. Knowing what to do in an encounter can help keep it a safe and enjoyable experience. The first thing you should know is that it is illegal to approach wildlife in the park. They are to be left undisturbed. You know that you've gotten too close when they turn to look at you. If you encounter wildlife along the trails, keep your distance and wait until they depart before continuing onward. For most animals, it is recommended that you keep a distance of two bus lengths; for potentially dangerous wildlife such as moose and bear, keep a distance of three bus lengths.

Along with this, you should not attempt to feed any of the animals, as human food can make them ill. The squirrel population in Rocky Mountain National Park has had a problem with the bubonic plague, which developed because of the way some types of human food decomposes. Not only does feeding animals cause them problems but also if you are bitten by one of them they can potentially transmit the bubonic plaque to you. I am fairly sure this would not be on most people's bucket list.

It is unlikely that you will run into a bear or mountain lion, though moose encounters are becoming more common. If you do come across one of these animals, here's what you should know:

BLACK BEAR

BULL MOOSE

Bear

In Rocky Mountain National Park live about twenty black bears. There are no grizzly bears in Rocky. Black bears generally avoid people unless there is food left out to attract them. This is why bear canisters are required for anyone camping in the backcountry. Often people who are new to Rocky buy bear bells to alert the bears that you are coming. These are not necessary and there is little evidence that they do anything other than alert other visitors that you are new here. In my many years of hiking this park I have not had a single encounter with a bear on a trail. It's not that it can't happen; it's just very rare. If, however, you do encounter a bear, stand up tall and make loud noises such as shouting or clapping. This will typically scare them away. If you have small children, keep them near you and if you are with others, group together. If attacked, fight back! Never try to retrieve anything once a bear has it.

Moose

Though not a native species to this area, moose are becoming more and more prominent in Rocky Mountain National Park since

TRAIL CREWS

While hiking on Rocky Mountain National Park's 350 miles of trails, it is easy to forget all the work that takes place to maintain these trails. It is tempting to think of them as just rough dirt trails that need no help. Yet each winter the howling winds knock trees all over the trails, erosion undermines them and takes entire sections out, bridges and stairs decay over time, and millions of visitors add their own wear and damage to the trails and the areas around them. It takes a small army to keep these trails open, especially considering that almost all the work must be done during the short season of summer.

The national park maintains a seasonal trail crew of about forty people who begin in May to clear fallen trees on the low-elevation trails and then work toward the higher-elevation trails as the snow melts. From June through mid-August they are often joined by volunteer crews from a number of different organizations such as the Rocky Mountain Conservation Corps, the Student Conservation Association, Larimer County Youth Corps, Rocky Mountain Youth Corps, and Eagle Rock School. There are also individual volunteers with the national park who assist with this work.

Each summer these crews embark on large trail-restoration projects that are very labor-intensive. For example, they may need to put in a new staircase on a section of trail. To do this they survey the surrounding land to identify the resources they can use and then create a plan of action for how to use the identified rocks, soil, and logs in such a way as to not do any long-term damage to the off-trail areas. Often they have to create highlines to carry the rocks and logs above the forest floor. As they are in a wilderness area, all the work is done using non-power tools. Building a simple five-step staircase can therefore take nearly two weeks of hard labor. Think of that the next time you are complaining about another upward climb!

Mother Nature ensures that there is more work to be done each year than can actually be done, so consider volunteering with the park or supporting the work of the trail crews with a donation to the Rocky Mountain Conservancy.

their introduction to Colorado in 1978 by the Colorado Department of Wildlife. While more numerous on the west side, sightings are becoming increasingly common on the east side as well. They can be found almost anywhere in the park but are most likely to be found in marshy areas, especially areas with an abundance of willows. In writing this book, I must have come across well over twenty either right on or right next to the trail. Unlike bears, there is a high likelihood you may encounter a moose.

While they seem slow and docile, they are not to be messed with and can be very unpredictable. If agitated, they can charge without warning. As they can weigh up to 1,500 pounds and are incredibly strong, they can easily knock the strongest person to the ground and trample them in seconds. Like other large animals, you want to give them a lot of space. It is recommended that you keep a distance of three bus lengths between you and a moose. If you accidently have a close encounter, try to put an object like a tree or large rock between you and the animal while you slowly back away. As long as you give them the required space, they are generally happy to ignore you.

Mountain Lion

There are only thought to be a small number of mountain lions in Rocky Mountain National Park, as they have very large territories. They are elusive and almost never seen. If you are lucky enough to see one, keep your distance. When out hiking on the trail remember to keep children close to you and don't let them run ahead. Jogging is not recommended, as it can trigger a mountain lion's attack response. If you do have a close encounter, hold your ground or back away slowly. Face the lion and stand upright. Do all you can to appear larger such as raising your arms or holding a stick over your head. If you have children, pick them up. If the lion behaves aggressively, wave your arms and throw objects at it to convince it that you are not prey and that you may be dangerous. If attacked, fight back! Afterward, notify a ranger of your encounter. Encountering a mountain lion is rare. You are much more likely to be hit by lightning or a falling tree than to be attacked by a lion.

UNDERSTANDING SEARCH AND RESCUE (SAR)

Each year there are over two hundred Search and Rescue (SAR) incidents in Rocky Mountain National Park. Some of these are as simple as rescuing a person who has fallen on a trail and sprained their ankle, while others are much more serious such as finding a missing hiker in a remote or rugged area. Due to limited funding of our national parks, there isn't a full-time rescue crew. Instead, search and rescue efforts are spearheaded by the park's Visitor Protection Rangers.

The park's Visitor Protection Rangers are not sitting around drinking coffee and waiting for an emergency but are out in the park busy with a wide variety of jobs, from controlling traffic to backcountry patrol. When a call comes in, those closest to the incident are contacted and make their way to the place of need. Often this involves hiking out of one location and hiking in to another. This can take a while. Sometimes there is no one nearby or no one available due to other crises and so they need to get help from elsewhere. As a result, when something happens, it isn't like calling for an ambulance at home and having it arrive ten minutes later. If you call for help, you should anticipate it taking a number of hours before help is able to arrive.

Surprisingly, even after the first responder arrives it may take many hours to get you out. This is because carrying someone out is a very labor-intensive activity in the mountains. It takes six people to carry the litter and they need to trade off to others every five to fifteen minutes, depending on the terrain. As a result it takes a large team of people, sometimes thirty or more, for a simple rescue. When large teams are needed the call goes out to the entire national park staff and those who can drop their other jobs, dress for the rescue, and make it to the place of the incident. Assembling such a team takes time. In some instances, particularly late in the day or during the winter season, a ranger may arrive only to inform you that they are going to stay with you overnight and in the morning a crew will arrive to start carrying you out.

Searches for missing persons are one of the most involved

activities. These can sometimes last for a week or more. These searches involve a team of thirty to forty in the field and a large support crew of perhaps twenty more working behind the scenes. They are a persistent group and in all the years of conducting searches have only had one person they couldn't find.

Rocky Mountain National Park does not have its own helicopter. Occasionally, when the situation is appropriate, they will call in a helicopter from outside the park. There are many variables that they consider in determining whether to do this or not. Most rescues occur without the use of a helicopter.

In order to avoid being the subject of a search and rescue incident, follow these recommendations:

- Tell someone exactly where you are going, when you plan to return, and the route you plan to take.
- Thoroughly research the hike you plan to do so you know where to go and what to expect.
- Research and compare multiple weather forecasts before you go.
- Bring proper footwear and proper clothing.
- Be prepared to spend a night with a little extra food, extra water, and extra clothing beyond what you need for the hike.

If you are injured:

- When you contact dispatch provide a good description of what happened, exactly where you are, and what you need.
- Do what you can to make at least some progress toward the trailhead, as that will help speed your rescue.

Other Concerns

Mosquitoes

As a general rule there are very few biting insects in Rocky Mountain National Park, which makes hiking here a real pleasure compared to other parks. However, there are times and places where you may encounter swarms of mosquitoes. Apart from the general discomfort they may cause, there is also the possibility that they could carry the West Nile virus. Generally it is the very young, the elderly, or those with suppressed immune systems who are most likely to be harmed. Nonetheless, it would be wise to protect yourself when you are hiking through areas with large mosquito populations. Cover your skin with clothing they can't bite through and use some form of mosquito repellent. I also carry a head net for these occasional but uncomfortable situations.

Ticks

During the spring, sometimes beginning as early as February, ticks will come out in force, particularly in the warmer low-elevation areas. They often hang on the long grasses or on the branches of trees, waiting for a meal to walk by. Ticks in the park may carry Colorado tick fever or Rocky Mountain spotted fever, both of which can cause serious illnesses. There are several things you can do to protect yourself. Firstly, reduce the amount of exposed skin and close off openings to the skin; for example, with long pants that are tucked in at the bottom. You can wear gaiters, put a rubber band around your pant leg, or pull your socks up around the outside of your pant legs. You will also want to wear a long-sleeve shirt, a hat, and something around your neck. Secondly, there are some tick repellents that can be used to make you less attractive. Some are designed for clothing and others for exposed skin. Thirdly and most importantly, as soon as you are done with your hike check your clothing carefully and then fully check your body. They like to crawl into areas like belly buttons, ears, hair, underarms, and genital areas. The CDC recommends that you put your hiking clothing in the dryer for at least ten minutes on high heat to kill any ticks that may have come home with you.

If you do find a tick, don't worry, as it generally takes up to a day before they can burrow in enough to transmit disease. If they have begun to bite, you'll want to remove them with a tweezer, being sure to grab them from the pinchers rather than from their body and making sure to remove all the mouth parts. I then recommend putting them in a ziplock bag with the date on it and put them in the

HIKER AT LAKE OF GLASS

freezer. That way if any symptoms develop you can bring the tick in with you for testing. If no illness appears you may use them as condiments. Just kidding! If you experience a fever within two weeks of the bite, see your doctor and let them know you were bitten by a tick.

APPROACHING LAKE NANITA

TYPES OF HIKES

This section contains lists of different types of hikes to help you find exactly the right one for you. I find that many people are looking for very specific things when they hike, be it wildflowers, a summit to conquer, a hike that is a loop so that everything they see is new, etc. The following lists address some of the most common things hikers ask about. Each of the hikes is listed in order of difficulty.

LOOP HIKES

These are hikes that start and end at the same place but don't repeat any of the same trail. They show you something different the entire way unlike the majority of hikes in this book, which are hikes up to a destination and then back down the same way you came.

* Lily Lake - 134
* Sprague Lake - 138
* Hidden Valley - 165
* Bear Lake - 146
* Upper Beaver Meadows Loop - 171

* Cub Lake Loop - 254
* Haiyaha Loop - 270
* Big Meadows Loop - 284
* Lumpy Loop - 376
* Western Loop - 444

ONE-WAY HIKES

The one-way hikes are hikes that most people only do in one direction and then get a ride back to their starting point. You'll need to arrange your ride back before you leave, as cell phone coverage is spotty. Any of these hikes can be done as a there-and-back hike or as a hike in the opposite direction, but be aware that I have recorded these hikes in their easiest direction. If you intend to do them both

TRAIL TO ODESSA LAKE

ways, I encourage you to do the hardest direction first and then do your return trip in the direction I've described in the book.

One of the really special things about Rocky Mountain National Park is the large number of lakes that can be found throughout the park. The vast majority of them have incredible views of the surrounding peaks, making them among the most beautiful places in the entire park. Below are some of the best lakes to visit in the park.

- Lily Lake - 134
- Sprague Lake - 138
- Bear Lake - 146
- Dream Lake - 205
- Bierstadt Lake Loop - 238
- Emerald Lake - 226
- Cub Lake - 246
- Mills Lake - 250
- The Loch - 266
- Haiyaha Loop - 270
- Fern Lake - 288
- Finch Lake - 330
- Black Lake - 302
- Ouzel Lake - 350
- Lawn Lake - 342
- Sandbeach Lake - 334
- Chasm Lake - 354
- Timber Lake - 368
- Pear Lake - 386
- Mirror Lake - 372
- Lake Verna - 382
- Bluebird Lake - 404
- Crystal Lakes - 418
- Lake Nanita - 438

SPRAGUE LAKE

TUNDRA HIKES

These are hikes that will take you up into the alpine zone where you can experience the world above the trees. On these hikes you need to be especially careful to watch the weather, as you should never be in this zone during a thunderstorm.

- Forest Canyon Overlook - 163
- Tundra Communities - 180
- Alpine Ridge Trail - 210
- Tombstone Ridge - 218
- Western Ute - 214
- Chasm Lake - 354
- Flattop Mountain - 362
- The Boulderfield - 400
- Bighorn Flats - 408
- Crystal Lakes - 418
- Bear Lake to Grand Lake (North Inlet) - 422
- Bear Lake to Grand Lake (Tonahutu) - 426
- Western Loop - 444

WILDFLOWER HIKES

This section lists trails where you may find wildflowers. These trails are listed not because the destination has flowers, though it may, but because you are likely to find wildflowers along the way as you hike these trails.

Be aware that the flowers can come and go quite quickly and that different areas tend to bloom at different times of year. You'll also find very different flowers in the tundra than you'll find in the meadows. As a general rule, you will start seeing flowers in the lower meadows beginning in mid-May usually until sometime in late July. While in the tundra you may see them from mid-June until as late as mid-August.

- Forest Canyon Overlook - 163
- Adams Falls & East Meadow - 175
- Tundra Communities - 180
- Summerland Park - 192
- Western Ute - 214
- Tombstone Ridge - 218
- Cub Lake - 246
- Ouzel Lake - 350
- Mirror Lake - 372
- Bluebird Lake - 404
- Crystal Lakes - 418

FERN FALLS

WATERFALL HIKES

Along each of the hikes listed you will find at least one waterfall. On most of these hikes the waterfalls are not at the destination but somewhere along the trail.

- Adams Falls & East Meadow - 175
- Alberta Falls - 188
- Calypso Cascades - 222
- Cascade Falls - 262
- Ouzel Falls - 258
- Fern Lake - 288
- Odessa Hike - 292
- Granite Falls - 320
- Black Lake - 302
- Sky Pond - 314

SUMMIT HIKES

For those of you who like to stand on top, these are the hikes in this book that will take you to an actual summit of a mountain. Most of the other summits in Rocky Mountain National Park can only be reached by going off trail and so are not covered in this book. Talk to a ranger before attempting any of those.

◆ Deer Mountain - 276
◆ Twin Sisters Peaks - 306
◆ Estes Cone - 326 & 358
◆ Flattop Mountain - 362

◆ Longs Peak - 462 (not a hike but rather a very serious climb)

BULL ELK IN SPRING COAT

WILDLIFE HIKES

Various forms of wildlife can be found throughout Rocky Mountain National Park. The following hikes are ones where there is a particularly good chance you may see wildlife, but there is never any guarantee. Coming early in the morning or late in the evening and being very quiet can certainly help improve your chances. Review the section about viewing wildlife on page - 87.

- Coyote Valley Trail - 142
- Holzwarth Historic Site - 150
- Adams Falls & East Meadow - 175
- Western Ute - 214
- Cub Lake - 246 & 254
- Lulu City - 280
- Big Meadows Loop - 284
- Ouzel Lake - 350
- Western Loop - 444

HISTORICAL HIKES

The following hikes are ones where you will pass by some of the human history of the area. At the back of this book I list a few resources that will help you to learn more about each of these areas.

- Sprague Lake - 138 (Sprague Lodge)
- Holzwarth Historic Site - 150 (former ranch and early tourist lodge)
- Lulu City - 280 (former mining town)
- Big Meadows Loop - 284 (old homestead ruin on Big Meadows)
- Fern Lake - 288 (former sites of Old Forest Inn and Fern Lodge)
- Estes Cone from Longs Peak Trailhead - 326 (Eugenia Mine)

AUTUMN HIKES

In the autumn the leaves are changing and the elk are in rut. Most trails are still great for hiking, but those listed below can be especially pretty at this time of year. The locations at higher elevations will change first and then the autumn colors will slowly make their way downward. Even though I don't list tundra hikes here, don't overlook autumn in the tundra in late August and early September. While there are no trees at that elevation, the colors of the grasses have their own beauty.

- Lily Lake - 134
- Bear Lake - 146
- Alberta Falls - 188
- Dream Lake - 205
- Bierstadt Lake Loop - 238
- East Shore Trail - 234

WINTER HIKES

Hiking in the winter is a very different experience. The trails could either be icy, meaning you'll need microspikes, or they could be snow covered,

WINTER NEAR DREAM LAKE

requiring snowshoes. Trails in the subalpine zone are likely to have more
snow, while lower trails, especially on the Estes Park side, may have none.
Navigating after heavy snows can be difficult, as there may be no sign of
the trail; the issue of encountering avalanches must also be taken seriously. Here are some hikes that are generally easy to navigate during the
winter—but you might still need microspikes or snowshoes. Accessible
hikes are no longer considered accessible in the winter. Also, the rating
system used in this book is not applicable for snow-covered trails.

Snowy Trails

- Sprague Lake - 138
- Bear Lake - 146
- Holzwarth Historic
  Site - 150

- Bear Lake to Park &
  Ride - 200
- Dream & Emerald lakes
  - 205 & 226
- Mills Lake - 250

Possibly Snow-free Trails

- Black Canyon Trail - 230
- Gem Lake - 242

EARLY SPRING HIKES

In April and May, while much of the United States is enjoying beautiful springlike conditions, much of Rocky Mountain National Park
is still in the midst of winter. Most hikes above 10,000' will have deep
snow, as this can be one of the snowiest times of the year, even at lower
elevations. To avoid most of the snow, consider the following hikes.

- Lily Lake - 134
- Sprague Lake - 138
- Coyote Valley - 142
- Holzwarth Historic
  Site - 150

- Adams Falls & East
  Meadow - 175
- The Pool - 197
- Black Canyon Trail - 230
- East Shore Trail - 234
- Gem Lake - 242

While not official trails you could also try, Wild Basin Road, Old
Fall River Road, Upper Beaver Meadows Road or Trail Ridge Road
before they open to traffic later in the spring or summer.

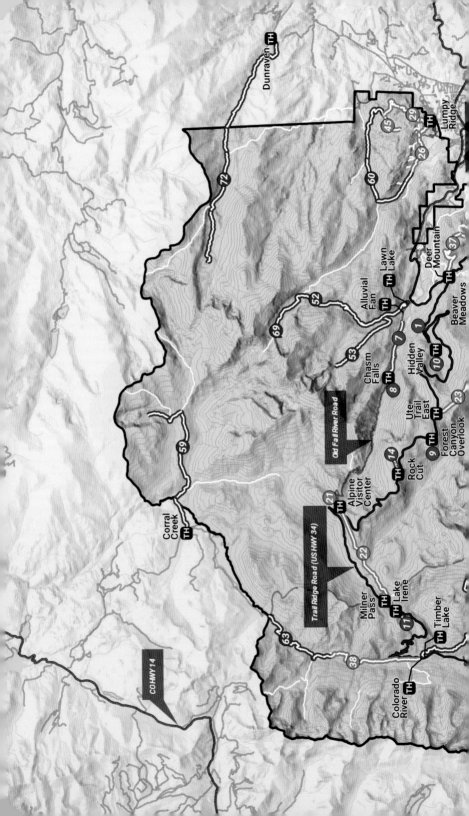

EAST INLET TRAILHEAD

THE TRAILHEADS

Many different hikes in Rocky Mountain National Park begin from the same trailhead, so in order to avoid repeating the same information again and again throughout this guide, I've created a trailhead section. Here you'll find: how to get there, how much parking is available, what amenities you'll find, if shuttle service is available, etc. At the beginning of each hike, I'll reference the page that has the appropriate trailhead information.

ALPINE VISITOR CENTER

One of the most popular places to visit in Rocky Mountain National Park is the Alpine Visitor Center on Trail Ridge Road. It is located twenty miles west of the main east entrance at an elevation of 11,796'. While the parking lot is very large, it is often filled by 10 a.m. during the busy season and stays busy until about 3:30 p.m. You'll find 158 standard parking spaces, four accessible spaces, and nine spaces for buses and RVs. On the south side of the parking lot you'll see two large buildings; the one farther to the west is the visitor center run by the national park and the Rocky Mountain Conservancy. They have exhibits about the alpine world and hold regular ranger programs, an information desk, and a small store with books and gifts. The building to the east of this is the Trail Ridge Store & Café, which offers primarily gifts and food with some great views out their back windows. These typically open around 9 a.m. and close about 5 p.m. There is one set of restrooms on the east end of the visitor center and there are vault toilets over on the north side of the parking lot. Hikes available from this location:

- Alpine Ridge Trail — starts on the northeast end of the parking lot (page 210)

- Western Ute Trail — starts on the southwest end of the parking lot just accross Trail Ridge Road (page 214)

ALLUVIAL FAN PARKING AREAS

There are two separate parking areas for the Alluvial Fan: an east parking area and a west parking area. These are located off of Highway 34 on Endovalley Road. The first parking lot is 0.4 miles from the intersection and the second is 0.7 miles. Both of these will get you onto the same trail, but for the directions given in the book and for accessible access I recommend the western parking area. The western parking lot is larger, with space for twenty-two vehicles parked side by side as well as room for a few parallel-parked vehicles and some accessible parking. This west parking lot has vault toilets and several picnic tables. It is located at an elevation of 8,585'.

The east parking lot has space for seventeen vehicles parked side by side as well as a few vehicles parked parallel and one accessible space. The east parking area has no facilities and is located at 8,756'.

Hikes avavailable from these trailheads:

- Alluvial Fan Trail - 154

- Chasm Falls (winter access) - 162

BEAR LAKE TRAILHEAD

This trailhead is located at the very end of Bear Lake Road, about 9.5 miles south of the Beaver Meadows Entrance Station. There are 215 standard spaces, seven accessible parking spots, and a small area for two or three motorcycles. While this is one of the largest parking areas in Rocky Mountain National Park, it fills rapidly due to its popularity. If you want to drive your own vehicle, I recommend arriving as early as possible, as it is usually full by 6:30 a.m. during summer days and autumn weekends, or arrive late in the day. Alternatively, during the summer and fall, you can take a shuttle from the Park & Ride up to Bear Lake.

Although this trailhead primarily serves the trails leading to Bear Lake, Dream Lake, Emerald Lake, Lake Haiyaha, Fern Lake, and Flattop Mountain, you can also access all the trails in Glacier Gorge from here. The Glacier Gorge Trails can be reached by turning left behind the ranger station and then in about 100 feet you'll turn left again at the next trail junction. Starting at Bear Lake adds an additional 0.1 miles each way plus 113' of additional elevation gain on your return to Bear Lake.

At the trailhead you will find a row of vault toilets on the southwest corner as well as a small ranger station that is typically staffed on most busy days of the year. The elevation at the Bear Lake Trailhead is 9,475'.

Hikes available from this trailhead:

- Bear Lake - 146
- Alberta Falls - 188
- Dream Lake - 205
- Bear Lake to Park & Ride - 200
- Emerald Lake - 226
- Mills Lake - 250
- The Loch - 266
- Haiyaha Loop - 270
- Black Lake - 302
- Sky Pond - 314
- Flattop Mountain -362
- Bighorn Flats - 408

FEBRUARY AT THE BEAR LAKE RANGER STATION

BIERSTADT LAKE TRAILHEAD

The Bierstadt Lake Trailhead is located about seven miles down Bear Lake Road on the right side. It has a smaller parking lot holding only twelve vehicles and one accessible vehicle but has a large covered bus shelter and vault toilets. Because this parking lot is so small it may fill very early. Fortunately, during the summer and early autumn you can take a shuttle bus here from the Park & Ride. The trailhead is located on the northwest corner of the parking lot. Its elevation is 8,850'. The only hike in this book available from this trailhead is:

◆ Bierstadt Lake - 238

CHASM FALLS PARKING AREA

The Chasm Falls parking area is located 1.3 miles up Old Fall River Road from the point at which it becomes a one-way dirt road. Be aware that if you start on this dirt road, you can't turn around after hiking the falls. You have to follow the road all the way up to the Alpine Visitor Center and return via Trail Ridge Road.

The parking area is on the left side of the road and can hold about thirty vehicles. There are no facilities. The trail for Chasm Falls begins on the southeast end of the parking area. The elevation here is 9,091'. The only hike available from this trailhead is:

◆ Chasm Falls - 160

COLORADO RIVER TRAILHEAD

The Colorado River Trailhead is located at the north end of the Kawuneeche Valley, 9.5 miles from the west entrance to Rocky Mountain National Park. It is on the west side of the road and has a very large parking area with room for approximately fifty vehicles. These parking spaces include a number of pull-through parking spots, ideal for large vehicles or vehicles with trailers. There are also three accessible parking places. Around the parking lot are a number of picnic tables, with some in the woods on the east side. There is a vault toilet as

COLORADO RIVER TRAILHEAD

well as a bear-proof trash can and recycling containers. The elevation at the trailhead is 9,010'.

Hikes in this guide available from this trailhead:

- Lulu City - 280
- La Poudre Pass - 390

CORRAL CREEK TRAILHEAD

Corral Creek is the most remote trailhead in Rocky Mountain National Park. It is located on the northern border of the park and is only accessed via Highway 14 from Walden to the west or Fort Collins to the east. This is a long drive from both Estes Park and Grand Lake. It requires following Long Draw Road, a gravel road that typically opens on July 1 and is maintained by the United States Forest Service. I recommend checking the road status before you make the drive, as this road is occasionally closed. You can find road status updates under the Canyon Lakes Area at https://www.fs.usda.gov/arp.

From Estes Park, drive down Highway 34 toward Loveland and then turn left on Buckhorn Road, which will take you through

CORRAL CREEK RANGER CABIN

Masonville. Follow this until you reach Highway 14. Turn left and follow this up the Poudre Canyon for thirty-eight miles. Turn left on Long Draw Road and follow this dirt road for 3.6 miles until you come to an unmarked intersection. Turn right and continue for another 5.0 miles. The trailhead will be on your left but it is easy to miss, so keep your eyes open for a log cabin on the right side of the road. The trailhead is on the opposite side of the road.

Alternatively, you can drive via Grand Lake. From Grand Lake head south to Granby, follow Highway 40 west for a short distance and then take Highway 125 north to Rand. Turn onto Highway 27 north until it intersects with Highway 14. Follow Highway 14 east until you reach Long Draw Road. Turn right and then follow the directions above.

The trailhead has a dirt parking lot. If everyone parks properly, there should be room for about fifteen vehicles. There are no facilities here at all. The small ranger cabin on the opposite side of the road is only used occasionally. The trailhead starts on the east end of the parking lot. The elevation here is 10,034'. The only trail in the book that is accessed from the Corral Creek Trailhead is:

- Mirror Lake Trail -372

COYOTE VALLEY TRAILHEAD

The Coyote Valley Trailhead is located on the west side of Trail Ridge Road in the Kawuneeche Valley between the Onahu Trailhead and the Bowen Baker Trailhead. This parking area heads down a short, steep hill and into the forest. It is pretty tight and is not suitable for large vehicles. Those towing trailers will likely get stuck if they attempt to drive down here. There is parking for eleven cars and also five accessible parking places. These fill quite quickly. There are wheelchair-accessible toilets here as well as a number of wheelchair-accessible picnic tables along the trail. The elevation here is 8,834'. The only hike available from this trailhead is:

 ◆ Coyote Valley Trail - 142

CUB LAKE TRAILHEAD

The Cub Lake Trailhead is located at the west end of Moraine Park, which is off of Bear Lake Road. Follow Bear Lake Road for 1.2 miles and then turn right opposite the museum onto Moraine Park Road. Follow Moraine Park Road about half a mile. Just before the campground, turn left and follow Fern Lake Road 1.3 miles to the Cub Lake Trailhead. You'll find a parking area on the right side of the road shortly after the pavement ends. This can hold about fourteen cars. Right next to the trailhead, farther down on the left, you'll find an area that holds about seven cars. If both of these are full, you can continue down to the next parking area, which also holds about seven cars. At the Cub Lake Trailhead there are no amenities but there is a shuttle bus stop just opposite. The elevation at the Cub Lake Trailhead is 8,080'.

Hikes available from this trailhead:

 ◆ Cub Lake- 246   ◆ Cub Lake Loop -254

DEER MOUNTAIN TRAILHEAD

This trailhead is found at Deer Ridge Junction on Trail Ridge Road, almost exactly three miles up the road from the Beaver Meadows

Entrance Station. There are places for about twenty-two vehicles and then a few more a bit farther down the road. This is a popular hike, as it is easy to access, so getting here early is key in securing a place to park. There are no toilets or other amenities to be found here. The elevation is 8,930'. The only hike in this book accessed from this trailhead is:

- Deer Mountain - 276

DUNRAVEN TRAILHEAD

The Dunraven Trailhead is located about ten miles east of Estes Park. From downtown Estes Park follow MacGregor Avenue for just over seven miles to the little town of Glen Haven. Make sure to pop in to the General Store and get a hot cinnamon roll. Continue past town for an additional mile and a half. You'll see a road on your left called Dunraven Glade Road. The area is known as the Retreat. Follow the dirt road for about two miles. Please respect the speed limit, as it is an attempt to keep the dust down for those who live there. The trailhead will be on the left-hand side and is very obvious. There is room for about thirty to forty cars if parked in two rows. There are usually horse trailers parked here as well. There is a vault toilet on the west side but no other facilities. The elevation at the trailhead is 7,789'. The only trail from here is the Lost Lake Trail, sometimes called the Dunraven Trail:

- Lost Lake Trail - 432

EAST INLET TRAILHEAD

The East Inlet Trailhead is located on the east end of Grand Lake (the lake, not the town) next to the boat launch. It is about 1.5 miles east of town on West Portal Road. When you arrive the boat launch parking is on your right and the trailhead parking is on your left. This is a large parking lot that holds approximately sixty vehicles. There are vault toilets here and bear-proof garbage and recycling cans. The trailhead is at an elevation of 8,400'. Hikes available from this trailhead:

EAST SHORE TRAILHEAD

This trailhead is located off of Jericho Road in the town of Grand Lake. It lies just south of the inlet dividing Grand Lake and Shadow Mountain Lake. To get here from the Grand Lake Visitor Center at the entrance to town, head east on the main road, which is Highway 278, and take a right on Lake Avenue, then take the next right onto Shadow Mountain Drive and follow it for about half a mile until you reach the bridge. Take a right onto the bridge, which is Jericho Road, and follow it for another half a mile until you see the East Shore Trail parking area on your right. The parking area can hold about fifteen cars. There are no toilet facilities here. You will, however, find a bike rack if you prefer to arrive via your own locomotion. The trail begins on the east side of the parking area where you will see a large information display. This trailhead is in the Arapahoe National Recreation Area rather than in the national park. Be aware that this trail will be multi-use, so keep your eyes open for people on bikes. The elevation at the trailhead is 8,440'. The only trail accessed from here is:

- East Shore Trail - 234

FERN LAKE TRAILHEAD

The Fern Lake Trailhead is located at the west end of Moraine Park, which is off of Bear Lake Road. Follow Bear Lake Road for 1.2 miles and turn right on Moraine Park Road opposite the museum and follow it down along the north edge of Moraine Park. At 0.5 miles, just before the campground, turn left and follow Fern Lake Road to its terminus, which is approximately 2.5 miles. Much of this road is gravel. The last stretch of road is usually only open during the summer and early autumn months. If it is closed or if the parking is full you can park at the Fern Lake bus stop and walk an extra 0.6 miles each way.

When you arrive at the Fern Lake Trailhead you'll find parking for only twenty-five to thirty vehicles, but just back down the road a short distance you'll find a few more parking spots. There are no toilets here and no amenities other than a garbage can. You'll also find a vault on the southwest corner designed to protect food from bears. If you have food or other items with an odor in your car, it would be wise to put it in this public vault until you return, as bears may tear the door off of your car to get to any food left behind. The elevation is 8,155'. From this location you can access the following hikes listed in this book:

- ◆ The Pool - 197
- ◆ Fern Lake - 288

FINCH LAKE TRAILHEAD

The Finch Lake Trailhead is located on Wild Basin Road just 0.3 miles before the main Wild Basin Trailhead. There are no facilities at the

FERN LAKE TRAIL

Finch Lake Trailhead other than food-storage lockers, which if used will help keep the bears out of your car. This gravel parking area has room for only seven vehicles. You may also park at the main Wild Basin parking area or other parking spots along Wild Basin road, but be aware that most of these generally fill quite early in the morning. The elevation at the trailhead is 8,476'. From this location you can access the following hikes listed in this book:

- Finch Lake - 330
- Pear Lake - 386

FOREST CANYON OVERLOOK

The Forest Canyon parking area is located fourteen miles up Trail Ridge Road from the eastern entrance to Rocky Mountain National Park. It is located above tree line and can be found on the south side of the road. At the parking area there are no facilities but there is parking for thirty-three standard vehicles and two accessible spots. The elevation is 11,699'. The only trail accessed from here is:

- Forest Canyon Overlook - 163

GLACIER GORGE TRAILHEAD

The Glacier Gorge Trailhead is one of the most popular trailheads in the park but has a relatively small parking lot with thirty-eight standard parking spots and two accessible parking spots. There are vault toilets and during the summer and early autumn it is not unusual to find a volunteer ranger standing near the trailhead ready to answer questions. The trailhead is located eight miles down Bear Lake Road on the left-hand side. The parking lot fills so quickly that I've had national park leaders joke with me that if you see an open parking spot you should take it whether or not you were planning to hike there, since a free parking spot is such a rare find. Parking is often full by 6 a.m. and sometimes even earlier and can stay full until late evening. Fortunately, it is serviced during the summer and autumn by the park shuttle.

All of the trails that are accessed from the Glacier Gorge Trailhead can also be accessed from the Bear Lake Trailhead, with a slight

0.1-mile addition each way and a total 113' of elevation gain that you'll climb on your return to Bear Lake, so save a little energy for the climb back up.

The elevation at the Glacier Gorge Trailhead is 9,175'. From this trailhead you can reach

- ◆ Alberta Falls - 188
- ◆ Mills Lake - 250
- ◆ The Loch - 266
- ◆ Haiyaha Loop - 270
- ◆ Black Lake - 302
- ◆ Sky Pond - 314
- ◆ All Bear Lake hikes - 110

GREEN MOUNTAIN TRAILHEAD

The Green Mountain Trailhead is located 2.6 miles north of the Rocky Mountain National Park Grand Lake Entrance Station on the east side of the road. The trailhead parking lot is paved and can accommodate about twenty-five vehicles. There are also vault toilets. The elevation at the trailhead is 8,794'. From here you can access the following trails:

- ◆ Big Meadows Loop - 284
- ◆ Granite Falls - 320
- ◆ Haynach Lakes - 412

HIDDEN VALLEY PARKING AREA

The Hidden Valley parking area is located 5.5 miles up Trail Ridge Road from the main east entrance. You'll take a right turn on a sharp switchback and then follow the paved road for about a third of a mile. The parking area for Hidden Valley is very large, holding 105 standard vehicles and six accessible parking spots. Hidden Valley used to be a downhill ski area until it was closed in 1990. Today it is a winter play area with a sledding hill during the winter months. In the summer it is the headquarters of the Junior Ranger program and one of the best picnic spots in the park, with numerous picnic tables throughout the area. There are flush toilets and running water in the main building and there are usually rangers on site to answer questions when they are not busy with Junior Ranger activities. The elevation is 9,412'. The only trail you can access here is:

GREEN MOUNTAIN
TRAILHEAD

- Hidden Valley Loop Trail - 165

HOLZWARTH HISTORIC SITE

This is a large parking area located on the west side of Trail Ridge Road in the Kawuneeche Valley about 7.5 miles north of the west entrance to Rocky Mountain National Park. There are spaces for thirty-two vehicles and four accessible vehicles. You'll also find about six picnic tables in the trees on the east side of the parking lot. There are vault toilets on the west side of the parking area. The trail begins on the south side of the parking area. The elevation is 8,911'. From here you can walk the trail to the:

- Holzwarth Historic Site - 150

LAKE IRENE TRAILHEAD

The Lake Irene Trailhead is located just off of Trail Ridge Road right below Poudre Lake. It has thirteen parking places as well as one accessible parking spot. There are a few picnic tables and a vault toilet. The trail to Lake Irene and the Lake Irene Overlook begins on the northwest corner and starts at an elevation of 10,664'. The only trail from this trailhead is:

- Lake Irene Overlook - 168

LAWN LAKE TRAILHEAD

The Lawn Lake Trailhead is located in the Endovalley, just a little west of Horseshoe Park. It is best accessed from the Fall River entrance to Rocky Mountain National Park via highway 34. There are spaces for about thirty cars in the parking lot. There is also a vault toilet and a few picnic tables. The elevation at this trailhead is 8,540'. From here you can hike to:

- Lawn Lake - 342
- Ypsilon Lake - 346
- Crystal Lakes - 418

LILY LAKE TRAILHEAD

This trailhead is located 6.1 miles south of Estes Park on the west side of Highway 7 right beside beautiful Lily Lake. There is room for twenty vehicles plus two accessible parking spots. There are trash bins, picnic tables, and vault toilets. If the parking here is filled, there is another parking area of similar size just on the opposite side of Highway 7. The elevation here is 8,931'. From here you can hike to

- Lily Lake - 134
- Lily Ridge Loop - 184
- Estes Cone - 358

LONGS PEAK TRAILHEAD

The Longs Peak Trailhead is located 8.6 miles south of Estes Park off of Highway 7. Turn right onto Longs Peak Road and follow it approximately one mile to the end of the road. There you will find a

parking lot that holds sixty-four cars, plus three accessible parking spaces.
There are vault toilets on the northwest end of the parking area as well as
vault toilets located a couple hundred feet to the south. There is a ranger
station at the trailhead, which is manned most summer days during business hours. The rangers here would be happy to answer any questions
you might have. There are picnic tables available near the ranger station
and also a couple on the northeast corner in the trees. You'll find a couple
of food-storage lockers just to the north side of the ranger station. The
trailhead is at an elevation of 9,400'. From this trailhead you can hike to

- Estes Cone - 326
- Chasm Lake - 354
- Longs Peak - 462

LUMPY RIDGE TRAILHEAD

The Lumpy Ridge Trailhead is located two miles north of Estes Park
off of Devil's Gulch Road. The paved parking area has vault toilets and
parking for about ninety cars. Despite this, on busy days the parking
lot can fill early and then it is necessary to park down on Devil's Gulch
Road. Please park on the dirt and **not** on the grass. This trailhead has two
different trails leading from the parking lot, so pay attention to which
trail you take. The elevation at the Lumpy Ridge Trailhead is 7,840'. This
trailhead provides access to

- Black Canyon Trail - 230
- Gem Lake - 242
- Balanced Rock - 310
- Lumpy Loop - 376

MILNER PASS TRAILHEAD

Right next to Poudre Lake, twenty-four miles from the main east
entrance along Trail Ridge Road and sixteen miles from the west
entrance, is the Milner Pass Trailhead. Many people stop here to have
their photo taken at the sign for the Continental Divide, which runs
right through the parking area. There is a vault toilet but no other
facilities. There is parking for twenty-two vehicles and one accessible
vehicle. About a quarter of a mile to the east of the trailhead is another

A QUIET DAY AT PARK & RIDE

parking area that holds about seven vehicles and another one a quarter of a mile east of that on the opposite side of the road where there is space for about ten cars if they are parked nose inward. The elevation here is 10,750'. Most hikers will begin up at the Alpine Visitor Center and then get picked up at this location. This is the ending of the:

- ◆ Western Ute Trail - 214

NORTH INLET TRAILHEAD

Within walking distance of the town of Grand Lake is the North Inlet Trailhead. The easiest way to get here by car is to head out of town on Garfield Road up to West Portal Road, turn right and about a quarter of a mile down on your left you'll see a dirt road named 663 with a sign for Shadow Cliff Lodge. Follow that very steep dirt road up to the top of the hill and turn right. That will bring you to the first parking lot for the North Inlet Trailhead. You'll find seven parking spots plus two accessible parking spots as well as a vault toilet. There is then another parking lot a little farther up the road with twenty parking spaces. The trailhead elevation is 8,520' and is

at the southeast end of the first parking area. From this trailhead you
can reach

- Summerland Park - 192
- Cascade Falls - 262
- Lake Nanita - 438

This is also the end point for

- Bear Lake to Grand Lake - 422
- The Western Loop Trail - 444

PARK & RIDE

Drive five miles down Bear Lake Road to reach the Park & Ride. This is the largest parking area in Rocky Mountain National Park. It has room for 338 standard vehicles, six accessible vehicles, and eleven spots for RVs and buses. Despite its size, on busy days it can fill by 9 a.m. or earlier. The Park & Ride has vault toilets and a small ranger station. There are no picnic areas or other facilities.

The Park & Ride is not only a parking area but also the main bus terminal in the park. From here you can take a bus up the Bear Lake Corridor with stops at the Bierstadt Lake Trailhead, the Glacier Gorge Trailhead, and Bear Lake. You can also catch the Moraine Park bus, which will take you to the Moraine Park Campground, the Cub Lake Trailhead, the Fern Lake bus stop, and other stops. There is also a bus that will take you into the town of Estes Park to the town visitor center.

The elevation of the Park & Ride is 8,635'. The Bierstadt Moraine Trailhead is located on the far west end of the parking lot. Both Bear Lake and Bierstadt Lake can be reached from this trailhead. This is the end point for the:

- Bear Lake to Park & Ride hike - 200

ROCK CUT

The Rock Cut parking area is located sixteen miles up Trail Ridge Road from the main east entrance. It is located directly on Trail Ridge Road. There are two sets of vault toilets on the north side of the road: one on the east end and one on the west. There are no other facilities here. There are a total of forty-two standard parking spaces; fourteen of them are parallel parking on the south side of the road. There are also two accessible parking spaces. The elevation here is 12,110'. The only trail that can be accessed from here is:

- ◆ Tundra Communities Trail - 180

SANDBEACH LAKE TRAILHEAD

The Sandbeach Lake Trailhead is right at the entrance to the Wild Basin area of the park, just off of Highway 7 and about twelve miles south of Estes Park. After you go through the entrance station, pull into the parking lot on your right and you will see the trailhead on the north end. There is room for thirteen vehicles on the pavement and about seven more on a dirt section located at the end of the parking lot. At the trailhead you will find a vault toilet on the west end and a food vault. The elevation at the trailhead is 8,316'. The only trail in the book that can be accessed from here is:

- ◆ Sandbeach Lake - 334

WILD BASIN VIEW

SPRAGUE LAKE TRAILHEAD

The Sprague Lake Trailhead is located off of Bear Lake Road. Drive down Bear Lake Road for six miles and turn left. It is the first left after passing the Park & Ride. The parking area has about fifty standard parking spots and five accessible parking spots. You'll find bathrooms with running water as well as another building with vault toilets in the parking area. There are also numerous picnic tables; some have fire pits with grills for roasting burgers or hot dogs. This area is also serviced by a shuttle bus that drops passengers off at Glacier Creek Stables. There is a short trail that leads from the stables to the lake. The Sprague Lake Trail begins on the southeast corner of the parking area. The elevation at Sprague Lake is 8,701'. The only trail here that is in this book is:

- Sprague Lake Trail - 138

TIMBER LAKE TRAILHEAD

The Timber Lake Trailhead is located on the north end of the Kawun-echee Valley on the east side of the road, just across from the Colorado River Trailhead. It is located 9.5 miles from the west entrance. It is a fairly large parking lot with thirty-six standard parking places and three accessible parking spaces. It tends to only fill on the busiest of days. The trail begins on the east side of the parking area. There is a nice picnic area as well as a vault toilet. There are tall aspens lining both the parking lot and the beginning of the trail, which are gorgeous in mid-September. The elevation at this trailhead is exactly 9,054'. This trailhead only provides access to:

- Timber Lake - 368

TONAHUTU CREEK TRAILHEAD

The Tonahutu Creek Trailhead is about half a mile east of the town of Grand Lake and only a few hundred feet from the North Inlet Trailhead. It is an easy walk into town from here. The simplest way to get here by car is to head out of town on Garfield Road up to West Portal Road, turn right, and about a quarter of a mile down on your left you'll see a dirt road named 663 with a sign for Shadow Cliff Lodge. Follow that very steep dirt road up to the top of the hill. The trailhead is located on the east end of the large industrial building. There is currently no parking here and no facilities, so you either need to park in the North Inlet parking area just a few hundred feet to the east (turn right) or park at the bottom of the hill on West Portal Road. The elevation at this trailhead is 8,552'. The only trail in this book that is accessed from here is:

- ◆ Western Loop - 444

TWIN SISTERS PEAKS TRAILHEAD

You can reach the Twin Sisters Trailhead by driving south from Estes Park on Highway 7 for six miles. Turn left onto the dirt road just opposite Lily Lake. Follow this dirt road up the hill for approximately 0.4 miles. There is space for about ten cars to parallel park on the side of the road. If these parking areas are full, there is parking at the bottom of the hill. The actual trail begins about 0.1 miles up the dirt road from the last parking spot. There are no facilities here, but you can find a vault toilet at the Lily Lake parking lot on the west side of the highway. The elevation at the trailhead is 9,206'. This trailhead only provides access to:

- ◆ Twin Sisters Peaks - 306

UPPER BEAVER MEADOWS TRAILHEAD

To reach the Upper Beaver Meadows Trailhead, pass through the main east entrance to Rocky Mountain National Park and continue west on Highway 36 for 0.7 miles. At the first sharp bend in the road, turn left onto the partially paved Upper Beaver Meadows Road. Follow this road for 1.5 miles to the Upper Beaver Meadows Trailhead. Here you will find a dirt parking area with space for fourteen vehicles. There is a vault toilet on the north end. You'll also see a few informational signs and on the southeast side of the parking lot you may notice a few strange metal stands. These hold telescopes for night-sky events held by the park. The trailhead is on the southwest corner of the parking lot. Here the trail

LONGS PEAK FROM NEAR UTE CROSSING

crosses a small stream beside a large and beautiful aspen tree. The elevation is 8,345'. Trails accessed from here:

- Upper Beaver Meadows Loop - 171
- Eastern Ute (finish point) - 298

UTE CROSSING TRAILHEAD

On Trail Ridge Road, thirteen miles from the main east entrance, is the Ute Crossing Trailhead. It is really just a small pull-over on the south side of the road right above tree line. You'll notice the view begin to open up on your left just as you reach the parking area. There are no facilities. There is space for seven vehicles to parallel park. If all the spaces are taken, there is another small parking area about a quarter of a mile up the road with room for an additional eight vehicles. The elevation at the trailhead is 11,438'. This trailhead provides access to

- Tombstone Ridge Trail - 218
- Eastern Ute Trail - 298

WILD BASIN TRAILHEAD

From the start of Highway 7 in Estes Park, drive south for 12.3 miles and turn right onto County Road 84W and follow for 0.3 miles. Just after you pass Wild Basin Lodge, the Wild Basin entrance will be on your right side. From the entrance station follow the bumpy dirt road for two miles. At 1.0 mile you will pass the winter parking lot. From mid-October through mid-May the road is closed here to all vehicles, so you'll need to walk an additional mile to get to the trailhead. During the rest of the year you can continue on to the main Wild Basin Trailhead, which is located in a large dirt parking lot. At the trailhead you'll find vault toilets, a storage vault for any food you might have in your car, and also a ranger station behind the vault toilets. At the trailhead there is room for seventy-five vehicles. Back down the road there are a number of additional parking places here and there, though you may have to walk a ways to get to the trailhead from these. On most days the parking is full by 8:30 or 9 a.m. The elevation at the trailhead is 8,500'.

From here you can access the following locations:

- Calypso Cascades - 222
- Ouzel Falls - 258
- Ouzel Lake - 350
- Bluebird Lake - 404
- Thunder Lake - 396

ACCESSIBLE HIKES

This section of hiking trails covers the few accessible trails in Rocky Mountain National Park. They are ideal trails for anyone who wants to experience the natural world but wants to stay on level terrain. This includes not only those who are using wheelchairs but also families with small children, especially those with strollers, people with walkers, crutches, or balance challenges as well as large groups with varying levels of fitness. Although these are the easiest of the trails in Rocky Mountain National Park, that doesn't make them any less worthwhile. There is beauty here to be seen that you can't see anywhere else.

PONDEROSA FOREST IN WINTER

ACCESSIBLE HIKES

BEAVER BOARDWALK

Overview

Take a very short stroll down a boardwalk and sit beside a gurgling stream while watching for birds and other wildlife in this marshland setting. You never know what might appear as you sit quietly.

The Stats

Distance Round Trip: 0.1

Difficulty Rating: 2

Hiking Time: 5 minutes

Time to Go: anytime

Season: April through October

Primary Ecosystem: montane

Views: marsh, stream

Possible Wildlife: birds, moose, elk

Trail Conditions: paved and wooden boardwalk

Reminder: Bring binoculars and plan to spend a while watching and listening.

Elevation Start: 9,146'

Highest Point: 9,146'

Total Elevation Gain: 10'

Trailhead: This walk starts at the boardwalk parking, which is located on the north side of Trail Ridge Road between Deer Ridge Junction and Hidden Valley. There is parking for about eight vehicles.

Waypoints

1.Begin	0.0	9,146'
2.End	0.06	9,136'

Hike Description

This trail leaves from the parking area and heads gently down a wide paved trail. At the bottom of the small hill the trail becomes boardwalk. Follow this out into the marshland and as you go, listen for the large variety of birds that make their home here.

Only 3 percent of Colorado is comprised of marshland, yet this is where the majority of the state's wildlife can be found. This boardwalk gives you a chance to pay attention and notice all the forms of life that thrive in this environment.

At the end of the boardwalk you'll find a nice viewpoint with seating around the edge. Just below the boardwalk is a gurgling stream, which is ever so relaxing, and if you sit still here you may be able to identify many different forms of life that thrive in this environment.

2 – LILY LAKE

Overview

Lily Lake is a delightful place to enjoy a gentle stroll around a mountain lake with stunning views of Longs Peak. It is located right below the towering spires of Twin Sisters Peaks and is popular with the local waterfowl and other birds. Lily Lake is easy to access and doesn't require going through an official park entrance.

The Stats

Distance: 0.8 miles

Difficulty Rating: 5

Hiking Time: 30 minutes

Time to Go: all day

Season: April through November

Primary Ecosystem: montane

Views: great views of Longs Peak and Twin Sisters Peaks with glimpses of the Mummy Range

Possible Wildlife: ducks, ground squirrels, moose, muskrats, frogs, other birds

Trail Conditions: gravel trail

Reminder: Do remember that it is illegal to feed the ducks, squirrels, and other animals in the national park. Help keep them wild.

Elevation Start: 8,931'

Highest Point: 8,942'

Total Elevation Gain: 17'

Trailhead: This hike begins at the Lily Lake Trailhead, with two accessible spaces; see page 122 for details.

Waypoints

1. Lily Lake Parking	0.00	8,931'
2. Right at Lily Lake	0.01	8,931'
3. Lily Ridge Jct.	0.05	8,928'
4. Bench under Douglas Fir	0.29	8,933'
5. Lily Ridge Trail Jct.	0.37	8,932'
6. Lily Extension Jct.	0.53	8,932'

Hike Description

Lily Lake is one of the newest additions to Rocky Mountain National Park. Purchased in 1992 by park partners, it has been a terrific asset being enjoyed by families, anglers, and those seeking a casual walk.

This hike begins on the west side of the parking lot. (**#1**) If you

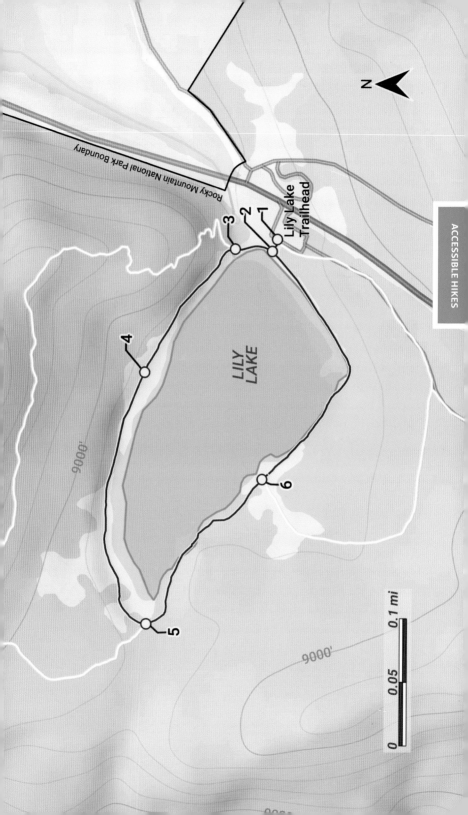

ACCESSIBLE HIKES

N

Lily Lake
Trailhead

1
2
3
4
5
6

LILY
LAKE

Rocky Mountain National Park Boundary

9000'

9000'

9000'

0   0.05   0.1 mi

turn right (**#2**) onto the trail and walk the lake in a counterclockwise direction, in about 250 feet you'll approach a small bridge. (**#3**) Just before the bridge is a trail on the right leading up to the Lily Ridge Loop Trail (see page 184). As you cross the bridge, be sure to look to your left for a spectacular view of Longs Peak looking down on the lake. This view is especially nice in the morning. As the trail continues it draws up next to the water, and you may be able to see some of the lake's inhabitants. As you continue along the north side of the lake, notice the trees growing right out of the rocks on your right as well as the lichen-covered granite, which is the primary rock here in the park. Along the trail you'll find numerous benches, many of them located in very peaceful locations.

At 0.3 you'll see a bench on your left (**#4**) under the trees that has one of the best views along the lake and is a great place to get family photos. Continue along for another minute and you'll pass a second junction with the Lily Ridge Trail. (**#5**) At this point we are at the far end of the lake, which is usually the calmest portion of the lake and so tends to attract wildlife. Spend some time sitting on one of the nearby benches. If you watch long enough you should spot a number of different animals, particularly during the mornings and evenings.

The trail begins to head back east toward the dramatic Twin Sisters Peaks. At 0.5 you'll reach the junction with the Lily Extension Trail. (**#6**) Continue straight and soon you'll be on a boardwalk with a marsh on your right and the lake on your left. This is a fabulous place to watch a wide variety of birds and other water life. At the right time of year, you may even hear the croaking of frogs. Be sure to spend some time in this area and see how many different species of birds you can count.

After the boardwalk the trail turns to the left and as it does, make sure to look across the lake and you'll get a glimpse of Chiquita, Ypsilon, and Fairchild mountains. You'll also have a wonderful view of the jagged rocks that tower over the north side of the lake. As you head back toward the starting point, you'll pass a small fishing dock that is often in use. Soon you'll arrive back at your starting point (**#2**) and may find that you can't resist doing it all again.

ACCESSIBLE HIKES

AUTUMN AT LILY LAKE

3 – SPRAGUE LAKE

Overview

Sprague Lake is one of those classic places that should be on everyone's list. It is a short, flat, accessible hike with wonderful views of the Continental Divide.

The Stats

Distance: 0.8 miles

Difficulty Rating: 7

Hiking Time: 30 minutes

Time to Go: anytime, but mornings are best

Season: June through October

Primary Ecosystem: montane

Views: mountain views from edge of the lake

Possible Wildlife: ducks, geese, moose, elk

Trail Conditions: gravel trail

Reminder: The morning is the best time for quiet and light on the mountains.

Elevation Start: 8,701'

Highest Point: 8,721'

Total Elevation Gain: 34'

Trailhead: This hike begins at the Sprague Lake Trailhead, with five accessible spaces; see page 127 for details.

HALLETT PEAK OVER SPRAGUE LAKE

1. Sprague Lake parking	0.0	8,701'
2. Right on Sprague Lake Trail	0.1	8,692'
3. Boardwalk	0.2	8,704'
4. Accessible camping junction	0.4	8,688'
5. Fishing dock	0.5	8,687'

Hike Description

The hike begins on the southeast corner of the parking lot. (**#1**) The first steps are across a wooden bridge and then the trail follows a stream that flows into the lake. If you look closely you may be able to see trout swimming in this area. In just a few hundred feet after starting your walk you'll reach an intersection. (**#2**) You can go around the lake in either direction, but for the purposes of this book, turn right, keeping the lake on the left.

This first section is through a stand of lodgepole pines. This area is one of the calmest sections of the lake and you'll often find ducks and geese swimming here. At 0.2 miles you'll leave the lodgepole forest and walk out on a boardwalk through marshland. (**#3**) This is a popular location for birds of all types. There are benches here where you can sit to watch and listen.

Sprague Lake is a very shallow lake built up by Abner Sprague to support the lodge he operated here until 1940. Most of the lake is no more than a few feet deep and you may see elk or moose out in the middle of it from time to time.

After the boardwalk the trail begins to head along the eastern shore. You'll often see golden-mantled ground squirrels scrambling over the rocks, begging for food. Help keep them wild by not feeding them. As the trail nears the end of the lake, you'll find a few benches on the left side on a section that juts out into the lake. Stop and take in the view back toward the mountains. Just a few feet past this point you'll see another trail heading into the woods. (**#4**) This is for a wheelchair-accessible campsite.

Continue straight and cross the outlet stream. This area provides some of the best views of the mountains, particularly in the mornings. Get a spot on the bench here and enjoy one of the best views

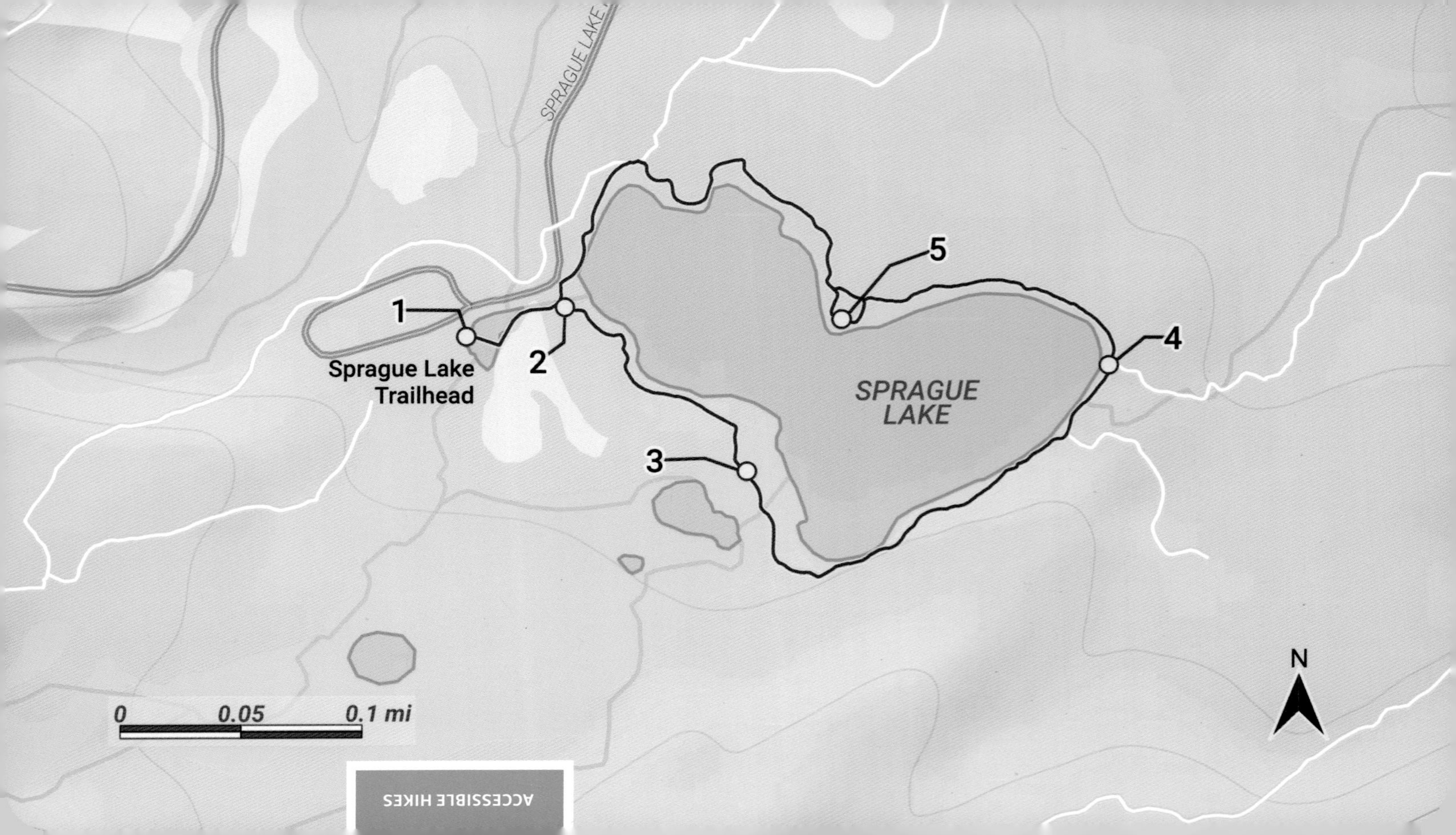

0

0.05

0.1 mi

Sprague Lake
Trailhead

1

2

3

SPRAGUE
LAKE

5

4

SPRAGUE LAKE

N

SUNRISE OVER SPRAGUE LAKE

in the park. The trail will begin to travel along the northern shore. You will often find folks fishing here. At 0.5 miles there's a short side trail that leads to a small fishing dock, which is a favorite location for family photos. (#5)

The trail continues along the shore, crossing over another small outlet stream before shortly arriving back at the junction next to the inlet stream. (#2) Turn right and this will lead you back to the parking lot. (#1)

4 – COYOTE VALLEY

Overview

This hike lets you experience the meadowlands of Rocky Mountain National Park, a place where life abounds. The trail crosses the Colorado River and heads out onto the open meadow with views of the Never Summer Mountains.

The Stats

Distance Round Trip: 1.3 miles

Difficulty Rating: 9

Hiking Time: 50 minutes

Time to Go: anytime

Season: June through October

Primary Ecosystem: montane

Views: meadow surrounded by mountains and the Colorado River

Possible Wildlife: moose, elk, deer, raptors, golden-mantled ground squirrels

Trail Conditions: well-maintained accessible trail with a grade of no more than 10%

Reminder: The moose can be quite active here in the mornings, so pay attention and give them a wide berth.

Elevation Start: 8,834'

Highest Point: 8,834'

Total Elevation Gain: 30'

Trailhead: This hike begins at the Coyote Valley Trailhead, with five accessible spaces; see page 115 for details.

Waypoints

1. Coyote Valley Trailhead	0.0	8,834'
2. Cross Colorado River	0.1	8,804'
3. Right at Picnic Loop junction	0.1	8,804'
4. Spur trail to water's edge	0.3	8,806'
5. End of trail	0.6	8,816'

Hike Description

This hike begins on the southwest corner of the parking lot, leading you first through a grove of majestic spruce trees. (#1) It then opens up and you arrive at the Colorado River. (#2) The trail goes over the river, allowing you to stop and admire this small stream that will become the great river that carves the Grand Canyon.

Just on the other side of the bridge is a small loop to your left. (#3) This loop is about 0.1 miles and will bring you past six accessible

A STROLL BELOW BAKER MTN.

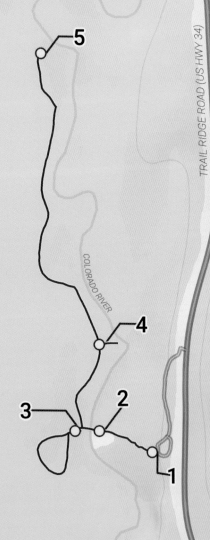

TRAIL RIDGE ROAD (US HWY 34)

COLORADO RIVER

9000'

8800'

5

4

3

2

1

N

0   0.1   0.2 mi

COYOTE VALLEY TRAIL

picnic tables out in the meadow. It then arrives back at the bridge. The trail continues to the north following the Colorado River. As you head north you'll have a great view of Mount Baker off to your left across the meadow. All the while, you are accompanied by the sound of the rushing river, giving you a chance to ponder the incredible journey that lies ahead.

At 0.3 miles there is a small accessible spur trail off to the right that will lead you down to the water's edge. (#4) It would be a great place to do a little fishing. If you continue onward, at 0.4 miles you'll pass a small pond on your right where you might find ducks or other birds. You may even find moose hanging out there.

Along the way, there are quite a few benches where you can sit and enjoy the peaceful silence of this place. There are also a number of informational signs that explain the wildlife, geology, and human history of this area. Then at 0.6 miles the trail reaches its end. (#5)

The Coyote Valley Trail is a place where it would be easy to spend a few hours, as it is so quiet and tranquil with many places to sit and admire the views.

5 – BEAR LAKE

Overview

Bear Lake is perhaps the most popular hike in Rocky Mountain National Park. A gentle trails leads you around a small mountain lake, giving you several very beautiful views of the surrounding mountains while also giving you a taste of the lower end of Rocky's subalpine zone.

The Stats

Distance: 0.6 miles

Difficulty Rating: 10

Hiking Time: 25 minutes

Time to Go: anytime

Season: mid-June through October

Ecosystem: subalpine

Views: forests and lake views

Possible Wildlife: golden-mantled ground squirrels and gray jays

Trail Conditions: dirt and gravel trail with some steeper sections

Reminder: This is a very popular hike best enjoyed early or late in the day.

Elevation Start: 9,475'

Highest Point: 9,522'

Total Elevation Gain: 71'

Trailhead: This hike begins at the Bear Lake Trailhead, with seven accessible spaces; see page 110 for details.

Waypoints

1. Bear Lake Trailhead	0.0	9,475'
2. Right at Lake Loop	0.04	9,467'
3. Fern Lake junction	0.1	9,481'
4. Longs Peak view	0.2	9,485'
5. Bridge crossing	0.4	9,486'
6. Highest point	0.4	9,522'

Hike Description

While this hike is accessible, it is not flat. There are a couple of climbs at the far side of the lake near waypoint #6 with a grade of up to 16%. To access those sections of trail with a wheelchair is doable but will likely require assistance. You can, however, access the rest of the trail without issue.

The trail begins on the west end of the parking lot right next to the ranger station. (#1) Walk past the ranger station, across the

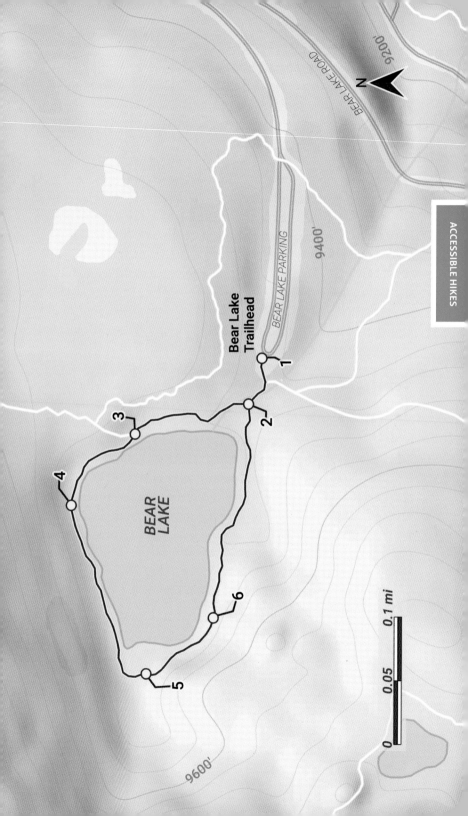

ACCESSIBLE HIKES

Bear Lake
Trailhead

BEAR LAKE

BEAR LAKE ROAD

BEAR LAKE PARKING

9200

9400'

9600'

N

1
2
3
4
5
6

0   0.05   0.1 mi

bridge, then follow the trail as it turns to the right. At the junction turn right, as you'll go around the lake in a counterclockwise fashion. (**#2**) At this intersection you'll also notice a little box where you can buy guides that explain to you in more detail what you're seeing on this hike.

Shortly after your turn to the right you'll arrive at a viewpoint over the lake. From here you can look across Bear Lake and see Hallett Peak looking down on you. You'll also find a sign that labels the entire scene in front of you. Continue on down the trail and notice a small side trail that leads out onto the lake. As you continue, remain on the trail to help prevent further erosion. In a short while you'll pass by the Fern Lake junction. (**#3**) Keep to the left to follow the trail around the lake.

At 0.2 miles, as you enter into an area of boulders, you should look to your left for a spectacular view of Longs Peak over Bear Lake. (**#4**) As you continue on, that view will open up farther. This entire north side of the lake provides great views to the south. As you reach the end of the lake, the trail begins to climb and then descends down into the woods. This is a marshy area where you can feel the moisture in the air and smell the earthy fragrances. (**#5**) You'll cross a couple of small seasonal streams and then the trail will bring you alongside a large granite wall that is usually covered with ice in the winter.

After the rock wall the trail climbs again quite steeply, reaching the highest point where you'll find a bench looking over the lake. (**#6**) There are a few small steps on the way down. The trail then follows the southern shore of the lake. In the autumn and spring there are terrific views of the colorful aspen trees from one of the openings to the lake, about 3/4ths of the way down. Just after this you will reach the main junction again. (**#2**) Turn right here to return to the parking area.(**#1**)

HALLETT PEAK OVER BEAR LAKE

6 – HOLZWARTH HISTORIC SITE

Overview

This is a gentle walk through the Kawuneeche Meadow and also through some of the history of the valley. Watch for moose and elk, cross the Colorado River, and visit a historic ranch to get a glimpse into life in the early 1900s. A number of the buildings are open during the summer months, allowing you to get a real taste of life back then.

The Stats

Distance Round Trip: 1.1 miles

Difficulty Rating: 10

Hiking Time: 45 minutes

Time to Go: morning

Season: June through October

Primary Ecosystem: montane

Views: meadows, Colorado River, historic cabins

Possible Wildlife: moose, elk, forest animals

Trail Conditions: gravel road

Reminder: Avoid the open meadows during storms.

Elevation Start: 8,911'

Highest Point: 8,931'

Total Elevation Gain: 49'

Trailhead: This hike begins at the Holzwarth Historic Site, with four accessible spaces; see page 121 for details.

Waypoints

1. Holzwarth Ranch Trailhead	0.0	8,911'
2. Colorado River crossing at Holzwarth	0.3	8,883'
3. Start of Holzwarth Loop	0.5	8,912'
4. Mama Cabin	0.6	8,911'

Hike Description

This hike begins on the south side of the parking lot. You'll find a path heading directly south to a small cabin about 100 feet down the trail. This is an old homestead cabin that you can visit and get a taste for what life was like for the first settlers. Continue with your back to the cabin, heading west into the Kawuneeche Meadow on the wide dirt path. (**#1**)

As you walk westward look up to the mountains in front of you

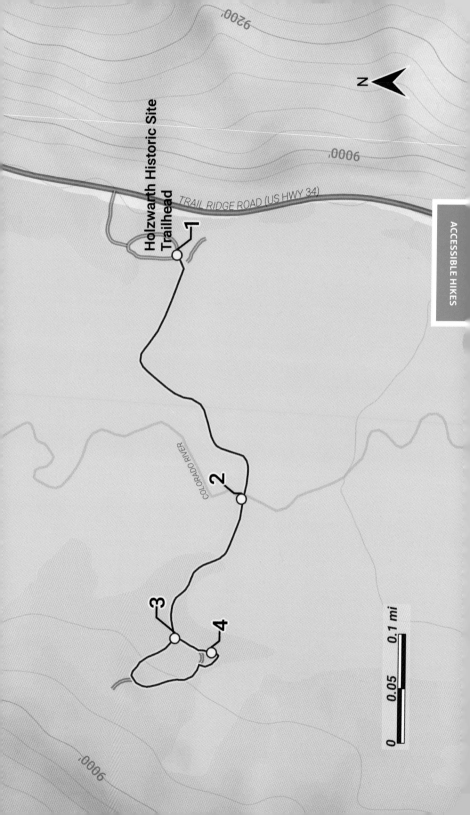

N

Holzwarth Historic Site
Trailhead

TRAIL RIDGE ROAD (US HWY 34)

1

2

3

4

COLORADO RIVER

9200'

9000'

9200'

9000'

9000'

0   0.05   0.1 mi

OLD HOMESTEAD

and notice the large gash along their side. This is the Grand Ditch, which diverts water from the west back to the east side of the mountains. It was built in the early 1900s and still operates today.

While you walk across the meadow, keep your eyes open for moose, especially in the mornings. It is also possible you may see elk or coyotes out there as well as a large variety of birds. Along this level path you'll see numerous educational signs and a few benches to sit and soak in the quiet beauty of this place. Soon the path crosses over the Colorado River, which is only about ten miles old at this point. (#2) It is amazing to think what this river will become and where it will go.

On the other side of the river you'll find a number of old farm implements and old fencing that suggests a small horse corral. Just beyond this the trail gently climbs up toward the trees and into the old

Holzwarth Ranch, which later became the Holzwarth Trout Lodge. You then reach an intersection. (#3) This is the start of a loop through the ranch. Turn to the right here and go around counterclockwise.

You'll pass a number of small cabins that were part of the Holzwarth Trout Lodge. Many of them are now used as housing for seasonal park staff, so don't try to visit any of these cabins. Soon the large path turns to the left and here you'll find a public vault toilet on your right. As you reach the south end of this loop and begin to turn again to your left you'll reach the historic buildings that are open to the public. The first one will be the tent house, which was built in 1919. Next you'll pass the Ice House and the taxidermy shop. Then you'll be at the main lodge called Mama Cabin, which was built in 1917 and served as the heart of the site. (#4) Be sure to go inside, as it is well preserved along with many artifacts from that era. As you loop around you'll find a couple of other guest cabins that you can also visit.

The trail then leads you back to the intersection; turn right to head back into the meadow and return to the parking area.

OLD WAGON WHEEL

7 – ALLUVIAL FAN

Overview

Take a gentle stroll along and across the Alluvial Fan, an area of debris that spreads out at the base of the Roaring River deposited by two major floods. Here you'll find delightful cascades, a roaring stream, and lots of large boulders for kids to climb on. It's an ideal family destination.

The Stats

Distance Round Trip: 0.8 miles

Difficulty Rating: 18

Hiking Time: 30 minutes

Time to Go: anytime

Season: May through November

Primary Ecosystem: montane

Views: cascades

Possible Wildlife: birds, squirrels, and fish

Trail Conditions: paved and boardwalk, accessible with exceptions

Reminder: Be aware that the stream can be very powerful. During May and June you must take extra precaution and keep children and childlike adults away from the water. Also be aware that wet rocks can be slippery.

Elevation Start: 8,585'

Highest Point: 8,651'

Total Elevation Gain: 211'

Trailhead: This hike begins at the Alluvial Fan West Trailhead for accessible access or alternatively the Alluvial Fan East Trailhead. See page 110 for details.

Waypoints

1. West parking	0.0	8,585'
2. Bridge	0.16	8,613'
3. Spur trail view point	0.21	8,651'
4. East parking	0.40	8,576'

Hike Description

The trail leaves the west parking area (**#1**) and gently climbs up onto a debris field. This area of scattered rocks was first created as a result of the Lawn Lake Flood in 1982. An earthen dam at Lawn Lake collapsed, sending a wall of water racing down the narrow valley, carving out the sides of the hills and depositing the debris at this spot. When seen from above you'll notice that the debris spilled

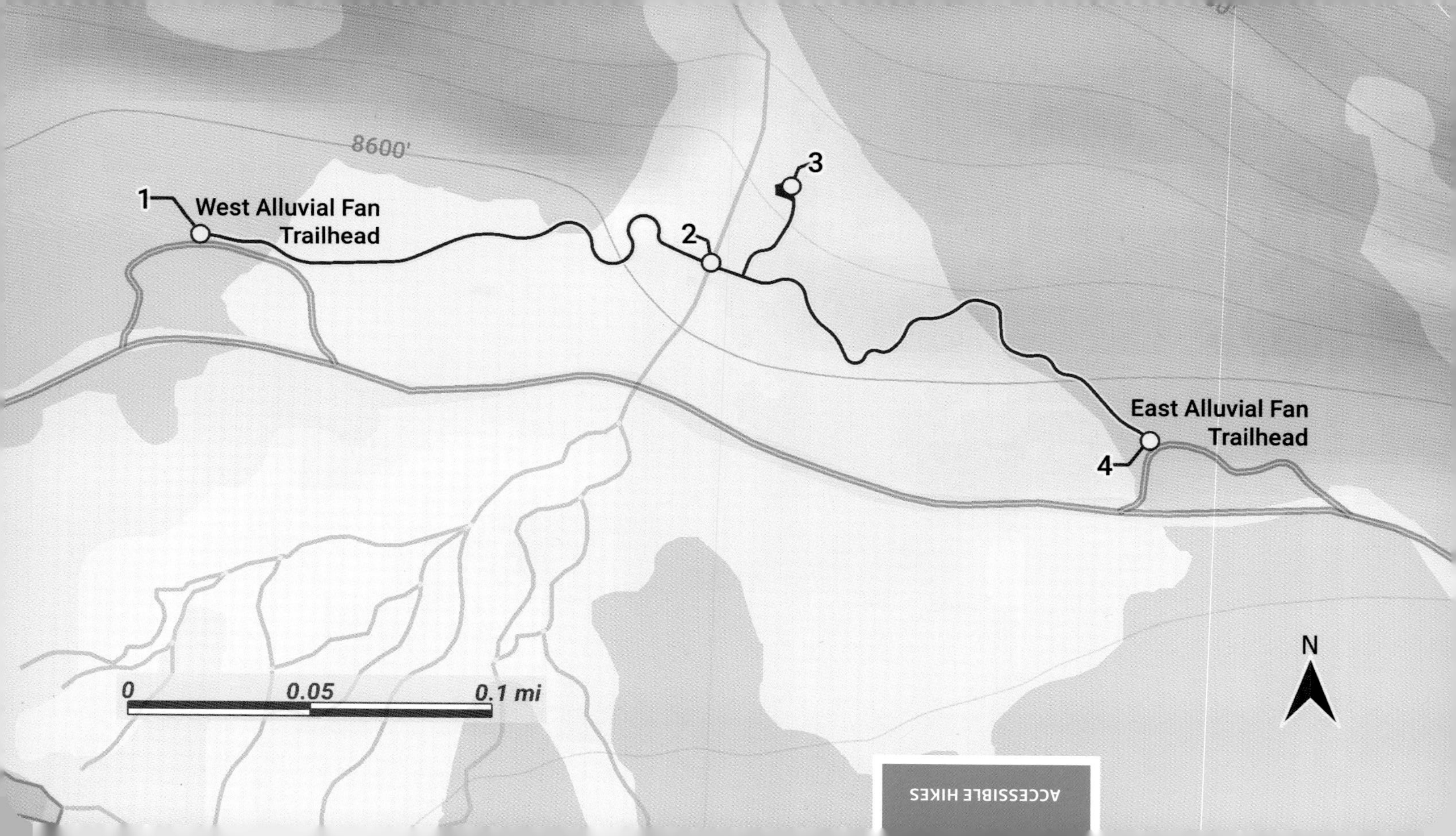

ACCESSIBLE HIKES

N

West Alluvial Fan
Trailhead

1

8600'

2

3

East Alluvial Fan
Trailhead

4

0   0.05   0.1 mi

out from the valley in the shape of a fan, hence its name. In the autumn of 2013 an intense storm created another flood that completely reshaped this area again, destroying the road, the bridges and this trail and changing the flow of the river. This entire area gives us a glimpse of how our world is constantly being shaped by natural forces that often go unseen.

After the 2013 flood the National Park Service left this area alone for numerous years before completely rebuilding the trail and bridge,

SPRING SNOW AT HORSESHOE FALLS

completing the work in 2020. This new trail was designed to allow easier access to this beautiful and interesting area. Be sure to take the time to read the educational signs along the trail.

After a short walk over the debris field, you will reach a bridge over the Roaring River (#2). Here you can enjoy the sound of the rushing stream and notice its crystal clear waters. If you look closely, you will notice the many multicolored rocks pulled out of different layers of the earth during the floods and if you are lucky you may even see trout swimming against the stream.

Be aware that during the spring and early summer the water here is extremely powerful and can easily sweep a person away. Don't approach the water's edge until the water flow is more gentle which usually happens from mid-summer through the autumn. Be especially careful with young children during the high-flow season.

Continue over the bridge and after a short distance take the spur trail to the left. This leads to a great viewpoint of Horseshoe Falls (#3). This area is particularly gorgeous in the spring and autumn, but regardless of the time of year this is a beautiful place to enjoy the views, sounds and smells of this dynamic place.

If you want to hike the full trail, continue back to the junction and then turn left. This next portion of the trail winds its way down to the east parking lot (#4). This section is not as gentle as the rest of the trail and is where you will find most of the elevation loss and gain. When you reach the parking lot you can turn around and return back the way you came.

Accessibility

This hike is considered to be accessible with exceptions. What this means is that while it may be possible to do this entire hike with a wheelchair, descending to the east parking lot may be challenging. My recommendation is that you begin at the west trailhead (#1) and enjoy the journey up to the bridge (#2) and the overlook (#3), as this section is fully accessible. You can then return back to the west parking lot (#1).

ACCESSIBLE HIKES

SUMMER BELOW LONGS PEAK

EASY HIKES

The hikes listed here are considered easy hikes. This does not necessarily mean they will be easy for you. It is simply a description of how they compare with the other hikes in this book. Each hike gets progressively more difficult, so the hikes at the start of this section will be considerably less difficult than those at the end of this section. These hikes are great for families with children. They are also good hikes that let you dip your toes into the water and get a taste of what it is like to hike in the wilderness. Even though they are listed as "Easy" doesn't make them any less enjoyable or beautiful than the later hikes. The hikes in this section will have limited elevation gain and are relatively short in comparison to the hikes listed later in this book.

ALBERTA FALLS TRAIL

8 – CHASM FALLS

Overview

Take a short but steep walk down to a viewing platform where you can get a great view of Chasm Falls flowing through a crack in the rocks.

The Stats

Distance Round Trip: 0.1 miles	**Trail Conditions:** short but steep trail with rock steps that may be wet and slippery
Difficulty Rating: 3	
Hiking Time: 10 minutes	**Reminder:** If you want to visit the falls between October and July, when the gate is closed at the West Alluvial Fan, you'll need to walk 2.3 miles each way.
Time to Go: all day	
Season: April through October	
Primary Ecosystem: montane	**Elevation Start:** 9,091'
	Highest Point: 9,091'
Views: waterfall	**Total Elevation Gain:** 48'
Possible Wildlife: ground squirrels and gray jays	**Trailhead:** This hike begins at the Chasm Falls parking area; see page 112 for details.

Waypoints

1. Begin	0.0	**9,091'**
2. End	0.06	**9,043'**

Hike Description

This hike begins on the east end of the Chasm Falls parking area. (**#1**) The trail follows a progression of rock stairs winding downward through a series of small switchbacks. At times the rocks can be wet and a bit slippery, so take your time. You'll also want to be sure that you keep children close by and not let them get near the water, as it is very powerful and dangerous.

After just a minute of climbing downward you'll reach a large flat platform with security railings. (**#2**) As you look to the west you'll see Fall River squeezed between the rocks, creating Chasm Falls, one of the more elegant waterfalls in Rocky Mountain National Park.

EASY HIKES

CHASM FALLS

The mist coming off of the falls is delightful on a hot day but can at times make it difficult to get a photo, as it coats your lens.

Visiting in the Off-season:

Old Fall River Road is normally only open from early July through mid-October, yet Chasm Falls remains a great hike during most of the year. If you would like to visit in the off-season, you'll begin the hike at the West Alluvial Fan parking lot. This is where the road is typically gated. From there you'll walk along the road, through the grove of aspens, past the willow-filled meadow, and to the start of Old Fall River Road. It is one mile to that point. From here follow the dirt road as it climbs upward. You'll make two switchbacks before arriving at the Chasm Falls parking area. It is a 2.3-mile hike each way, making it a total of 4.6 miles round trip with about 560' of elevation gain. Just be aware that if you are visiting in the winter that the trail down to the falls can get icy, so be sure to have microspikes on your shoes.

CHASM FALLS IN APRIL

Overview

This is a very short ten-minute walk that lets you get a quick taste of the alpine zone. You'll walk beside the incredible and delicate alpine tundra, look down on Forest Canyon and out toward the Never Summer Mountains.

The Stats

Distance Round Trip: 0.25 miles	**Reminder:** Do not attempt if there is any possibility of storms due to lightning danger. Stay on the paved trail to protect the delicate tundra. Also, like all other trails, no pets are allowed.
Difficulty Rating: 4	
Hiking Time: 10 minutes	
Time to Go: morning or late in the day	
Season: June through October	**Elevation Start:** 11,699'
Primary Ecosystem: alpine	**Highest Point:** 11,738'
Views: grand vistas	**Total Elevation Gain:** 40'
Possible Wildlife: marmots, pikas, ptarmigan, elk	**Trailhead:** This walk begins at the Forest Canyon Overlook parking area; see page 119 for details.
Trail Conditions: wide paved path	

EASY HIKES

Waypoints

1. Parking lot	0.0	11,699'
2. Viewing area	0.13	11,654'

Hike Description

This hike is actually more of a brief walk than an actual hike, but I mention it here for those who want to get out of their cars and quickly experience being in the alpine zone.

From the parking area the paved trail heads westward. (**#1**) Take advantage of being in this harsh zone and get down on your knees to have a close look at the great variety of plants that have learned to thrive in this intense high-altitude environment. Many of these are miniature versions of plants found elsewhere.

The trail quickly climbs a small hill from which you'll have the best view. Look down to your left. This is Forest Canyon. It is deep, dark, and wild. There are no trails down there and some parts of

SUNSET AT THE OVERLOOK

this valley have not burned in many hundreds of years, making the forest very thick and difficult to traverse. Across that valley you'll be looking up at Hayden Spire high above Hayden Gorge.

Along the trail you'll find a number of informational signs. Be sure to stop and read them, as they each have something very interesting to communicate about life at this elevation.

From here the trail slopes downward and terminates at a round viewpoint with three-feet-high stone walls. (**#2**) Here you can look west toward the Never Summer Mountains. This perspective is especially beautiful at sunrise and at sunset. There are a couple of benches here where you can sit and rest as you take in this incredible alpine environment. Please remember to stay on the paved trail.

10 – HIDDEN VALLEY LOOP TRAIL

Overview

Take a gentle stroll through a mountain meadow and follow a gurgling stream. This short and gentle hike heads up through the former ski area of Hidden Valley, just off of Trail Ridge Road. The meadows are often filled with wildflowers. There are many picnic tables throughout the area, inviting you to spend some time. You'll also find Junior Ranger Headquarters here during the main summer months, which is perfect for the younger kids in your party.

The Stats

Distance: 0.4 miles	**Trail Conditions:** wide and smooth gravel path
Difficulty Rating: 8	
Hiking Time: 15 minutes	**Reminder:** Bring a book or a picnic lunch.
Time to Go: anytime	**Elevation Start:** 9,412'
Season: June through October	**Highest Point:** 9,479'
Primary Ecosystem: montane	**Total Elevation Gain:** 76'
Views: meadow and forest	**Trailhead:** This hike begins at the Hidden Valley Trailhead; see page 120 for details.
Possible Wildlife: forest animals, elk, deer	

EASY HIKES

Waypoints

1. Hidden Valley parking	0.0	**9,412'**
2. Bridge at top of trail	0.2	**9,479'**

Hike Description

At the west end of the parking lot, in front of the building you'll find the path heading to the west. (**#1**) Follow it as it gently turns to the right and climbs. The trail comes alongside Hidden Valley Creek, which gently cascades downward. This stream will accompany you all the way up and down.

At the top of the first little rise you'll see a grassy meadow on your left. In the winter this serves as Rocky Mountain National Park's sledding area, but in the summer it is usually filled with wildflowers rather than snow. At the end of this first meadow you'll find picnic

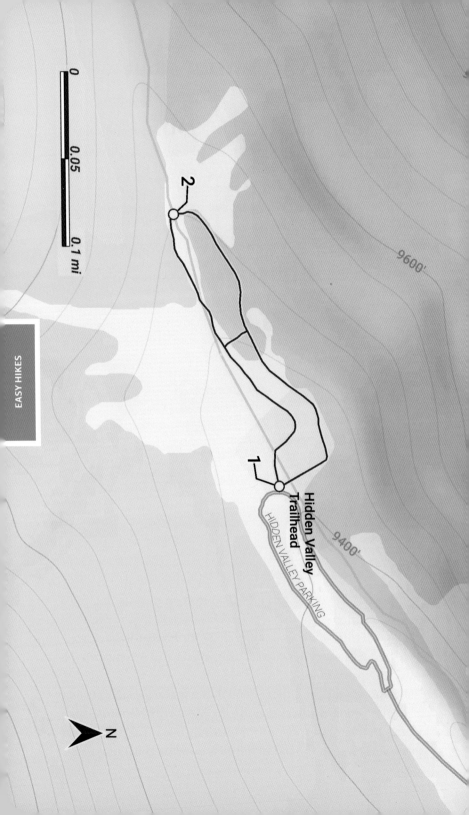

2

1

Hidden Valley Trailhead

HIDDEN VALLEY PARKING

9400'

9600'

0

0.05

0.1 mi

N

tables and just above them you'll see a sharp cut straight up through the trees. This is where there was once a ski lift during the time when Hidden Valley was a ski resort (from 1955 through 1990). A number of the old ski runs are still used today, though skiers have to make their own way to the top before they can ski down. You would be surprised by how many skiers are out here in the winter.

The trail then passes an intersection where you can cross over the stream and cut your journey in half. Continue up the trail. As you head up, you'll see a ski run ahead of you that runs all the way to the very top of the mountain, crossing Trail Ridge Road on its way up. These days it takes skiers about an hour to make their way to the top and only about fifteen minutes to ski back down.

At about 0.2 miles the trail turns to the right and crosses a bridge over the stream. (**#2**) This is the top of the trail. It now turns back and slowly heads down the other side of the stream. Just after you cross the bridge you'll see a great picnic spot, one of many scattered along this trail.

The walk back down is very gentle and peaceful. The sound of the stream beside you and meadows filled with wildflowers create a beautiful and restorative walk in the national park.

As the trail reaches the bottom, it actually passes right through the building. You'll find very nice restrooms here, Junior Ranger Headquarters, and usually rangers who, if they aren't busy helping kids, might have time to answer a question or two. You then arrive back out front where you began this walk.

EASY HIKES

HIDDEN VALLEY TRAIL

11 – LAKE IRENE

Overview

This is a short, gentle trail that leads down past a small forested lake, beside a meadow, then through the forest to an overlook of a small marshy meadow where wildlife might be seen at the edges of the day.

The Stats

Distance Round Trip: 0.8 miles

Difficulty Rating: 14

Hiking Time: 30 minutes

Time to Go: anytime

Season: June through October

Primary Ecosystem: subalpine

Views: lake and meadows

Possible Wildlife: moose

Trail Conditions: wide, smooth gravel with a stretch of steps

Reminder: This hike goes down, so save energy for the walk back up. You may want to bring a book and stay awhile in this peaceful area.

Elevation Start: 10,664′

Highest Point: 10,664′

Total Elevation Gain: 115′

Trailhead: This hike begins at the Lake Irene picnic area; see page 122 for details.

Waypoints

1. Lake Irene parking	0.0	10,664′
2. Lake Irene	0.1	10,634′
3. Overlook	0.4	10,554′

Hike Description

This hike begins by heading down a few stairs and then across a meadow. (**#1**) During the month of June this is often snow covered,

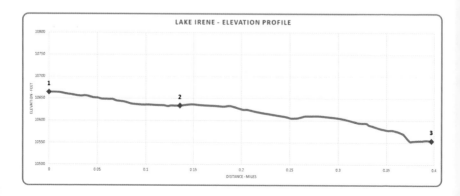

EASY HIKES

Lake Irene
Trailhead

1

2

LAKE
IRENE

3

TRAIL RIDGE ROAD (US HWY 34)

10800'

11000'

10800'

10600'

10400'

10200'

EASY HIKES

N

0   0.05   0.1 mi

LAKE IRENE

making it difficult to traverse. Please try to stay on the trail to protect the delicate mountain meadow. There may be wildflowers growing here during July and early August.

You'll very quickly arrive at the southern end of Lake Irene. It is a lovely example of the many little lakes tucked into the forest throughout Rocky Mountain National Park. The trail follows the lake's northern edge as the trees open to meadow. At the edge of the lake you'll be at 0.1 miles. During this first stretch there are several benches where you might want to sit and simply soak in the peace of this place.

If you have energy, continue following the trail downward, following the outlet stream for another 0.3 miles through the trees. It will eventually lead to an overlook of a small marshy meadow. (#2) If you are here in the early morning or in the evening you may catch sight of wildlife grazing. If it is a clear day you may be able to see the Gore Range way in the distance.

While there is another trail marked here that says "Ute Trail," the trail actually disappears about half a mile farther down, leaving you in rough terrain without a trail. It is best to return to the Lake Irene parking lot.

Overview

This is a gentle and pleasant stroll through a mountain meadow with views of Longs Peak. Here you may see elk, deer, and coyotes. During the late spring and early summer you may see numerous species of wildflowers. You'll also walk through a wonderfully scented ponderosa pine forest as you make this loop.

The Stats

Distance: 1.1 miles

Difficulty Rating: 15

Hiking Time: 40 minutes

Time to Go: anytime

Season: May through October

Primary Ecosystem: montane

Views: meadows, ponderosa pine forest, Longs Peak

Possible Wildlife: elk, deer, coyotes, forest animals

Trail Conditions: sandy

Reminder: Keep your distance from any wildlife.

Elevation Start: 8,437'

Highest Point: 8,544'

Total Elevation Gain: 108'

Trailhead: This hike begins at the Upper Beaver Meadows trailhead; see page 128 for details.

EASY HIKES

LONGS PEAK OVER BEAVER MEADOWS

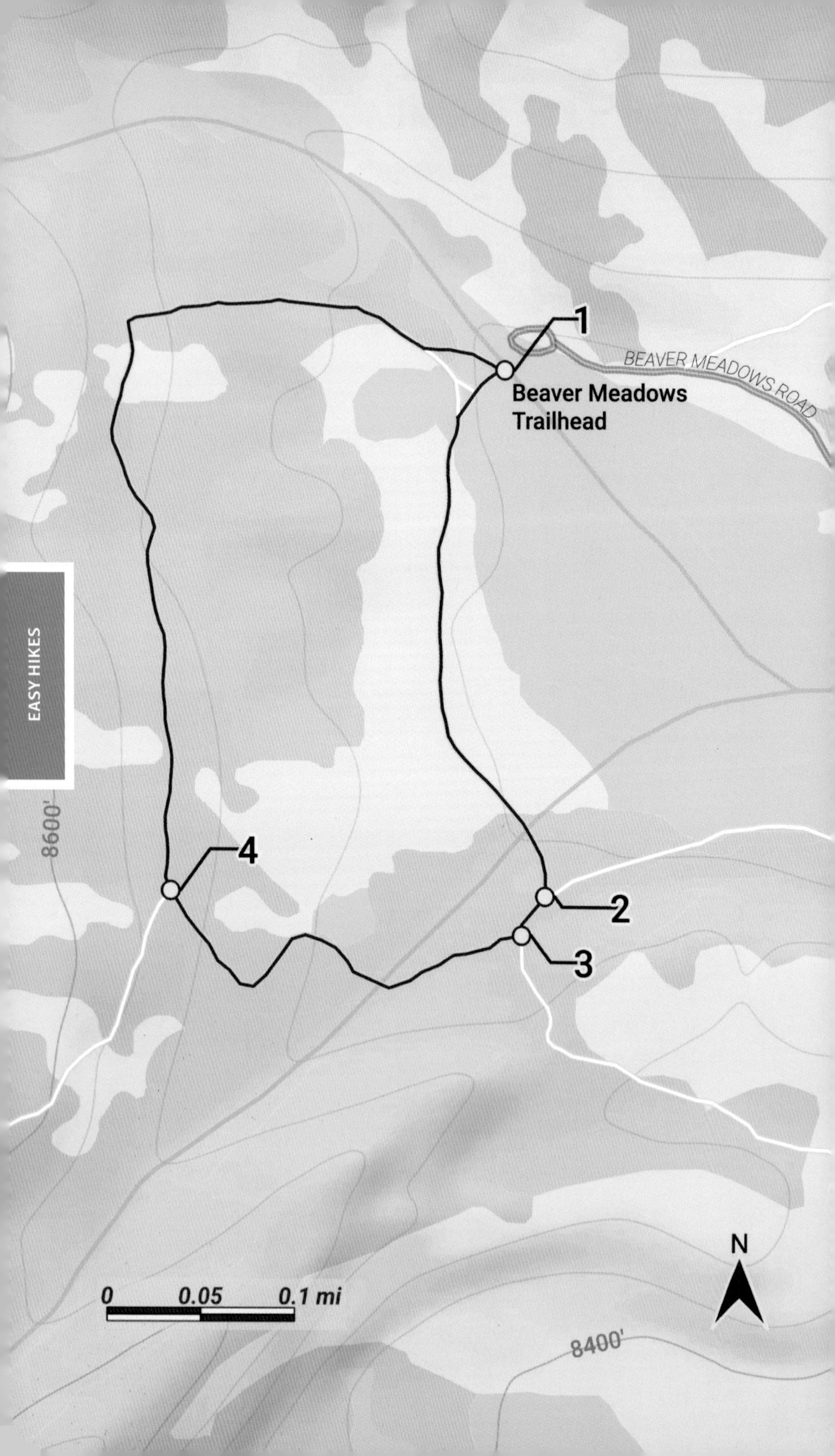

1

BEAVER MEADOWS ROAD

**Beaver Meadows
Trailhead**

EASY HIKES

4

2

3

8600'

0   0.05   0.1 mi

N

8400'

1. Upper Beaver Meadows Trailhead	0.0	8,437'
2. Right at first junction	0.3	8,454'
3. Right at second junction	0.3	8,464'
4. Right onto the Ute Trail	0.6	8,542'

Hike Description

This hike begins on the south side of the parking lot just beneath the large aspen tree. (**#1**) Begin by heading across the log bridge. Continue straight, following the level path that winds through the meadow. In the distance you can see Longs Peak high above the trees. This area of meadow is often frequented by elk, mule deer, and coyotes. Look out for all the other forms of life that thrive in a meadow like this, including a wide variety of plants as well as insects, birds, and small mammals.

As you begin to walk through the meadow look to your right and you may see a fenced enclosure. This is one of many in the lower meadows of Rocky Mountain National Park. They preserve the vegetation behind the fence, allowing it to thrive without being continually eaten back by the herds of elk. Pay attention to the many things growing inside the fence and the few growing outside and you'll immediately understand the impact that the elk have on the foliage.

Continue on this sandy trail as it heads directly toward Longs Peak. Off to your left the summit of Deer Mountain is clearly visible from this perspective. The trail enters the trees, climbs a small hill, and then reaches an intersection. (**#2**) At the intersection turn right. This section of trail is north facing and so it is comprised of more

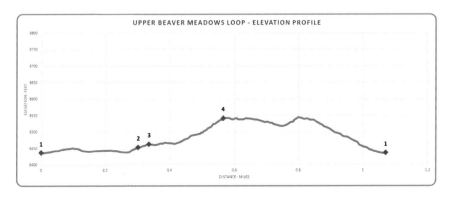

174 lodgepole pine. Because of the many horses that use the trail, it is very sandy. In a short distance you'll reach a second intersection. (#3) Again you should turn to the right.

The trail soon reenters the meadow and wanders as it makes its way around the occasional ponderosa pine and aspen tree. In this section the trail gently climbs. As you reach the shade of the ponderosa take a moment to inhale. If the sun is shining you'll smell the sweet fragrance of drying needles. If it is shining on a ponderosa tree trunk, smell it and enjoy the delicious butterscotch aroma, though some think it smells more like vanilla.

The trail will reach one last intersection where it meets the Ute Trail, an ancient trail that was used for nearly 10,000 years by ancient peoples to cross the mountains. (#4) Turn right on this trail. It leads you northward along a gentle but sandy trail through ponderosa pines at the edge of the meadow. You may notice a number of dead trees along this stretch. These are a result of the bark beetle epidemic as discussed on page 74. Eventually the trail will turn to the right and will descend back down to the parking lot where you started.

ELK HERD IN BEAVER MEADOWS

Overview

Enjoy a picturesque short walk up to Adams Falls and East Meadow. This walk is popular with families. The trail climbs gently for about a third of a mile, then descends to Adams Falls and continues another third of a mile to the very large East Meadow with the East Inlet stream gently flowing through it.

The Stats

Distance Round Trip: 1.1 miles

Difficulty Rating: 15

Hiking Time: 40 minutes

Time to Go: anytime

Season: May through October

Primary Ecosystem: montane

Views: waterfall; large, open meadow with a stream running through it and mountain in the background

Possible Wildlife: forest animals and moose

Trail Conditions: very wide, easy-to-follow trail with some rock steps near the falls

Reminder: Keep your eyes open for moose and give them a wide berth.

Elevation Start: 8,400'

Highest Point: 8,501'

Total Elevation Gain: 111'

Trailhead: This hike begins at the East Inlet Trailhead; see page 116 for details.

EASY HIKES

Waypoints

1. East Inlet Trailhead	0.0	8,401'
2. Right to Adams Falls	0.3	8,469'
3. Adams Falls	0.3	8,426'
4. Right on East Inlet Trail	0.5	8,501'
5. East Meadow	0.6	8,498'

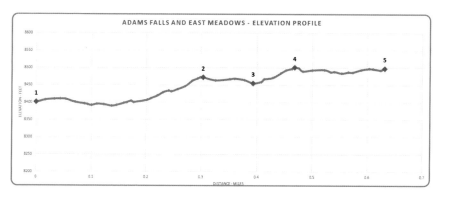

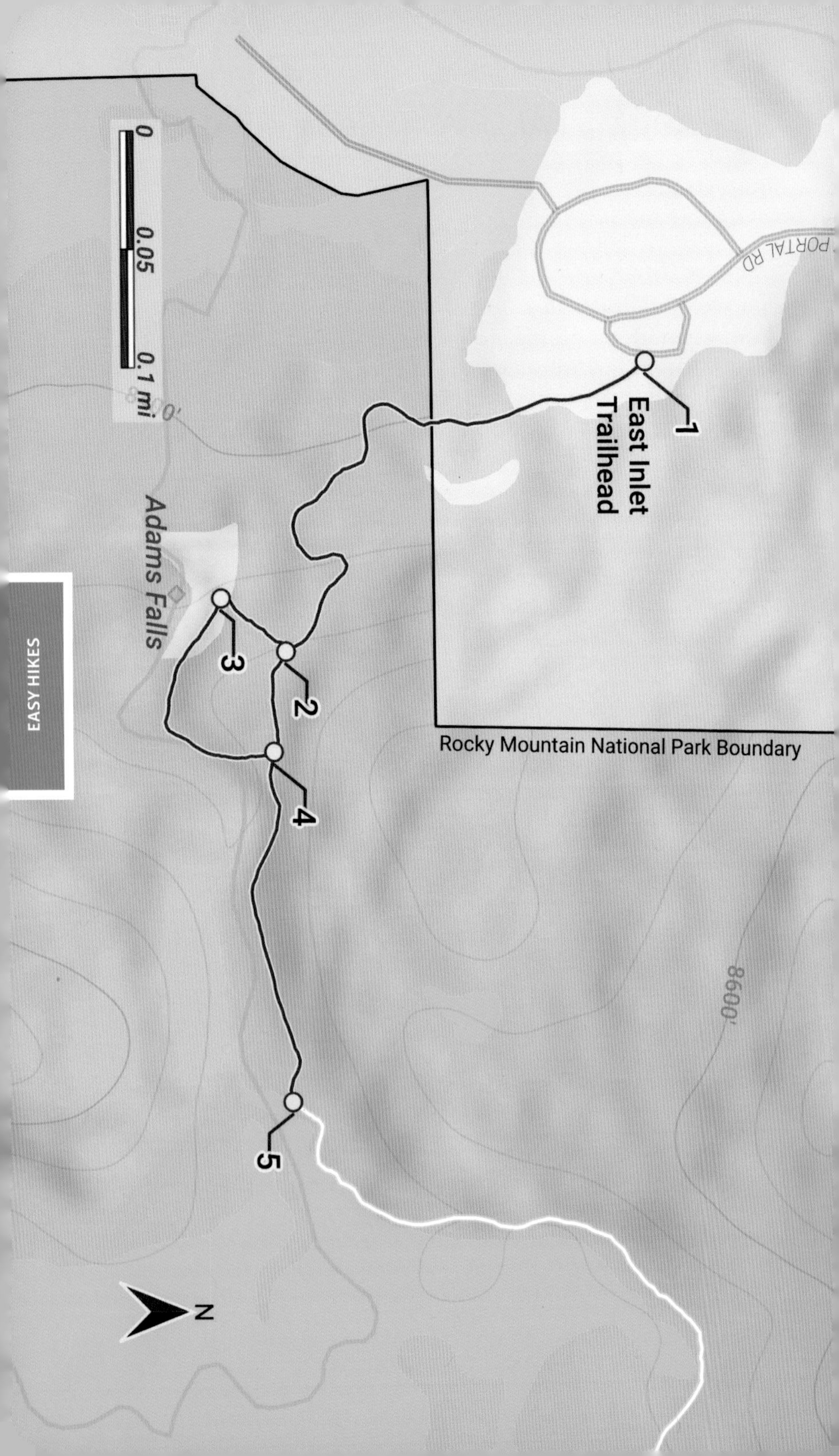

0
0.05
0.1 mi

EASY HIKES

Adams Falls

East Inlet
Trailhead

1

2

3

4

5

PORTAL RD

Rocky Mountain National Park Boundary

8600'

N

EASY HIKES

ADAMS FALLS

This hike begins on the south end of the parking lot. (**#1**) Follow the wide and gentle trail through a field of sagebrush and then into the forest. Here the trail winds its way upward with a few small turns. The trail is a bit rocky. Fortunately, this section isn't very long. Soon you'll arrive near the top of the hill and here you'll find a wooden trail sign pointing to the right for Adams Falls. (**#2**)

Walk down the stone steps for about 150 feet and you'll arrive at Adams Falls. (**#3**) There is a large stone wall protecting you and your children from the steep drop. Crawling on the wall or over to the other side is not recommended, as the drop is significant.

Here you can enjoy watching the East Inlet stream make its way around a small island before it plummets to a ledge below, where it turns and then falls off of another ledge as it makes its way down to Grand Lake.

The trail continues upward alongside the stream. This is a very pleasant and shaded section of trail. Be aware that in the spring the streams in Rocky will be flowing very powerfully and so you'll want to keep your distance and especially keep children away from the dangerous currents.

The trail then turns and climbs a series of stone steps and rejoins the main trail. (**#4**) Turn right here and continue along the gentle and mostly level trail through the forest. Soon you'll arrive at East Meadow. (**#5**) Here you can walk out to the edge of the East Inlet stream as it lazily makes its way through the meadow. As you look out across the meadow, you'll see Mount Craig at the far end, known by locals as "Baldy," looking down on this idyllic scene. It's a peaceful place to sit, listen to the birds, and watch for moose.

If you have time and energy, continue on up the trail from East Meadow for another 0.8 miles to the East Meadow Overlook. This is described in detail in the Lone Pine Lake section, which begins on page 338. Along this stretch you have a good chance of spotting moose grazing in the meadow or hiding in the forest.

To return from East Meadow, continue back the way you came. Stay on the main trail and it will lead you directly back to the trailhead.

EASY HIKES

MOUNT CRAIG OVER EAST MEADOW

14 – TUNDRA COMMUNITIES TRAIL

Overview

A short, steep climb at the beginning, followed by a gentle stroll through open tundra with vast views in every direction. Along the way, take time to get down low and examine the delicate and beautiful tundra vegetation that is similar to what you would find in the arctic regions. This is an enjoyable walk for the entire family.

The Stats

EASY HIKES

Distance Round Trip: 1.1 miles

Difficulty Rating: 20

Hiking Time: 45 minutes

Time to Go: morning or late in the day

Season: June through October

Primary Ecosystem: alpine

Views: delicate alpine foliage, open tundra, and grand vistas

Possible Wildlife: marmots, pikas, ptarmigan, elk, bighorn sheep

Trail Conditions: wide and paved but a little steep at the beginning

Reminder: Remember that you are starting at a very high elevation, so it will feel more difficult. Head down if you develop any signs of altitude sickness: headache, weakness, nausea, etc. Do not hike if there is any threat of a storm. Also, be certain to stay on the paved trail to protect the tundra.

Elevation Start: 12,110'

Highest Point: 12,286'

Total Elevation Gain: 176'

Trailhead: This hike begins at the Rock Cut parking area on Trail Ridge Road; see page 125 for details.

Waypoints

1. Rock Cut Trailhead	0.0	12,110'
2. Hoodoo Rock Junction	0.4	12,278'
3. Toll Memorial	0.6	12,286'

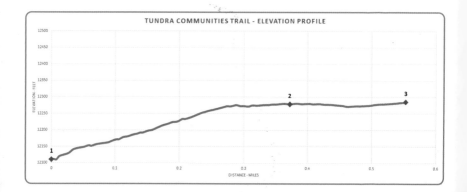

N

3

2

12200'

TRAIL RIDGE ROAD (US HWY 34)

1

Rock Cut

EASY HIKES

Rock Cut
Trailhead

12000'

11800'

11200'

11000'

0   0.05   0.1 mi

This hike begins on the north side of the road at the Rock Cut parking area just west of the east vault toilets. (**#1**) This trail is wide and paved, though not ideal for wheelchair access, as it does climb quite steeply at the beginning and has a few areas where there are large cracks in the pavement.

As you begin to head up the trail please remind everyone in your party to stay on the pavement, as the vegetation is very delicate. While it may look like rough grass, it actually consists of special plants that have evolved to survive the intense cold and high winds that this region experiences for most of the year. However, they have not evolved to handle footsteps! As the growing season is usually just six to eight weeks a year it can take decades and in some cases over a hundred years for a damaged area to regrow. Please do not take this hike if there is any chance of storms. The trail is fully exposed and there is a real danger of getting struck by lightning, as has happened to a number of unfortunate people along Trail Ridge Road over the years. You don't want to be one of them.

Soon after starting, the path is joined by another trail coming from the left. That trail starts just west of the restroom and has stairs rather than a slope. Continue upward as the trail heads to the north. You'll see many educational signs along the way. Stop and read these, as they will give you insight into this unique terrain. Get down on your knees at some point and look closely at the many different plants growing here.

The trail begins to level out, providing expansive views out toward the Mummy Range to the north. Along this stretch pay attention to the many alpine flowers growing up here, and in the rock piles beside the trail look for marmots and pikas.

At 0.4 miles there is a short paved trail that heads off to the right. (**#2**) Follow it, staying on the paved trail, up to Mushroom Rock, one of the very few hoodoos to be found in Rocky Mountain National Park. The upper darker rock is schist and below that is a layer of whitish granite. The schist is actually harder than the granite, which has begun to erode underneath, creating this unusual mushroom formation. Stay off of these rocks, as they are quite delicate. Up next to

Mushroom Rock you can look off to the southeast and enjoy a great view of Longs Peak.

Return to the main path and continue westward along this level stretch of trail. It leads out toward a large pile of rocks in the distance. As you walk, the view to the east opens up and you'll see the blocky summit of Longs Peak in the distance and cars traveling along Trail Ridge Road below you.

The trail stops right at the base of what appears to be a large pile of rocks but is actually a single rock formation. (**#3**) If you are nimble, you can scramble up the rock. On your way up you'll find a plaque honoring former RMNP superintendent Roger Toll and then at the top of the rock you'll not only find great views but also a large metal disc that shows you an overview of the area. It also points to where other national parks are located from here. After carefully making your way back down the rocks, enjoy a gentle stroll back. Note that this hike is especially beautiful in early morning and late evening.

EASY HIKES

VIEW FROM TUNDRA COMMUNITIES TRAIL

15 – LILY RIDGE LOOP

Overview

Enjoy a different view of Lily Lake by taking the Lily Ridge Trail for a view from above. This rough trail climbs up the hill on the north side of the lake, offering you spectacular views of Longs Peak over Lily Lake. It then adds a little distance and quiet by taking you around an outer trail.

The Stats

Distance: 1.3 miles

Difficulty Rating: 23

Hiking Time: 55 minutes

Time to Go: all day

Season: April through November

Primary Ecosystem: montane

Views: great views of Longs Peak and Twin Sisters with glimpses of the Mummy Range

Possible Wildlife: ducks and ground squirrels

Trail Conditions: rocky and sandy on the ridge section of the hike

Reminder: Always pay attention to the weather and if there is lightning return to your car.

Elevation Start: 8,931'

Highest Point: 9,114'

Total Elevation Gain: 189'

Trailhead: This hike begins at the Lily Lake Trailhead; see page 122 for details.

Waypoints

1. Lily Lake parking	0.0	8,931'
2. Right onto Lily Ridge Trail	0.05	8,928'
3. Lily Overlook 1	0.1	9,015'
4. Lily Overlook 2	0.3	9,114'
5. Lily Overlook 3	0.4	9,104'
6. Turn left onto trail	0.7	8,954'
7. Right onto main trail	0.8	8,931'
8. Right onto extension trail	0.9	8,932'
9. Maintenance road junction	1.2	8,953'

Hike Description

This hike begins at the Lily Lake Trailhead on the west end of the parking lot. (**#1**) You'll start by heading toward the lake and turning to the right. You'll be circling the lake in a counterclockwise direction. In about 260 feet, immediately before the first bridge, notice

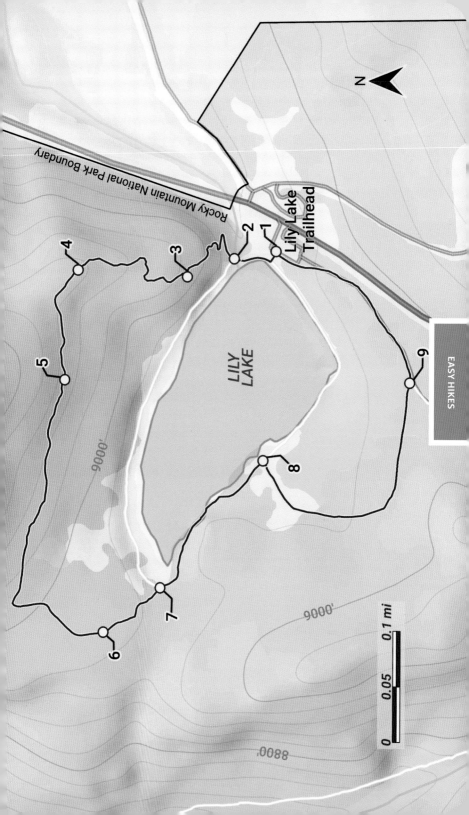

LILY
LAKE

Lily Lake
Trailhead

Rocky Mountain National Park Boundary

EASY HIKES

9000'

9000'

8800'

N

0   0.05   0.1 mi

the small Lily Ridge Trail on the right side. (#2) It heads off to the northeast. This junction is a little indistinct, so you'll have to pay attention. If you cross the bridge you've gone too far.

Follow the sandy trail and it will quickly climb up the ridge, gaining about a hundred feet with the first three switchbacks. At just a little over 0.1 miles you'll come across an open viewpoint on your left over Lily Lake. (#3) Then the trail begins to level out and heads into the woods. The trail is quite sandy and at times can be a bit difficult to discern. Keep your eyes open for rocks that have been set out to guide your way. At one point you'll have a small scramble over a large rock. At 0.3 miles you'll reach a high point and if you look off to your left down a small path you'll find a bench overlooking the lake. (#4) Be sure to stop here and spend some time. This is one of the highlights of the hike.

The trail begins to descend gently before climbing again to a third overlook. (#5) While there is no bench here, there are large rocks that you can crawl out on to enjoy the view. From here the trail descends the sandy trail and winds its way downward. At 0.7 miles it will connect with another small trail. (#6) Keep left and you will soon be back at the far side of Lily Lake, reconnecting with the main Lily Lake Trail at 0.8 miles. (#7)

Turn right and follow the main Lily Lake Trail along the south end of the lake. At one mile you'll intersect with the extension trail. (#8) Turn right here and follow it southward. Shortly after you begin on this section of trail, look off to your right and you'll notice a large picnic area that is often used as a wedding venue, which you can book with the national park. In a few minutes you will see a maintenance road heading off to your right, also the Storm Pass Trail (page 358). (#9) Near this intersection look left to get a great view of the Mummy Range. You then return to the Lily Lake Trailhead and can do it again.

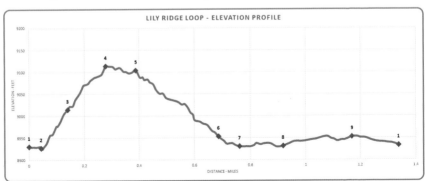

EASY HIKES

LILY RIDGE VIEWPOINT #1

16 – ALBERTA FALLS

Overview

Alberta Falls is one of the most popular hikes in Rocky Mountain National Park, as it is one of the easiest-to-reach waterfalls in the park. This hike leads you through forest, across small mountain streams, and up to Alberta Falls where you can watch Glacier Creek crash over the rocks.

The Stats

Distance Round Trip: 1.6 miles

Difficulty Rating: 28

Hiking Time: 1 hour 5 minutes

Time to Go: anytime

Season: May through October

Primary Ecosystem: montane

Views: forest, streams, and a waterfall

Possible Wildlife: pine squirrels, gray jays, Steller's jays

Trail Conditions: well defined but rocky

Reminder: Avoid the crowds by hiking this either early or late in the day.

Elevation Start: 9,175'

Highest Point: 9,394'

Total Elevation Gain: 234'

Trailhead: This hike begins at the Glacier Gorge Trailhead; see page 119 for details. It can also be started from the Bear Lake Trailhead (page 110).

Waypoints

1. Glacier Gorge Trailhead	0.0	9,175'
2. Bridge over Chaos Creek	0.2	9,176'
3. Glacier Creek Trail junction	0.3	9,228'
4. Left at junction with trail to Bear Lake	0.3	9,249'
5. Overlook of Glacier Creek	0.6	9,332'
6. Alberta Falls	0.8	9,394'

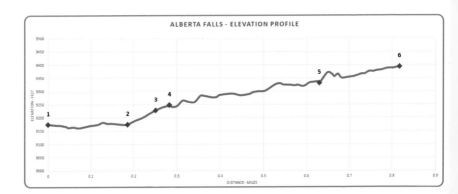

EASY HIKES

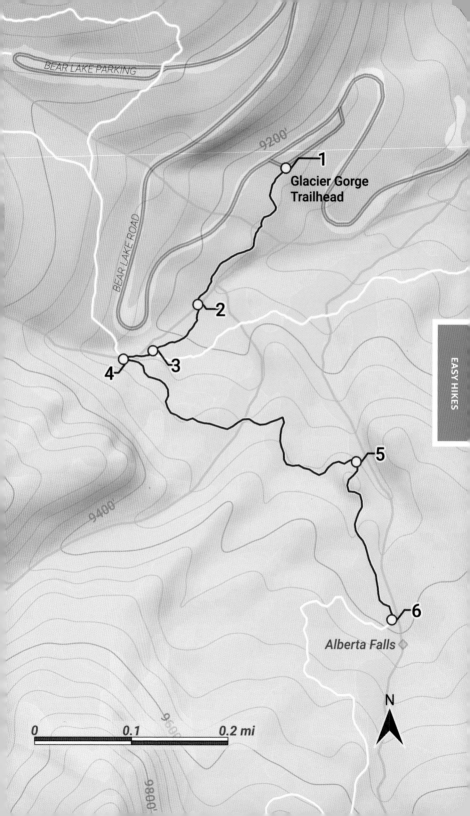

BEAR LAKE PARKING

9200'

1

Glacier Gorge Trailhead

2

3

4

EASY HIKES

5

9400'

6

Alberta Falls

9600'

9800'

N

0   0.1   0.2 mi

EASY HIKES

SPRING AT ALBERTA FALLS

The trail begins on the southwest side of the Glacier Gorge parking lot. (**#1**) At the beginning it is wide and smooth heading downhill through aspen trees. Soon you'll pass a small meadow with wildflowers and you'll begin to hear the roar of Chaos Creek below you. You'll cross a small bridge over a seasonal stream. The trail eventually levels out and then climbs a bit before reaching a bridge over Chaos Creek. (**#2**) From here the trail climbs steeply up stone steps. Soon it passes the intersection with the Glacier Creek Trail and continues to climb. (**#3**) At the top you'll reach the junction with the trail from Bear Lake. (**#4**) Take a sharp left here to continue on the Glacier Gorge Trail.

Here the trail levels out and winds through a canopy of small aspen trees that are gorgeous in early June and late September. At about 0.4 miles there is a bridge to get you across a small, shallow stream. Alternatively you can use the rocks in the stream to cross over. After this is another bridge and then you'll walk across a rock slab. At the far end of this slab look to your right and notice the big rock that has a smile.

You'll now begin to gently climb as the trail winds its way through the woods. It arrives at an overlook of Glacier Creek at a spot that is a bit of a canyon with high rock walls on the far side. (**#5**) You'll want to keep your eyes on kids here and keep them away from the edge. The trail turns to the right and follows the creek upstream. This stretch is relatively gentle. Keep your eyes open on the left for a nice view of the stream. At 0.8 miles you arrive at Alberta Falls. (**#6**) Here, Glacier Creek pours through a crack in the rocks and falls about twenty-five feet. There are large rock slabs around here for the kids to climb on or to sit and relax in the sun.

If you have energy, you can continue up the trail to destinations such as Mills Lake (page 250), Black Lake (page 302), the Loch (page 266), and Sky Pond (page 314). Just be sure you have enough food and water with you for a longer hike.

EASY HIKES

17 – SUMMERLAND PARK

Overview

This is a great family hike. It first takes you by a horse pasture, then through aspen trees, along a gentle river, beside marshland where there may be moose, then into the forest until you reach a wooden bridge over a stream. There are often many flowers growing along this route.

The Stats

Distance Round Trip: 3.3

Difficulty Rating: 33

Hiking Time: 2 hours and 10 minutes

Time to Go: morning or late afternoon

Season: May through October

Primary Ecosystem: montane

Views: meadows, marshland, forest

Possible Wildlife: marmots, moose, forest animals

Trail Conditions: large dirt road for most of the way, then a forest trail

Reminder: This hike is quite exposed. It can be very hot at midday and is not protected from storms.

Elevation Start: 8,520'

Highest Point: 8,583'

Total Elevation Gain: 165'

Trailhead: This hike begins at the North Inlet Trailhead just outside of Grand Lake; see page 124 for details.

Waypoints

1. North Inlet Trailhead	0.0	8,520'
2. Horse pasture	0.2	8,469'
3. Alongside North Inlet Creek	0.8	8,505'
4. Summerland Park Cabin	1.2	8,507'
5. Stream Crossing	1.6	8,576'

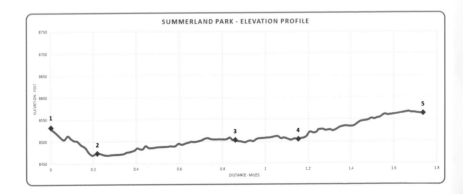

SUMMERLAND PARK - ELEVATION PROFILE

EASY HIKES

N

EASY HIKES

North Inlet
Trailhead

RMNP Boundary

WEST PORTAL RD

0   0.25   0.5 mi

1
2
3
4
5

9800'
9600'
9400'
9600'
9600'
9600'
9600'
9400'
9200'
9000'
8800'
9000'
9200'
9400'
9000'
9800'

This hike begins on the southeast corner of the first parking lot. (**#1**) You'll make your way around a metal gate and then head downhill on a large dirt road lined by aspen trees. At the bottom of the hill the trees open up on your right-hand side, revealing a large meadow. (**#2**) That side of the road is private property and there is a large wooden fence separating the road from the meadow. Behind the fence you can often find horses peacefully grazing. Sometimes they will come up to the road to say hello.

As you continue you'll notice a wide variety of flowers growing on both sides of the road. In the early morning, as the fog lifts from the meadow and the first light begins to awaken the grasses, it is especially delightful. The road here is flat and the walking is easy, making it ideal for families with younger children. As you continue onward along this entire hike, keep your eyes open for moose. I've seen them on nearly every part of this trail at one time or another, both in the meadow and in the trees. If you see them, give them plenty of space. Often in the rock piles on the left side of the road I've seen marmots playing and keeping watch on passing hikers.

EVENING LIGHT IN THE MEADOW

HAPPY HORSE AT WAYPOINT #2

At about 0.8 miles the trail will come alongside the North Inlet Creek, which lazily wanders through the meadow. (#3) This is a great place to stop for a while. As you continue on, the stream flows alongside the road. This area can be quite wet and muddy in the spring and early summer when the creek breaks its banks, but as the summer continues it does dry out.

After this section you'll soon arrive at the cabin at Summerland Park. (#4) This is a private residence, so be sure to stay on the road. You'll notice to your right that the meadow has become marshland and it is very possible you may see moose. Just past the cabin the road changes into a trail and heads into the woods. Here you will often find wildflowers abounding, especially columbine. To your right, from time to time you'll get a glimpse of the marshy meadows. After 0.4 miles of gentle walking you'll reach a bridge over a small stream, which is shaded by the surrounding trees. (#5) This is the end of the Summerland Park hike. Beyond here the trail begins to climb quite steeply.

If you are continuing on to Cascade Falls or beyond, If you are continuing on to Cascade Falls or beyond, turn to page 262.

EASY HIKES

SPRING AT THE POOL

Overview

This is a relatively gentle family-friendly hike through the woods and alongside the Big Thompson River. It ends at a bridge over rushing water where there is a deeper pool in the river. The trail is peaceful and has a large variety of foliage. There seems to always be something blooming along this trail.

The Stats

Distance Round Trip: 3.4 miles	**Reminder:** Keep children and adults away from the river during the spring, as it is extremely powerful and dangerous at this time of year.
Difficulty Rating: 37* (51)	
Hiking Time: 2 hours and 15 minutes	
Time to Go: anytime	**Elevation Start:** 8,155'
Season: May through October	
Primary Ecosystem: montane	**Highest Point:** 8,350'
Views: forest and stream views	**Total Elevation Gain:** 380'
Possible Wildlife: forest animals	**Trailhead:** This hike begins at the Fern Lake Trailhead; see page 117 for details.
Trail Conditions: easy to follow and relatively gentle	

EASY HIKES

Waypoints

1. Fern Lake Trailhead	0.0	8,155'
2. Cross Windy Gulch Creek	0.4	8,195'
3. Small pond	0.6	8,212'
4. Arch Rocks	1.2	8,238'
5. The Pool	1.7	8,319'

Hike Description

This hike leaves from the west side of the parking lot. (**#1**) The trail is narrow and level and surrounded by thick vegetation. Though you can't see it, the Big Thompson River is just off to the left. If you pay attention you'll see wild roses, vine maples, Douglas fir trees, mountain junipers, aspens, etc. This area is simply verdant.

After the first rise, the trail descends and meets the Big Thompson before heading back into deep forest. At just under half a mile you'll cross a small stream coming down from Windy Gulch and then another small stream just after that. (**#2**) The forest then opens up and you're likely to find lots of wildflowers growing. When you reach 0.6 miles be sure to look off to your left and notice the small pond below you. (**#3**) You never know if a moose might be grazing there. If you see one, be sure to give it plenty of space.

A little later the trail again comes alongside the river. At about one mile you'll see a large rock wall on your right. This is often used by folks who enjoy the sport of bouldering, so it is likely you'll see white powder on the rock, which climbers use to improve their handholds. The trail then visits the river again. Be aware that in the spring it can be extremely powerful, so be sure to stay clear and keep kids away at this time.

You'll reach a long, flat sandy stretch and you will notice a giant long boulder that juts into the trail. This came down during the big flood of 2013. Look up the hill to your right to see where it came from and try to imagine what it was like when this came down.

Just 0.1 miles farther the trail winds between some towering boulders. This area is known as Arch Rocks. (**#4**) The kids really enjoy this spot and if you are lucky you might find some rock-climbers practicing their skills. Shortly after Arch Rocks the trail climbs gently up some stairs. For a little while you'll be fairly high above the river. It then slowly descends and arrives at a bridge. (**#5**) This is the Pool. You can see how on the upstream portion it is quite deep. On the far side of the bridge there are rocks to climb on and places to have a picnic.

From here you can continue on up to Fern Falls and Fern Lake; see page 288 for details.

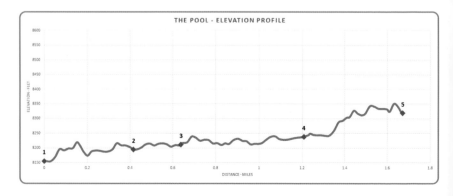

THE POOL - ELEVATION PROFILE

EASY HIKES

Fern Lake
Trailhead

CUB
LAKE

THE
POOL

Fern Falls

Steep
Mountain
9541ft
2908m

N

8800'
8600'
8400'
8800'
9400'
9600'
10200'
10000'
9800'
10400'
8600'
8800'
9800'
9200'
8800'
8600'
8400'

0   0.25   0.5 mi

19 – BEAR LAKE TO PARK & RIDE

Overview

Skip the shuttle bus and hike from Bear Lake down to Park & Ride via the beautiful Bierstadt Lake. This hike can be done in reverse if the shuttle lines are too long. You also have the option to simply follow this trail up and around Bierstadt Lake and back to your starting point. This is a quiet forest hike with wonderful views at the lake.

The Stats

Distance One Way: 3.6 miles

Difficulty Rating: 46

Hiking Time: 2 hours and 25 minutes

Time to Go: anytime

Season: June through October

Primary Ecosystems: subalpine and montane

Views: mostly forest with beautiful mountain views from Bierstadt Lake

Possible Wildlife: forest animals

Trail Conditions: Much of this trail is quite rocky.

Reminder: This is a one-way hike. Don't forget to stop and listen to the sounds of the forest from time to time.

Elevation Start: 9,475'

Highest Point: 9,765'

Total Elevation Gain: 290' (1,131' elevation loss)

Trailhead: This hike begins at the Bear Lake Trailhead; see page 110 for details.

Waypoints

1. Bear Lake Trailhead	0.0	9,475'
2. Bierstadt Lake Trail junction	0.5	9,712'
3. Mill Creek west junction	1.2	9,606'
4. Lake Loop junction	1.7	9,442'
5. Access to Bierstadt Lake	2.0	9,433'
6. Left onto trail to Park & Ride	2.1	9,422'
7. Steep trail section	2.8	9,193'
8. Park & Ride	3.6	8,635'

Hike Description

Head past the ranger station toward Bear Lake. (**#1**) When you get to the loop trail around the lake, turn right and follow the trail along the eastern edge of the lake. At 0.1 miles turn right onto the

EASY HIKES

CONTINENTAL DIVIDE AND BIERSTADT LAKE

EASY HIKES

Alberta Falls

BEAR LAKE

Bear Lake Trailhead

1

2

3

4

BIERSTADT LAKE

5

6

7

BEAR LAKE ROAD

9000'

9400'

9200'

SPRAGUE LAKE

8

Park and Ride Trailhead

8800'

8600'

8600'

8800'

9800'

9600'

9400'

9200'

N

0   0.25   0.5   0.75   1 mi

Fern Lake Trail. Here the trail begins to climb upward, entering an aspen grove filled with boulders. As you climb, notice the orange markers located high up in the trees. These are to guide skiers and those on snowshoes who want to visit Bierstadt Lake in the winter.

At about half a mile you'll reach the junction with the Bierstadt Lake Trail. (**#2**) Continue straight ahead up the hill toward the lake. The trail begins to turn to the north and becomes quite a bit rockier before turning toward the northwest and leveling out. It reaches its highest point at about 0.6 miles and then begins gradually sloping downward. Soon it will take a sharp switchback to the right and descend more steeply.

At the bottom of the hill the trail winds gently back and forth through the trees. This is a very peaceful section of forest and somewhere I sometimes come to think and pray. Then when you least expect it you pass the western junction for the Mills Creek Basin Trail on your left. (**#3**) Continue straight ahead past the junction. The trail will begin to descend soon and is quite rough here due to erosion.

You'll next reach the junction for the loop trail around Bierstadt Lake. (**#4**) This is about the halfway point on your hike. You'll want to head to the left, as the best viewpoint is on this side of the lake. (The trail around the lake is one mile long and relatively flat. You have the option of simply going around the lake and returning to Bear Lake instead of heading down to Park & Ride.)

As you head through the woods just north of the lake, you'll pass a second junction for Mills Creek Basin; keep going straight past it. Then at two miles you'll see a junction and horse tie-up on your right. (**#5**) Turn here and follow the trail for a short distance to the edge of the lake. Allow yourself to be captured by the incredible view of the

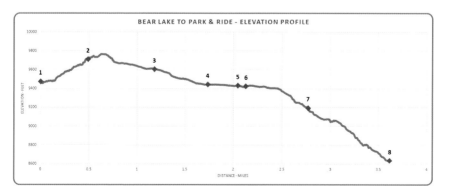

Continental Divide looking down on the lake. After you've spent some time here head back to the main trail and turn right to continue on.

In a short ways you'll cross a small bridge over the outlet stream that may or may not be running. Just past this you reach the junction with the trail to the Park & Ride. (**#5**) Turn left here. (If you are returning to Bear Lake, continue around the lake.)

As you make your way toward Park & Ride the trail becomes quite rough as it descends through a tight section of lodgepole pine and many fallen trees. At about 2.8 miles there is one very short and very steep section; fortunately it is less than 0.1 miles long. (**#6**) In less than half a mile the trail begins to change from thick lodgepole to aspen. You'll begin to get views to your right of Glacier Creek Stables and behind it Sprague Lake.

As you make your way down the rocky hillside, you'll pass another junction on your right. (**#7**) This is a trail that follows Bear Lake Road. Continue past it and in a few minutes the trees will open and you'll find yourself at the Bierstadt Moraine Trailhead at the Park & Ride. (**#8**) During the summer months and early autumn you can take a shuttle back up to Bear Lake or down to Estes Park.

EASY HIKES

HALLETT PEAK AND FLATTOP MOUNTAIN

20 – DREAM LAKE

Overview

This is one of the most popular hikes in Rocky Mountain National Park, as it provides you with quick and relatively easy access to one of the park's most beautiful lakes. Dream Lake lives up to its name with its stunning views of Hallett Peak and Flattop Mountain.

The Stats

Distance Round Trip: 2.2 miles

Difficulty Rating: 47

Hiking Time: 1 hour and 30 minutes

Time to Go: anytime but it's most beautiful in the morning

Season: June until first snow

Primary Ecosystem: subalpine

Views: Enjoy views over Glacier Basin and Glacier Gorge followed by a stunning mountain lake.

Possible Wildlife: forest animals

Trail Conditions: The trail is quite wide and smooth compared to most in RMNP. The first half is roughly paved.

Reminder: This is one of the most popular hikes in the park, so it pays to visit very early or late in the day. The light is best in the morning.

Elevation Start: 9,475'

Highest Point: 9,921'

Total Elevation Gain: 503'

Trailhead: This hike starts at the Bear Lake Trailhead; see page 110 for details.

Waypoints

1. Bear Lake Trailhead	0.0	9,475'
2. Nymph Lake	0.5	9,706'
3. Nymph Lake Overlook	0.8	9,805'
4. Haiyaha junction	1.0	9,904'
5. Dream Lake	1.1	9,920'

Hike Description

The trail begins next to the ranger station at the west end of the Bear Lake parking lot. (**#2**) From the ranger station begin walking west toward Bear Lake. Take the left turn just a few steps past the ranger station. In a couple hundred feet you'll pass a junction that leads down to the Glacier Gorge Trail. Keep to the right and head uphill. You'll initially be going south, but slowly the trail will turn to the west. This section of trail is partially paved. This is a gentle climb

JUNE AT DREAM LAKE

up through the trees, but if you are not acclimatized or particularly fit, you may find it to be challenging. The key is to take it slow and steady, walking at a pace at which you can comfortably breathe. Remember to allow room for others to pass.

At 0.5 miles you'll arrive at Nymph Lake, a small body of water surrounded by trees. (#2) Be sure to respect the Restoration Area signs and stay off of the vegetation around the edges of the lake. During the summer this little pond is filled with lily pads, often with big yellow flowers. As the trail moves toward the north side of the lake, look both to the west and south for great views. On the north side there is a small trail leading down to a bench beside the lake. This

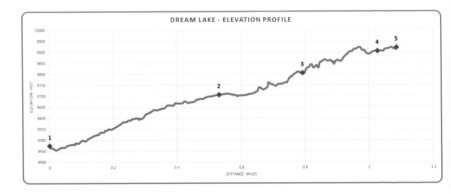

DREAM LAKE - ELEVATION PROFILE

EASY HIKES

BEAR LAKE ROAD

9200

9400'

N

Bear Lake
Trailhead

1

BEAR
LAKE

9600'

9600'

2

NYMPH
LAKE

3

9800'

4

5

DREAM
LAKE

10200'

10400'

600'

0   0.25   0.5 mi

is a nice detour if you have time. It's a great place to sit and take in an impressive view of Longs Peak.

The trail continues up the hill alongside a large rock outcropping and then at 0.7 miles it reaches a switchback that sends you hiking south up a section of stairs. This particular stretch can sometimes avalanche after heavy snows in the winter, so if the avalanche danger is high, you may want to go back to Nymph and find the winter trail. At the top of these stairs on your left side is a terrific overlook you shouldn't miss. (#3) It looks out over Nymph Lake and into Glacier Gorge with Longs Peak standing high above it.

The trail continues up through aspen trees with beautiful views to the south. As you continue upward you'll begin to get views of Hallett Peak looking like the prow of a mighty ship up ahead of you. At the first switchback you may notice a small cascade at the end of a short detour trail. In the summer there are often flowers growing around this cascade.

From here the trail makes a couple of short switchbacks and then levels out, crossing a small bridge. Be sure to look out to your left as you cross the bridge to see Longs Peak perfectly framed.

At exactly one mile you'll reach a junction for Lake Haiyaha. (#4) Stay to the right and cross a log bridge across the outlet stream. Just beyond the bridge you'll climb a small rise, and the main Dream Lake viewpoint will be on your left. (#5) When you get to the viewpoint look to the west and you'll see the imposing summit of Hallett Peak, though what you are seeing is actually well below the summit. To the right you'll see Flattop Mountain, which from this perspective looks anything but flat. This is a great place to spend some time enjoying this dramatic scene.

If you have energy to continue on up to Emerald Lake, turn to page 226. It is only an additional 0.6 miles each way and an additional 200' of elevation gain.

MODERATE HIKES

I f you enjoy hiking and want the thrill of being out in the mountains without doing anything crazy, then these will be the hikes for you. They are good for people who are relatively fit and acclimated to the elevation of Rocky. Most of these can be enjoyed by older kids who are happy walking a few miles. As you look through this section, realize that each hike is progressively more difficult, with the first hikes in this section being closer to Easy and the later hikes being closer to Strenuous. These hikes will involve a fair amount of elevation gain and distance.

MODERATE HIKES

FERN LAKE TRAIL NEAR BEAR LAKE

21 – ALPINE RIDGE TRAIL

Overview

This is a very short hike up into the tundra above the Alpine Visitor Center. Although short, it is deceptively difficult. Because it starts at nearly 12,000' many people who are not acclimated to the elevation can really struggle on it. So take it easy on this hike unless you are fully acclimated.

The Stats

Distance Round Trip: 0.6 miles

Difficulty Rating: 50* (16)

Hiking Time: 25 minutes

Time to Go: morning

Season: July through October

Primary Ecosystem: alpine

Views: grand vistas over the tundra and over the Alpine Visitor Center area

Possible Wildlife: marmots and pikas

Trail Conditions: well-maintained stairs and paved path

Reminder: This hike begins at nearly 12,000' and so is much more difficult than it looks, so listen to your body. Also, don't attempt if there is any potential for storms. You are a lightning target up here.

Elevation Start: 11,796'

Highest Point: 12,005'

Total Elevation Gain: 209'

Trailhead: This hike begins at the Alpine Visitor Center; see page 109 for details.

Waypoints

1. Alpine Ridge Trailhead	0.0	11,796'
2. Top of stairs	0.2	11,911'
3. End of trail	0.3	12,005'

MODERATE HIKES

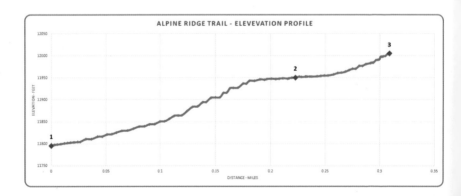

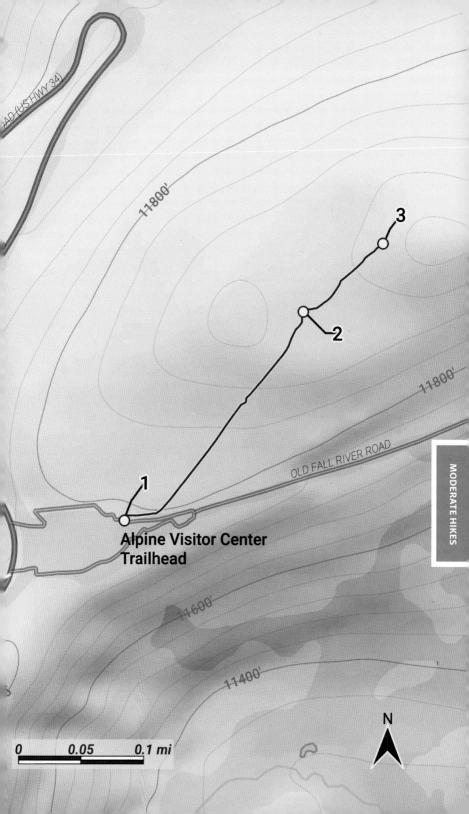

11800'

3

2

1

11800'

OLD FALL RIVER ROAD

MODERATE HIKES

Alpine Visitor Center
Trailhead

11600'

11400'

AD (US HWY 34)

N

0   0.05   0.1 mi

STAIRS TO 12,000'

This hike starts from the northeast corner of the parking lot. (#1) It climbs a short flight of twelve steps and then makes its way eastward on a fairly gentle paved path before climbing more steeply northward. It then reaches the second set of steps, which heads directly up the hill. There are about seventy-four steps in this section.

As you ascend notice the incredible tundra plants that line the path. In late June and early July you'll likely find many different species of wildflowers growing and giving off the most delightful aromas. Fortunately, the National Park Service has many of these flowers and other plants labeled with small signs letting you to know what you are looking at.

After those steps you'll reach a small, flat section of trail with signage about life at this elevation. Then the trail continues straight up another 150 steps to the top. (#2) Take your time and don't walk faster than you can breathe. If you feel a headache or chest pains or any other physical symptoms, head back down. All the park staff working at the Alpine Visitor Center (building with log roof) are trained medics.

At the top of this third section of stairs the path levels out and continues to head northwest. There are numerous signs along the path describing what you are seeing. After a very short walk the trail comes to an end at a viewpoint. (#3) Here you have a 360-degree view and can see not only the Never Summer Mountains to your west but also the plains out to the east. Here you are at an elevation of 12,005'. Do not go beyond this point, as the tundra is extremely delicate and any footsteps can quickly kill the plant life. Some estimates say that damaged areas require nearly one hundred years to recover due to the harsh environment and the very limited growing season. From here you can slowly make your way back to the Trail Ridge Store & Café and grab a refreshing drink or attend a talk by one of the rangers at the Alpine Visitor Center.

MODERATE HIKES

22 – WESTERN UTE TRAIL

Overview

Enjoy a delightful downhill stroll through the alpine tundra, down through tree line and into the forest. All the way you'll enjoy fantastic views of the Never Summer Range and Forest Canyon. Pay attention and you'll see an extensive variety of miniature plant life growing in the tundra. You are also likely to see elk, pikas, and marmots along this hike. This is a one-way downhill hike. You'll either need to leave a car or be picked up at Milner Pass, unless you feel up for a workout and want to hike back up.

The Stats

Distance One Way: 4.0 miles

Difficulty Rating: 51* (36)

Hiking Time: 2 hours and 40 minutes

Time to Go: morning

Season: late June through October

Primary Ecosystems: alpine and subalpine

Views: grand vistas on both sides, tarns, wildlife

Possible Wildlife: elk, marmots, pikas, bighorn sheep

Trail Conditions: well-defined trail with a few steep switchbacks at the end; muddy second half in early summer

Reminder: This is a one-way hike. You'll either need to leave a car at the bottom (Milner Pass) or get picked up. If you want to walk both ways, I recommend starting at Milner Pass. In June or early July ask a ranger before attempting, as there may be snowfields. Do not attempt if storms are likely. Early morning is best.

Elevation Start: 11,796'

Highest Point: 11,796'

Total Elevation Gain: 163' (1,209' elevation loss)

Trailhead: This hike begins at the Alpine Visitor Center; see page 109 for details.

Waypoints

1. Alpine Visitor Center parking	0.0	11,796'
2. Tarns	1.5	11,522'
3. Enter forest	2.0	11,335'
4. Stream crossing	2.7	11,240'
5. Right at Ida junction	3.4	11,089'
6. Spires	3.8	10,780'
7. Milner Pass	4.0	10,750'

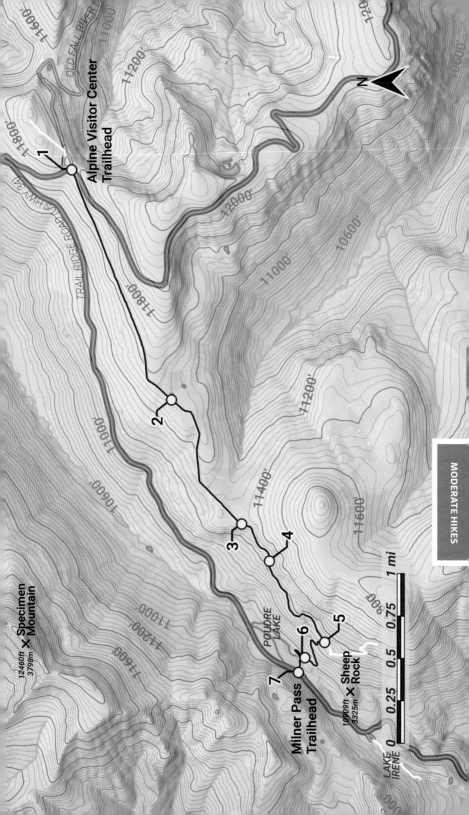

N

MODERATE HIKES

Alpine Visitor Center
Trailhead

1

OLD FALL RIVER

11200'

12000'

10600'

11000'

11200'

11400'

11600'

11600'

2

3

4

5

6

7

POUDRE
LAKE

Milner Pass
Trailhead

Sheep
Rock

10909ft
3325m

TRAIL RIDGE ROAD / US HWY 34

11800'

11800'

11000'

10600'

Specimen
Mountain

12460ft
3798m

11200'

11000'

11400'

11600'

900'

900'

LAKE
IRENE

0   0.25   0.5   0.75   1 mi

Be aware that this trail can have snow through early July some years. In early summer it's best to ask a ranger about trail conditions before beginning.

This hike begins opposite the western entrance to the Alpine Visitor Center parking lot, on the other side of Trail Ridge Road. (**#1**) Just after you begin on the trail, you'll see a large orange sign with the letter *H* on the ground. This is a designated helicopter-landing site used in emergencies. The trail begins ever so gently and smoothly. As you continue down this trail, remember to protect the delicate tundra and keep the trail from expanding by walking in the center of the trail.

As I was recording this hike, I was treated to the sight of a coyote hunting just below this trail while marmots behind him squeaked loud warnings to the others. In the distance elk were lying in the tundra, watching the show. Along the side of the trail I can usually spot a dozen different flowers blooming. The aromas they give off are better than any perfume.

The trail gradually descends, occasionally interrupted by a small rise. At a little over a mile you'll encounter *krumholz*, which is a German word for "crooked wood" used to describe the small deformed trees you'll find around tree line. The deformity comes from the harsh conditions and many of these trees can be hundreds of years old.

Continue on and at 1.5 miles you'll see a few small alpine tarns (ponds) overlooking Forest Canyon. (**#2**) You can get some very nice photos of them from the trail, so there is no need to trample the delicate tundra. You'll find tarns like these scattered throughout the high country across Rocky Mountain National Park.

About a tenth of a mile farther on you'll come across a sign for Forest

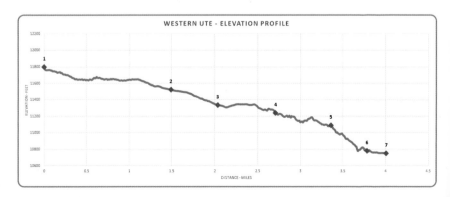

POOLS NEAR NEAR WAYPOINT #2

Canyon Pass. This is where the Big Thompson River begins. A short distance farther the krumholz closes in and hides the views. Eventually you descend into another open area. This will be your last taste of the tundra before entering into the forest. (**#3**) Here it is interesting to see how quickly the trees grow in height as you head downward, showing how even very small changes in temperature have a big impact on the growth of trees. At 2.7 miles you'll cross a couple of small streams. (**#4**) Along this next stretch you may encounter some mud through mid- to late July.

At 3.4 miles you'll reach an intersection with the Ida Trail. (**#5**) Here you'll take a sharp right and begin a steep descent with five sharp turns before the bottom. This section is not only quite steep but the trail is also rough with a lot of exposed tree roots and some areas where there is a drop-off on one side. Hiking poles are recommended.

After four sharp turns the trail levels out and begins its final descent. Notice on the right side of the trail several very tall rock spires that reach about forty-five feet. (**#6**) These are ancient pegmatite dikes. Just opposite them is a good view of Poudre Lake. Head down the trail and it will soon come alongside the western edge of the lake before arriving at the Milner Pass Trailhead on the Continental Divide. (**#7**) Here the waters of the lake flow into the Atlantic Ocean and everything to the west of the lake flows into the Pacific Ocean.

23 – TOMBSTONE RIDGE

Overview

This hike follows a portion of the ancient Ute Trail out across the tundra to Timberline Pass. It is all above tree line and is a great way to see and experience this unique environment. The trail is relatively gentle and good for the entire family as long as everyone stays on the trail and off the delicate tundra.

The Stats

Distance Round Trip: 3.9 miles

Difficulty Rating: 61

Hiking Time: 2 hours and 40 minutes

Time to Go: morning

Season: mid-June through October

Primary Ecosystem: alpine

Views: grand vistas in every direction

Possible Wildlife: marmots, pikas, elk, ptarmigan

Trail Conditions: rocky trail with some smoother sandy sections

Reminder: This hike is completely exposed to the elements—not only rain, hail, and wind but also lightning—so do not attempt this hike if there is any chance of a storm. Turn back at the first sign of a storm brewing. Consider bringing a plant guide to identify tundra flowers and plants.

Elevation Start: 11,437'

Highest Point: 11,659'

Total Elevation Gain: 481'

Trailhead: This hike begins at the Ute Crossing Trailhead on Trail Ridge Road; see page 129 for details.

Waypoints

1. Trailhead at Ute Crossing	0.0	11,437'
2. Top of first climb	0.2	11,554'
3. Bottom of hill	0.9	11,557'
4. Top of second hill	1.4	11,658'
5. Timberline Pass	1.9	11,461'

Hike Description

Begin by heading south over very rocky terrain. (**#1**) While you may be tempted to find the smoothest way, in order to protect the fragile tundra try to find the main path and walk in the middle of it. At the very least, walk on rocks rather than vegetation. The trail soon begins to ascend, climbing one hundred feet in 0.2 miles. Take it slowly and it isn't too bad. (**#2**) It then reaches the top and levels

Ute Trail East
Trailhead

TRAIL RIDGE ROAD (US-34)

N

MODERATE HIKES

0   0.25   0.5   0.75   1 mi

out. As the trail heads eastward take the time to get down on your knees and take a close look at the impressive variety of plants that are growing here. Tundra life is amazing, as it has adapted to this incredibly harsh terrain where the bitter wind howls for most of the year and the growing season is not much more than two months.

As you continue on you can see the block-shaped summit of Longs Peak in the distance ahead of you. To your far right and far below you are Forest Canyon and Hayden Gorge. The trail continues on fairly gently. It is a mixture of sand and larger rocks. If you keep your eyes open you may see a herd of elk in the tundra below you or marmots and pikas in the rocks to your left.

As you reach the half-mile mark you'll notice rocky hills off to your left and farther in the distance to your right. Some of these ridges have rocks that stand almost straight up, reminiscent of tombstones, giving this area its name.

The trail reaches a low point at around 0.9 miles. (#3) Here you can look off to your left and see a great view of the Mummy Range. To your right you can see Longs Peak as well as Flattop, Notchtop, and Gabletop mountains. This lower portion of the hike can sometimes get quite wet and muddy in the spring, so be prepared.

After climbing the next hill the trail begins to level out with wide-open views. (#4) Quite often I see large herds of elk here. Around 1.6 miles you'll see a really interesting ridge off to your left that is covered in precariously balanced rocks. Here the trail begins to descend. (If you are already getting tired you may want to turn around here rather than continuing downhill and having to climb back up again.) As the trail continues downhill it begins to get a bit rough and rocky. It also becomes a little more difficult to find. From here you will have views

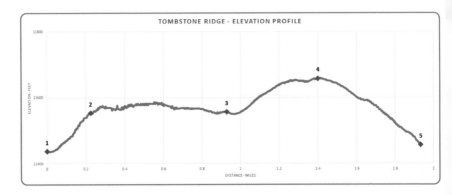

TOMBSTONE RIDGE - ELEVATION PROFILE

LONGS PEAK FROM TOMBSTONE RIDGE

of the east side of the park including Moraine Park far below. Here you arrive at your destination, Timberline Pass. (#5)

From here the trail descends very steeply and then makes its way to Beaver Meadows. If you are planning to continue, you can find trail information on page 298. Otherwise, it is time to turn around and make your way back to the Ute Crossing.

24 – CALYPSO CASCADES

Overview

Hike along a gentle path by the side of North Saint Vrain Creek as it makes its way through the deep forests of Wild Basin. At the top you'll enjoy the dramatic scene of Cony Creek cascading down about 150 feet before tumbling under the bridge you'll be standing on. This is a good hike for families and anyone wanting a refreshing walk in the woods.

The Stats

Distance Round Trip: 3.6 miles

Difficulty Rating: 68

Hiking Time: 2 hours and 25 minutes

Time to Go: anytime

Season: June through October

Primary Ecosystem: montane

Views: forest and stream views as well as a large cascade

Possible Wildlife: forest animals

Trail Conditions: relatively wide trail with rocky sections and some stairs

Reminder: Parking fills quickly, so arrive early. Be aware that the water can be very powerful and dangerous during the spring runoff; keep yourselves and your children at a distance.

Elevation Start: 8,500'

Highest Point: 9,142'

Total Elevation Gain: 642'

Trailhead: This hike begins at the Wild Basin Trailhead; see page 130 for details.

Waypoints

1. Wild Basin Trailhead	0.0	8,500'
2. Copeland Falls junction	0.3	8,576'
3. Rock slab	1.0	8,802'
4. Campsite Trail – east junction	1.4	8,886'
5. Calypso Cascades	1.8	9,139'

Hike Description

The hike departs on the south end of the main Wild Basin parking lot. (#1) It crosses a small stream, heads through a small section of forest, and then enters a meadow that often has wildflowers. At the end of the meadow it reenters the forest. Here the trees reach over the trail like a very tall canopy. The trail here is wide and gentle. Soon it

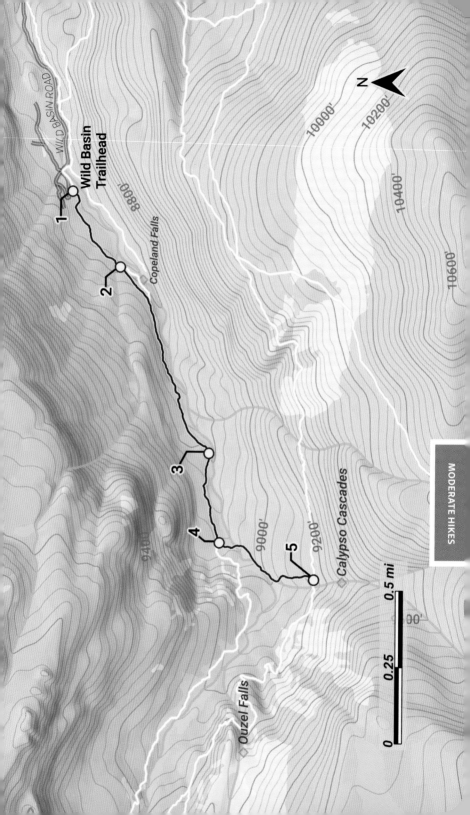

WILD BASIN ROAD

Wild Basin Trailhead

1

2

Copeland Falls

8800'

3

4

5

9000'

9200'

9200'

Calypso Cascades

Ouzel Falls

9400'

10000'

10200'

10400'

10600'

N

MODERATE HIKES

0   0.25   0.5 mi

400'

arrives at a junction for Copeland Falls, which is not much of a waterfall (being only a few feet in height), but this trail lets you get down by the water and then brings you back to the main trail. (**#2**) If you don't go down the Copeland Falls Trail and instead stay on the main trail, you'll enjoy an often flower-filled meadow on your right side.

After a little while the trail draws near to the stream, with a few places where you can get right down by the water. This is not recommended in the spring when the water is dangerous but can be enjoyable later in the summer when the flow has slowed. At about one mile the trail climbs a large rock slab. (**#3**) Here you get your first glimpse of the valley with the high hills surrounding it. Along this rocky area are places where you can get off the trail and relax in the sun with a good book.

At 1.4 miles you'll reach an intersection with a trail heading off to your right. (**#4**) This trail leads to a number of wilderness camping sites, which can be reserved at Rocky Mountain National Park's Wilderness Office. Most of them are more than a mile up the branch trail. You, however, will stay on the main trail that soon leads across a large bridge over the North Saint Vrain Creek. Here you can watch the water crashing over the rocks as it hurries downward.

Just after the bridge the trail begins to climb. Many people find this section of trail a bit challenging, but the key is to take your time and don't walk faster than you can comfortably breathe. In a little while you'll reach the top and the trail will begin to level off. It's not far from here to Calypso Cascades. When you pass a horse tie-up on your left, you know you are nearly there.

When you reach the long bridge, you've arrived at Calypso Cascades. (**#5**) Here Cony Creek puts on a show as its waters tumble down, creating this great roaring fury of water. There are a few large

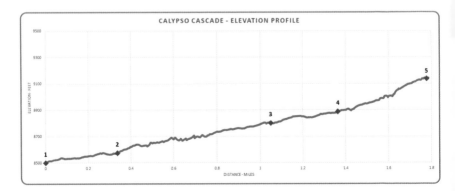

BRIDGE BELOW CALYPSO CASCADES

boulders here where you can sit and enjoy the sounds, scenes, and the gentle mist coming off of the cascade.

If you have energy, continue on to Ouzel Falls. It is another 1.8 miles round trip from here with another 243' of elevation gain. You can find details for that hike on page 258.

25 – EMERALD LAKE

Overview

This is one of the most popular hikes in Rocky Mountain National Park, as it provides you with quick and fairly easy access to two of the park's most beautiful lakes. You will first pass Dream Lake and then continue up to Emerald Lake, which lies right below two awe-inspiring peaks that rise up dramatically from the edge of the lake.

The Stats

Distance Round Trip: 3.3 miles

Difficulty Rating: 78

Hiking Time: 2 hours and 10 minutes

Time to Go: anytime, but it's most beautiful in the morning

Season: June until first snow

Primary Ecosystem: subalpine

Views: dramatic mountain lakes that will take your breath away

Possible Wildlife: forest animals

Trail Conditions: The trail is comparatively wide and smooth but there are a number of stairs to climb.

Reminder: This is one of the most popular hikes in the park, so it pays to visit very early or late in the day.

Elevation Start: 9,475'

Highest Point: 10,132'

Total Elevation Gain: 906'

Trailhead: This hike begins at the Bear Lake Trailhead; see page 110 for details.

Waypoints

1. Bear Lake Trailhead	0.0	9,475'
2. Nymph Lake	0.5	9,706'
3. Dream Lake	1.1	9,920'
4. Emerald Lake	1.7	10,111'

Hike Description

The first part of this hike up to Dream Lake is described in detail on page 205.

From Dream Lake continue westward toward the mountains. (#3) The trail follows the north shore of the lake. This section is fairly gentle and wide. As you head down the north side of Dream Lake notice the many twisted trees right by the lake, formed by the winds that howl here for much of the year.

At 1.2 miles you'll cross a wooden boardwalk over a marshy area.

Bear Lake Trailhead

BEAR LAKE ROAD

9400'

1

BEAR LAKE

9600'

2

NYMPH LAKE

9800'

3

DREAM LAKE

10400'

10600'

LAKE HAIYAHA

4

EMERALD LAKE

11200'

9800'

N

MODERATE HIKES

0   0.25   0.5 mi

228 The trail heads back toward the lake and soon will come right alongside the lake. Here you can look directly down into the water and you may even see trout swimming in the cool waters. I always enjoy looking

HALLETT AND FLATTOP ABOVE EMERALD LAKE

MODERATE HIKES

back to the east from here, especially early in the morning when the sun is just rising.

At about 1.4 miles you'll reach the end of Dream Lake and will hear the inlet stream coming down from Emerald Lake. The trail now starts to climb somewhat steeply. As you climb you'll see a few small cascades and even a little waterfall. There are often many bluebells growing all around these cascades in the summer. As you make your way upward you'll reach a very rocky area and here the trail will make a sharp turn to your right before continuing to climb again. Notice how Flattop Mountain peeks over the rock slab. Soon you'll pass over an area where the trail is often muddy during the early summer.

After this the trail winds up an area of rock steps. At the top you are greeted by an imposing view of Hallett Peak, which seems to be looking right down on you. The trail here begins to level out, crossing an area of rock slab, and then makes one last small climb before beginning its descent to the lake. (#4)

As you reach the lake you'll find yourself at the foot of these giant peaks that tower over you. Once you adjust to the scene you'll probably hear and then see a waterfall coming down from the side of Hallett Peak. There are large rock slabs and boulders all around the area where you can sit and enjoy the view. If you have binoculars with you, look up at Hallett Peak and you may be able to see climbers making their way up the sheer face to the top. This is a popular climbing route. Then to your right on Flattop Mountain have a look at those steep gullies. It's hard to believe that these are skied during the winter by some of the more skilled backcountry skiers. These activities are best enjoyed vicariously.

MODERATE HIKES

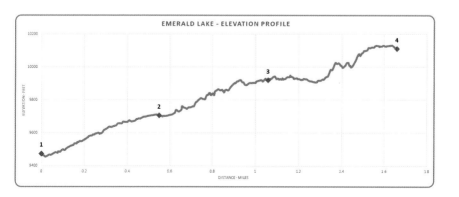

EMERALD LAKE - ELEVATION PROFILE

26 – BLACK CANYON TRAIL

Overview

This is a relatively gentle and beautiful hike close to downtown Estes Park. The first half a mile of trail winds through open ponderosa forest and then the trail enters the open meadows of MacGregor Ranch. Here you have wide-open views of Longs Peak and the unusual rock formations of Lumpy Ridge.

The Stats

Distance Round Trip: 4.1 miles	**Trail Conditions:** Apart from one steep hill near the parking area, the rest of the trail is fairly gentle and smooth.
Difficulty Rating: 80	
Hiking Time: 2 hours and 45 minutes	**Reminder:** This trail crosses private property, so stay on the trail. It can also get quite hot in the meadow, as there is no shade, so bring a hat and extra water. Avoid hiking during the heat of the day.
Time to Go: morning or late afternoon	
Season: year round	
Primary Ecosystem: montane	**Elevation Start:** 7,840'
	Highest Point: 7,963'
Views: great views of Longs Peak, surrounding mountains, Lumpy Ridge	**Total Elevation Gain:** 770'
Possible Wildlife: elk, raptors, coyotes, ground squirrels	**Trailhead:** This hike begins at the Lumpy Ridge Trailhead; see page 123 for details.

Waypoints

1. Lumpy Ridge Trailhead	0.0	7,840'
2. Junction with trail to Gem Lake	0.6	7,903'
3. Climbers Access to Batman	0.7	7,927'
4. Enter MacGregor Ranch	0.9	7,860'
5. Climbers Access to The Book	1.5	7,833'
6. Climbers Access to The Pear	1.9	7,886'
7. MacGregor Ranch gate	2.1	7,963'

Hike Description

The trail starts on the northwest side of the parking lot next to the vault toilets. (**#1**) There are two different trails here. Take the one on the left and follow the Black Canyon Trail up the hill. In just a couple

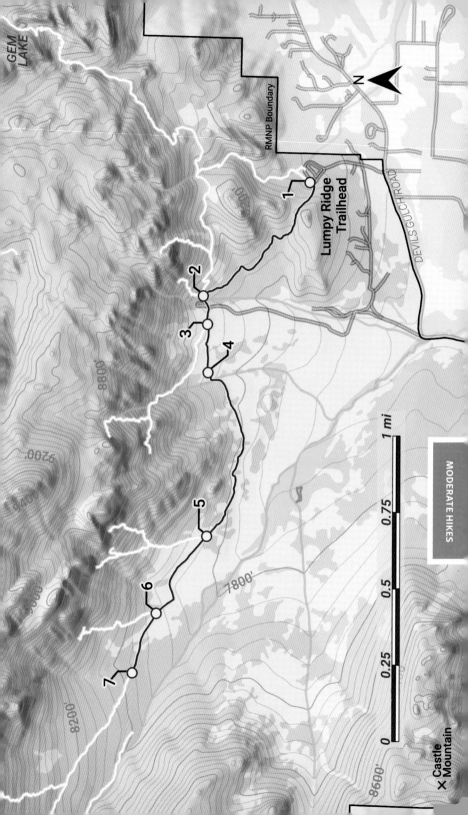

GEM
LAKE

N

RMNP Boundary

1

Lumpy Ridge
Trailhead

DEVILS GULCH ROAD

2

3

4

5

6

7

9000'

8800'

9200'

7800'

8200'

8600'

MODERATE HIKES

1 mi

0.75

0.5

0.25

0

X Castle
Mountain

hundred feet you'll pass through a gate that leads you out of Rocky Mountain National Park and on to private property. Much of this hike will be on private property, so please stay on the trail. The trail continues uphill and into the ponderosa forest. The climb is a bit steep but it doesn't last long. Before you get to the top, take a look at the rock formation known as Hen and Egg straight ahead and a bit to the right. At the top of the hill you get to a rather steep descent, which you'll have to climb on your return. In the winter this section can be icy.

After you reach the bottom of the hill the rest of the trail becomes fairly gentle, wandering around large boulders and through the open forest. Pay attention to all the plant and animal life flourishing here. You may get glimpses to your right of the Twin Owls rock formation. At 0.6 miles you pass through another fence and enter back into Rocky Mountain National Park. Just a few steps farther and there's an intersection where another trail will take you to Gem Lake. (#2) There is an emergency telephone at the intersection in case of climber accidents. Stay to the left and continue on. In just a minute you'll step out of the forest and onto a paved road.

Cross the road to where the trail continues on the other side. The National Park Service has done such a great job restoring the area that it is almost impossible to tell that this section of trail was once a large parking lot and trailhead. On the right side you'll find a memorial to a climber; it incorporates a water fountain but it is not maintained by the national park, so if you use the water from here be sure to filter it first.

Just past the memorial you'll reach an intersection. (#3) Take the left fork, as the other direction is simply an access point for rock climbers. You'll then find a sign describing the raptors that call Lumpy Ridge home. From here onward you will be treated to

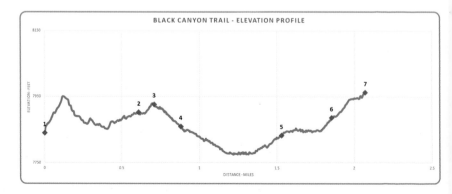

BLACK CANYON TRAIL - ELEVATION PROFILE

wide-open and inspirational views of Longs Peak, part of the Continental Divide, Twin Sisters Peaks, and also of the formations of Lumpy Ridge. You'll continue to enjoy these views as you head through the meadow. At 0.9 miles you pass through an opening in a fence and onto MacGregor Ranch property. (**#4**) Be aware that there are often cattle grazing out in these meadows. They generally stay away from people but if you run into them, be sure to give them plenty of space. At 1.9 miles you'll pass a climbers access to the Pear formation. (**#6**) Straight in front of you there will be a great view of the Sundance Buttress. At 2.1 miles, just after entering back into the ponderosa trees, you'll reach a metal gate. (**#7**) This is the end of MacGregor Ranch property and where your journey will end. This is a great place to just sit in the shade and listen to the sounds of the forest. If you were to continue onward, the trail would soon rise steeply and you would be on the Lumpy Loop Trail, which you can learn more about on page 376.

MODERATE HIKES

AUGUST ON THE BLACK CANYON TRAIL NEAR WAYPOINT #4

27 – EAST SHORE TRAIL

Overview

This is a gentle hike along Shadow Mountain Lake, through forest, meadows, and marshland. It begins on the south end of Grand Lake and goes to the dam on the south end of Shadow Mountain Lake. The southern portion of this hike has a loop that can be used during the drier months of the year but should be avoided in wetter seasons.

The Stats

Distance Round Trip: 6.5 miles

Difficulty Rating: 81

Hiking Time: 4 hours and 20 minutes

Time to Go: all day

Season: May through November

Primary Ecosystem: montane

Views: lake and meadow views

Possible Wildlife: forest animals, ospreys, moose

Trail Conditions: The lakeshore portion of the trail is well maintained and clear, but the Ranger Meadows portion can be wet and muddy.

Reminder: The inland loop portion of the trail should be avoided during spring and wet conditions. Be aware that the trail along the shore will become multi-use, so keep watch for bicycles.

Elevation Start: 8,440'

Highest Point: 8,500'

Total Elevation Gain: 512'

Trailhead: This hike begins at the East Shore Trailhead; see page 117 for details.

see page 117 for details.

Waypoints

1. East Shore Trailhead	0.0	8,440'
2. Enter RMNP	0.7	8,381'
3. Shadow Mountain Trail junction	1.5	8,424'
4. Left onto Ranger Meadows Trail	1.6	8,406'
5. Right onto Continental Divide Trail	3.0	8,424'
6. CDT junction #2	3.3	8,341'
7. Right at Shadow Mountain Dam	4.1	8,379'

Hike Description

The trail begins by heading into the forest and uphill as it bypasses a residential area. (#1) It then descends toward the lake, descending farther than the initial climb. At the bottom of the descent, the trail levels out and winds through the forest. You will be treated to views

MODERATE HIKES

GRAND
LAKE

1
East Shore
Trailhead

2

RMNP Boundary

9800

9400

8800

SHADOW
MOUNTAIN
LAKE

3

4

7

6

5

8400

MODERATE HIKES

US HWY 34

N

0   0.25   0.5   0.75   1 mi

TRAIL ALONG SHADOW MOUNTAIN LAKE BEFORE WAYPOINT #3

of Shadow Mountain Lake just beyond the trees. A few years ago, the pine beetle epidemic ravaged this forest, but now new trees, including many aspens, are beginning to grow, providing gorgeous color during the autumn. At mile marker 0.7 you leave Arapahoe National Forest and enter Rocky Mountain National Park. (#2)

About half a mile later the trail comes out of the trees and you'll get a view of Shadow Mountain Lake. In the distance you can see the Shadow Mountain Dam, where the hike eventually takes you. You'll then pass a junction for the Shadow Mountain Trail, which leads steeply up to a lookout tower that is closed at the time of this writing. (#3) Soon after the junction you'll reach another. Here the trail splits into two routes, creating the option of a loop. (#4) The inland trail is often called the Ranger Meadows Trail and is part of the Continental Divide Trail that runs from the Mexican border to Canada. This trail provides a gorgeous hike through forest, marshland, and meadow.

However, it has the potential to be very wet and muddy, so I only recommend it during the late summer and autumn when it is likely to be dry. The other option, which goes along the lake, will keep your feet drier.

For the purpose of this guide, I'm going to turn left and follow the Ranger Meadows Trail, taking the loop in a clockwise direction. Soon the trail leaves the forest and enters into a marshland filled with willows that even create a tunnel. This is the area that is the most likely to be wet and muddy and there is no way to bypass it. This is also moose territory, so be aware and keep your eyes open.

After crossing the small Ranger Creek, the trail enters a large, open meadow. On the far end of the meadow are elegant aspen trees. The trail continues through other large meadows. These are delightful, wide-open spaces with views for quite some distance. Through these meadows the trail is generally quite level and smooth, although on a hot day there is no shelter from the sun.

At 3.0 miles you will reach an intersection where the Continental Divide Trail continues on south toward Lake Granby. (**#5**) Turn right here. At the next intersection continue straight ahead onto a stretch of boardwalk through the marsh. (**#6**) Watch for the many birds that thrive here. On the other side of the marsh, you'll reach the Shadow Mountain Dam. (**#7**) Turn right here and follow the East Shore Trail to the north alongside Shadow Mountain Lake.

This section of the trail follows the edge of the lake and provides open views of Baker Mountain, which overlooks the lake. The far shore of the lake is lined with aspen trees, a particularly beautiful sight in the autumn. At 5.1 miles we return to the intersection of the Ranger Meadows Trail. (**#4**) Simply continue straight ahead to return to the trailhead. (**#1**) It's time to get an ice cream cone in Grand Lake!

MODERATE HIKES

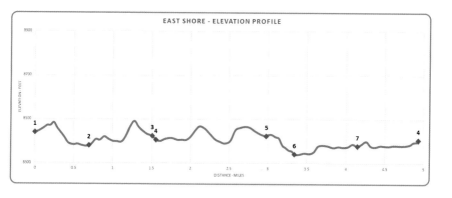

28 – BIERSTADT LAKE LOOP

Overview

Take a very steep hike up to Bierstadt Lake and then around the lake to enjoy a gorgeous view. On the way up you'll enjoy grand vistas of Longs Peak and the Continental Divide. In the early spring and autumn the aspens on the way up can be very colorful.

The Stats

Distance Round Trip: 3.1 miles

Difficulty Rating: 82

Hiking Time: 2 hours and 5 minutes

Time to Go: morning

Season: June through October

Primary Ecosystem: montane

Views: great views of Longs Peak and the Continental Divide followed by a peaceful lake view

Possible Wildlife: forest animals

Trail Conditions: steep, rocky, sandy trail with eleven switchbacks

Reminder: This hike is quite steep and should be avoided if there is a potential for thunderstorms. It can also be quite hot on sunny days, so bring extra sun protection and water.

Elevation Start: 8,850'

Highest Point: 9,454'

Total Elevation Gain: 699'

Trailhead: This hike begins at the Bierstadt Lake Trailhead; see page 112 for details.

see page 112 for details.

Waypoints

1. Bierstadt Lake Trailhead	0.0	8,850'
2. Switchback #11	0.9	9,401'
3. Right at Lake Loop	1.1	9,447'
4. Junction with trail to Park & Ride	1.4	9,425'
5. Left to Bierstadt Lake access	1.7	9,435'
6. Mill Creek junction	1.9	9,445'
7. Left on Lake Loop	2.0	9,445'

Hike Description

This hike begins on the northwest corner of the parking area. (#1) It heads up into a dark lodgepole forest and then turns to the right. The trail soon emerges from the forest as it continues to climb a good number of steps. Shortly after, you enter a large aspen grove that continues all the way to the top of this hill. This entire hillside can be

MODERATE HIKES

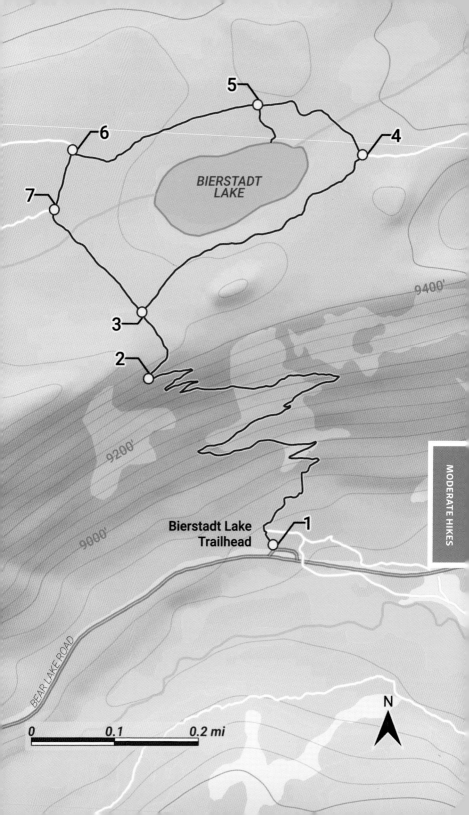

BIERSTADT LAKE

9400'

MODERATE HIKES

9200'

9000'

Bierstadt Lake
Trailhead

BEAR LAKE ROAD

0   0.1   0.2 mi

N

spectacular in early June and early October when the aspen leaves show off their best colors.

At just over a tenth of a mile you reach the first of eleven switchbacks. After your third switchback you can start to look down over the valley and see just how far you've already climbed. After the fourth switchback you'll get your first glimpse of Sprague Lake ahead of you and to the right. Switchbacks three through five have longer stretches between them, and the other switchbacks are much shorter. As you get near the top, make sure to take some time to stop and admire the amazing view. There are a few locations where you can see that people have taken shortcuts to avoid making the full switchback. Please stay on the main trail, as short-cutting leads to increased erosion on the hillsides and trail.

After the eleventh and final switchback the trail soon turns to the north and enters into a lodgepole forest. (**#2**) Here the trail becomes much less steep and in just a minute you will reach the highest point. From here you descend and in another minute you'll see a junction on your right. (**#3**) This is the Bierstadt Loop Trail that goes all the way around the lake. Turn right here and continue down the trail through the forest. There are not any great views here but be patient. At 1.4 miles you'll pass the junction for the trail to the Park & Ride. (**#4**)

BIERSTADT LAKE FROM WAYPOINT #5

After crossing a small bridge continue along for another 550 feet until you see a horse tie-up on the left. (**#5**) Follow the trail beside it down to the water's edge. Here you will enjoy a spectacular view that explains why this lake was named after the famous painter Albert Bierstadt.

Return to the main trail and turn left, continuing westward. In 0.2 miles you'll pass by a junction on your right (**#6**) and then in a few hundred feet you'll reach a second junction that leads to Bear Lake. (**#7**) Turn left here and in just a few minutes you'll pass the place where you started the loop trail. (**#3**) Continue straight up the hill and then follow the switchbacks down to the parking area. (**#1**)

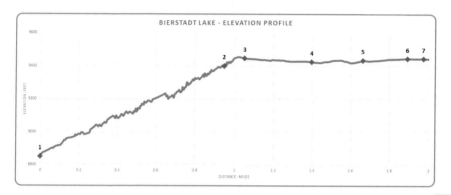

MODERATE HIKES

29 – GEM LAKE

Overview

This hike begins just two miles north of Estes Park and leads through the unusual rock formations of Lumpy Ridge, providing views over the Estes Valley. It climbs steeply up to a small pond with a large sandy beach tucked between towering rock formations. Many people choose this hike for their families, but the large rock stairs make this a bit challenging for those with shorter legs.

The Stats

Distance Round Trip: 3.5 miles

Difficulty Rating: 85

Hiking Time: 2 hours and 20 minutes

Time to Go: anytime

Season: most of the year

Primary Ecosystem: montane

Views: unusual rock formations as well as views of Longs Peak and the Estes Valley

Possible Wildlife: forest animals

Trail Conditions: The trail is very well marked and easy to follow. There are, however, a number of large stone stairs that can be tiring, especially for those with shorter legs.

Reminder: This is a popular hike, so start early. It involves a fairly steep climb, so take it slow and steady. Avoid the lake and exposed areas during storms.

Elevation Start: 7,840'

Highest Point: 8,844'

Total Elevation Gain: 1,054'

Trailhead: This hike begins at the Lumpy Ridge Trailhead; see page 123 for details.

Waypoints

1. Lumpy Ridge Trailhead	0.0	7,840'
2. Right at junction	0.5	8,171'
3. Estes Park Overlook	0.9	8,398'
4. Das Boot	1.3	8,555'
5. Gem Lake	1.7	8,844'

Hike Description

There are two different trails that leave from the trailhead, so be sure to take the Gem Lake Trail, which heads east (right). (**#1**) The trail first runs parallel to the parking lot, passes through a gap in a wooden fence, then heads north into the woods. Be aware that this first section of trail goes through private property and so you must

MODERATE HIKES

8800'

5

GEM
LAKE

4

8600'

8400'

RMNP Boundary

3

8200'

2

MODERATE HIKES

8200'

1

Lumpy Ridge
Trailhead

7800'

0   0.25   0.5 mi

N

GULCH ROAD

LONGS PEAK OVER GEM LAKE

stay on the trail. The journey begins with a gentle climb through a small aspen grove after which you need to climb some large stone steps. At 0.5 miles is the junction for the trail leading to MacGregor Ranch. (#2) Turn right to continue up to Gem Lake.

During this next stretch it is easy to get off-trail, especially on the way down. On the way up, the trail stays more to the left than it might sometimes appear. Pay attention to logs and rocks that have been laid out to help keep you on the trail. At the top of this stretch, take a look back down to identify your route for the way back.

At 0.9 miles, after a couple of switchbacks, you will reach an open flat area that provides an amazing view of the Estes Valley. (**#3**) This is a great place for a picnic or to come and watch the sunrise. From here the trail levels out a bit and soon turns to the north, heading farther into Lumpy Ridge. To your right you might see French Fry Rock, which as the name suggests looks like a box of French fries, high above on the far side of the valley.

As the trail heads back into the woods, it crosses a small log bridge over a seasonal stream. The area in here is quite shaded and so during the winter months it can be icy. Microspikes are a good idea. There are some beautiful aspens in here that turn to vibrant hues in late September and early October.

The trail then begins a series of steps again that make their way up the mountain. After a couple of switchbacks the trail reaches a level dirt area. Be sure to stop here and look to your left. (**#4**) You'll see a rock formation known as Das Boot. It looks exactly like a giant boot with a big hole in it. It is a fun spot, especially for kids.

Continue up more stone steps. As you climb, make sure to stop from time to time to look behind you to see the stunning views out toward Longs Peak and the Continental Divide. Finally, after climbing over one thousand feet, the trail levels out and you reach Gem Lake. (**#5**) It is more of a pond with a large sandy beach than a lake but it's the setting that makes it special; it is surrounded by huge, whimsically shaped granite rocks that are great for exploring.

MODERATE HIKES

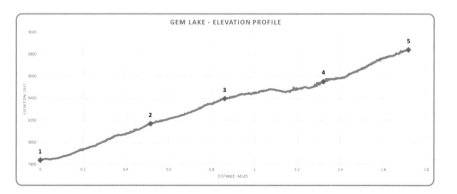

GEM LAKE - ELEVATION PROFILE

30 – CUB LAKE

Overview

This is a very enjoyable hike for the entire family. It passes by numerous ponds where you might spot wildlife. It then goes through an aspen grove and up to Cub Lake with Stones Peak towering above it. On this hike you'll pass by some of the area burned by the 2012 Fern Lake Fire.

The Stats

Distance Round Trip: 4.7 miles

Difficulty Rating: 87

Hiking Time: 3 hours and 10 minutes

Time to Go: morning

Season: May through October

Primary Ecosystem: montane

Views: towering peaks, marshy meadows, burn areas, river

Possible Wildlife: elk, moose, forest animals

Trail Conditions: well defined but rocky

Reminder: Be prepared to encounter wildlife on the trail.

Elevation Start: 8,080'

Highest Point: 8,676'

Total Elevation Gain: 802'

Trailhead: This hike begins at the Cub Lake Trailhead; see page 115 for details.

see page 115 for details.

Waypoints

1. Cub Lake Trailhead	0.0	8,080'
2. Trail turns west	0.5	8,094'
3. First pond	0.8	8,111'
4. Begin climb	1.7	8,316'
5. Cub Lake	2.4	8,671'

MODERATE HIKES

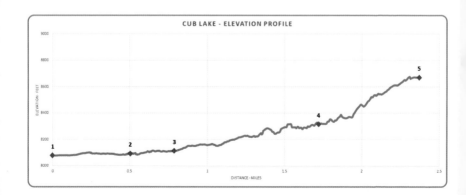

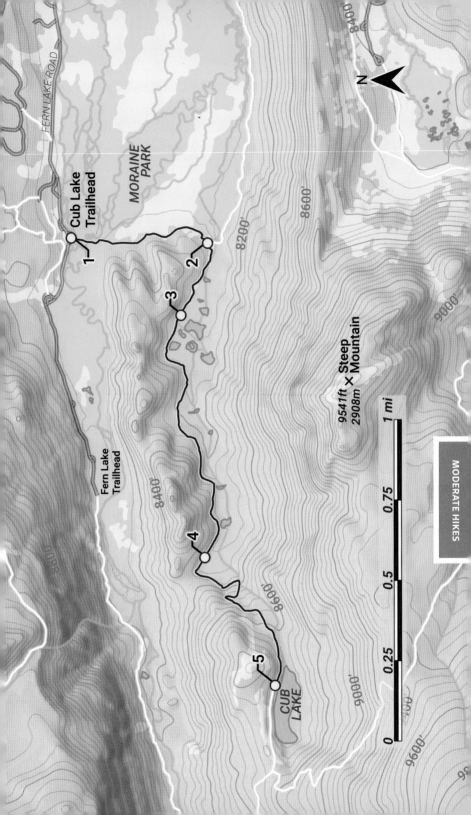

FERN LAKE ROAD

Cub Lake
Trailhead

1

MORAINE PARK

2

3

8200'

8600'

8400'

9000'

Fern Lake
Trailhead

9541ft × Steep
2908m × Mountain

4

8600'

5

CUB LAKE

9000'

9600'

N

MODERATE HIKES

0   0.25   0.5   0.75   1 mi

This hike begins by heading south, crossing a couple of small bridges. (**#1**) One of them crosses over the Big Thompson River, which eventually flows through downtown Estes Park. The trail follows the western edge of Moraine Park, providing good views into the meadows where you can often see herds of grazing elk. Along this stretch the trail climbs up and down small hills and winds around large boulders that kids will want to stop and climb on. You'll see a lot of ponderosa pines as well as occasional mountain juniper trees. Be sure to stop and smell the sweet bark of the ponderosa. On a warm morning they can smell like butterscotch, although some people think it smells more like vanilla.

At about half a mile the trail turns westward and intersects with a trail that runs along the south end of Moraine Park. (**#2**) Continue due west toward the mountains. The main mountain you'll see in front of you is Stones Peak with an elevation of almost 13,000'. This majestic mountain will accompany you to Cub Lake. As the trail heads westward it can get a bit uneven and rocky. You will also notice a great deal of trail erosion. Where it was once just over a foot wide, it is now eight feet wide or more in places and is a good reminder to stay in the center of the trail. From here to Cub Lake you'll encounter the remains of a large fire that burned through here in December of 2012, the result of an illegal campfire. It spread all the way from Forest Canyon down this valley and across Moraine Park, covering much of this distance in one night.

As you continue on this trail, you'll pass beside a series of ponds. (**#3**) Approach them quietly, especially in the morning, and you may find moose enjoying them as well as a wide variety of birds. Keep your distance and stay quiet and you can enjoy watching them go about their day.

After the last pond, the trail begins to climb uphill, making a couple of switchbacks as it winds through a beautiful aspen grove. (**#4**) Notice how cool and moist the air is in this area and how lush the vegetation is due to the way this area is sheltered. Take your time on this climb and before you know it you will be at the top. Near the top look around and see areas where the forest is coming back to life after the fire.

As the trail begins to level out you arrive at Cub Lake. (**#5**) There are a lot of fallen trees around here, but there are a few spots where, if you are careful, you can get down to the lake and find a big rock to sit on. During the summer the lake fills with lily pads and they often put out lovely yellow flowers. This is a great place to spend some time watching the ducks and enjoying the dramatic view of Stones Peak in the distance.

If you have the energy, consider returning via the Pool, which adds an additional 1.4 miles to your return hike. You'll find details on page 254.

MODERATE HIKES

STONES PEAK OVER CUB LAKE

31 – MILLS LAKE

Overview

This is one of the classic hikes to take in Rocky Mountain National Park. It leads to a beautiful lake that was named after Enos Mills, known as the "Father of Rocky Mountain National Park." The trail passes through deep forest, over rushing streams, and across rock slabs to the side of Mills Lake with its dramatic backdrop of Longs Peak and Keyboard of the Winds.

The Stats

Distance Round Trip: 5.4 miles

Difficulty Rating: 95

Hiking Time: 3 hours and 35 minutes

Time to Go: morning

Season: June through October

Primary Ecosystems: montane to subalpine

Views: forest, streams, a waterfall, and a dramatic mountain lake

Possible Wildlife: forest animals

Trail Conditions: well defined but rocky

Reminder: You don't want to be up at the lake during a thunderstorm due to the lightning danger, so turn around if the weather turns bad.

Elevation Start: 9,175'

Highest Point: 9,962'

Total Elevation Gain: 840'

Trailhead: This hike begins at the Glacier Gorge Trailhead; see page 119 for details. It can also be started from the Bear Lake Trailhead; see page 110 for details.

Waypoints

1. Glacier Gorge Trailhead	0.0	9,175'
2. Left at junction with trail to Bear Lake	0.3	9,245'
3. Alberta Falls	0.8	9,394'
4. North Longs Peak Trail junction	1.6	9,744'
5. Left at main junction in Glacier Gorge	2.0	9,786'
6. Mills Lake	2.7	9,957'

Hike Description

The first section of this hike up to Alberta Falls is described in detail on page 188.

At Alberta Falls the trail turns sharply to the right and wraps around to the northwest. At this point the trail begins to get rockier.

BEAR LAKE

9600'

BEAR LAKE ROAD

9000'

1 Glacier Gorge Trailhead

2

3 Alberta Falls

4

5

6

MILLS LAKE

9800'

MODERATE HIKES

N

0   0.25   0.5 mi

11400'

11600'

10600'

11800'

10800'

12000'

11200'

It winds back and forth as it climbs through the forest, moving away from the stream and then later drawing alongside it again. At 1.1 miles the view on your left side opens up and you get a gorgeous view of a cascade down below. Shortly after, the trail will begin to head directly west toward a large granite wall. Look behind you to see back down the valley toward the trailhead and out to the Mummy Range. This section of trail consists mostly of rock slabs and stone steps. The trees turn to limber pine here, probably due to their exposed location.

Next you'll pass a junction on your left for the North Longs Peak Trail. This is another and considerably longer route to Granite Pass on Longs Peak. If you have some extra time, head down that trail about 0.1 miles to the bridge over Glacier Creek and watch the raging waters plunge beneath the bridge.

After passing this junction the trail soon reaches a level area with open views to both the east and the west. This is a great place for a break. Then continue due west and you'll have views of jagged peaks ahead. This is a beautiful section of trail. It is a little rocky but has almost no elevation change. After a few minutes the trail reenters the forest and soon arrives at the main junction in Glacier Gorge. Here you'll want to take the trail on the left.

Shortly after this, you pass a horse tie-up. The trail will cross a stream with a few small cascades and ascend a series of rock stairs before emerging onto flat granite. Simply walk down the center of the slab and soon you'll reenter the forest. Before you enter the forest look to your left and notice the ancient limber pine on the edge of the rock.

Next you'll cross a bridge over Glacier Creek and begin to climb a rough section of trail that requires some care. Once you are at the top, the trail alternates between path and rock slabs. If you get

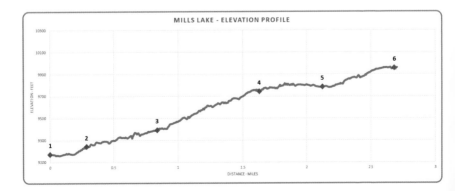

MILLS LAKE - ELEVATION PROFILE

LONGS PEAK OVER MILLS LAKE

confused, simply look for areas of wear on the rock from the many feet that have passed this way. The backside of Longs Peak will soon appear ahead and a bit to the left. Directly in front you'll get some glimpses of Pagoda Mountain. Soon you'll see the outlet stream of Mills Lake. Continue over the rock slabs and it will lead you along the east side of the lake. Eventually the trail will bring you to a large flat rock that juts out into the lake. Here you will have one of the best views of this stunning place.

From this vantage point, as you look across the lake, you'll see from left to right: Longs Peak, Pagoda, Chiefs Head, and just below, a sharp rock formation known as the Spearhead.

If you still have energy, consider heading on to Black Lake. Details can be found on page 302.

32 – CUB LAKE LOOP

Overview

This is a very enjoyable loop hike leading beside numerous ponds where you might spot wildlife, through an aspen grove, and up alongside Cub Lake. After this you'll walk through an area of abundant wildflowers and down through the site of a recent fire to the Pool, where you will follow the Big Thompson River back to the trailhead.

The Stats

Distance: 6.1 miles

Difficulty Rating: 104

Hiking Time: 4 hours

Time to Go: morning

Season: May through October

Primary Ecosystem: montane

Views: towering peaks, marshy meadows, burn areas, river

Possible Wildlife: elk, moose, forest animals

Trail Conditions: well defined but rocky

Reminder: Above Cub Lake there is some exposure in the burn area to be avoided during afternoon storms.

Elevation Start: 8,080′

Highest Point: 8,751′

Total Elevation Gain: 884′

Trailhead: This hike begins at the Cub Lake Trailhead; see page 115 for details.

Waypoints

1. Cub Lake Trailhead	0.0	8,080′
2. Trail turns west	0.5	8,094′
3. Cub Lake	2.4	8,671′
4. Trail junction	2.6	8,744′
5. The Pool	3.5	8,317′
6. Arch Rocks	4.0	8,238′
7. Fern Lake Trailhead	5.2	8,156′
8. Fern Lake bus stop	5.8	8,117′

Hike Description

This hike begins by heading south across two small bridges. (**#1**) One of them crosses over the Big Thompson River, which is one of the most important rivers in the area. The trail then follows the western edge of Moraine Park, providing good views into the meadows where

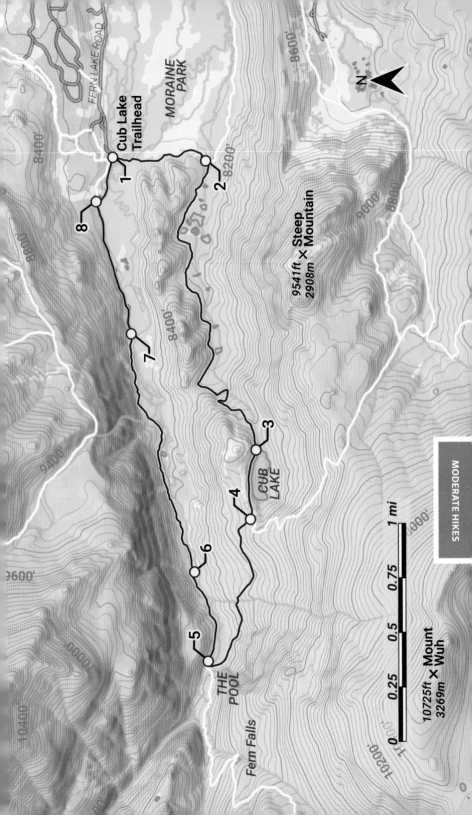

you can often see herds of elk grazing. Along this stretch the trail undulates and winds around large boulders that kids will love to climb on. You'll see a lot of ponderosa pines, as well as occasional mountain juniper trees. Be sure to stop and smell the sweet bark of the ponderosa, as on a warm morning they can smell like butterscotch.

At about half a mile in, the trail turns westward and intersects with another trail that runs along the south end of Moraine Park. (#2) Turn right and head due west toward the mountains. The main mountain you'll see in front of you is Stones Peak with an elevation of almost 13,000'. This majestic mountain will accompany you beyond Cub Lake and almost until you reach the Pool. As the trail heads westward it can get a bit uneven and rocky. You will also notice a great deal of trail erosion. Where it was once just over a foot wide, the trail is sadly now eight feet wide or more in places. Let it be a reminder to stay in the center of the trail. From here to the Pool you'll encounter the remains of a large fire that burned through the area in December of 2012. You'll also pass alongside a series of ponds. Approach them quietly, especially in the morning, and you may see moose as well as a large variety of birds.

After the last pond the trail begins to climb uphill, making a couple of switchbacks as it passes through a beautiful aspen grove. At the top of this hill you arrive at Cub Lake. (#3) There are a lot of fallen trees around the lake, but there are a few spots where you can get down close to the water. During the summer the lake fills with lily pads that are often adorned by lovely yellow flowers.

After your time here continue westward on the trail in the direction of Stones Peak. Along this stretch during the summer months you may find many wildflowers, particularly fireweed. At the top of

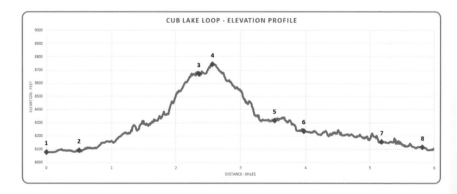

BRIDGE BETWEEN WAYPOINT #4 & #5

the hill you reach the highest point and then pass an intersection. (**#4**) Stay to the right. Our trail now begins a long descent through the burn area. Be aware that in the winter this area of trail can be difficult and dangerous to follow. As you descend, notice all the different forms of life that are reappearing after the fire.

Just after you reach the bottom you'll cross a large bridge at an area known as the Pool because of the deeper water to be found here. (**#5**) After the bridge, the trail turns back to the east and follows the Big Thompson River. This portion of trail is quite gentle, though a bit rocky. Along the way you'll enter an area named Arch Rocks for the way the boulders tower above you as you walk between them. (**#6**) Later you'll notice ponds on your right where you might see a moose. At 5.2 miles you'll arrive at the Fern Lake Trailhead. (**#7**) Here the trail joins the dirt road. Follow it through an aspen grove and alongside a meadow. Be sure to be alert for traffic if the road is open. At 5.8 miles the road reaches the Fern Lake bus stop with vault toilets and parking. (**#8**) Continue along the road just a little farther and you'll arrive back at the Cub Lake Trailhead. (**#1**)

33 – OUZEL FALLS

Overview

Hike along a gentle path by the side of North Saint Vrain Creek as it makes its way through the deep forests of Wild Basin. The trail passes by the impressive Calypso Cascades and then winds through open forest before climbing up to beautiful Ouzel Falls.

The Stats

Distance Round Trip: 5.4 miles

Difficulty Rating: 106

Hiking Time: 3 hours and 35 minutes

Time to Go: anytime

Season: June through October

Primary Ecosystem: montane

Views: forest and stream views, a 150-feet cascade, a waterfall

Possible Wildlife: forest animals and moose

Trail Conditions: relatively wide trail, with rocky sections, some stairs, and a few switchbacks

Reminder: Parking fills quickly, so arrive early. Be aware that the water can be very powerful and dangerous during the spring runoff, so keep an eye on children and maintain a safe distance.

Elevation Start: 8,500'

Highest Point: 9,387'

Total Elevation Gain: 1,037'

Trailhead: This hike begins at the Wild Basin Trailhead; see page 130 for details.

see page 130 for details.

Waypoints

1. Wild Basin Trailhead	0.0	8,500'
2. Copeland Falls junction	0.3	8,576'
3. Rock slab	1.1	8,802'
4. Campsite Trail junction	1.4	8,886'
5. Calypso Cascades	1.8	9,139'
6. Ouzel Falls	2.7	9,382'

Hike Description

Follow the trail that begins on the southeast corner of the Wild Basin parking area. (**#1**) It leads through meadow and forest up past Copeland Falls. (**#2**) The trail follows the north side of North Saint Vrain Creek. After a series of short climbs, the trail crosses over the creek and ascends more steeply, making its way up to Calypso

MODERATE HIKES

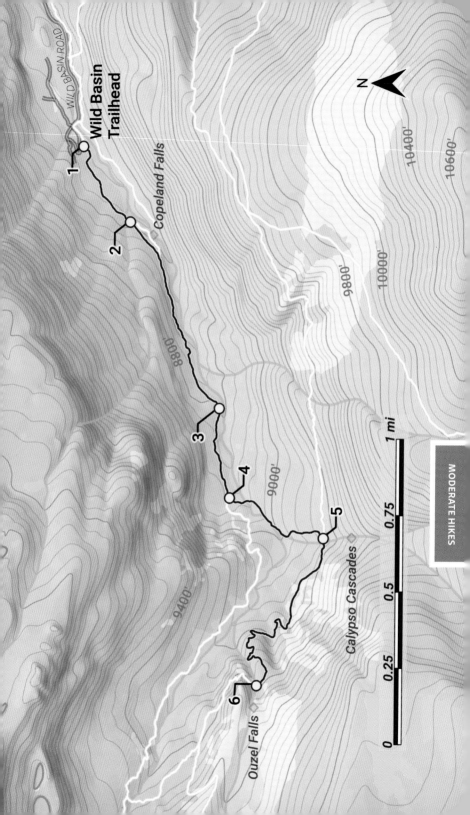

WILD BASIN ROAD

Wild Basin Trailhead

1

2

Copeland Falls

8800'

3

4

9000'

5

Calypso Cascades

6

Ouzel Falls

9400'

9600'

9800'

10000'

9800'

10400'

10600'

N

MODERATE HIKES

0   0.25   0.5   0.75   1 mi

Cascades. (**#5**) This first section is described in more detail on the Calypso Cascades hike on page 222.

From Calypso Cascades continue across the bridge to the north. Around the corner there is another bridge with a pretty stream coming down the hillside. The trail continues through a pleasant section of forest and is relatively level as it gently winds its way through the trees. If you keep your eyes open you may catch glimpses of Mount Meeker and Longs Peak. After crossing two small streams the trail begins to ascend.

This next section is a bit of a climb, winding sharply back and forth as it makes its way up the hillside. There are a number of very large steps, which can be a challenge for smaller legs. Simply take your time and you'll eventually get there. The last sharp left turn takes you to the south and then the trail gradually turns to the right until it heads back to the north. Just as it heads north you arrive at Ouzel Falls.(**#6**)

You'll see a large bridge in front of you, but take the spur trail slightly off to the left. This will give you a better view toward the falls. Where this spur trail meets the water is where the old bridge used to be before it was washed away in the flood of 2013. The NPS with great effort built the new bridge much higher over the water just downstream.

Head back to the main trail. Next to the sign for Ouzel Falls you'll find a rough and muddy path heading to the base of the falls. This is not an official trail and is definitely not maintained. It is only for the adventurous and sure-footed. It has many fallen trees, rocks, mud, and other obstacles that you'll have to negotiate, but if you're careful you can follow it and get right next to the waterfall. Be especially aware that the rocks and logs are extremely slick when wet.

OUZEL FALLS - ELEVATION PROFILE

Ouzel Creek was named by Enos Mills for the small ouzel birds that can often be found along the edge of fast-running streams. The falls later took the name of the stream. Keep your eyes open and perhaps you'll see an ouzel either here or elsewhere along the water's edge.

If it's early in the day and you are still full of energy, consider continuing on up the trail to either Thunder Lake (page 396), which is an additional 7.8 miles round trip and 1,300' of elevation gain. Alternatively, head on to Bluebird Lake (page 404), which adds an additional 7.4 miles and 1,600' of elevation gain.

MODERATE HIKES

OUZEL FALLS

34 – CASCADE FALLS

Overview

Enjoy a delightful hike through gentle meadows and then up through the forest alongside the North Inlet Creek to arrive at Cascade Falls, which doesn't quite know if it is a waterfall or a cascade. Here you can sit in the shade beside this roaring water feature and feel the cool mist refresh you.

The Stats

Distance Round Trip: 6.7 miles

Difficulty Rating: 107

Hiking Time: 4 hours and 30 minutes

Time to Go: morning or late afternoon

Season: June through October

Primary Ecosystem: montane

Views: meadows, forest, streams, a large cascading waterfall

Possible Wildlife: marmots, moose, forest animals

Trail Conditions: It begins with a wide road and then becomes a typical Rocky hiking trail. It is well defined and easy to follow.

Reminder: The first and last part of this hike is very exposed to sun and storms. Bring plenty of water and avoid this section during thunderstorms.

Elevation Start: 8,520'

Highest Point: 8,861'

Total Elevation Gain: 854'

Trailhead: This hike begins at the North Inlet Trailhead; see page 124 for details.

see page 124 for details.

Waypoints

1. North Inlet Trailhead	0.0	8,520'
2. Summerland Park Cabin	1.1	8,507'
3. Stream crossing 1	1.6	8,578'
4. Stream crossing 2	2.7	8,646'
5. Cascade Falls	3.4	8,814'

Hike Description

The first portion of this hike is described in detail in the Summerland Park hike on page 192. In summary, it follows the North Inlet Trail up through Summerland Park and past the Summerland cabin.

From the first bridge (**#3**) after the cabin at Summerland Park the trail continues on fairly gently for another 0.2 miles before it begins to climb. It soon comes out onto a large granite rock slab. It is clear

MODERATE HIKES

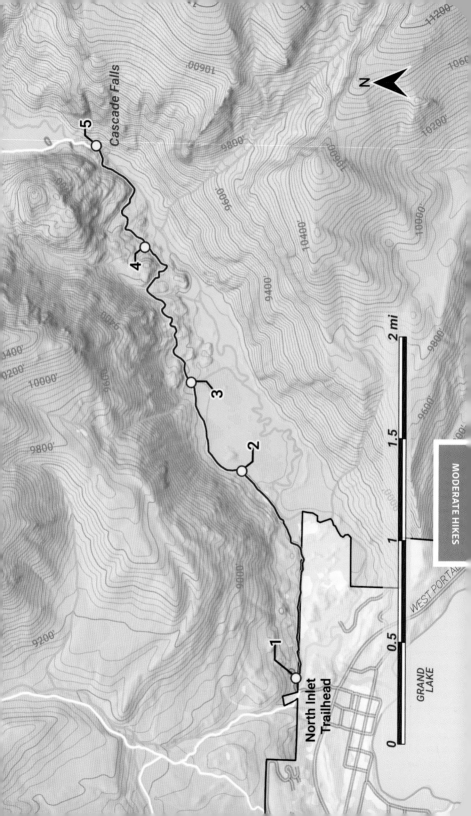

Cascade Falls

5

4

3

2

1

North Inlet
Trailhead

N

WEST PORTAL

GRAND
LAKE

0   0.5   1   1.5   2 mi

that many people get confused at this point and have walked all over trying to find the trail again. When you reach this point turn left on the rock and you'll find the trail continues out in that direction. It will then climb and descend and climb again as it weaves its way eastward through the forest, sometimes in the shade and sometimes in the open.

Eventually you'll reach your second stream crossing. (#4) This one is tucked under a grove of very stately trees and is heavily shaded. This is a pleasant place to take a little break. Then at a little over three miles the trail again draws alongside the North Inlet. You'll hear its roar as you make your way upward. Here the trail begins to climb more steeply. There is one area where you'll have to make your way over a rock section and you may need to use your hands for balance. Then just a little farther up the trail you'll see a section where a rock wall was cut away at the bottom to allow the trail through. This spot provides a nice cool place to sit and rest. While you are up here have a look down at the trees below you. They are not only beautiful but also some of them are quite large. This verdant valley makes for ideal growing conditions and as a result these trees can reach impressive sizes.

Up the trail a little farther is a junction. The trail to the left is a bypass trail for horses. Hikers should take the right-hand trail. Soon after this junction you'll hear the roar of the falls and see a sign announcing that you've arrived at Cascade Falls. (#5) Right at the sign there is a rough trail that descends to the base of the falls. You'll have to climb over rocks, some fallen trees, and even some small pools of water to get out to the stream. Be aware that in the spring and early summer the flow of water can be very powerful and dangerous. Down next to the falls in the shade of the trees it is usually quite cool and refreshing, especially on a hot day.

CASCADE FALLS - ELEVATION PROFILE

You also have the option to continue up the main trail to the viewpoint above. This top area provides a nice place to sit on the rocks, enjoy the sunshine, and look down on Cascade Falls.

If you are continuing on up to Lake Nanita, turn to page 438.

NEARING CASCADE FALLS

MODERATE HIKES

35 – THE LOCH

Overview

The Loch is a fabulous destination and one of the more popular hikes in Rocky Mountain National Park. The trail leads you from the Glacier Gorge parking area up past Alberta Falls. It then makes its way up between Glacier Greek and the Glacial Knobs. From here it follows a stream called Icy Brook up to the Loch, a large mountain lake surrounded by high peaks.

The Stats

Distance Round Trip: 6.0 miles

Difficulty Rating: 114

Hiking Time: 4 hours

Time to Go: morning

Season: June through October

Primary Ecosystem: subalpine

Views: forest, stream, waterfall, cascades, mountain lake

Possible Wildlife: forest animals

Trail Conditions: average

Reminder: Make sure you are not near the lake during thunderstorms.

Elevation Start: 9,175'

Highest Point: 10,208'

Total Elevation Gain: 1,081'

Trailhead: This hike begins at the Glacier Gorge Trailhead; see page 119 for details. It can also be started from the Bear Lake Trailhead, page 110.

Waypoints

1. Glacier Gorge Trailhead	0.0	9,175'
2. Left at junction with trail to Bear Lake	0.3	9,245'
3. Alberta Falls	0.8	9,394'
4. North Longs Peak Trail junction	1.6	9,744'
5. Main junction in Glacier Gorge	2.0	9,786'
6. The Loch	3.0	10,195'

Hike Description

The first part of this hike up to Alberta Falls is described on page 188.

At Alberta Falls (**#3**) the trail turns sharply to the right and wraps around to the northwest. Starting here the trail begins to get rockier. It winds back and forth as it climbs through the forest, moving away from the stream and then later drawing near again. At 1.1 miles the

MODERATE HIKES

BEAR LAKE

DREAM LAKE

9600'

9400'

9400'

BEAR LAKE ROAD

9200'

9000'

9000'

1 ○ **Glacier Gorge Trailhead**

2 ○

3 ○

Alberta Falls

4 ○

10000'

5 ○

6 ○

Glacier Falls

THE LOCH

10800'

11200'

10200'

10600'

MILLS LAKE

12000'

MODERATE HIKES

N

| 0 | 0.25 | 0.5 | 0.75 | 1 mi |

view on your left side opens and you get a gorgeous view of a cascade below. In a short while the trail will begin to head directly west toward a large granite wall. At this point the view will open up a bit behind you, allowing you to see back down the valley to where you started and out to the Mummy Range. This section of trail is mostly rock slabs and stone steps. The trees in this area are limber pine due to the exposed position of this spot.

Next you'll pass a junction on your left for the North Longs Peak Trail. (**#4**) This is a considerably longer way up to Granite Pass on Longs Peak. If you have some extra time, head down that trail about 0.1 miles to the bridge over Glacier Creek and watch the impressive cascade from the bridge.

A short distance past the junction, the trail reaches a level area with open views to both the east and the west. This is a nice spot for a break. The trail continues due west with views of jagged peaks ahead. This beautiful section of trail is rocky but has little elevation change. After a few minutes the trail reenters the forest and soon arrives at the main junction in Glacier Gorge. (**#5**) At the junction you will continue on the path that leads straight ahead. (The left turn leads to Mills Lake, and the sharp right turn leads to Lake Haiyaha.)

From here the trail begins to gently climb and soon meets Icy Brook, where it becomes a little steeper. Then you'll reach the first of four switchbacks. When you get to the third switchback, stop and admire the view. Here you can see Icy Brook tumbling down over the rocks for about a quarter of a mile.

After the fourth switchback the trail winds a bit through the woods and then veers to the left as you climb a series of stone stairs. In a short while the trail begins to level out and you arrive at the

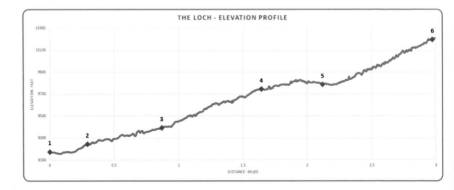

THE CATHEDRAL ABOVE THE LOCH

Loch. (**#6**) According to the book *High Country Names*, this lake was named after a Kansas banker whose last name was Locke, though Abner Sprague, who gave it the name, chose instead to use the Scottish spelling.

This lake looks out to the west toward the dramatic rock formation known as the Cathedral. If you look closely you may also be able to see Timberline Falls in the distance. There are lots of rocks to climb on both directly to your left and along the northern shore. You may also find some quiet corners where you can enjoy gorgeous views and a good book.

36 – HAIYAHA LOOP

Overview

This hike is a great way to get introduced to a few of the more popular and beautiful lakes of Rocky Mountain National Park such as Nymph Lake, Dream Lake, and Lake Haiyaha. These lakes are right near tree line, providing spectacular views of the surrounding mountains. There are also a couple of dramatic overlooks.

You can turn this into a five-lake hike by incorporating a walk around Bear Lake (page 146) before you begin and then continuing on to Emerald Lake (page 226) from Dream Lake before continuing on up to Lake Haiyaha. This adds 1.8 miles and about 209' of elevation gain. Adding the Loch (+1.6) and Mills Lake (+1.2) to this hike to make it a seven-lake hike is also an option.

The Stats

MODERATE HIKES

Distance: 5.3 miles

Difficulty Rating: 121

Hiking Time: 3 hours and 30 minutes

Time to Go: best in the morning just after sunrise but can be done throughout the day

Season: mid-June until first snow

Primary Ecosystem: subalpine

Views: dramatic lake view with peaks rising above

Possible Wildlife: mostly forest animals, occasionally moose

Trail Conditions: The trail is well maintained, though a few areas below Haiyaha can be a little rough and also muddy in the spring.

Reminder: There are some steeper sections and the last half a mile is uphill, so pace yourself. This hike should not be attempted in the winter.

Elevation Start: 9,475'

Highest Point: 10,265'

Total Elevation Gain: 1,399'

Trailhead: This hike begins at the Bear Lake Trailhead; see page 110 for details.

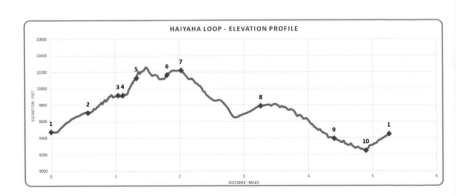

MODERATE HIKES

HALLETT PEAK OVER SMALL POND BETWEEN WAYPOINTS #7 & #8

1. Bear Lake Trailhead	0.0	9,475'
2. Nymph Lake	0.5	9,706'
3. Haiyaha Trail junction	1.0	9,916'
4. Dream Lake	1.1	9,920'
5. Glacier Gorge Overlook	1.3	10,129'
6. Lake Haiyaha junction	1.8	10,164'
7. Lake Haiyaha	2.0	10,220'
8. Main junction in Glacier Gorge	3.1	9,786'
9. Alberta Falls	4.4	9,394'
10. Left onto trail to Bear Lake	4.9	9,249'

Hike Description

The first portion of this hike up to Dream Lake is recorded in detail on page 205.

After you've enjoyed a few minutes at Dream Lake (**#4**), return to the Haiyaha Trail junction(**#3**), which is 0.1 miles back down the trail. From here, turn right at the junction and follow the Haiyaha trail westward. It will lead you into the dark forest and will begin to climb steeply upward. You'll likely see the crowds begin to thin as you start on this trail, as most people stop at Dream and Emerald lakes. As you head upward, the trail makes one steep switchback before turning to the east. Soon the hillside drops away quite precipitously on your left, which may make you a little uncomfortable if you are afraid of heights, but it doesn't last long. The trail then turns to the south and dramatic views over Glacier Gorge slowly begin to open up. At 1.3 miles there is a terrific overlook next to a large boulder where you may want to stop to enjoy the views. (**#5**) There is a second overlook just another 0.1 mile later and this is the highest point of today's hike at 10,265' with great views of Longs Peak.

The trail continues downhill, turns left, and levels out. It soon crosses a stream coming out of Lake Haiyaha. Not long after this you'll reach the Lake Haiyaha junction, which you'll return to later. (**#6**) For now continue straight. This trail will wander through an increasingly rocky terrain. Eventually, the trees give way and the views open up as you pass a small pond on your left. Continue along the rocky trail, paying attention to where you step, as it is quite uneven. You'll now

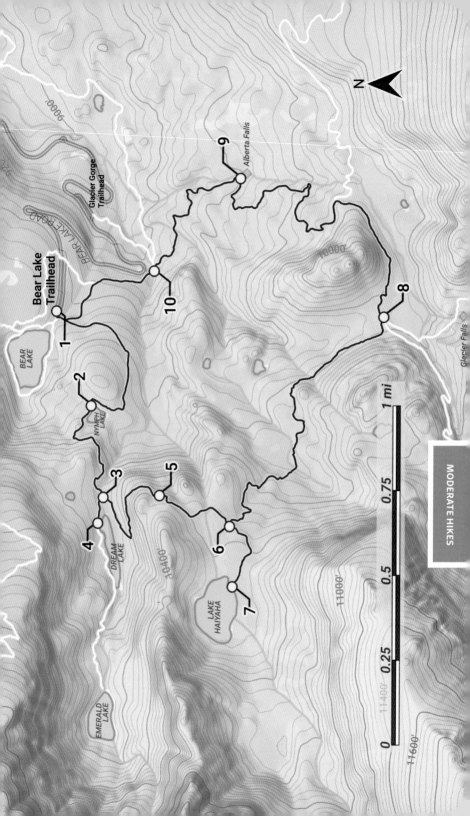

MODERATE HIKES

N

Bear Lake
Trailhead

Glacier Gorge
Trailhead

BEAR LAKE ROAD

BEAR
LAKE

EMERALD
LAKE

NYMPH LAKE

DREAM
LAKE

LAKE
HAIYAHA

Alberta Falls

Glacier Falls

9000'

10000'

10400'

11000'

11400'

11600'

1
2
3
4
5
6
7
8
9
10

0   0.25   0.5   0.75   1 mi

be heading north, passing by a couple of ancient limber pines that are worth admiring. Just past the second one, you'll reach the end of the trail and you will be able to look out on Lake Haiyaha. (#7) *Haiyaha* is an Arapahoe word that means "big rocks." You will understand how appropriate this name is when you see it. This is such a beautiful location with views of the south side of Hallett Peak.

After you've spent some time at the lake, follow the trail back 0.2 miles to the Lake Haiyaha junction. (#6) When you reach the junction, turn to the right and follow the trail downhill. Eventually it becomes less steep and enters a marshy area where you may see moose, so be alert. The trail in this area can become a bit rough and even a little muddy in the spring.

At 3.1 miles the trail intersects with the Glacier Gorge Trail. (#8) From here it isn't too far to Mills Lake (0.6) or the Loch (0.8) if you want to add additional lakes to your hike. For our loop, though, turn left at this intersection and head east. Follow this through a rocky stretch and past the junction with the North Longs Peak Trail. Continue straight and you'll soon reach Alberta Falls and hear its delightful roar. (#9) About half a mile later you'll reach the junction with the trail to Bear Lake. (#10) Continue straight to hike the final half-a-mile stretch back up to Bear Lake. It is somewhat of a steep climb, so take it slowly. At the top of the hill you'll connect with the Dream Lake Trail. From here turn right. It is just about a hundred yards back to the Bear Lake Ranger Station. (#1)

MODERATE HIKES

HALLETT PEAK FROM JUST BEFORE LAKE HAIYAHA

37 – DEER MOUNTAIN

Overview

This hike leads you up to one of the easier mountain summits in Rocky Mountain National Park, providing wonderful views in almost every direction. You'll want to bring a lunch with you and spend some time at the top taking in the fabulous scenery.

The Stats

Distance Round Trip: 6.2 miles

Difficulty Rating: 132

Hiking Time: 4 hours and 5 minutes

Time to Go: anytime

Season: April through November

Primary Ecosystems: montane and subalpine

Views: impressive vistas of the eastern portion of Rocky Mountain National Park

Possible Wildlife: forest animals

Trail Conditions: The trail is well traveled and easy to follow. There are numerous switchbacks and some rock steps.

Reminder: Bring a pair of binoculars, as there is a lot to see from the top.

Elevation Start: 8,930′

Highest Point: 10,006′

Total Elevation Gain: 1,410′

Trailhead: This hike begins at the Deer Mountain Trailhead; see page 115 for details.

Waypoints

1. Deer Mountain Trailhead	0.0	8,930′
2. Little Horseshoe Park junction	0.1	8,929′
3. First switchback	0.8	9,176′
4. Start of numerous switchbacks	1.1	9,322′
5. Last switchback	2.1	9,835′
6. False Summit	2.4	9,928′
7. Right to Deer Mountain summit	2.9	9,846′
8. Deer Mountain summit	3.1	10,006′

Hike Description

The trail begins on the north side of Trail Ridge Road, (**#1**) heading up a wide path with wooden stairs into a ponderosa pine forest that can smell absolutely dreamy on days when the sun warms the pine needles covering the forest floor. Just a short distance up the

Deer Mountain Trailhead

ROAD (US HWY 34)

Deer Mountain
10006ft
3050m

US HWY 36

N

MODERATE HIKES

0   0.25   0.5   0.75   1 mi

trail, you'll pass by a junction to Little Horseshoe Park. (**#2**) Continue up the trail and soon it begins to level out. It then descends before climbing again. As it begins this next climb, the views to the south provide grand vistas over Rocky.

At just under a mile, the trail reaches the first of many switchbacks. (**#3**) This stretch of trail has some of the most dramatic and easily accessible views in Rocky Mountain National Park. Even if you only come this far, you will have a great reward for your effort. Shortly past the first switchback, you leave the open meadows and begin to head into the forest, but just before you enter the forest take a moment and look down to where this trail began, far below you to the southwest.

After entering the forest, you will start climbing a series of switchbacks. (**#4**) Over the next mile you'll climb thirteen switchbacks. While it may be tempting to short-cut some of these, please stay on the trail to avoid causing erosion and damage to the trail system. As you travel through this section you will notice the forest change from ponderosa pine to lodgepole pine. You can tell this change is taking place by watching the forest floor. The lodgepole block most of the light, preventing other plants from growing below them. At just over two miles and over nine hundred feet of elevation gain, you finish the last switchback. (**#5**) The trail now begins to straighten out as it climbs a series of rock steps. Along this next stretch, look to the right for some lovely views. The trail begins to level out a little and it's tempting to think that you are almost at the summit. Don't get your hopes up yet. Even though it seems like the summit should be close, you still have some distance to go. Follow the trail northward into the forest and then downhill. (**#6**)

The next half a mile of trail winds down through the forest seemingly aimlessly. It seems so wrong to head down when climbing a mountain,

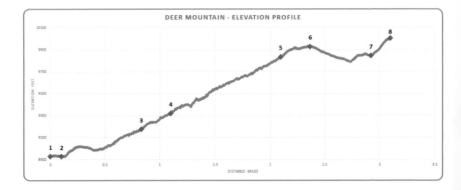

AUTUMN ON THE DEER MOUNTAIN TRAIL

but that is the only way to reach this particular summit. There is one small climb along this section before you get to the next junction. During the winter, this back section of trail tends to hold on to snow and ice, so be prepared with microspikes and poles, perhaps even snowshoes.

At 2.9 miles you reach the final junction. (#7) Turn right and head up the steep hill, climbing the many stone steps. You're on the last stretch and in about ten minutes you'll reach the top. The official summit is about a hundred feet to the west of the top of the stairs. (#8) From up here you can enjoy spectacular views in almost every direction. Now is the time to get out the binoculars and enjoy the view. Take the time to drink it in or even have a picnic. Just remember not to feed the birds, squirrels, or other animals no matter how much they beg. Also remember that this is not a safe place to be when storms move into the area.

38 – LULU CITY

Overview

Follow the Colorado River along a gently-climbing trail until you reach Lulu City, the site of an abandoned village that was used as a base for gold mining in the late 1800s. Though there is little sign of the village today, the meadow setting with the river running through it is a great place for a picnic and watching wildlife.

The Stats

Distance Round Trip: 7.1 miles

Difficulty Rating: 132

Hiking Time: 4 hours and 45 minutes

Time to Go: anytime but best in morning

Season: June through October

Primary Ecosystems: montane and subalpine

Views: forest views with occasional views of the river and some open meadows

Possible Wildlife: marmots, deer, bighorn sheep, moose, forest animals

Trail Conditions: at the start wide and smooth but becomes rocky at times

Reminder: To have the best chance of seeing wildlife, go early and walk quietly. Remember not to approach wildlife.

Elevation Start: 9,010'

Highest Point: 9,492'

Total Elevation Gain: 1,230'

Trailhead: This hike begins at the Colorado River Trailhead; see page 112 for details.

Waypoints

1. Colorado River Trailhead	0.0	9,010'
2. Red Mountain Trail junction	0.5	9,057'
3. Alongside Colorado River	0.9	9,090'
4. Shipler Cabins	2.1	9,247'
5. Left at junction	3.3	9,457'
6. Lulu City	3.5	9,363'

Hike Description

The hike departs on the north end of the parking lot on a wide and gentle trail that heads into the woods. (**#1**) In just a few hundred feet you'll take a short but steep climb with one switchback and then the trail will gradually descend through deep woods. You'll be able to hear the Colorado River off to your left. After you cross some

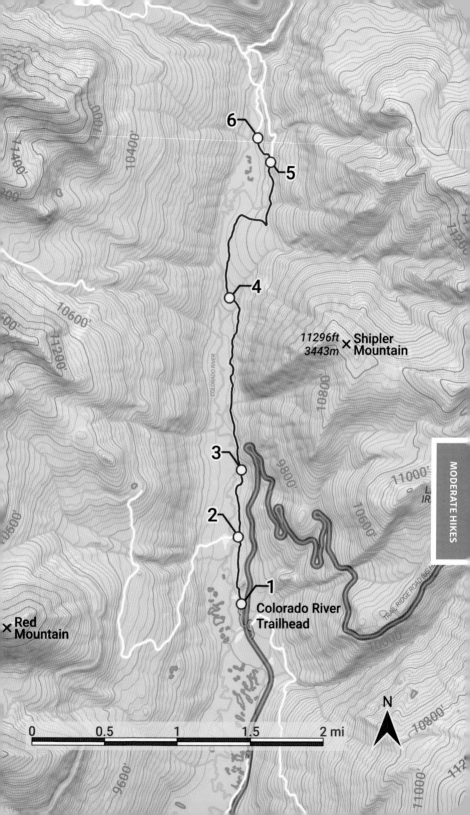

6

5

4

11296ft
3443m ✕ Shipler
Mountain

3

2

1

Colorado River
Trailhead

✕ Red
Mountain

COLORADO RIVER

N

| 0 | 0.5 | 1 | 1.5 | 2 mi |

small streams, you'll enter a beautiful meadow and pass an intersection with a trail leading up to the Grand Ditch. (#2) While that trail may look gentle, just beyond eyesight it is anything but that. So continue straight through the meadow. As you reenter the trees you may notice some abandoned mines on your right. These are blocked off for safety and are a reminder of the failed mining in the area.

At about 0.9 miles the trail will meet the Colorado River and can get a bit muddy in the spring. (#3) The trail then undulates as it heads northward. You'll notice that the forest is very lush and in some ways resembles the Pacific Northwest with the higher levels of moisture.

At about 1.7 miles the trail opens up somewhat. If you look to the right you may see marmots or bighorn sheep, while in the marshy meadows to your left you may find moose. Birds are abundant in this area as well. After reentering the woods you'll cross Crater Creek coming down from Specimen Mountain and just after this you'll enter another large meadow. At the far end of this meadow on the right side you'll find the remains of Shipler Cabins built by Joe Shipler, who spent nearly thirty years mining for silver but never found riches. (#4)

The trail reenters the woods and is quite wide for a while, though a bit rough. It gives you a chance to imagine what the old wagon road leading up to Lulu City might have been like and how very remote this would have felt. This is a peaceful section of trail but you are unlikely to see much wildlife, as they tend to prefer the meadow areas. At 2.8 miles the trail turns to the right and begins to climb a bit more. You continue through dense forest, crossing numerous streams.

Eventually at 3.3 miles you'll reach a junction. (#5) Turn left here and continue down the very steep trail toward Lulu City even if your

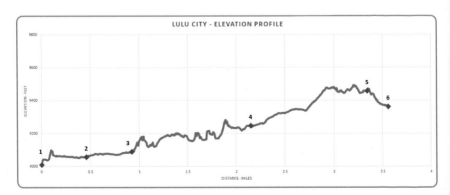

LULU CITY - ELEVATION PROFILE

end goal is La Poudre Pass. The view is much better this way and the distance is not much more than the other trail.

At 3.75 miles you'll arrive at the place where two hundred people lived in the late 1800s as they searched in vain for gold. (**#6**) Today, you can explore the area and see the foundations and logs of a few of those early cabins, but there is very little else remaining. Enjoy a picnic in the meadow or follow the trail leading down to the river. This is a great place to spend an hour or two with a good book.

If you are continuing on to La Poudre Pass, turn to page 390.

MODERATE HIKES

MEADOW AT LULU CITY

39 – BIG MEADOWS LOOP

Overview

This is a loop hike that takes you from the Green Mountain Trailhead up to the expansive Big Meadows where you can sometimes find moose grazing. It then travels alongside the meadow before connecting with the delightful Onahu Trail, which winds through the forest and along Onahu Creek before returning to the Kawuneeche Valley and the Green Mountain Trailhead. This is primarily a forest walk with all the silence and solitude that goes with it.

The Stats

Distance: 7.3 miles

Difficulty Rating: 139

Hiking Time: 4 hours and 55 minutes

Time to Go: anytime

Season: May through November

Primary Ecosystems: montane and subalpine

Views: forest and meadow

Possible Wildlife: forest animals and moose

Trail Conditions: The trail is clearly marked and generally smooth with some rocky sections.

Reminder: Enjoy and preserve the silence of the forest and give moose plenty of space.

Elevation Start: 8,794'

Highest Point: 9,922'

Total Elevation Gain: 1,325'

Trailhead: This hike begins at the Green Mountain Trailhead; see page 120 for details.

see page 120

Waypoints

1. Green Mountain Trailhead	0.0	8,794'
2. Left onto Tonahutu Trail	1.7	9,403'
3. Old Homestead	2.0	9,422'
4. Left onto Onahu Creek Trail	2.3	9,467'
5. Highest point	3.2	9,921'
6. Long Meadows Trail junction	3.8	9,604'
7. Big bridge	5.3	9,244'
8. Bowen Gulch junction	6.4	8,883'
9. Onahu Creek Trailhead	6.7	8,794'

Hike Description

The trail begins on the east side of the parking lot, heading through

MODERATE HIKES

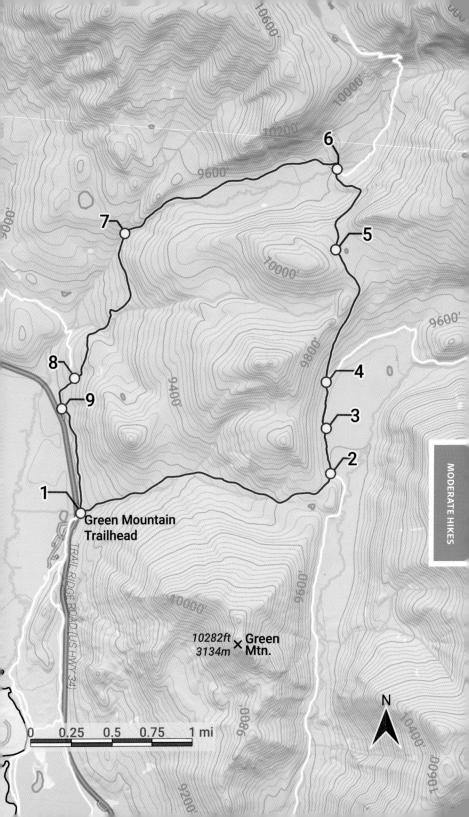

MODERATE HIKES

10600'

10600'

10200'

10000'

9600'

6

5

7

10000'

9600'

10000'

8

9

9400'

4

3

10800'

9600'

2

1 Green Mountain
Trailhead

TRAIL RIDGE ROAD (US HWY 34)

10000'

9800'

10282ft × Green
3134m   Mtn.

9800'

9600'

9200'

10400'

10600'

N

0   0.25   0.5   0.75   1 mi

a grove of aspen trees and up into the forest. (**#1**) The first half a mile of the trail climbs fairly steeply, about 300' gain in elevation before leveling off a bit at the half-mile mark. So be sure to start with a slow, gentle pace. As the trail heads up through the trees, it passes some mountain meadows on the right side that might occasionally have moose grazing in them, so walk quietly and keep your eyes open. At 1.7 miles you will have climbed 609 feet. At this point you'll connect with the Tonahutu Trail. (**#2**) Take a left turn on the trail and follow it to the north. About a hundred feet down the trail, there will be a spur trail heading down the hill and into the meadow. This is a delightful place to take a break and watch for moose and other wildlife. From here you can look out to the north to get a nice view of Mount Ida.

A little farther down the main trail you'll come across the remains of an old homestead at the edge of the meadow. (**#3**) You'll find another one a bit farther along the trail. Try to imagine what life was like out here in the early 1900s. At just over two miles the trail leaves the meadow and begins to head uphill back into the woods. It then reaches the junction with the Onahu Creek Trail, which heads uphill to the left. (**#4**) Follow the Onahu Creek Trail as it climbs quite steeply up the side of a ridge through a forest of lodgepole pine. Although many lodgepole pines have died due to the mountain pine beetle, many new trees are now growing up in their place.

At about three miles the trail begins to level out and turn toward the west, making its way through an open forest with lots of lush undergrowth, where it tops out at 3.2 miles and an elevation of 9,922'. (**#5**) This section of trail is one of my favorite sections of forest in the whole park. At times it feels like you've entered a fairyland with the deep red trunks, the bright green undergrowth, and

MODERATE HIKES

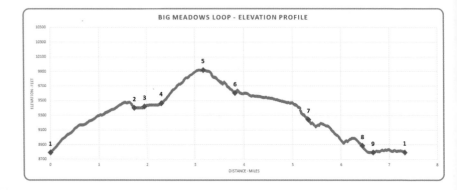

the airy feel. Soon the trail begins to descend, at times quite steeply. It then crosses a boulder field and then heads back into the forest. At 3.8 miles you reach the junction with Long Meadows Trail, which I don't recommend you take, because the trail vanishes into marshy meadow. (**#6**) Instead, continue down the Onahu Creek Trail and you'll soon cross the large Onahu Creek Bridge. (**#7**) The trail wanders delightfully through another open and airy forest, gently winding through the trees with little elevation change. After about a mile the forest begins to close in around you and the trail begins to descend more steeply. Soon the trail crosses a small bridge over a stream coming down from the north, followed shortly after by another bridge that is my favorite in the park. I often feel like I'm in something of a hall of worship here as the trees reach for the sky and there is an air of ancient solemnity in this space. The trail then winds up and down small hills, eventually passing the junction with the Bowen Gulch Trail. (**#8**) Just beyond this you arrive at the Onahu Creek Trailhead. (**#9**) From here you will turn left and follow the trail through the trees parallel with the highway. This rolling trail will lead you back to your starting point at the Green Mountain Trailhead. (**#1**)

MODERATE HIKES

ONAHU CREEK TRAIL AFTER
WAYPOINT #5

40 – FERN LAKE

Overview

This hike takes you along a gentle path beside the Big Thompson River up to the Pool. From here the trail climbs upward through deep forest, past Fern Falls, and then up to Fern Lake, with views of the Continental Divide high above. Here you'll find a ranger cabin and one of the park's popular fishing spots.

The Stats

Distance Round Trip: 7.5 miles

Difficulty Rating: 151

Hiking Time: 5 hours

Time to Go: anytime

Season: June through October

Primary Ecosystem: montane

Views: forest and stream views, a waterfall, a beautiful mountain lake

Possible Wildlife: forest animals

Trail Conditions: The trail is easy to follow and is relatively smooth for

Rocky, though there are plenty of rocky sections.

Reminder: This hike involves is a steep uphill climb, so give yourself plenty of time.

Elevation Start: 8,155'

Highest Point: 9,528'

Total Elevation Gain: 1,523'

Trailhead: This hike begins at the Fern Lake Trailhead; see page 117 for details.

see page 117 for details.

Waypoints

1. Fern Lake Trailhead	0.0	8,155'
2. Arch Rocks	1.2	8,238'
3. The Pool	1.7	8,317'
4. Fern Falls	2.6	8,824'
5. Fern Lake	3.7	9,527'

Hike Description

The first section of this hike is described in detail on page 197, the Pool.

Cross the bridge at the Pool (**#3**) and then about twenty feet after the bridge, look for a trail sign and a trail heading up the rocks to the right. It can be a little difficult to spot but once you are on it, it's very easy to follow. The trail starts by climbing up a series of rock stairs

MODERATE HIKES

Fern Lake Trailhead

Steep Mountain
9541ft ×
2908m

N

BIERSTADT LAKE

CUB LAKE

10000'

9000'

8200'

8200'

1

2

3

THE POOL

Fern Falls

4

8600'

Mount Wuh
10725ft ×
3269m

9400'

9800'

5

FERN LAKE

9800'

10000'

ODESSA LAKE

MODERATE HIKES

0   0.25   0.5   0.75   1 mi

and then it reaches a plateau. Just off the path from this flat section of trail, there used to be a big lodge called Old Forest Inn. It was dismantled by the park service as part of their effort to restore the park to its natural condition. I like to imagine what life might have been like at the lodge when it was in operation.

Soon you'll cross a log bridge over Fern Creek before heading through an open area. The trail reaches Spruce Creek Canyon and then turns left to follow the creek upstream. It winds back and forth upward through Douglas fir and Engelmann spruce. The trail gets quite steep at times in this dark forest and it often feels like you aren't making any progress. Just take it slow and steady. Eventually you reach Fern Falls on one of the switchbacks, where I often take a break. (#4) The falls are probably thirty or forty feet tall and the spray they give off as they crash onto the rocks below feels wonderful on a hot day.

Continue upward on the trail. Just after the three-mile mark the trail begins to turn westward. Here it becomes less steep. This section continues for some ways and is a very enjoyable forest walk. You'll know you are getting close to your destination when you see a horse tie-up on your left. Just after this you'll reach the junction with the Spruce Lake Trail. Continue straight ahead and in just another minute you'll climb a very short but steep hill and arrive at Fern Lake.(#5)

On your right is a ranger cabin. This is one of about five ranger cabins located in the national park where there were rangers stationed when the parks were better funded. They are still used occasionally by rangers. There are many places to get down by Fern Lake where you will have a view of Notchtop Mountain, Gabletop, Knobtop, and the Little Matterhorn. If you have time, continue around the lake following the trail along its east side to enjoy more great views.

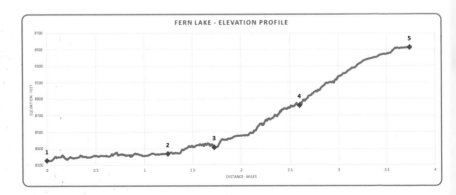

FERN LAKE - ELEVATION PROFILE

FERN LAKE OUTLET

41 – ODESSA HIKE

Overview

This hike leads from Bear Lake to near Moraine Park through some of the most spectacular terrain in Rocky Mountain National Park, visiting Odessa Lake and Fern Lake on the way. It requires either leaving a car at the Fern Lake Trailhead or catching the shuttle from the Fern Lake bus stop (additional 0.6 miles) back to Park & Ride and then another shuttle to Bear Lake. (Remember that the shuttles only operate during the summer and early autumn.) Nearly six miles of this hike is downhill or on relatively flat terrain.

The Stats

Distance One Way: 8.6 miles

Difficulty Rating: 153

Hiking Time: 5 hours and 45 minutes

Time to Go: early to late morning

Season: mid-June through October

Primary Ecosystems: subalpine to montane

Views: dramatic mountain valleys, beautiful lakes, waterfall, quiet forest

Possible Wildlife: mostly forest animals

Trail Conditions: The trail is very well defined but some sections are quite rocky and there is a bit of exposure just as you begin the descent.

Reminder: This hike is long and the extensive downhill stretch can be hard on the knees and ankles, so consider bringing hiking poles. This hike requires you to either leave a car at the Fern Lake Trailhead or take a shuttle back to Bear Lake. Be sure to know the current shuttle schedule before you depart.

Elevation Start: 9,475'

Highest Point: 10,700'

Total Elevation Gain: 1,358' (2,677' elevation loss)

Trailhead: This hike begins at the Bear Lake Trailhead; see page 110 for details.

Waypoints

1. Bear Lake Trailhead	0.0	9,475'
2. Right at Fern Lake Trail	0.1	9,481'
3. Left at Bierstadt Lake junction	0.5	9,701'
4. Flattop junction	0.9	9,964'
5. Boulderfield crossing	2.2	10,459'
6. Viewpoint access	2.9	10,676'
7. Odessa Lake junction	4.1	10,025'
8. Odessa Lake	4.2	9,967'

MODERATE HIKES

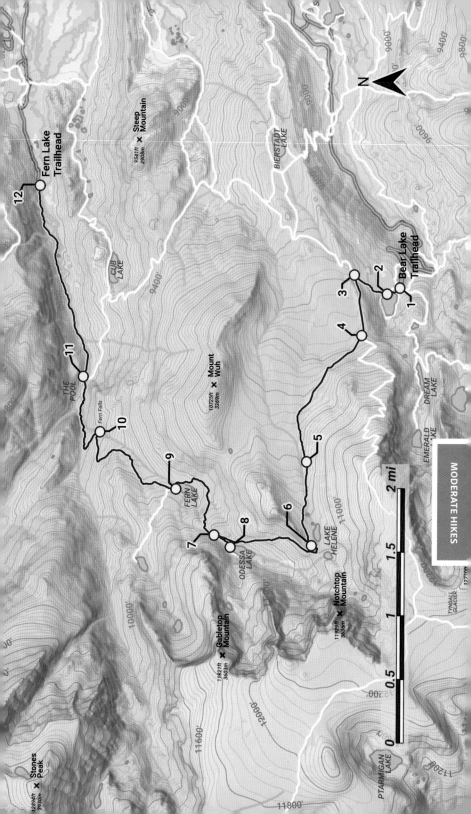

N

Fern Lake
Trailhead

12

Steep
Mountain
9541ft
2908m ×

BIERSTADT
LAKE

Bear Lake
Trailhead

2

3

1

CUB
LAKE

9400'

11

THE
POOL

Fern Falls

10

Mount
Wuh
10725ft
3269m ×

4

5

9

FERN
LAKE

8

6

7

ODESSA
LAKE

LAKE
HELENE

11000'

EMERALD
LAKE

DREAM
LAKE

Gabletop
Mountain
11821ft
3603m ×

Notchtop
Mountain
11989ft
3655m ×

TYNDALL
GLACIER

MODERATE HIKES

Stones
Peak
12894ft
3930m ×

PTARMIGAN
LAKE

0   0.5   1   1.5   2 mi

9. Fern Lake	5.0	9,527'
10. Fern Falls	6.1	8,824'
11. The Pool	6.9	8,319'
12. Fern Lake Trailhead	8.5	8,156'

Hike Description

Begin by following the trail to Bear Lake (**#1**) and follow the trail around to the right (east) side of the lake. In 0.1 miles turn right onto the Fern Lake Trail. (**#2**) This section will lead you up through a beautiful aspen grove, which is usually vibrant during the last weeks of September. At 0.5 miles you'll reach the Bierstadt Lake junction. (**#3**) Here you will take a sharp left turn to begin a rather steep climb. At the top of the hill it begins to level out, allowing you to catch your breath. At 0.9 miles you will reach the junction for the Flattop Mountain Trail. (**#4**) Continue straight at this junction on the Fern Lake Trail as it continues to climb. In about half a mile you will reach an overlook where you can see Bierstadt Lake in the forest below. The trail now levels out and winds its way through the forest before reaching open meadow. Until mid-July there can be a large snowdrift you may have to scramble over in this meadow. The trail then heads back into the forest.

At 2.2 miles you will reach a boulder field with your first view of Notchtop Mountain. (**#5**) Just before three miles the trail reaches its apex and then gradually begins to descend. At this point look for a very wide trail leading off to the right. (**#6**) This goes up to a ridge that provides incredible views of Lake Helene, Notchtop Mountain, Grace Falls, Odessa Lake and Fern Lake. It is a great place to have a break and eat a snack while you inhale the views and fresh air.

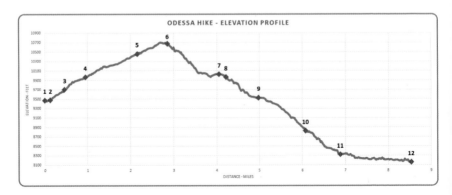

ODESSA HIKE - ELEVATION PROFILE

Soon after this the trail takes a sharp turn to the right and then begins its steep descent toward Odessa Lake. This portion of trail is one of the most dramatic and scenic you will find in Rocky Mountain National Park. The first bit hugs the edge of a steep drop-off but it doesn't last long. During the winter months this stretch of trail fills with snow, making it avalanche prone and extremely dangerous until sometime in mid-June, so don't attempt if there is snow. Also, be aware that the trail is very rocky and so make regular stops to enjoy the views, as you'll want to watch your footsteps on this section.

At about four miles you will reach the junction for Odessa Lake. (#7) While it may be tempting to continue on and ignore this side trail, that would be a significant mistake. Turn left and follow the level trail alongside the stream for 0.1 miles until it leads you to the lakeshore. (#8) The approach to the lake is nothing short of dramatic and once you reach the lake there is a great place to sit and enjoy a rest while you take in the views. You most certainly won't regret making this short detour from the main trail, and the listed mileage assumes you made this detour.

At five miles the trail joins the east shore of Fern Lake. (#9) The trail then crosses the stream. Be sure to look back over the water and take in the expansive view from this spot before you continue on. The trail then makes its way up near the ranger's cabin. It used to be staffed during the summers but due to limitations in park staff and budgeting, it is only used as staffing allows. Just before the cabin, the trail turns to the right and then drops into the woods, soon passing the intersection with the Spruce Lake Trail. Continue down the main trail as it gently winds through the woods. In just over a mile you'll reach the impressive Fern Falls. (#10)

After winding through the woods and crossing a log bridge over a stream, you will arrive at the Pool, a popular destination for families. (#11) From here the trail is much gentler as it follows the north shore of the Big Thompson River. This section always seems to take longer than I expect it to, but eventually you'll arrive at the Fern Lake Trailhead. (#12) If you need to catch the shuttle back to Bear Lake, continue along the dirt road for another 0.6 miles to arrive at the parking area and shuttle stop.

MODERATE HIKES

APPROACHING ODESSA LAKE

42 – EASTERN UTE TRAIL

Overview

Follow in the footsteps of ancient peoples who used this route for nearly ten thousand years to cross over the mountains. This is a one-way hike, starting high in the tundra and descending to Upper Beaver Meadows Trailhead. Watch the terrain and vegetation transition from alpine to subalpine to montane.

The Stats

Distance One Way: 6.2 miles

Difficulty Rating: 163* (62)

Hiking Time: 4 hours and 10 minutes

Time to Go: morning

Season: mid-June through October

Primary Ecosystems: alpine to subalpine to montane

Views: At the top you'll experience grand vistas followed by forest and meadow views.

Possible Wildlife: marmots, pikas, elk, mule deer, forest animals

Trail Conditions: The trail is a bit rocky and narrow up to Timberline Pass but easily traveled by almost anyone. From Timberline Pass to Ute Meadows is one of the roughest trails in this book. It is very steep with a lot of loose rock. It is not recommended for those with knee problems or balance issues, or for children.

Reminder: This is a one-way hike. You'll need to leave a car at the Upper Beaver Meadows Trailhead or arrange to be picked up there when you arrive.

Elevation Start: 11,438'

Highest Point: 11,659'

Total Elevation Gain: 306' (3,276' elevation loss)

Trailhead: This hike begins at the Ute Crossing Trailhead on Trail Ridge Road (page 129) and ends at the Upper Beaver Meadows Trailhead (page 128).

Waypoints

1. Ute Crossing Trailhead	0.0	11,438'
2. Timberline Pass	1.9	11,461'
3. Ute Meadow	3.3	9,534'
4. Beaver Mountain Trail junction	4.7	9,041'
5. Moraine Trail junction	5.7	8,542'
6. Upper Beaver Meadows Trailhead	6.2	8,437'

Hike Description

The first part of this hike is explained in detail as the Tombstone Ridge hike on page 218. In summary, follow the trail from Ute

Crossing for about two miles across the tundra till you arrive at Timberline Pass just above tree line. (**#2**)

From Timberline Pass the trail is quite rocky and a bit difficult to follow. It drops quite steeply over loose rock and this continues far beyond the stretch you can see from the top. I recommend that you have a good pair of hiking boots with ankle support as well as hiking poles to help you keep balance. If you have knee issues, turn around at this point; this is the wrong trail for you. If not, make your way down the faint trail and in about 0.2 miles you'll leave the alpine zone and enter the krumholz. As the krumholz grows into large trees, the trail unfortunately does not improve. Erosion has had its way with this trail, making it tricky at times to tell where the trail is, so look for large historic rock cairns to guide you. This rough climb down takes some time and feels rather endless but at just over three miles it all changes.

At around the three-mile point you'll reach a small meadow. Here the trail becomes much less rocky and descends less steeply. In just a minute the trail enters back into the trees but only for a short visit before opening up at the top of Ute Meadows. (**#3**) In the distance you can see Longs Peak looking down on the meadow that in the early summer overflows with wildflowers. This is a delightful spot for a picnic. Here the trail is quite sandy but gentle. At the bottom of the meadow, you'll reach a junction for a campsite off to your right (permits required for camping). Continue straight and you'll soon be back in the forest. Off to your right you'll hear the roar of Windy Gulch Creek.

The trail now is much broader and gentler. After a little while alder trees line the trail as it follows the edge of a marshy meadow. As

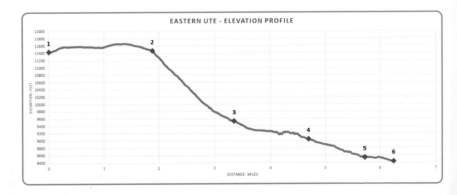

LONGS PEAK FROM NEAR TIMBERLINE PASS

with all marshy meadows, be on the lookout for wildlife. At a little over four miles you'll hear the sound of a waterfall. This is Windy Gulch Cascades just out of sight below. Here the trail takes a sharp left turn and opens up to the south with terrific views of Longs Peak, Pagoda, Chiefs Head, Notchtop, and many other mountains. Not a bad place to take a break and enjoy the views. The trail then follows the edge of the valley. This is a rather rough but short section with one short, steep climb.

After leaving the edge of the valley, the trail reenters the woods. You'll then cross a muddy section, followed by a steep descent. Then at just under five miles you'll pass an intersection. (#4) This is for a loop trail that is popular with horse tours. Just to the right of this intersection is a short trail that leads to an overlook. You may want to walk out and take a peek, though the views you had previously are better.

Continue straight ahead. From here the forest begins to open more as it transitions to a ponderosa pine forest. I especially enjoy this section and sometimes spot mule deer here. At 5.7 miles you'll pass a junction on your right. (#5) From here continue straight for 0.5 miles to arrive at the Beaver Meadows Trailhead. (#6)

43 – BLACK LAKE

Overview

Enjoy a hike up past Alberta Falls, up to Mills Lake, and then deeper into Glacier Gorge to Ribbon Falls and Black Lake. On this hike you cover a lot of beautiful territory, though the trail is quite rough from Mills Lake to Black Lake.

The Stats

Distance Round Trip: 9.4 miles

Difficulty Rating: 164

Hiking Time: 6 hours and 15 minutes

Time to Go: morning

Season: July through October

Primary Ecosystem: subalpine

Views: forest, streams, three mountain lakes

Possible Wildlife: forest animals

Trail Conditions: Beyond Mills Lake this trail can be very rough with lots of tree roots and rocks. There are also a few long wooden planks to balance on as you walk through marshland.

Reminder: You don't want to be up at the lake during a thunderstorm due to the lightning danger, so turn around if the weather turns bad.

Elevation Start: 9,175'

Highest Point: 10,611'

Total Elevation Gain: 1,436'

Trailhead: This hike begins at the Glacier Gorge Trailhead; see page 119 for details. It can also be started from the Bear Lake Trailhead; see page 110 for details.

Waypoints

1. Glacier Gorge Trailhead	0.0	9,175'
2. Alberta Falls	0.8	9,394'
3. Main junction in Glacier Gorge	2.0	9,786'
4. Mills Lake	2.6	9,957'
5. Jewel Lake	3.0	9,954'
6. Meadow area	4.0	10,246'
7. Black Lake	4.7	10,611'

Hike Description

The first half of this hike is described in detail first on the Alberta Falls hike (page 188) and then on the Mills Lake hike (page 250). In summary, follow the Glacier Gorge Trail (**#1**) just under a mile to Alberta Falls (**#2**) and then continue past it. Wind your way up the rocky trail past the North Longs junction and on to the main junction

1 Glacier Gorge Trailhead

2 Alberta Falls

3

4

5

6

7

BEAR LAKE

BEAR LAKE

DREAM LAKE

LAKE HAIYAHA

THE LOCH

Timberline Falls

GLASS LAKE

12654ft 3857m ✕ Thatchtop

MILLS LAKE

Ribbon Falls

BLACK LAKE

FROZEN LAKE

LAKE POWELL

MODERATE HIKES

9600'
9800'
9000'
9200'
9400'
10000'
10200'
10400'
11000'
10800'
10280'
11800'
11200'
11600'
10600'
11400'
12600'
12400'
13000'
12800'
13400'
13600'

N

0   0.25   0.5   0.75   1 mi

in Glacier Gorge. (**#3**) Turn left and follow the trail over streams and across rock slabs until you reach the spectacular Mills Lake. (**#4**)

Continue along the east shore of Mills Lake, heading south toward the distant mountains. Along the way you'll see a number of great spots where you can get alongside Mills Lake or out onto rocks that jut into the lake. About three-quarters of the way down the lake the trail will begin to climb a number of rock stairs before returning to the lake. You'll then be at the end of the lake and will have a nice view of the inlet stream with Chiefs Head Peak in the background.

The trail then reenters the woods and comes out alongside Jewel Lake on its north end and then follows the shoreline southward. (**#5**) At the far side of the lake you'll encounter your first boardwalk. These are wood planks that help you avoid walking in the marshland. They are quite narrow, so using hiking poles will help you maintain balance.

After the boardwalks you will notice an incredible number of downed trees. This was the result of a powerful windstorm that swept through here in November of 2011. Following the storm the trail was completely covered in fallen trees, and they had to cut a new trail through the downfall, hence the trail here is quite rough with lots of tree roots and rocks. You'll be walking through this area of fallen trees for quite some distance, so plan for it to take extra time. You'll have to watch your footing, as tripping is easily done in this area.

On your right you'll pass the bridge leading to the Glacier Gorge Campsite. Immediately after this the trail climbs steeply. You'll have a number of these climbs over the next couple of miles. The forest continues to look really rough, almost as if a bomb went off here. The power of the wind that took these large trees down is hard to imagine. If you look closely, however, you'll see that life is returning. At about

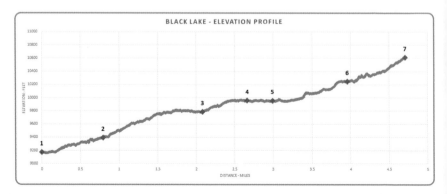

four miles you'll enter a small meadow with a very peaceful Glacier Creek running through it. (#6) This meadow has a terrific view of Chiefs Head Peak and is one of my favorite parts of this hike. Sometimes you'll find elk grazing in this meadow. The trail continues along the edge of this meadow and crosses a boardwalk over a marshy section.

At the end of the meadow the trail climbs steeply up to the left. At the top you'll pass right next to a small waterfall coming down from Blue Lake. It's a truly refreshing place to pause. The trail then makes its way down to the valley. At times it can be a bit rough and there could even be snow in this section until midsummer. Having a pair of hiking poles can really help if you encounter snow.

Eventually the trail will come out of the trees and join Glacier Creek just below Ribbon Falls, a beautiful cascade coming out of Black Lake. Follow the rocky trail up alongside the falls and then over a series of rock slabs to arrive at Black Lake. (#7) Here you can both hear and see a very large waterfall pouring down over the cliff at the south end of the lake. Above you Chiefs Head Peak, McHenry's Peak, and the Arrowhead look down on you in granite majesty. As you sit and look up at them, it is easy to feel very small.

MODERATE HIKES

RIBBON FALLS AND MCHENRYS PEAK

44 – TWIN SISTERS PEAKS

Overview

This steep hike leads you from the Lily Lake area up through deep forest to the summits of Twin Sisters Peaks above tree line where there are stunning views in every direction: over the Front Range, out across the Estes Valley and the Mummy Range, views of Longs Peak, and out toward Wild Basin.

The Stats

Distance Round Trip: 6.4 miles

Difficulty Rating: 168

Hiking Time: 4 hours and 15 minutes

Time to Go: morning

Season: mid-June until first snow

Primary Ecosystems: subalpine and alpine

Views: forest views, the Front Range, Estes Valley, Longs Peak

Possible Wildlife: forest animals, pikas, marmots

Trail Conditions: The trail is very well established and easy to follow. There is a very steep section after you pass the old landslide area, and the last stretch is very rocky.

Reminder: This trail leads above tree line, so be sure to be down in the trees as early in the day as possible during the summer months to avoid lightning. It can be quite cool and windy up there. There is no water along the way, so bring enough.

Elevation Start: 9,206'

Highest Point: 11,350' (saddle)

Total Elevation Gain: 2,212' (saddle)

Trailhead: This hike begins at the Twin Sisters Trailhead; see page 128 for details.

Waypoints

1. Twin Sisters Trailhead	0.0	9,206'
2. Re-enter RMNP	0.7	9,604'
3. Overlook of Tahosa Valley	1.0	9,789'
4. Landslide area	1.3	9,832'
5. Re-enter Roosevelt National Forest	2.2	10,620'
6. Enter the Talus	2.7	11,016'
7. Saddle between summits	3.1	11,350'

Hike Description

The trail begins just up the dirt road from the last parking spot. (**#1**) The trail begins in Rocky Mountain National Park but within a

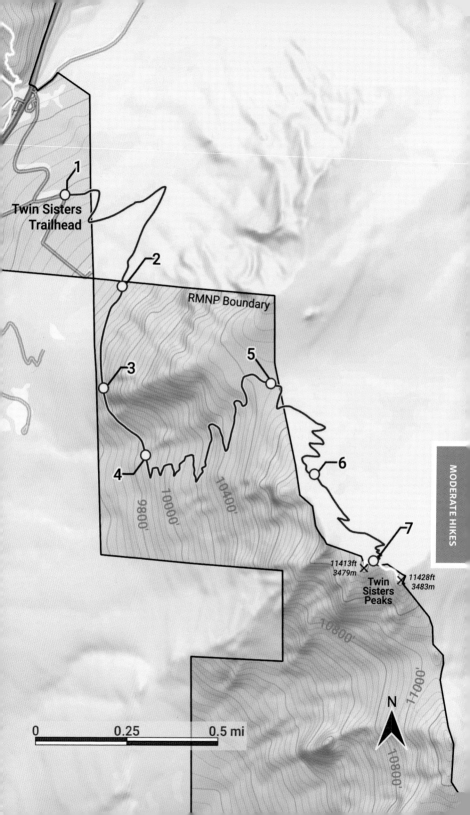

1

Twin Sisters
Trailhead

2

RMNP Boundary

5

3

4

6

7

11413ft
3479m

11428ft
3483m

Twin
Sisters
Peaks

10800'

11000'

10800'

9800'

10000'

10400'

MODERATE HIKES

N

0   0.25   0.5 mi

few steps it is in Roosevelt National Forest, bouncing back and forth between the two land management organizations on the way up.

From the trailhead, it heads right into a lodgepole forest. These trees grow so close together that they block out the light, preventing other plants from gaining hold. This section of dark forest has a couple of switchbacks and the trail is rocky and uneven. (**#2**) At one mile, you reach a break in the trees with a terrific viewpoint looking out on Longs Peak, Mount Meeker, and Estes Cone. (**#3**) This is a great place to stop for a snack.

Just beyond this you'll reach a portion of the mountain that washed away in a huge landslide during the Great Flood of 2013. (**#4**) The trail has now been reestablished over this slide, but immediately after the landslide you reach a section of trail about 0.3 miles in length that consists of a number of very steep, short switchbacks with some loose rock and sand. The trail then resumes a gentler climb.

In a short while the forest begins to thin out and the trail begins to head around the north side of Twin Sisters, gradually winding its way upward. You'll now start to notice that many of the trees have been stunted and twisted by the intense winds they experience up here.(**#5**)

At 2.7 miles you'll break through the trees and enter the alpine zone. (**#6**) The rest of the way is over sharp talus and requires more concentration to find the trail through the rocks. From here you can see the summits and the radio tower that sits between them. Be aware that this area often experiences extremely strong winds. If the winds feel too strong, turn back.

After winding through the talus, you finally reach the saddle between the two summits of Twin Sisters Peaks. (**#7**) Here you will find an old stone cottage that has an attached radio tower. From

MODERATE HIKES

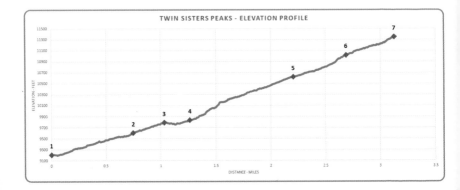

here you can climb either or both of the summits, as they are very near each other and don't take more than a few minutes to climb. The east summit is slightly higher at 11,428' and the west summit is 11,413'. The west summit is a little easier to climb, as there is a trail that begins beside the stone hut.

To reach the east summit, you have to head out across the jagged talus to the base of the summit pile. From here you need to scramble up the rocks to reach the summit. If you are not very agile, it is recommended that you walk up the west summit instead.

The views from both summits are very similar, with the west summit providing a bit better view to the north where the Estes Valley lies, and the east summit provides a little better view to the south, down the Tahosa Valley. From the top of both of these summits you can see for miles in every direction: to the east you can see the cities of the Front Range; to the west you can see Longs Peak and Mount Meeker; behind them you can see the mountains of the Continental Divide; and to the northwest you can see the Mummy Range. Once you are up here, it is tempting to stay all day; just be aware of storms that can build quickly if you are not paying attention.

MODERATE HIKES

LONGS PEAK FROM WAYPOINT #3

45 – BALANCED ROCK

Overview

This hike begins two miles north of Estes Park and leads through the unusual rock formations of Lumpy Ridge, providing views over the Estes Valley. It first leads up to Gem Lake, a small pond encircled by cliffs, and ends at a very large boulder precariously balanced on top of another. The hike up to Gem Lake is very popular but the second half of this hike is generally quiet and peaceful.

The Stats

Distance Round Trip: 7.7 miles

Difficulty Rating: 169

Hiking Time: 5 hours and 10 minutes

Time to Go: anytime

Season: May through November

Primary Ecosystem: montane

Views: unusual rock formations and views of Longs Peak and the Estes Valley

Possible Wildlife: forest animals

Trail Conditions: The trail is very well marked and easy to follow. There are many large stone stairs on the way up to Gem Lake; beyond the trail is sandy.

Reminder: The hike up to Gem Lake is very popular, so start early. This is a longer hike and there are not many good places to filter water, so bring enough with you.

Elevation Start: 7,840′

Highest Point: 8,847′

Total Elevation Gain: 1,839′

Trailhead: This hike begins at the Lumpy Ridge Trailhead; see page 123 for details.

Waypoints

1. Lumpy Ridge Trailhead	0.0	7,840′
2. Right at junction	0.5	8,171′
3. Estes Park Overlook	0.9	8,398′
4. Das Boot	1.3	8,555′
5. Gem Lake	1.7	8,844′
6. Left at Balanced Rock Trail	2.8	8,650′
7. Balanced Rock	3.9	8,744′

Hike Description

The first portion of this hike is described in detail as the Gem Lake hike on page 242.

From Gem Lake, (**#5**) continue along the western shore of the lake

8400'

8200'

6

8600'

8800'

8800'

7

5 GEM LAKE

8400'

8600'

8200'

4

3

8200'

2

RMNP Boundary

8200'

1

Lumpy Ridge
Trailhead

MODERATE HIKES

DEVILS GULCH ROAD

0   0.25   0.5   0.75   1 mi

N

and keep heading north. The trail will eventually appear as you get past the lake. Here you will say good-bye to the crowds and enjoy a much quieter trail. It first winds its way up through rocks and trees past a horse tie-up to the highest point of the hike. You are now about halfway there.

From here the trail begins to gently descend. In that first tenth of a mile there are some large boulders nestled in the trees where you can take a break away from the crowds of Gem Lake. After this level area the trail heads steeply down. Later the trail winds back and forth through the forest as well as both up and down. The trail is not always in great condition and you'll encounter some areas where the trail has eroded due to heavy rains and some areas where there is loose rock. This trail is much more narrow and rough than the trail to Gem Lake.

As there are not many views and little to judge your sense of progress, this section of trail feels longer than it actually is. Fortunately, it is very quiet and peaceful. After a little over a mile of winding your way through the forest, you eventually arrive at the junction for the Balanced Rock Trail. (**#6**) This is on a level and sandy area in a ponderosa forest. It's a perfect place to get away from the crowds and sit under a tree with a good book. In the spring and early summer remember to check for ticks when you get back.

At the intersection, turn left and you are only one mile from your destination. You'll begin by winding your way through this cheery ponderosa pine forest. In just under half a mile the sandy trail makes a very steep and uneven drop, which you'll need to descend with care. It then heads through the woods, where it can sometimes be a little muddy, then climbs back up the other side. Finally the trail descends again and reaches its end right at the base of Balanced Rock. (**#7**) You won't be able to see it until you reach it, as it is tucked into the forest.

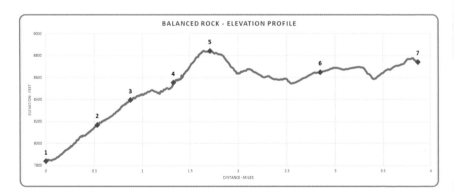

BALANCED ROCK

When you arrive you can't help but admire this amazing formation of granite as this huge boulder sits precariously balanced on top of a rock pedestal. There isn't a lot else to see here deep in the woods, but the silence and peacefulness of the place more than make up for the view.

46 – SKY POND

Overview

This is one of the classic hikes of Rocky Mountain National Park, providing a great deal of variety and beauty in a fairly reasonable distance. On this hike you'll visit three gorgeous lakes, two waterfalls, and hike up above tree line. This hike also involves a bit of adventure, with a steep climb up a section of rock that sometimes has a small stream cascading down it.

The Stats

Distance Round Trip: 8.4 miles

Difficulty: 172

Hiking Time: 5 hours and 35 minutes

Time to Go: morning

Season: mid-June through October

Primary Ecosystem: subalpine

Views: forest, streams, waterfalls, lakes

Possible Wildlife: forest animals

Trail Conditions: There are some rough sections of trail and one section of scrambling.

Reminder: This hike involves climbing up a steep section of rock that may have water flowing down it. There is also a bit of way-finding at the top of this section.

Elevation Start: 9,175′

Highest Point: 10,831′

Total Elevation Gain: 1,750′

Trailhead: This hike begins at the Glacier Gorge Trailhead; see page 119 for details. It can also be started from the Bear Lake Trailhead; see page 110 for details.

Waypoints

1. Glacier Gorge Trailhead	0.0	9,175′
2. Left at junction with trail to Bear Lake	0.3	9,249′
3. Alberta Falls	0.8	9,394′
4. North Longs Peak Trail junction	1.6	9,744′
5. Main junction in Glacier Gorge	2.0	9,786′
6. The Loch	2.8	10,197′
7. Timberline Falls	3.8	10,740′
8. Sky Pond	4.2	10,877′

Hike Description

The first section of this hike is described in detail in the Alberta Falls hike on page 188. The next section of this hike is described in the

1

Glacier Gorge
Trailhead

2

3

Alberta Falls

4

5

6

Glacier Falls

THE
LOCH

MILLS
LAKE

EMERALD
LAKE

DREAM
LAKE

LAKE
HAIYAHA

BEAR
LAKE

7

Timberline Falls

GLASS
LAKE

8

SKY
POND

9600'

9200'

9000'

BEAR LAKE

11000'

10200'

11400'

12200'

12400'

12600'

12000'

11800'

11200'

N

0   0.25   0.5   0.75   1 mi

hike up to the Loch, page 266. In summary, you'll follow the Glacier Gorge Trail up past Alberta Falls (#3) and continue on to the main junction. (#5) Here you'll take the trail that goes straight ahead. After a bit of a climb and a few switchbacks you'll arrive at the Loch. (#6)

From the Loch, take the trail around to the right alongside the lake. The trail follows the north side of the lake, providing a couple of good views out over the lake as well as several spots where you can climb out onto the rocks. The trail then heads around the western edge of the lake. If you are looking, you might notice two small islands. The trail turns to the southwest and follows the inlet stream into the forest. This entire stretch along the lake is very gentle.

Just after the trail begins following the inlet stream, it begins to climb and heads up a steep stretch of rock stairs. It then levels out and later climbs steeply up another section of stairs. Just past the top of this second section, you'll cross two log bridges over Andrews Creek. Look for Parry's primrose growing at the water's edge. You'll then head through a marshy section over a series of single-log bridges. The trail begins to climb and as it does, you can start to hear the roar of Timberline Falls ahead. This is a long climb, mostly up stairs. As you ascend, the trees transition to krumholz and then just before four miles, you break through the trees and have a clear view up toward Timberline Falls.

Follow the rock stairs that lead up to the base of Timberline Falls. (#7) There is sometimes a small stream running down the trail, so be prepared to get your feet a little wet. You'll then reach the base of the top tier of falls. You can walk around and get a good view of the falls, but then come back to continue your journey. You're going to scramble up the gash in the rock. There may be water running down it, and that can make the rock a bit slick. Don't worry about getting wet; just go

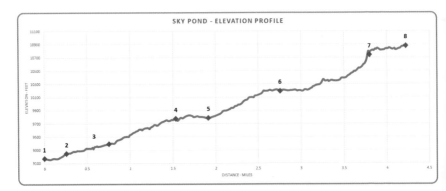

SKY POND - ELEVATION PROFILE

TIMBERLINE FALLS

slowly, making sure you have good handholds and footholds. You'll only be in the water for a short ways and then you'll be above it. If this climb makes you too uncomfortable, don't attempt it, as coming down is a bit more difficult than going up.

At the top of the scramble, you arrive at the outlet of Lake of Glass. This is a beautiful alpine lake with a great view out to the north over the Loch. You can also look to the south and see Taylor Peak keeping watch. From here you're going to follow the edge of the lake to its south end, but you can't do that directly, as there is a large rock wall blocking the way. So, from the outlet of the lake you'll need to turn right and walk along the edge of that rock wall. On the northwest side you'll find a point where it is easy to climb up. Once you are on top of it, turn left and travel parallel to the lake, heading toward its far end. You'll soon find bits of a trail.

This next section of trail gets a little rough. You'll climb over boulders, through thick krumholz and willows before coming out to a more clearly defined trail through a boulder field at the far end of Lake of Glass. After passing through a small meadow you'll see a gorgeous cascade off to your left. From here it is just a short climb and you'll arrive at Sky Pond. (#8) Here the granite spires of the Sharkstooth tower high above, while Taylor Peak looks down from the south end. This is truly one of the more dramatic views in Rocky Mountain National Park.

CATHEDRAL SPIRES FROM SKY POND

47 – GRANITE FALLS

Overview

Hike through quiet woods up to Big Meadows tucked into the forest, where you may very likely find moose grazing. Walk around the giant meadow and then follow the Tonahutu Creek upstream, passing by several other meadows and through a large burn area before arriving at Granite Falls.

The Stats

Distance Round Trip: 10.1 miles

Difficulty Rating: 177

Hiking Time: 6 hours and 40 minutes

Time to Go: anytime

Season: June through October

Primary Ecosystem: montane

Views: Enjoy views out across Big Meadow and the crashing waters of the Tonahutu Creek at Granite Falls.

Possible Wildlife: moose and forest animals

Trail Conditions: average

Reminder: Keep your eyes open for moose, as most of this is through moose territory. Be careful near the falls during the spring runoff; the streams are powerful and deadly at this time of year.

Elevation Start: 8,794'

Highest Point: 9,834'

Total Elevation Gain: 1,556'

Trailhead: This hike begins at the Green Mountain Trailhead; see page 120 for details.

Waypoints

1. Green Mountain Trailhead	0.0	8,794'
2. Left at Tonahutu Trail	1.8	9,403'
3. Old Homestead	2.0	9,412'
4. Right at Onahu Creek Trail junction	2.3	9,467'
5. Enter burn area	3.9	9,558'
6. Granite Falls	5.0	9,834'

Hike Description

The trail begins on the east side of the parking lot, (**#1**) heading through a grove of aspen trees and up into the forest. The first half a mile of the trail climbs fairly steeply, about 300' in elevation gain, before leveling off some at the half-mile mark, so be sure to start with a slow, gentle pace. As the trail heads up through the trees, it passes a few mountain meadows on the right side that might occasionally

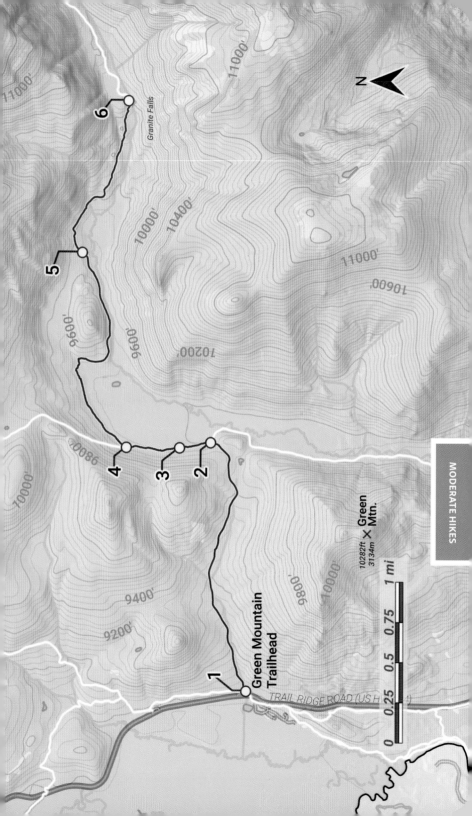

MODERATE HIKES

Granite Falls

6

5

4

3

2

1

Green Mountain
Trailhead

TRAIL RIDGE ROAD (US H---)

10282ft ✕ Green
3134m   Mtn.

11000'

11000'

10600'

10400'

10000'

10200'

9600'

9600'

9800'

9800'

10000'

9400'

9200'

9800'

10000'

11000'

N

0   0.25   0.5   0.75   1 mi

have moose grazing in them, so walk quietly and keep your eyes open. At 1.8 miles you will have climbed 609 feet and here you'll connect with the Tonahutu Trail. **(#2)** Take a left turn on the trail and follow it to the north. About a hundred feet down the trail you'll find a spur trail heading down the hill and into the meadow. This is a delightful place to take a break and watch for moose and other wildlife. From here you can look out to the north to get a nice view of Mount Ida. You'll realize that Big Meadows really does live up to its name.

Just a short ways down the trail, you'll come across the remains of an old homestead at the edge of the meadow **(#3)**; the remains of another building is located just a bit farther along. Imagine what it was like homesteading here in the early 1900s. About ten minutes later the trail leaves the meadow and begins to head uphill back into the woods. It then reaches the junction with the Onahu Creek Trail. **(#4)** Keep to the right at this junction, and the trail will soon head back downhill. From here Big Meadows can be seen through the trees but the trail no longer follows right at its edge. Slowly the trail wraps around the north end of the meadow as it begins to head eastward. You'll get one more good view of the meadow right at its end and then you'll head up the valley along the Tonahutu.

At about 3.7 miles the creek will almost meet the trail in a small but beautiful meadow. As the trail heads on you'll soon follow the edge of a larger meadow and then enter a burn area, from the Big Meadows Fire in 2013. **(#5)** Just after leaving the burn area you'll cross a stream coming down from Nakai Peak. Here the trail begins to climb more steeply and becomes a little more rough for a bit. There are intermittent short, steep climbs followed by more level

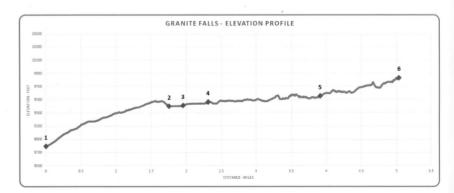
GRANITE FALLS - ELEVATION PROFILE

sections of trail. Finally, you arrive at a sign announcing that you are at Granite Falls. (**#6**)

From here you can climb down the steep, rough trail that leads to the base of the falls. Down at the edge of the water are a couple of large granite slabs that are perfect for a picnic. Here you can watch the waters of Tonahutu Creek crash over a couple of different steps totaling about fifty feet. Be careful around the fast-running water and be especially aware that wet granite can be very slippery.

MODERATE HIKES

TONAHUTU CREEK

GRANITE FALLS

STRENUOUS HIKES

This section contains the hardest hikes in the book. Like the other sections, each hike is progressively more difficult than the previous one, so the last hike listed is the hardest of all. These are serious hikes that require not only physical strength but also knowledge of the mountains and the wisdom to use that knowledge. These hikes take you back into the wilderness where you will face the elements and be far from help. You need proper equipment (see page 62) as well as the know-how of what to do if something goes wrong (page 79). The hikes on these pages take you into some of the most dramatic and beautiful areas of Rocky Mountain National Park.

FINAL CLIMB TO CHASM LAKE

STRENUOUS HIKES

48 – ESTES CONE *(from Longs Trailhead)*

Overview

Estes Cone is an impressive hill next to Longs Peak that just reaches tree line, allowing for incredible views of Longs Peak as well as views in every direction. The first part of this hike is great for families; after Moore Park the trail climbs steeply and then from Storm Pass to the top it is a challenging scramble that requires good footing and good way-finding skills.

The Stats

Distance Round Trip: 6.4 miles

Difficulty Rating: 180* (159)

Hiking Time: 4 hours and 15 minutes

Time to Go: morning

Season: May through October

Primary Ecosystem: subalpine

Views: incredible views in every direction, including Longs Peak, Mummy Range, Continental Divide, the Front Range

Possible Wildlife: gray jays, ground squirrels, forest animals

Trail Conditions: The trail to Storm Pass is typical; beyond that it is more of a scramble than a hike, with loose sand and rock and over tree roots and boulders.

Reminder: The last section of this hike is not for everyone. It is very steep and at times difficult to follow, requiring good route-finding skills and agility. You can start this hike from two different locations—either the Longs Peak Trailhead or from Lily Lake. Starting at the Longs Peak Trailhead is shorter and has less elevation gain.

Elevation Start: 9,400'

Highest Point: 11,010'

Total RT Gain: 1,976'

Trailhead: This hike begins at the Longs Peak Trailhead; see page 122 for details.

Waypoints

1. Longs Peak Trailhead	0.0	9,400'
2. Right onto Eugenia Mine Trail	0.5	9,682'
3. Eugenia Mine	1.4	9,841'
4. Moore Park	1.7	9,706'
5. Storm Pass	2.6	10,236'
6. Summit of Estes Cone	3.2	11,010'

Hike Description

Begin at the Longs Peak Trail located on the west side of the parking lot next to the ranger station. **(#1)** Follow the wide trail

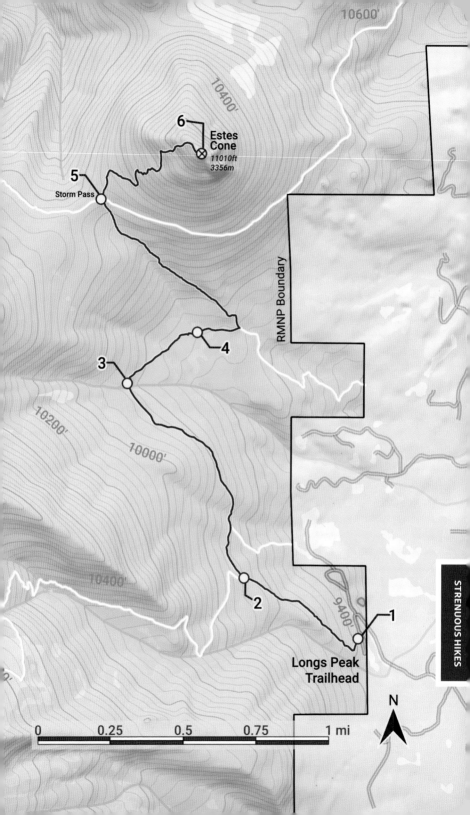

10600'

10400'

6

Estes
Cone
11010ft
3356m

5

Storm Pass

4

3

10200'

10000'

10400'

RMNP Boundary

STRENUOUS HIKES

2

1

9400'

Longs Peak
Trailhead

0   0.25   0.5   0.75   1 mi

N

upward for half a mile. This section is fairly steep, so you'll want to take it slowly. At the half-mile mark you'll reach an intersection; here you'll turn right and follow the Eugenia Mine Trail. (#2) This trail winds up and down through the forest. Be sure to stop from time to time to listen to the sounds of the forest.

At just under a mile from when you left the main trail, you cross a log bridge and arrive at the Eugenia Mine, the site of an old and unsuccessful mining operation. (#3) Take a few minutes to look around this area to find remnants of their time here. Then continue on the main trail. In a few minutes you'll reach Moore Park, a delightful grassy meadow surrounded by forest that invites you to stop and have a picnic. (#4) On the other side of the meadow you'll reenter the forest and soon will take a sharp left turn. Here the trail will climb steeply for about half a mile. As the trail begins to level off it arrives at Storm Pass. (#5) At Storm Pass a couple of trails converge. Look at the sign to identify the one that leads to Estes Cone, lest you accidently end up in Glacier Basin or Lily Lake.

Note: From here to the top of Estes Cone, the hike changes from an easy hike to something much more challenging. You'll have to really keep your eyes open, as the trail can be hard to find. Look for the most open path, the wear of many feet, rock piles guiding your way, and also notice logs and rocks that have been placed to help keep you on the trail. If you lose the trail, stop and look around before you take another step, or even go back to where you last saw it.

Begin by following the path in the direction of Estes Cone. It should be straight ahead and a bit to your right. The trail begins fairly gently but in a few minutes turns into more of a scramble, getting steeper the farther up you get. The trail will also become quite sandy

ESTES CONE VIA LONGS PEAK TRAILHEAD - ELEVATION PROFILE

with loose rock. You'll be climbing over tree roots, between trees, and over large rocks. Take it slow. I find that the actual trail heads farther to the south (right) than I had expected.

As you approach the top area you'll notice a lot of old twisted limber pine. Once you reach the top area, keep to the right and work your way around on the right-hand side until you get to the last major rock outcropping on your left. You'll see a way to scramble up fairly easily. It definitely is a scramble, though, and you'll need to use both hands to climb up. If you are afraid of heights, you may want to skip this portion. At the top of that climb, you are just a few feet shy of the highest point. To reach the very highest point, continue down the other side and then climb up the next rock outcropping. This will bring you to the summit. (**#6**) Any of these rock outcroppings will provide you with jaw-dropping views in every direction. Be very careful descending the rock outcroppings and down again to Storm Pass. Be sure to take your time. Also, be sure to be well below the summit before thunderstorms arrive.

STRENUOUS HIKES

FINAL CLIMB TO ESTES CONE SUMMIT

49 – FINCH LAKE

Overview

Head up into the deep forest of Wild Basin and experience the silence of the wilderness. This trail passes through a large burn area before descending to beautiful Finch Lake tucked into the trees.

The Stats

Distance Round Trip: 8.6 miles

Difficulty Rating: 183

Hiking Time: 5 hours and 40 minutes

Time to Go: anytime

Season: mid-June until first snow

Primary Ecosystems: montane and subalpine

Views: alpine lake with towering peaks, deep forest, small streams, views across to Longs Peak

Possible Wildlife: dusky grouse, gray jays, Abert squirrels, moose

Trail Conditions: well maintained and easy to follow, though some sections are very rocky

Reminder: Be aware that parking is limited, so arrive early or late.

Elevation Start: 8,470'

Highest Point: 10,119'

Total Elevation Gain: 1,954'

Trailhead: This hike begins at the Finch Lake Trailhead; see page 118 for details.

Waypoints

1. Finch Lake Trailhead	0.0	8,470'
2. First intersection	1.4	8,989'
3. Confusion Junction	2.3	9,610'
4. Enter burn area	2.5	9,763'
5. Leave burn area	2.8	9,876'
6. Descend to Finch Lake	3.9	10,119'
7. Finch Lake	4.3	9,925'

Hike Description

The trail heads straight into the woods and begins to climb almost immediately. (**#1**) It then turns to the east running parallel to the valley as it climbs. You'll head upward and eastward for just under a mile with a couple of nice view points along the way. When trail takes a sharp right turn it finally levels out and continues level for quite a while as it heads through a delightful aspen grove. The

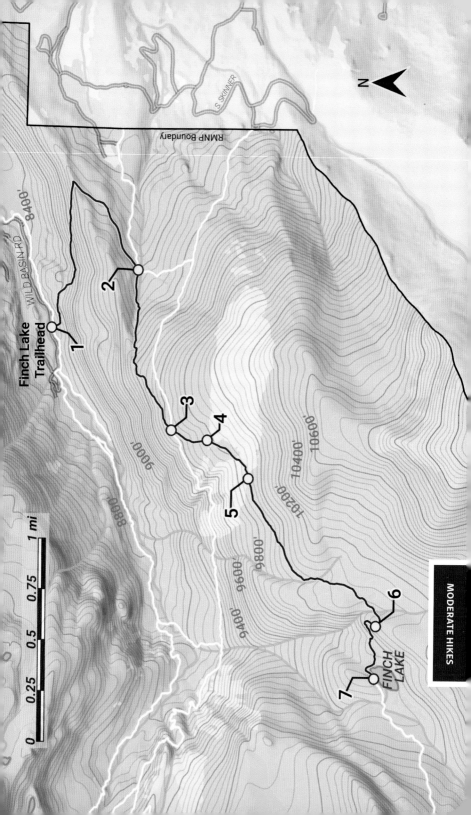

FINCH LAKE PANORAMA

trail then reaches its first intersection. (**#2**) Continue straight. Climb through deep woods while climbing numerous stairs along the way.

Eventually you'll reach an intersection known by locals as "Confusion Junction." (**#3**) Here, two trails cross each other at an angle, making it easy to feel a bit confused about which way to turn. Continue straight uphill (south-heading trail), following the sign toward Finch and Pear lakes. From here the trail begins to climb farther up and enters a burn area left by a large wildfire in 1978, known as the Ouzel Fire. (**#4**) Much of this area burned so hot that it was many years before plants were able to regain a foothold. Today, vegetation

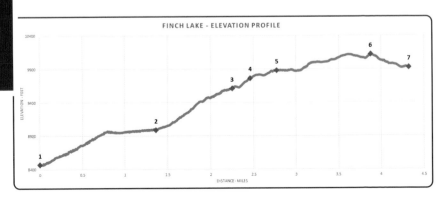

FINCH LAKE - ELEVATION PROFILE

is back and there are even a few trees that are twenty feet tall or more. Slowly the forest is returning, but for now you can still enjoy open views to the north looking out to Longs Peak and Mount Meeker. After a short while you leave the burn area and reenter the older-growth forest. (**#5**) The trail levels out and follows the top edge of the valley, providing occasional views through the trees. This gentle stretch gives you a chance to catch your breath and enjoy the subalpine forest. On one of my last walks through this area, I spotted a dusky grouse watching me just off the trail.

At 3.6 miles the trail begins to slowly descend, soon crossing a log bridge over a small stream. Then it begins a steep descent with two switchbacks(**#6**), arriving at beautiful little Finch Lake tucked into the forest. When you reach the Finch Lake sign, you'll find a path leading down to the shore. (**#7**) Here you can enjoy views toward Copeland Mountain. Be sure to take time to find a rock and sit in the stillness in this incredibly peaceful setting.

If you are continuing on to Pear Lake, turn to page 386.

50 – SANDBEACH LAKE

Overview

This hike heads up along a ridgeline that provides great views over Wild Basin. It then enters into deep forest, winding up and down small hills until it delivers you to Sandbeach Lake, located just below tree line. Here you'll find a great view of Mount Meeker towering above the lake to the north, and Copeland Mountain can be seen in the distance. Sandbeach Lake was used as a reservoir for many years until the park removed the artificial dam, which dropped the water level and created the ring of sand around the lake. Bring your beach towel, sunscreen, and a good book, as this is a great place to enjoy both the mountains and the beach well away from the busy crowds to be found elsewhere.

The Stats

Distance Round Trip: 8.7 miles

Difficulty Rating: 187

Hiking Time: 5 hours and 45 minutes

Time to Go: anytime

Season: mid-June until first snow

Ecosystems: montane and subalpine

Views: Look down over the Wild Basin valley and enjoy high peaks around a mountain lake.

Possible Wildlife: mostly forest animals

Trail Conditions: The trail is generally in great shape, though it can be a bit rocky during the climb along the ridge at the end of the first mile.

Reminder: If you are spending any time on the beach, don't forget your sunscreen and either extra water or a water filter.

Elevation Start: 8,345'

Highest Point: 10,343'

Total Elevation Gain: 2,028'

Trailhead: This hike begins at the Sandbeach Lake Trailhead; see page 126 for details.

Waypoints

1. Sandbeach Lake Trailhead	0.0	8,345'
2. Meeker Park junction	1.3	8,989'
3. Cross Campers Creek	2.4	9,557'
4. Cross Hunters Creek	3.5	9,837'
5. Sandbeach Lake	4.3	10,313'

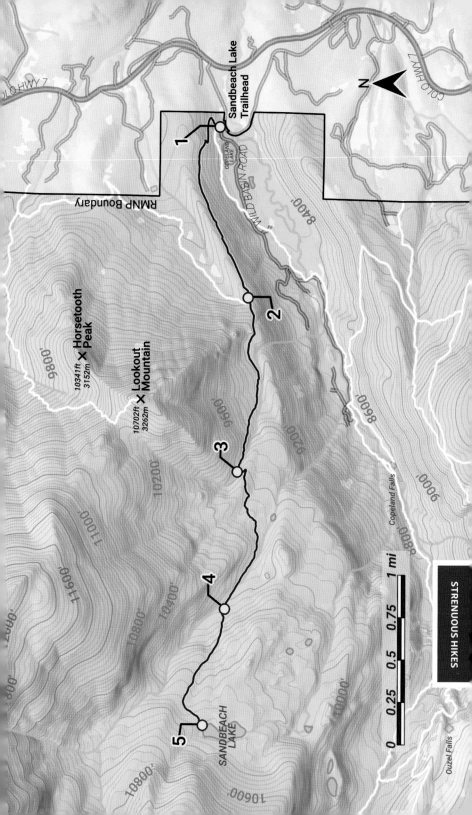

Sandbeach Lake Trailhead

1

Copeland Lake

WILD BASIN ROAD

COLO HWY 7

N

COLO HWY 7

RMNP Boundary

8400'

2

Horsetooth Peak
10341ft X 3152m

Lookout Mountain
10702ft X 3262m

9800'

9600'

9200'

9600'

8600'

9000'

8800'

Copeland Falls

3

10200'

11000'

11600'

11800'

10400'

10800'

4

10000'

10200'

9600'

10800'

10600'

SANDBEACH LAKE

5

Ouzel Falls

STRENUOUS HIKES

1 mi   0.75   0.5   0.25   0

The trail begins on the north side of the parking lot and heads due north. (**#1**) After just a couple hundred feet you'll pass a junction with another trail that leads through the woods to the main Wild Basin Ranger Station. You'll want to continue straight ahead up the hill and follow it as it turns to the left heading westward and gradually makes its way up the north side of the valley as it moves through a fragrant ponderosa forest. Along the way you will get terrific views down across the whole of Wild Basin. In one section it gets a bit rough, rocky, and sandy as it hugs the side of the hill. At 1.3 miles the trail reaches two very short switchbacks before reaching the junction with the Meeker Park Trail. (**#2**) At this point you will have climbed 655' in elevation.

Continue uphill to the west. Soon the trail begins to head away from the edge of the ridge and into the forest. Here you'll find lots of giant boulders reaching high above the trees, and the trail becomes much more peaceful and level. This section of trail heads through an aspen grove that can be brilliant yellow in mid- to late September. After a short respite, the trail begins to climb again. At about two miles it reaches the crest of a hill and gradually begins to descend until it reaches Campers Creek. (**#3**) It then follows the creek upward. At this point the forest becomes much denser as it transitions from ponderosa pine to Douglas fir. After almost half a mile the trail finally crosses the creek.

Just before the three-mile mark the trail enters another aspen grove. To the south you can see small meadows and ponds, which must make this a favorite location for the larger wildlife in the area, so keep your eyes open. Just as you pass the junction for the Hunters

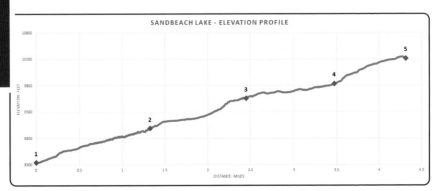

STRENUOUS HIKES

MOUNT MEEKER FROM SANDBEACH LAKE

Creek Campsite (wilderness camping permit required) the trail begins climbing steeply upward and in a short while it crosses a log bridge over Hunters Creek. (#4) This is a delightful spot with the crystal clear water that cools the air around it and a great place to have a rest and filter superb-tasting icy water.

From here the trail continues to climb about 500' in elevation over the next 0.8 miles before leveling out and arriving at Sandbeach Lake. (#5) As the trail leads down to the lake, the trees come to an end and the world opens up around you. You'll find a very large sandy beach that stretches around much of the lake. This beach is the result of the lake having been previously dammed to create a larger reservoir. It was dismantled by the National Park Service in 1988 following the breach at the Lawn Lake reservoir. Despite being drained from its previous size, it is still considered to be one of the deepest lakes in Rocky Mountain National Park.

In the distance you'll see Copeland Mountain keeping watch to the south. For the best views, continue south along the east edge of the lake at least halfway and then look back to see Mount Meeker looking down on you. It is a very impressive view. This is a terrific area to simply relax with a good book and enjoy being out in the best of the wilderness.

51 – LONE PINE LAKE

Overview

This hike leads from the east end of Grand Lake into East Meadows, where you may often find wildlife. It then heads into deep forest and takes you past numerous cascades and alongside the East Inlet stream up to Lone Pine Lake tucked into the forest. If you have additional time, consider continuing on up to Lake Verna (page 382) for spectacular views.

The Stats

Distance Round Trip: 10.1 miles

Difficulty Rating: 189

Hiking Time: 6 hours and 45 minutes

Time to Go: morning

Season: June through October

Primary Ecosystems: montane and subalpine

Views: beautiful meadows, forest streams, overlook of Grand Lake, cascades, a forested lake

Possible Wildlife: moose, deer, forest animals

Trail Conditions: The first two miles of this trail are fairly gentle and then it climbs quite steeply, some areas with steep drop-offs. The trail is well marked and easy to follow.

Reminder: Be aware that moose frequent the area all along this trail but especially the first couple of miles. Simply stay aware and avoid approaching them.

Elevation Start: 8,400'

Highest Point: 9,890'

Total Elevation Gain: 1,772'

Trailhead: This hike begins at the East Inlet Trailhead; see page 116 for details.

Waypoints

1. East Inlet Trailhead	0.0	8,400'
2. Adams Falls	0.3	8,426'
3. East Meadow	0.5	8,498'
4. East Meadow overlook	1.3	8,563'
5. Grand Lake overlook	2.9	9,163'
6. Water access	3.3	9,120'
7. Bridge over East Inlet	4.1	9,374'
8. Lone Pine Lake	5.0	9,878'

Hike Description

The first portion of this hike leads to Adams Falls and East Meadow. This section is described in detail on page 175. In summary, follow the

STRENUOUS HIKES

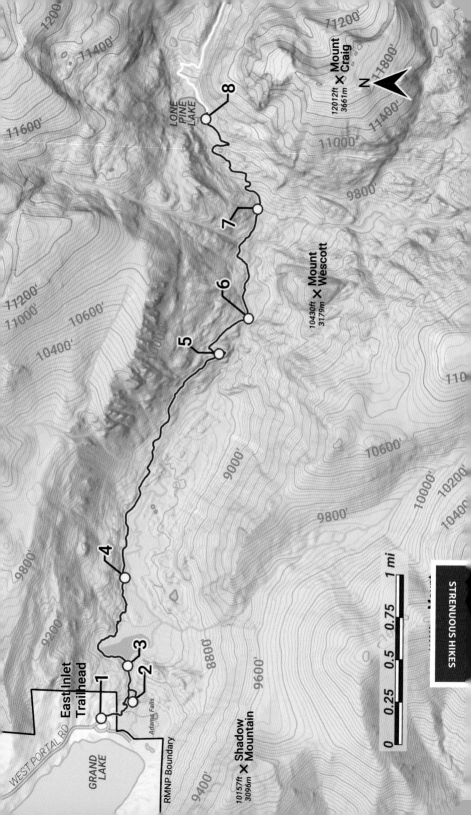

STRENUOUS HIKES

East Inlet
Trailhead

WEST PORTAL RD

GRAND
LAKE

Adams Falls

RMNP Boundary

10157ft ✕ Shadow
3096m   Mountain

LONE
PINE
LAKE

10430ft ✕ Mount
3179m   Wescott

12012ft ✕ Mount
3661m   Craig

N

0   0.25   0.5   0.75   1 mi

East Inlet Trail, taking the short detour to visit Adams Falls. (**#2**) In just over half a mile you arrive at the start of East Meadow. (**#3**)

Follow the trail as it turns to the north, following the western edge of the meadow. You'll pass a small pond and then the trail heads into the woods and turns to the east, following the northern edge of the meadow. Keep your eyes wide open, as moose are sometimes found on either side of the trail. Also, take time to stop and just listen to the many birds that make their home here. At 1.1 miles there is a little rise with a bit of a view and then it heads back down into the forest. At 1.3 miles, shortly after the turn for the East Meadow campsite (wilderness camping permit required), you'll come to an overlook that I refer to as East Meadow overlook. (**#4**) It is a great place to watch for wildlife in the meadow.

After climbing and descending a second little rise, the trail enters into the woods. It then crosses a stream coming down from Mount Enentah. Soon it begins climbing. Over the next mile and a half you'll encounter a number of stone stairs and switchbacks. There are a few places where there is a significant drop-off but the trail is pretty wide, so there is little likelihood of falling. As you near the top, you'll find a large overlook on your left with great views out over Grand Lake. (**#5**) This is a good place for a break.

From the top the trail descends a number of rock steps and then in just a bit it climbs back up a large number of rock steps. A great deal of work went into these. At about 3.2 miles the trail again descends a series of rock steps. At the bottom of these steps there is a rock slab leading out to the stream. (**#6**) This is a good place to filter water and fill up your water bottle. The trail continues much more gently on the north side of the stream. This is a forested section of

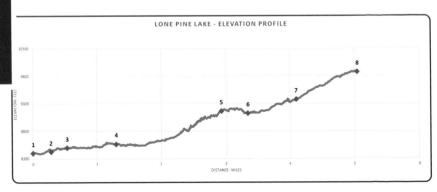

LONE PINE LAKE - ELEVATION PROFILE

trail that is really wonderful; you can hear the stream for most of the way. Eventually the trail begins climbing and will lead you across a stream coming down from Ptarmigan Mountain. This is a delightful place to stop. Then you'll climb again before arriving at a large bridge that finally leads you to the south side of the East Inlet. (#7)

From here you have your last big climb up to Lone Pine Lake. The trail winds its way upward quite steeply. After a while you'll pass a couple of pretty cascades right by the intersection for Gray Jay campsite (wilderness camping permit required). From here the trail skirts a large rock wall and then makes a last gentle climb before arriving at Lone Pine Lake. (#8) When you arrive you'll notice a small island in the lake with one large lone pine tree on it. I assume this is where the lake got its name. Here you can relax and enjoy the beauty of the forest or, if you still have energy, consider continuing on to enjoy the dramatic views of Lake Verna only 1.6 miles farther up the trail (see page 382).

STRENUOUS HIKES

A LONE PINE AT LONE PINE LAKE

52 – LAWN LAKE

Overview

This hike leads you six miles through the forest along the edge of the Roaring River. When you think it will never end, the trees begin to thin and the world begins to open. As you approach Lawn Lake, its delightful meadows and surrounding peaks welcome you to this idyllic hideaway.

The Stats

Distance Round Trip: 12.2 miles

Difficulty Rating: 190* (251)

Hiking Time: 8 hours and 5 minutes

Time to Go: most anytime

Season: mid-June until first snow

Primary Ecosystems: montane and subalpine

Views: forest and stream views followed by a large lake near tree line surrounded by mountains

Possible Wildlife: forest animals and marmots

Trail Conditions: The trail is generally wider and smoother than most in Rocky but it does have some rougher sections.

Reminder: This is a longer hike, so be sure to have some way to filter water, bring plenty of food, and stay out of the open during storms.

Elevation Start: 8,540'

Highest Point: 11,010'

Total Elevation Gain: 2,600'

Trailhead: This hike begins at the Lawn Lake Trailhead; see page 122 for details.

Waypoints

01. Lawn Lake Trailhead	0.0	8,540'
02. Roaring River overlook	0.9	9,021'
03. Ypsilon Lake Trail junction	1.3	9,218'
04. Switchbacks	2.1	9,494'
05. Stream access	4.3	10,298'
06. Black Canyon junction	5.5	10,832'
07. Lawn Lake	6.1	11,007'

STRENUOUS HIKES

Hike Description

The trail begins on the northeast side of the parking lot. (#1) Just a few steps up the trail and you'll need to turn left at the first intersection. Continue on up four switchbacks that quickly lead you higher. As the trail begins to head westward, parallel to the Endovalley, it

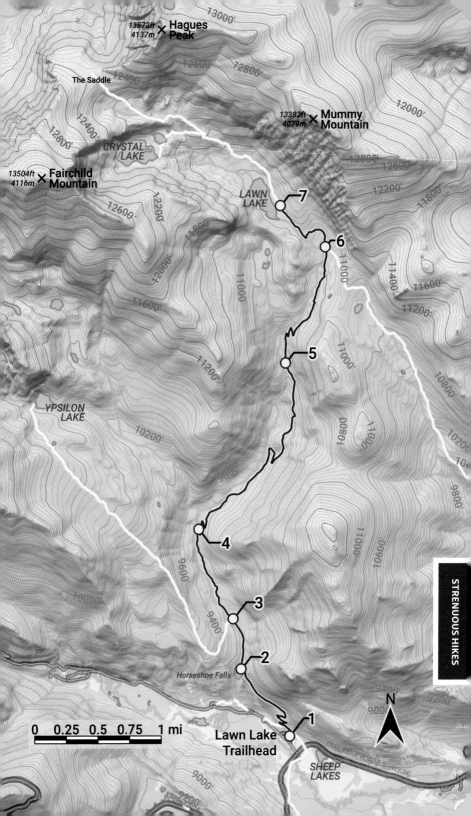

13573ft
4137m ✕ Hagues
Peak

13000'
12600'
12800'

The Saddle

12400'

12800'
12400'

CRYSTAL
LAKE

13382ft
4079m ✕ Mummy
Mountain

12000'

13504ft
4116m ✕ Fairchild
Mountain

12600'

LAWN
LAKE ⑦

⑥

11000'

YPSILON
LAKE

⑤

10200'

④

9600'

③

9400'

②

Horseshoe Falls

①

Lawn Lake
Trailhead

SHEEP
LAKES

0   0.25   0.5   0.75   1 mi

N

provides views on the meadows below. This first section of trail is wide and fairly steep. Just before the one-mile mark you reach the edge of the Roaring River and the trail turns to the north, following the river upstream. (**#2**) It will be your companion all the way to Lawn Lake. Here the Roaring River is in a deep chasm that it carved out during the Lawn Lake Flood and again during the flood of 2013. The edges of this bank are quite dangerous, as it is still eroding, so avoid walking anywhere near the edge and be sure to keep children well back. As the trail follows the river, it will become a little less steep. In a short while it heads into an aspen grove, which can be brilliant in late September and early October.

At 1.3 miles you pass the junction for the Ypsilon Lake Trail. (**#3**) For the next half a mile the trail continues very gently and peacefully alongside the river. At around two miles it begins to climb and soon starts the next set of switchbacks. (**#4**) After four turns it begins to level out. The trail often feels rather long as it makes its way through the woods, with little in terms of views beyond the forest. Fortunately, almost all of this hike is accompanied by the sound of the Roaring River, which is never too far away. This is a great hike for hot, sunny days or windy days, as neither will bother you much here in the deep forest.

You'll cross a few streams and traverse a couple more switchbacks as you make your way through the woods. At about 4.3 miles the trees on the left open and you have a chance to go down to the stream to dip your toes in or filter some additional water. (**#5**) Soon you'll reach the start of the last switchbacks. At the top of those four switchbacks you'll notice the trees getting shorter and things beginning to open up. The trail levels out and you'll begin to get glimpses of Mummy Mountain. Eventually the trail will come right alongside

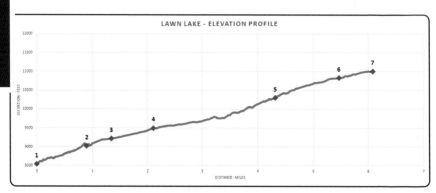

the stream and you'll notice lots of debris. This was the result of the Lawn Lake Flood in 1982 when a dam at the lake broke. As you move through this area you'll pass a junction on your right. (**#6**) This is the Black Canyon Trail, which leads a long ways back to Lumpy Ridge.

Shortly after the junction, the trail enters a marshy area that can be a bit muddy and which during the early summer is filled with a great variety of wildflowers. Continue on up and eventually the forest will open for you at the outlet of Lawn Lake, the start of the Roaring River. From here you'll walk through beautiful meadows with views of the lake. When you reach the junction for the campsite trail (wilderness camping permits required), turn left and follow the small path down to the water's edge. (**#7**) I'm certain this is a place you'll want to stay for quite a while as you soak in the beauty of this special place.

If you have energy and the weather shows no sign of storms, consider continuing on to Crystal Lakes, which is another 1.4 miles up trail from here. You can find details on page 418.

STRENUOUS HIKES

ARRIVING AT LAWN LAKE

53 – YPSILON LAKE

Overview

This hike takes you from the low meadow of Horseshoe Park up to a lake just below tree line surrounded by high peaks. It is a very steep hike through thick forest, so it is generally not very crowded.

The Stats

Distance Round Trip: 8.6 miles

Difficulty Rating: 206

Hiking Time: 5 hours and 40 minutes

Time to Go: mornings

Season: late June until first snow

Primary Ecosystems: montane and subalpine

Views: forested trails and mountain lakes

Possible Wildlife: forest animals and bighorn sheep

Trail Conditions: The trail is rocky and steep but easy to follow.

Reminder: This is a steep hike, so be sure to take it slow and steady. Bring plenty of water and give yourself enough time.

Elevation Start: 8,540'

Highest Point: 10,744'

Total Elevation Gain: 2,491'

Trailhead: This hike begins at the Lawn Lake Trailhead; see page 122 for details.

Waypoints

1. Lawn Lake Trailhead	0.0	8,540'
2. Roaring River overlook	0.9	9,016'
3. Left onto Ypsilon Lake Trail	1.3	9,218'
4. Opening in forest	2.5	10,009'
5. Begin descent	3.7	10,744'
6. Chipmunk Lake	3.9	10,680'
7. Ypsilon Lake	4.3	10,559'

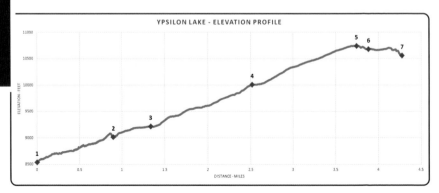

SPECTACLE
LAKES

11400'

11000'

10800'

11200'

10800'

YPSILON
LAKE

7

6

CHIPMUNK
LAKE

10200'

10400'

5

4

9600'

9400'

3

2

Horseshoe Falls

10000'

8800'

10600'

10000'

10800'

1

Lawn Lake
Trailhead

STRENUOUS HIKES

S
L

N

0   0.25   0.5   0.75   1 mi

8600'

TRAIL RIDGE ROAD (US HWY 34)

8800'

EAST END OF YPSILON LAKE

Hike Description

The trail begins on the northeast side of the parking lot. (**#1**) Just a few steps up the trail and you'll need to turn left at the first intersection. Very soon you'll encounter four switchbacks that quickly lead you higher. As the trail begins to head westward, parallel to the Endovalley, it provides views of the meadows below. This first section of trail is wide and fairly steep. At around the one-mile mark you reach the edge of the Roaring River and the trail turns to the north, following the river upstream. (**#2**) Here the Roaring River is in a deep chasm that it carved out during the Lawn Lake Flood and again during the flood of 2013. The edges of this bank are quite dangerous, as it is still eroding, so avoid walking anywhere near the edge and be sure to keep children well back. As the trail follows the river it will slowly begin to level out a little. In a short while it heads into an aspen grove, which can be brilliant in late September and early October.

At 1.3 miles you reach the junction for the Ypsilon Lake Trail. (#3) Turn left here and you'll soon cross a log bridge over the Roaring River. If you look upstream from this point you will see a beautiful view of Fairchild Mountain at the end of the valley. On the other side of the bridge, the trail begins its steep climb upward. The first section has well-made wooden stairs to ease your climb. This section of trail is through thick lodgepole forest with little undergrowth. For over a mile the trail climbs upward through the dark forest. At about 2.5 miles you'll reach an opening in the forest where the trail begins to level out for a little while, giving you a bit of a reprieve. (#4) Over the next half a mile the forest begins to change. The canopy becomes less dense, allowing more light to penetrate to the forest floor, resulting in more undergrowth.

At 3.6 miles you'll come across a beautiful old tree on the side of the trail that shows signs of the fires that have passed through here over the years. Soon after this tree the trail briefly levels out and winds through the open forest. You'll begin to get more and more glimpses of the mountains beyond. From this point onward snow will sometimes remain until late June.

Soon the trail will begin to descend fairly steeply, with a gorgeous view of Ypsilon towering above. (#5) A little ways down the hill you'll reach Chipmunk Lake on your right side. (#6) It is just a small pond but provides some of the best views of the hike, looking up at the towering Ypsilon Mountain and out toward Fairchild Mountain. Although you are not far from your destination, take a moment to savor the view. It is actually better here than at the destination.

From Chipmunk Lake the trail descends, then climbs and then steeply descends to Ypsilon Lake. You'll arrive at this forested lake right on the edge of tree line. (#7) It is a very peaceful place far from the crowds, where you can sit and meditate on the things that truly matter. For a better view, make your way along the southern shore to the far end of the lake where you can sit on the rocks and see Ypsilon Mountain looking down from above.

54 – OUZEL LAKE

Overview

Ouzel Lake is an especially peaceful place where you can sit and enjoy views of Ouzel Peak and Copeland Mountain towering high above this grass-lined lake. The hike up here brings you along rushing streams, past Calypso Cascades and Ouzel Falls, and then through a former fire zone, which is springing back to life.

The Stats

Distance Round Trip: 10.0 miles

Difficulty Level: 207

Hiking Time: 6 hours and 40 minutes

Time to Go: morning

Season: June through October

Primary Ecosystem: montane

Views: streams, forests, cascades, waterfall, mountain lake

Possible Wildlife: forest animals and moose

Trail Conditions: average

Reminder: Don't be in the open burn area if storms are threatening. Also, keep your eyes open in the burn area, as this is moose territory, particularly as you get closer to the lake.

Elevation Start: 8,500'

Highest Point: 10,025'

Total Elevation Gain: 2,141'

Trailhead: This hike begins at the Wild Basin Trailhead; see page 130 for details.

Waypoints

1. Wild Basin Trailhead	0.0	8,500'
2. Calypso Cascades	1.8	9,139'
3. Ouzel Falls	2.7	9,382'
4. Left at Bluebird Lake junction	3.1	9,403'
5. Ouzel Lake junction	4.5	9,978'
6. Ouzel Lake	5.0	10,025'

STRENUOUS HIKES

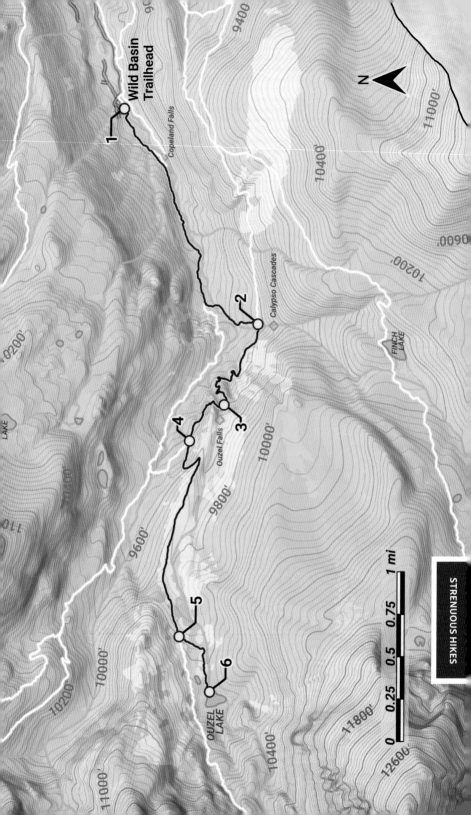

Wild Basin
Trailhead

Copeland Falls

Calypso Cascades

FINCH
LAKE

LAKE

Ouzel Falls

OUZEL
LAKE

N

9400'

9600'

9800'

10000'

10200'

10400'

10600'

10800'

11000'

11800'

12600'

1
2
3
4
5
6

STRENUOUS HIKES

0   0.25   0.5   0.75   1 mi

The first portion of this hike is up to Calypso Cascades. (#2) This is described in detail on page 222. You can then follow the Ouzel Falls hike on page 258. In summary, follow the Wild Basin Trail through deep woods along the edge of the North Saint Vrain Creek. This is a popular hike and tends to be quite busy. From here continue on the trail along a beautiful flat stretch through woods and meadow. In a short ways the trail will begin to climb up a series of switchbacks to Ouzel Falls. (#3)

From Ouzel Falls, head across the bridge. The trail will turn to the east and head up to a point where there is a large rock slab and overlook. Here you can get a glimpse over the Wild Basin valley. The trail then takes a sharp left and heads downhill. After a couple of switchbacks it winds its way through some very large boulders, then hugs the side of a large rock wall on your left. This section is generally cool and moist. You'll probably even find moss growing here. The trail continues on relatively gently through the forest. At about three miles it intersects with the Bluebird Lake Trail. (#4) You'll need to pay attention on the left side of the trail, as it could be easy to miss. At the intersection you'll turn left and follow it uphill.

From the intersection you'll climb quite steeply to the west and then it will take a sharp turn to the south. It then becomes a little less steep and by the time you take the next sharp turn to the right, the trail gives you a momentary break. From here you can look out across Wild Basin and get some great views of Longs Peak and Meeker to the south and Mount Alice to the west. Soon the trail begins to climb again quite steeply for another 0.2 miles.

This area is much more open than the forests you've hiked so far, since this was the scene of a large wildfire in 1978. The wildfire burned so hot that it sterilized the soil. As a result it took many years for life to return to this area, but now it is thriving again. It won't be long until the forest returns.

The trail becomes much gentler as it continues to head westward. As you look to the southwest you can see Ouzel Peak and Copeland Mountain, and straight ahead you'll see Mahana Peak. Be aware that this trail is quite sandy and very exposed. As a result it can get quite hot here on a sunny day, and if there are thunderstorms in the area it

OUZEL LAKE AND MAHANA PEAK AT SUNRISE

can be very dangerous to be here. But if the weather is nice, there are few better places to be.

Eventually the trail arrives at a junction with the Ouzel Lake Trail. (**#5**) Turn left here and the trail will first take you downhill over a rather rough section and across a small stream. You'll have to rock hop to get across. Some areas in this section could get muddy. The trail then winds back and forth and gently up and down, passing Chickadee Pond to the north, eventually coming alongside the outlet stream. This will take you up to the edge of Ouzel Lake. (**#6**) If you continue all the way on the trail it brings you farther along the northern shore of the lake to a place with a rock outcropping where you can sit and spend the rest of the day soaking in the peaceful silence of this beautiful place. The lake is lined with lush vegetation. To the south Copeland Mountain's spires add a sense of drama, and to the west Ouzel Peak keeps watch. You should keep your eyes open, too, as this is moose country and it is very possible you may see one or more in the lake or alongside the trail.

55 – CHASM LAKE

Overview

This is a spectacular hike up to a high mountain lake at the base of Longs Peak. The trail leads you through deep forest, out across open tundra, and into a dramatic valley with Longs Peak rising above you. You'll walk past waterfalls, through an alpine meadow, and then to a lake surrounded on three sides by imposing granite walls.

The Stats

Distance Round Trip: 8.5 miles

Difficulty Rating: 209

Hiking Time: 5 hours and 40 minutes

Time to Go: morning

Season: late June until first snow

Ecosystems: subalpine and alpine

Views: stunning views of the sheer east face of Longs Peak as well as views down over Colorado's Front Range

Possible Wildlife: forest animals during the first half and then you may see ptarmigan, pikas, and marmots above tree line

Trail Conditions: The trail is very much uphill. It's generally smooth for a Rocky trail until tree line and then you can expect a very rocky trail with large rock steps. The last section requires a bit of scrambling with hands and feet.

Reminder: The second half of this trail is completely exposed and so should not be hiked if there is a potential of thunderstorms. It is best hiked early in the morning. Carefully check weather conditions. If traveling in June or earlier, ask rangers about the safety of crossing the snowfield near Chasm Meadows.

Elevation Start: 9,400'

Highest Point: 11,806'

Total Elevation Gain: 2,566'

Trailhead: This hike begins at the Longs Peak Trailhead; see page 122 for details.

Waypoints

1. Longs Peak Trailhead	0.0	9,400'
2. Eugenia Mine junction	0.5	9,682'
3. Alpine Brook switchback	0.9	9,934'
4. Lightning Bridge	1.9	10,577'
5. Joe Mills Junction	2.5	10,947'
6. Left at Chasm Junction	3.3	11,533'
7. Chasm Meadows	3.8	11,530'
8. Chasm Lake	4.2	11,797'

Hike Description

The trail begins right beside the ranger station on the west side of the

STRENUOUS HIKES

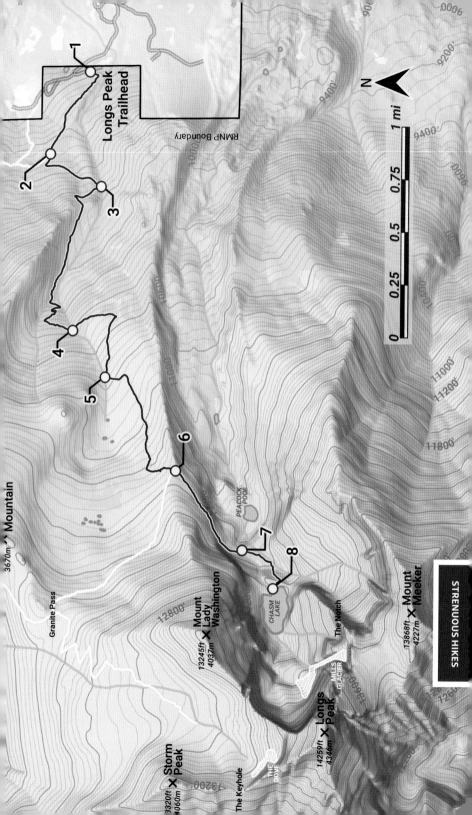

Longs Peak Trailhead

RMNP Boundary

N

3670m ✗ Mountain

Granite Pass

PEACOCK POOL

13245ft ✗ Mount Lady
4037m   Washington

CHASM LAKE

The Notch

13868ft ✗ Mount Meeker
4227m

MILLS GLACIER

Storm ✗ Peak
13320ft
4060m

The Keyhole

THE DOVE

14259ft ✗ Longs Peak
4346m

STRENUOUS HIKES

1
2
3
4
5
6
7
8

0   0.25   0.5   0.75   1 mi

parking lot. (**#1**) It climbs quite steeply through lodgepole forest, so it is best to begin this hike at a slow pace. At 0.5 miles you'll pass the intersection for the Eugenia Mine Trail. (**#2**) Continue straight and you'll soon take a sharp left turn. At 0.9 miles you'll reach a switchback that is right next to Alpine Brook. (**#3**) This is a pleasant place to stop and catch your breath. After one more switchback the trail will begin to level off somewhat in Goblins Forest. After a short break it slowly heads upward. In just over half a mile you'll begin to climb steeply again through several switchbacks. At 1.9 miles and nearly 1,200' of elevation gain you'll reach Lightning Bridge, named for the warning signs about the weather that are placed on both sides of the bridge. (**#4**) This is the last stop before reaching tree line. If it's a cold and windy day, consider stopping here in the relative shelter of the trees to put on your warmer clothes and windproof shell before continuing into the exposed tundra.

Just after the bridge, you begin the transition from forest to tundra. You'll begin to get views down toward the Front Range cities of Longmont and Boulder as well as glimpses of Longs Peak. This transition lasts for about 0.3 miles as you pass through fully-grown trees that have been stunted by the extreme weather. Many of them are hundreds of years old and have adapted to survive brutal winter conditions. When you reach the next junction, known as Joe Mills Junction, you're just leaving that transition zone. (**#5**) You'll want to turn left at the sign and begin your way up the carefully built rock stairs. Many feet have created new trails along this stretch, so try to walk on the official rock trail rather than the new dirt trails in order to give the vegetation a chance to come back. From here onward you'll be the tallest object around, so pay attention to the weather and head back down if storms are approaching.

At 3.3 miles and about 2,130' of elevation gain you reach Chasm

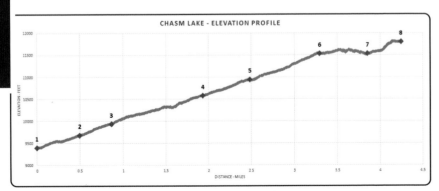

CHASM LAKE - ELEVATION PROFILE

LONGS PEAK FROM
CHASM JUNCTION · WAYPOINT #6

Junction. (#6) Here you'll find a place to tie up your horse and nearby you'll find one of the most scenic privies on the planet. This area also has one of the most spectacular views of Longs Peak. Even if this is as far as you go, this view itself is worth the climb. (To continue up to the Boulderfield and Longs Peak, turn to page 400.)

To continue to Chasm Lake, you'll head straight toward the imposing east face of Longs Peak along a narrow trail with a steep drop on your left side. As it gently descends, you can see Peacock Pool down below you and Columbine Falls pouring into the lake. There is one section along here at nearly 3.8 miles where snow tends to stay until mid- to late June. This is sometimes icy and dangerous to cross, so if in doubt do not attempt it. Assuming that the trail is clear you arrive at Chasm Meadows. (#7)

At Chasm Meadows you'll find a gentle stream flowing through lush green tundra grass. Be sure to stay on the trail to protect this idyllic place. Above you and to the right you'll see another waterfall coming out of the rocks from Chasm Lake. Follow the trail to the end of the meadow. You'll pass an intersection for another privy and then you'll reach the sign pointing you up the rocks to Chasm Lake. From here it is a bit of a scramble. The best way up follows the area of broken rock. Look for crushed rock and the wear of many feet. There is one point near the top where you will need to use your hands and climb up a short, steep section. Once you pass that, you'll be at the top admiring one of the most dramatic views you have probably ever seen, with the granite face of Longs Peak towering nearly 2,500 feet above you. (#8)

56 – ESTES CONE (from Lily Trailhead)

Overview

This hike is for those who are willing to put in the work to enjoy a stunning 360-degree view of Rocky Mountain National Park. Estes Cone is an outcropping on the side of Longs Peak, which feels like a mountain in its own right. It is a long, hard climb through the trees with a very rough scramble up the last 0.6 miles. A slightly easier version of this hike can be done by starting at the Longs Peak Trailhead, but this approach is quieter and provides a better workout.

The Stats

Distance Round Trip: 7.5 miles

Difficulty Level: 210* (188)

Hiking Time: 5 hours

Time to Go: morning

Season: May through October

Primary Ecosystems: montane to subalpine

Views: incredible views in every direction, including Longs Peak, Mummy Range, Continental Divide, the Front Range

Possible Wildlife: gray jays, ground squirrels, other forest animals

Trail Conditions: The trail up to Storm Pass is steep but in excellent shape, though rocky at times. The top section is more of a scramble than a hike, with loose sand and rock and over tree roots and boulders; this is not an easy hike.

Reminder: The last section of this hike is not for everyone. It is very steep and at times difficult to follow, requiring good route-finding skills and agility.

Elevation Start: 8,931'

Highest Point: 11,010'

Total Elevation Gain: 2,361'

Trailhead: This hike begins at the Lily Lake Trailhead; see 122 for details.

Waypoints

1. Lily Lake Trailhead	0.0	8,931'
2. Left on dirt road	0.2	8,953'
3. Right on Storm Pass Trail	0.2	8,961'
4. Bridge crossing	0.6	8,869'
5. Storm Pass	3.1	10,241'
6. Estes Cone summit	3.7	11,010'

Hike Description

This trail begins on the south end of the Lily Lake parking lot. (**#1**) Heading south, the trail follows a dirt road through a grove of

STRENUOUS HIKES

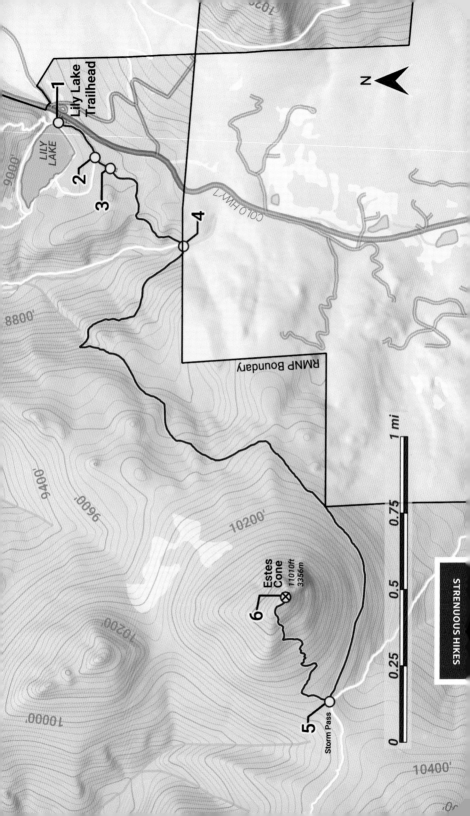

STRENUOUS HIKES

N

LILY LAKE

9000'

Lily Lake
Trailhead

1

2

3

4

COLO.HWY.7

RMNP Boundary

8800'

9400'

9600'

10200'

10200'

10000'

10400'

10200'

Estes Cone
11010ft
3356m

6

5

Storm Pass

0   0.25   0.5   0.75   1 mi

aspen. In 0.2 miles, leave the path and follow the dirt road around to the left. (**#2**) This leads to a national park maintenance area. Just before you get to this dumping area, take the small trail that heads off to the right. (**#3**) This is the Storm Pass Trail, which you will be following for the next several miles. Quickly the trail turns westward and heads into the trees. It then begins to descend. At the bottom you'll cross a big bridge to the other side of the valley. (**#4**)

The trail then begins its climb. It is a fairly wide and gentle trail that is mostly dirt. In about half a mile from the bridge, you'll pass through large boulders. Stop and notice the great views of Twin Sisters Peaks to the east. As you continue, you'll notice that this trail is very well designed with hundreds of carefully built steps created by trail crews over the years.

At about 2.5 miles the trail begins to work its way around the south end of Estes Cone on its way to Storm Pass. During this stretch you'll start to get occasional views on your left of Longs Peak and Mount Meeker. Soon the trail will become gentler and then it will begin its descent down to Storm Pass, which is simply an intersection in the forest at the top of a ridge. (**#5**) There are no views at Storm Pass itself.

Note: From here to the top of Estes Cone, the hike changes from an easy hike to something much more challenging. You'll have to really keep your eyes open, as the trail can be hard to find. Look for the most open path, the wear of many feet, rock piles guiding your way, and also notice logs and rocks that have been placed to help keep you on the trail. If you lose the trail, stop and look around before you take another step, or even go back to where you last saw it.

Begin by following the path in the direction of Estes Cone. It should be straight ahead and a bit to your right. The trail begins fairly

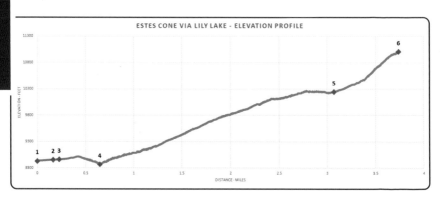

ESTES CONE VIA LILY LAKE - ELEVATION PROFILE

ESTES CONE FROM HIGHWAY 7

gently but in a few minutes turns into more of a scramble, getting steeper the farther up you get. The trail will also become quite sandy with loose rock. You'll be climbing over tree roots, between trees, and over large rocks. Take it slow. I find that the actual trail heads farther to the south (right) than I had expected.

As you approach the top you'll notice a lot of old twisted limber pine. Once you reach the top area, keep to the right and work your way around on the right-hand side until you get to the last major rock outcropping on your left. You'll see a way to scramble up fairly easily (see photo on page 329). It is definitely a scramble, though, and you'll need to use both hands to climb up. If you are afraid of heights you may want to skip this portion. At the top of that climb, you are only a few feet shy of the highest point. To reach the very highest point, continue down the other side and then climb up the next rock outcropping. This will bring you to the summit. (#6) Any of these rock outcroppings will provide you with jaw-dropping views in every direction. Be very careful descending the rock outcroppings and down again to Storm Pass. Be sure to take your time. Also, be sure to be well below the summit before thunderstorms arrive.

57 – FLATTOP MOUNTAIN

Overview

On this hike you'll get to experience the transition from forest to tundra and the accomplishment of climbing up to the top of the Continental Divide. Along this hike you'll have views that you'll never forget.

The Stats

Distance Round Trip: 8.5 miles

Difficulty Rating: 221

Hiking Time: 5 hours and 40 minutes

Time to Go: early morning to avoid afternoon storms

Season: mid-June until first snow

Primary Ecosystems: subalpine and alpine

Views: grand views over much of Rocky Mountain National Park and the Front Range

Possible Wildlife: forest animals, marmots, pikas, elk

Trail Conditions: In the forest it is a typical rocky trail, though not as rocky as many. Above tree line the trail is sandy and rocky with some larger steps.

Reminder: There is no water on this hike, so bring enough. It is also very exposed, so don't attempt if there is a chance of bad weather.

Elevation Start: 9,475'

Highest Point: 12,326'

Total Elevation Gain: 2,866'

Trailhead: This hike begins at the Bear Lake Trailhead; see page 110 for details.

Waypoints

1. Bear Lake Trailhead	0.0	9,475'
2. Right at Fern Lake Trail	0.1	9,486'
3. Left at Bierstadt Lake junction	0.5	9,701'
4. Left onto Flattop Trail	1.0	9,972'
5. Dream Lake Overlook	1.6	10,479'
6. Rest Rock	2.4	10,983'
7. Emerald Lake Overlook	2.9	11,348'
8. Horse tie-up	3.9	12,163'
9. Flattop summit	4.2	12,326'

Hike Description

Head past the ranger station toward Bear Lake. (**#1**) When you reach the junction with the lake trail, turn right and follow the trail

STRENUOUS HIKES

Bear Lake
Trailhead

BEAR
LAKE

Alberta Falls

DREAM
LAKE

LAKE
HAIYAHA

EMERALD
LAKE

LAKE
HELENE

11929ft × Notchtop
3636m   Mountain

12720ft × Hallett
3877m   Peak

Flattop
Mountain
12326ft
3757m

TYNDALL
GLACIER

0   0.25   0.5   0.75   1 mi

along the eastern shore. Before you reach the end of the lake, you'll come to a junction on your right with the Fern Lake Trail. (**#2**) Turn right here and follow the trail upward. It will lead through a boulder field with aspen trees and then up to the junction with the Bierstadt Lake Trail. (**#3**) Here you'll take a sharp left and continue upward. This section is one of the steepest you'll climb today, so take it slowly. It climbs for 0.2 miles before leveling out. Continue another 0.3 miles through the woods to the junction on the left with the Flattop Mountain Trail. (**#4**) Here you'll turn left. There are no more junctions between here and the top of the mountain.

This next section climbs through thick forest. It begins with two sharp turns and then there are two switchbacks. After the second switchback the trail climbs in a southerly direction for about 0.3 miles before arriving at the Dream Lake Overlook. (**#5**) Here you can look down and see part of Dream Lake. In the distance Longs Peak stands impressively and if you look closely you may be able to see Mills Lake below it.

As you follow the trail back into the forest you may notice that it is changing as you climb higher, with a lot more sunlight penetrating the forest floor. The trail will head north for a while and then begin a series of switchbacks. By the fourth switchback you'll notice the trees becoming a bit smaller, and then the sixth switchback is your final one. If you hear the wind howling through the tops of the trees, this might be a good time to put on some additional layers before you come out of the trees. As you head up this final stretch, you'll notice somewhat in the distance directly up in front of you that one tree stands higher than the others. Up there is a spot I call "Rest Rock." (**#6**) It is just above the trees and provides fantastic views in all directions.

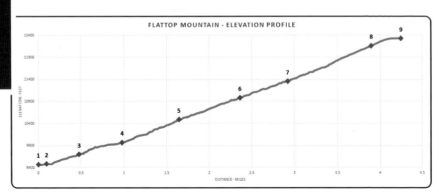

FLATTOP MOUNTAIN - ELEVATION PROFILE

SUNRISE FROM NEAR FLATTOP SUMMIT

From here onward you will be above the trees, so if you see any potential bad weather moving in, be sure to head back down. At first you'll pass through sections of ancient krumholz and then you'll be fully exposed. The trail here is sandy and rocky with a number of large steps. As it climbs you'll encounter six sharp turns, most of them are actual switchbacks. This brings you to another set of five very short switchbacks that are quickly climbed. You'll then be at the Emerald Lake Overlook. (#7) This is a good place to stop, enjoy the view, and catch your breath.

From here the trail heads directly north and then wraps around the north side of Flattop Mountain. Along this stretch keep your eyes and ears open for marmots and pikas, as they are usually quite active here. Once the trail makes that turn around to the north side of the mountain, it begins to feel rugged and dramatic, as you are in a very rocky area with views out toward Notchtop and Stones Peak. Eventually it turns less rocky and there is more vegetation. After two more switchbacks, you'll take a long stretch up to the horse tie-up. (#8) From here the trail often crosses a large snowbank. Look for the historic rock cairns higher up to help find the trail again. That section of trail soon becomes almost level as it makes its final gentle approach to the meadow summit of Flattop Mountain. The only way you'll know you've reached the summit is when you reach the sign.(#9)

STRENUOUS HIKES

VIEW FROM REST ROCK · WAYPOINT #6

58 – TIMBER LAKE

Overview

This hike leads you from the Kawuneeche Valley up through deep forests for nearly five miles. You then emerge into delightful mountain meadows that lead you to Timber Lake, which quietly sits at the final transition from forest to tundra.

The Stats

Distance Round Trip: 9.9 miles

Difficulty Rating: 221

Hiking Time: 6 hours and 35 minutes

Time to Go: anytime

Season: mid-June until first snow

Primary Ecosystem: subalpine

Views: deep forest, cascading streams, mountain meadows, and then an alpine lake

Possible Wildlife: forest animals and moose

Trail Conditions: The majority of the trail is well maintained and relatively smooth, though a landslide has made a challenging scramble necessary until the hill can be stabilized and the trail fixed.

Reminder: Check with a ranger for current trail conditions before attempting this hike due to the impact of the landslide.

Elevation Start: 9,054'

Highest Point: 11,091'

Total Elevation Gain: 2,475'

Trailhead: This hike begins at the Timber Lake Trailhead; see page 127 for details.

Waypoints

1. Timber Lake Trailhead	0.0	9,054'
2. Beaver Creek crossing	0.6	9,103'
3. Trail veers east	1.4	9,537'
4. Landslide area	2.4	10,033'
5. Long Meadow Trail junction	3.3	10,200'
6. Enter the meadow	4.2	10,788'
7. Timber Lake	5.0	11,088'

STRENUOUS HIKES

Hike Description

The trail begins by heading east into a small aspen grove and then through a small meadow before turning south. (**#1**) It gently winds through a pine forest, smoothly undulating for about 0.6 miles until it reaches Beaver Creek. (**#2**) I could be perfectly content enjoying

N

TIMBER LAKE

7

11693ft × Jackstraw
3564m   Mountain

6

5

4

2

3

1

Timber Lake
Trailhead

TRAIL RIDGE ROAD (US HWY 34)

STRENUOUS HIKES

0   0.25   0.5   0.75   1 mi

just this section of trail, as it is so peaceful. The trail soon crosses a log bridge over this cascading stream and then begins to climb quite steeply as it continues southward along the edge of the Kawuneeche Valley. As you hike through the forest, one of the things you may notice is the abundant green undergrowth, something you won't see on the east side of the park. Here on the west side it is much more lush, which almost gives the trail a feeling of being in the Pacific Northwest. At about two miles the trail begins to briefly level out as it turns to the east and makes its way toward the Timber Creek Valley. (**#3**) At this point you have already gained about 500' of elevation.

At just under two and a half miles the trail crosses a small stream. It is a delightful place to sit and have a snack in the cool shade of the trees. Here it is deeply forested with lots of moss on the trees and undergrowth. Just a few hundred feet farther on you reach the site of a large landslide. (**#4**) At the time of writing, the National Park Service is assessing the stability of this area to determine whether to build a bypass trail or rebuild the existing trail. Check with a ranger for current trail conditions before attempting this hike.

After the slide, the trail resumes as if nothing happened and continues quietly until it crosses another small stream at around three miles. Just a short while later the trail finally comes alongside Timber Creek. It is a small gently-flowing stream that gurgles and babbles in this verdant valley. Then the trail reaches a junction with the Long Meadows Trail. (**#5**) Please note that this trail is not recommended, as it disappears into a marsh except on the driest of years.

Soon a beautiful meadow opens up on the right side, surrounded by deep forest in every direction. (**#6**) On some days you might be lucky enough to encounter a moose or elk grazing in the meadow

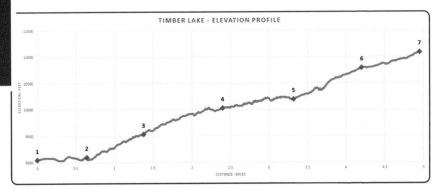

TIMBER LAKE - ELEVATION PROFILE

or wandering through the edge of the forest. The meadows ahead are dotted with small pine trees and from here you can now see the rolling tundra just beyond the trees in front of you. This section of trail is simply delightful.

Eventually the trail reaches Timber Lake, which lies in a bowl surrounded by high ridges on three sides. (#7) Here you can sit by the edge of the water while the sound of a gurgling stream and the scent of alpine grass and wildflowers fill the air.

STRENUOUS HIKES

NEARING TIMBER LAKE - WAYPOINT #6

59 – MIRROR LAKE

Overview

Hike to a beautiful remote lake surrounded by towering peaks. On the way, cross numerous streams, walk through meadows, and hike through gorgeous open forest. This hike is on the very northern border of Rocky Mountain National Park and is only accessed by a three-hour drive to the trailhead.

The Stats

Distance Round Trip: 12.5 miles

Difficulty Rating: 228

Hiking Time: 8 hours and 20 minutes

Time to Go: anytime

Season: June through October

Primary Ecosystem: subalpine

Views: rushing streams, open forests, large meadows, alpine lake

Possible Wildlife: moose, deer, marmots, forest animals

Trail Conditions: better than most trails but rough at the end

Reminder: There are numerous sections of this trail that are through moose terrain, so keep your eyes open.

Elevation Start: 10,034'

Highest Point: 11,033'

Total Elevation Gain: 2,071'

Trailhead: This hike begins at the Corral Creek Trailhead; see page 113 for details.

Waypoints

1. Corral Creek Trailhead	0.0	10,034'
2. Enter Comanche Peak Wilderness	0.4	9,946'
3. Bridge into RMNP	1.3	9,678'
4. Left onto Mummy Pass Trail	1.8	9,713'
5. Begin climb	2.4	9,894'
6. Top of climb	4.3	10,730'
7. Left onto Mirror Lake Trail	4.8	10,713'
8. Comanche Peak Trail junction	5.4	10,683'
9. Mirror Lake	6.3	11,028'

Hike Description

This hike begins outside of Rocky Mountain National Park in Roosevelt National Forest. (**#1**) The trail departs the Corral Creek Trailhead and gently heads downhill. It then levels out and heads

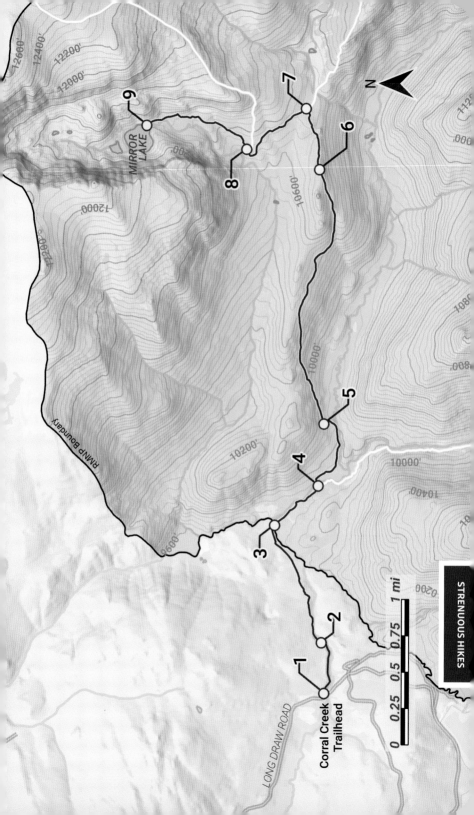

N

MIRROR LAKE

RMNP Boundary

12600'
12400'
12200'
12000'
12200'
12000'
12000'
12200'
10600'
10000'
10600'
10200'
10000'
10400'
10000'
10200'

LONG DRAW ROAD

Corral Creek Trailhead

9
8
7
6
5
4
3
2
1

STRENUOUS HIKES

0   0.25   0.5   0.75   1 mi

through a forest before continuing its descent. You'll cross a section of the Comanche Peak Wilderness (**#2**), and despite one small climb the trail will continue to descend. It descends a total of nearly four hundred feet before leveling out. Remember to save energy for the climb on your return. After it levels out you'll pass one small intersection on your left; keep to the right here. In just a short ways you'll cross a bridge over the roaring La Poudre Pass Creek coming out of Long Draw Reservoir. (**#3**) As you cross the creek, you'll enter Rocky Mountain National Park.

After entering the park, the trail is very gentle and quickly comes alongside the Cache la Poudre River. In just half a mile you'll reach a junction where you'll turn left. (**#4**) The trail straight ahead follows the river all the way back to Poudre Lake on Trail Ridge Road, but this trail is often too wet to travel and the trail is not maintained. Turn left here onto the Mummy Pass Trail. Almost immediately the trail crosses the Cache la Poudre. It follows the stream for a short ways until it comes alongside Hague Creek, which it then follows. After climbing two sets of wooden stairs, the trail comes briefly alongside a large willow-filled meadow. Take a moment to walk to the edge of this large meadow. (**#5**) From here the trail begins its steepest climb, climbing over 550 feet before giving you a break. Once it does level out, take a break and enjoy the very open forest. As the beetle kill has hit this area hard, the sunlight now penetrates the forest floor, allowing the ground cover to thrive. This makes for an absolutely delightful trail. After about half a mile of gentle walking the trail again climbs quite steeply for another 300' of elevation gain. (**#6**) The trail then arrives at a junction in the woods. (**#7**) Turn left

MIRROR LAKE - ELEVATION PROFILE

here, but before you do, take a moment to follow the other trail into the meadow and have a look up toward Mummy Pass.

Turn left at the intersection and you'll now be on the Mirror Lake Trail, which winds through the woods as if it has gotten lost, slowly dropping a bit of elevation. You then reach a meadow, and the views begin to open up. In just a minute you'll reach the junction with the Comanche Peak Trail, which heads off to the right. (#8) Continue straight ahead. Soon you'll have a glimpse of where you're going before heading into the woods.

This next section of trail is at times a little steep and can be somewhat rough with tree roots, rocks, and mud, but don't give up. As you get past the campsites (wilderness camping permit required) and closer to the lake, the forest opens up as the land begins its transition to tundra. The trail makes its final climb up the rocks, and you find yourself standing at the edge of Mirror Lake right beside the outlet stream. (#9) You'll notice that this lake is surrounded by high mountains, with the highest one towering over the lake on its west side. Unfortunately, this peak remains unnamed. Once you get here you're going to want to stay awhile to soak in the views and enjoy the sound of the rushing water beginning its downward journey.

STRENUOUS HIKES

SUMMER AT MIRROR LAKE

60 – LUMPY LOOP

Overview

This is a long loop trail along the eastern edge of Rocky Mountain National Park that circles an area of unusual rock formations known as Lumpy Ridge. Enjoy a spectacular view of the Estes Valley as well as intimate forest, stream, and meadow scenes along this ten-mile loop.

The Stats

Distance: 10.7 miles

Difficulty Rating: 236

Hiking Time: 7 hours and 5 minutes

Time to Go: anytime

Season: May to November

Primary Ecosystem: montane

Views: meadows, forests, views of Longs Peak and the Estes Valley

Possible Wildlife: elk, mule deer, gray jays, ground squirrels

Trail Conditions: Most of the trail is excellent. There are some large steps on the way up to Gem Lake and a short area of steep terrain with loose rocks on the way down from the Balanced Rock junction to Cow Creek.

Reminder: This is a long hike, so bring plenty of food, water, and a way to filter additional water. This trail can get very hot in the summer, as there are long stretches without shade. Fill up at Cow Creek.

Elevation Start: 7,840'

Highest Point: 9,122'

Total Elevation Gain: 2,604'

Trailhead: This hike begins at the Lumpy Ridge Trailhead; see page 123 for details.

Waypoints

1. Lumpy Ridge Trailhead	0.0	7,840'
2. Right at junction	0.5	8,174'
3. Gem Lake	1.7	8,844'
4. Balanced Rock junction	2.8	8,628'
5. Left onto Cow Creek Trail	4.4	8,071'
6. Left at Bridal Veil junction	5.2	8,266'
7. Left onto Black Canyon Trail	6.8	9,023'
8. Sundance Climbers Access	8.1	8,210'
9. MacGregor Ranch fence	8.6	8,210'
10. Right at Twin Owls junction	9.8	7,894'

Hike Description

This is a loop hike that begins and ends at the Lumpy Ridge

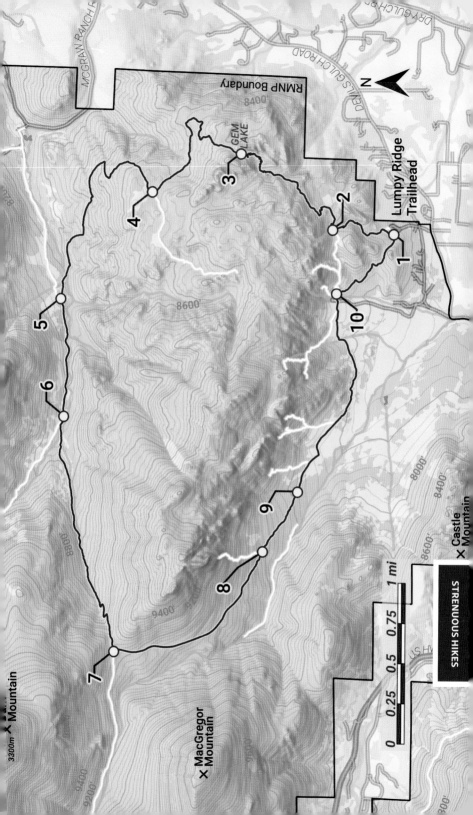

Trailhead. (#1) It can be done in either direction, but for the purpose of this book you're going to do it counterclockwise, as this seems to be the easier way to do it. The first portion of the hike leads up to Gem Lake (#3) and is described in detail on page 242. The trail continues down to the junction with the Balanced Rock Trail, which is explained in detail beginning on page 310. In summary, from the trailhead (#1)turn right and follow the well-marked trail up to Gem Lake. (#3) Pass by the lake on its western side and you'll find the trail again on the back end of the lake. Follow this winding trail down through the forest until you reach the Balanced Rock Trail junction. (#4)

After reaching the Balanced Rock Trail junction, continue straight ahead, heading northeast. This section is quite flat with widely spaced trees. It reminds me of a delightful park. In a few minutes it all changes as the trail heads steeply downward with a number of short switchbacks and loose rock. Hiking poles and good boots would help here. You'll notice as you descend that the forest becomes much denser as it transitions from ponderosa pine to Douglas fir. Eventually the trail reaches the bottom where there is a small log bridge crossing Cow Creek. This is a good place to filter additional water and enjoy a break in the shade before continuing on. As soon as you leave the bridge, you emerge from the forest into the meadow and bright sunlight. In just a minute you'll intersect with the Cow Creek Trail. Here you'll turn left and head westward. (#5)

This section of trail is relatively gentle as it heads through a beautiful meadow with scattered aspen trees. Watch for wildflowers and all sorts of birds enjoying this sanctuary. In 0.8 miles you'll reach the Bridal Veil Falls junction. (#6) If you have time, take the one-mile detour (two miles round trip) up to the falls to admire their beauty. Once you return to this junction, take the lesser-traveled left fork down and across the stream. This trail is called the Dark Mountain Trail and this stream is the last you'll cross, so if you don't have full water bottles, be sure to filter water here before continuing onward.

This trail then begins to climb through the meadows. As you go along, the valley gets narrower until eventually you reenter the very dark forest at around six miles. It then climbs quite steeply, nearly 500' in elevation gain, with four switchbacks. This section of trail is the first to get covered in snow and the last to melt. Eventually you'll reach the saddle, the highest point of this hike. From here the trail will descend and in a minute you'll reach the junction with the Black Canyon Trail. (**#7**) Be sure to turn left here, heading downhill and to the south, as the other direction will lead you six miles up to Lawn

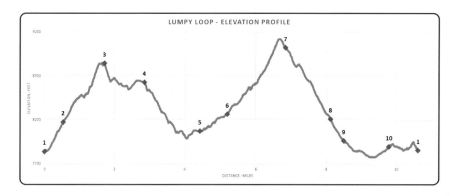

Lake, which is probably farther than you want to go today. The Black Canyon Trail will descend quite steeply at times through the thick forest. As you head downward you may get occasional glimpses of the Sundance Buttress high above you to your left, a major climbing area in Lumpy Ridge. At about eight miles you'll cross the remains of a landslide that occurred during the 2013 flood and shortly after that you'll pass the climbers access trail to Sundance, which means you are nearly at the bottom. (**#8**) In half a mile you'll reach the fence that marks the border of MacGregor Ranch. (**#9**) The fence will be secured with a chain but you can remove it to let yourself through; just remember to secure the chain again before you leave, as they have cattle roaming on their property. From here the forest begins to open up into meadow, and the trail becomes quite gentle. The trail winds through the open meadows of MacGregor Ranch with great views of Longs Peak and the Estes Valley. You'll then reenter the forest (**#10**) and make one last climb before arriving back at the trailhead. (The section from the fence to the trailhead is described in detail under the Black Canyon hike found on page 230.)

LUMPY RIDGE BETWEEN WAYPOINTS #9 & #10

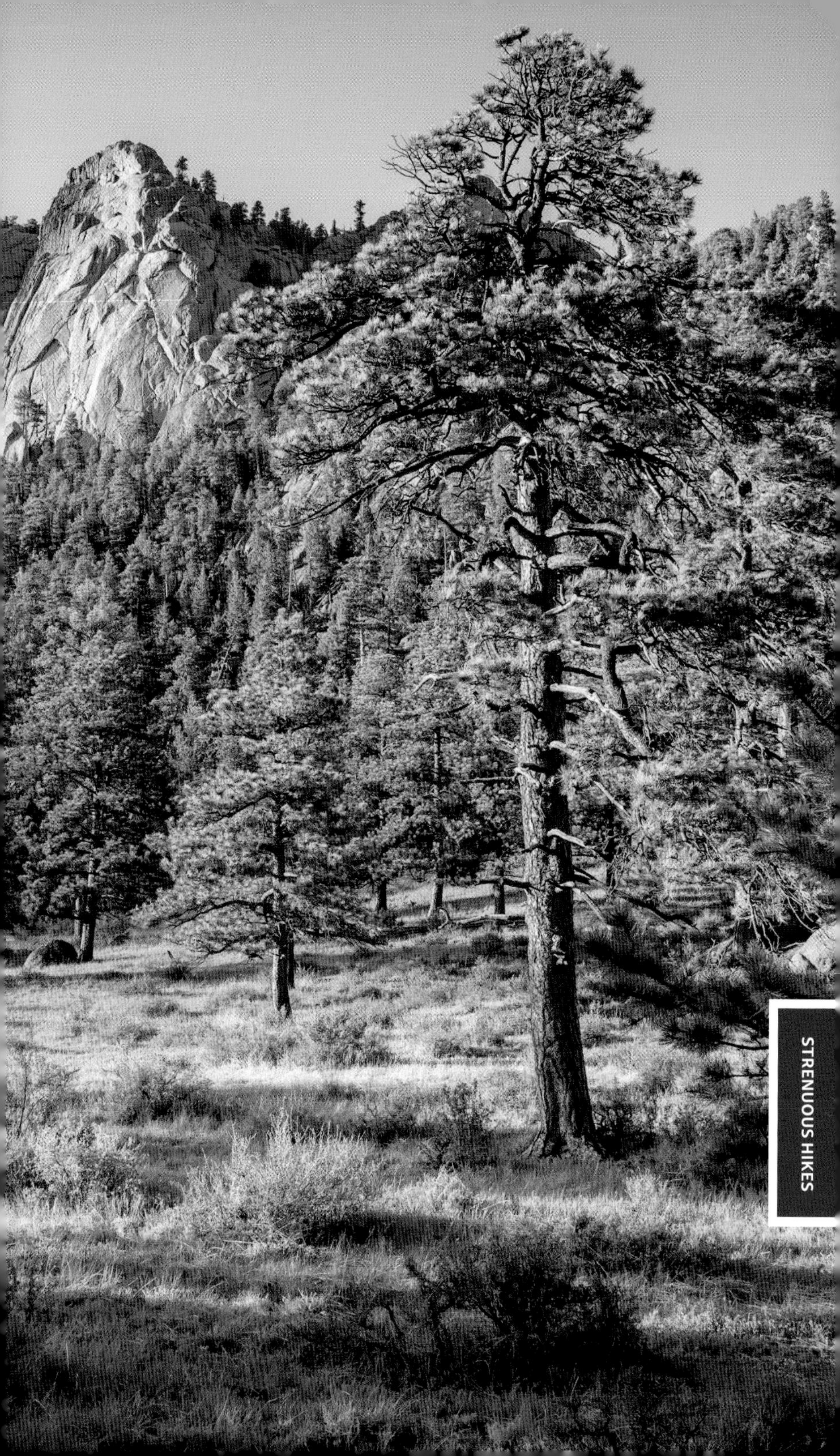

61 – LAKE VERNA

Overview

This is a long hike through dense forest to a quiet and beautiful lake with a dramatic backdrop. Along the way you'll visit Adams Falls, pass through East Meadow, walk through deep forest accompanied by the East Inlet stream, and stop at little Lone Pine Lake.

The Stats

Distance Round Trip: 13.1 miles

Difficulty: 244

Hiking Time: 8 hours and 45 minutes

Time to Go: morning

Season: mid-June to first snow

Primary Ecosystems: montane and subalpine

Views: Early on you get great views of Mount Baldy from East Meadow. You'll then have a great view looking over Grand Lake. You'll see cascades, streams, forest, and it all culminates in the dramatic views at Lake Verna.

Possible Wildlife: moose, deer, forest animals

Trail Conditions: The first two miles of this trail are fairly gentle and then it climbs quite steeply, some areas with steep drop-offs. The trail is well marked and easy to follow.

Reminder: Be aware that moose frequent the area all along this trail but especially the first couple of miles. This is a long hike; you will need to give yourself plenty of time and bring adequate food and a way to filter water.

Elevation Start: 8,400'

Highest Point: 10,266'

Total Elevation Gain: 2,259'

Trailhead: This hike begins at the East Inlet Trailhead; see page 116 for details.

Waypoints

1. East Inlet Trailhead	0.0	8,400'
2. Adams Falls	0.3	8,426'
3. East Meadow overlook	1.3	8,575'
4. Grand Lake overlook	3.0	9,167'
5. Water access	3.4	9,120'
6. Bridge over East Inlet	4.1	9,367'
7. Lone Pine Lake	5.0	9,844'
8. Lake Verna	6.6	10,227'

Hike Description

The first portion of this hike leads to Adams Falls and East

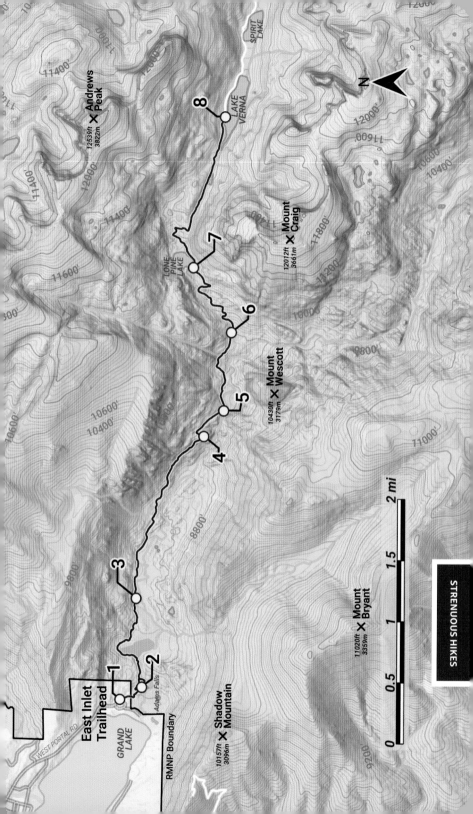

STRENUOUS HIKES

2 mi

1.5

1

0.5

0

11020ft × Mount
3359m   Bryant

10157ft × Shadow
3096m   Mountain

East Inlet
Trailhead

GRAND
LAKE

WEST PORTAL RD.

RMNP Boundary

Adams Falls

1
2

3

4

5

6

7

8

LAKE
VERNA

SPIRIT
LAKE

LONE PINE LAKE

10430ft × Mount
3179m   Wescott

12012ft × Mount
3661m   Craig

12539ft × Andrews
3822m   Peak

N

Meadow. This section is described in detail on page 175. It then continues to Lone Pine Lake, detailed on page 338. In summary, the hike begins at the East Inlet Trailhead (**#1**), heads up to East Meadow via Adams Falls (**#2**), and heads around the north end of the meadow. At the end of the meadow the trail climbs quite steeply for about a mile. It then becomes a little gentler for just under a mile as it follows the East Inlet stream closely through dense forest. The trail then climbs more steeply for the last mile up to Lone Pine Lake. (**#7**)

From Lone Pine, the trail continues along the southern edge of the lake. There can sometimes be snow along this section until sometime in late June; alternatively, it could be quite muddy from the recently melted snow, so come prepared. At the far end of the lake, the trail reaches a boulder field. Here the trail crosses the East Inlet, which crashes through here quite violently. The trail then heads into the woods and begins its third and final climb. You'll pass several very attractive cascades as the trail switchbacks upward, crossing one small stream a couple of times. You'll then reach a section where the trail hugs the side of a steep rock face as it continues upward. Right near the top of this stretch you'll find a large granite slab where you can rest and enjoy a great overlook of Lone Pine Lake.

The trail levels out and you'll enjoy a gentle walk looking down on the East Inlet, which is now moving at a much slower pace. In some areas the stream has been dammed by fallen rock, creating large pools. This stretch of trail is often overflowing with a variety of wildflowers between late June and early August. As you head eastward you'll start to get a glimpse of the Continental Divide in the distance.

When the trail reaches a short but very steep climb, you know you're nearly there. Just after the trail descends from that climb, you'll see the

LAKE VERNA - ELEVATION PROFILE

westernmost section of Lake Verna. It is very narrow at this point, but if you look up the lake from here you'll see it is quite long, stretching about 0.6 miles. Continue just a short ways farther down the trail and you'll arrive at your destination. (**#8**) There are a number of rock outcrops that look out on the lake where you can drink in the view. At the far end of the lake you'll see the Continental Divide. If you are like me, once you get to this beautiful and peaceful place you won't want to leave.

STRENUOUS HIKES

SUNRISE AT LAKE VERNA

62 – PEAR LAKE

Overview

Head up into the deep forest of Wild Basin and experience the silence of the wilderness. This trail passes through a large burn area before descending to beautiful Finch Lake tucked into the trees. It then climbs up to near tree line where Pear Lake lies surrounded by rugged peaks.

The Stats

Distance Round Trip: 12.5 miles

Difficulty: 259

Hiking Time: 8 hours and 20 minutes

Time to Go: morning departure

Season: mid-June until first snow

Primary Ecosystems: montane and subalpine

Views: mountain lake with towering peaks, deep forest, small streams, views across to Longs Peak

Possible Wildlife: dusky grouse, gray jays, Abert squirrels, moose

Trail Conditions: well maintained and easy to follow, though some sections are very rocky

Reminder: This is a long hike, so bring plenty of food, water, and a way to filter additional water.

Elevation Start: 8,470'

Highest Point: 10,605'

Total Elevation Gain: 2,690'

Trailhead: This hike begins at the Finch Lake Trailhead; see page 118 for details.

Waypoints

1. Finch Lake Trailhead	0.0	8,470'
2. Confusion Junction	2.3	9,610'
3. Enter burn area	2.5	9,763'
4. Finch Lake	4.3	9,925'
5. Cony Creek bridge	4.5	9,902'
6. Small pond	5.5	10,249'
7. Pear Lake	6.3	10,594'

Hike Description

The first portion of this hike is described in detail on the Finch Lake hike, page 330. In summary, follow the Finch Lake Trail for 2.3 miles to the main intersection, known as Confusion Junction, continue straight up hill. (#2) You'll climb up through an old burn area, with great views to the south. (#3) The trail returns to the forest, continuing to climb upward. At about 3.9 miles you'll descend steeply to Finch Lake. (#4)

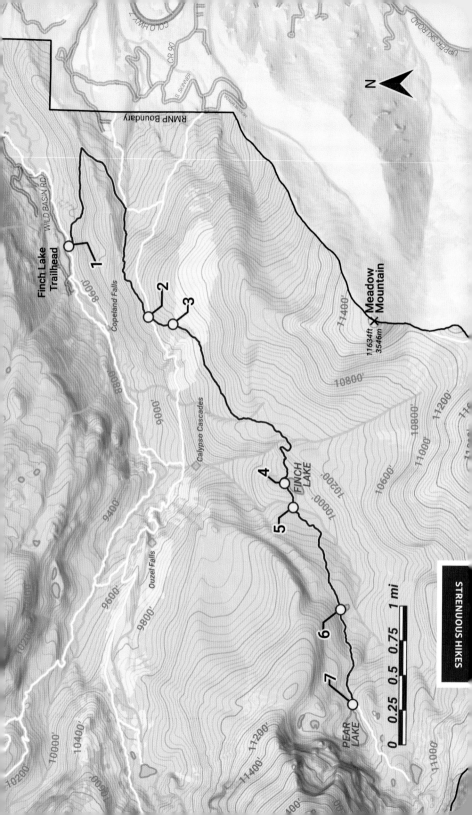

N

COLO. HWY.

UPPER SKI ROAD

CR 90

S. SKINNER

RMNP Boundary

Finch Lake
Trailhead

WILD BASIN RD.

9600'

Copeland Falls

1

2

3

Calypso Cascades

9000'

9800'

9600'

Ouzel Falls

9400'

9600'

10000'

10200'

10200'

Meadow
Mountain
11634ft
3546m

10800'

11400'

11200'

11000'

10800'

10600'

10400'

11000'

4

FINCH
LAKE

10000'

10200'

5

6

7

PEAR
LAKE

11200'

11400'

11000'

11400'

STRENUOUS HIKES

0   0.25   0.5   0.75   1 mi

At the sign for Finch Lake turn right. The trail continues along the north side of the lake. The trail here is level and provides some nice views of the lake through the trees. You'll pass by a few trails on your right leading to campsites. Stay to your left and you'll remain on the main trail. After it passes the end of the lake, the trail heads into the forest.

It soon crosses a bridge over Cony Creek and ascends upward through the forest. (**#5**) About half a mile later the trail climbs very steeply up the side of a hill. This is the steepest climb of the entire hike. Fortunately there are no more big climbs after this one.

At about five and a half miles there is a small pond on the south side that looks like ideal moose habitat. (**#6**) Keep your eyes open! It is possible that you could encounter them anywhere in this area and you'll want to give moose a very wide berth.

Soon the landscape begins to open up on your left side (south), providing views out toward Saint Vrain and Meadow mountains. Then you'll cross another stream coming out of Pear Lake. At this point you are nearly there. During the last stretch the trees begin to thin out and the terrain begins to look more alpine. There is a sense of release as the thick forest gives way to more open sky. During the summer this meadow is often filled with wildflowers.

Finally the trail leads you through a narrow gap in a group of trees, and as you come through the other side, Pear Lake appears before you. This large alpine lake lies just down the hill from where you are standing. (**#7**) It is surrounded by Ogallala Peak and Copeland Mountain, which tower above it. From here follow the sandy path down to the edge of the lake and find a rock to sit on as you soak in the dramatic beauty of this special place.

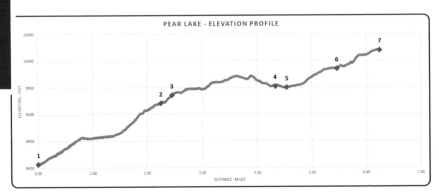

PEAR LAKE - ELEVATION PROFILE

COPELAND MOUNTAIN OVER PEAR LAKE

63 – LA POUDRE PASS

Overview

Follow the Colorado River back to its starting point at La Poudre Pass. Along the way, travel by the remains of old mining settlements, watch for moose, bighorn sheep, and other wildlife and travel through a section of the park known as Little Yellowstone for its geology.

The Stats

Distance Round Trip: 14.5 miles

Difficulty Rating: 264

Hiking Time: 9 hours and 40 minutes

Time to Go: morning

Season: late June through October

Primary Ecosystem: subalpine

Views: forest views with occasional views of the river, open meadows, grand vistas, marshes

Possible Wildlife: pikas, marmots, deer, bighorn sheep, moose

Trail Conditions: Begins wide and smooth but becomes rougher though easy to follow. There are about three miles on a dirt road.

Reminder: You'll be in exposed terrain from the Grand Ditch onward, so plan to complete this before storms arrive.

Elevation Start: 9,010'

Highest Point: 10,194'

Total Elevation Gain: 2,410'

Trailhead: This hike begins at the Colorado River Trailhead; see page 112 for details.

Waypoints

1. Colorado River Trailhead	0.0	9,010'
2. Shipler Cabins	2.1	9,247'
3. Left at junction	3.3	9,457'
4. Lulu City	3.5	9,363'
5. Straight to Little Yellowstone	3.8	9,402'
6. Left on Colorado River Trail	3.9	9,410'
7. Right on Yellowstone Trail junction	4.2	9,552'
8. Yellowstone waterfall	5.1	9,834'
9. Right onto Grand Ditch	6.0	10,185'
10. La Poudre Pass Ranger Station	7.0	10,188'
11. Colorado River – official source	7.3	10,184'

Hike Description

The first half of this hike is described in detail in the section on Lulu City (page 280). In summary, follow the Colorado River Trail

12027ft
3666m ✕ **Thunder Mountain**

11683ft
3561m ✕ **Mount Neota**

12201ft
3719m ✕ **Lulu Mountain**

LONG DRAW ROAD

10

11

9

8

7

5

6

4

3

12460ft
3798m ✕ **Specimen Mountain**

2

PINNACLE POOL

POUDRE LAKE

10909ft
3325m ✕ **Sheep Rock**

LAKE IRENE

TRAIL RIDGE ROAD (US HWY 34)

STRENUOUS HIKES

1

Colorado River Trailhead

ft
n ✕ **Red Mountain**

| 0 | 0.5 | 1 | 1.5 | 2 mi |

N

11693ft
3564m ✕ **Jackstraw Mountain**

along the eastern edge of the Colorado River as it leads primarily through deep forest with the occasional meadow. The trail is quite clear and easy to follow. At 3.3 miles you'll reach a junction (#3); turn left and head downhill to arrive at Lulu City. (#4)

From Lulu City continue on the trail heading north through the meadow. As you walk through the last of the meadow, you can see the scar of the Grand Ditch on the hills in front of you; that's where you're headed. Shortly after you climb out of the meadow, you'll reach a sign that says Thunder Pass to the left and Little Yellowstone straight ahead. (#5) Actually, you could go either way, as they join up again, but for simplicity's sake, head straight ahead. In just a couple of minutes you'll reach another intersection with the main Colorado River Trail; turn left here. (#6) Soon you'll cross a bridge over the Colorado River. As you cross, notice all the debris both above and below you, which is the result of a breach in the Grand Ditch in 2003. The NPS is working to restore some of the damage. In just 0.2 miles you'll reach another intersection; this is the one I mentioned you would reconnect with. (#7) You will want to turn right and cross over Lulu Creek, but before you do, look back at the intersection and sign so you aren't confused on your way back.

The trail climbs quite significantly and then levels out again. It is a very pretty trail with lots of undergrowth. It's also quiet, with birds singing and the Colorado River roaring in the distance. At about 4.8 miles the trail enters the area known as Little Yellowstone because some of the geology is reminiscent of the Grand Canyon of Yellowstone National Park. Here the canyon drops away and you may notice a few interesting rock formations in the canyon. The trail will switchback upward, and you might notice an area where there was once a bridge that was washed away in a flood. When the trail levels out a bit you might notice another rock formation through the trees. Continue onward and you'll get a better look at it soon. At the next stream crossing, which at the time of writing was still under repair after a recent flood incident, continue straight across. In 0.1 miles as the trail juts out to the right, stop and turn around. (#8) You'll see a beautiful sixty-foot waterfall just below that last crossing you made. If you look to your left you'll see the rock formation you saw earlier but much more clearly now. In another 0.1 miles you'll reach your last big overlook of Little Yellowstone.

From here the trail turns away from the Colorado River and heads upward. It crosses Lady Creek and wanders through a verdant section of forest. It then emerges at the Grand Ditch, a water-diversion project started in the late 1800s to take the water from the Never Summer Mountains (which previously flowed into the Colorado River) and send it across to the west side of the Continental Divide. (**#9**) The trail here is basically a dirt road. Turn right and follow it. This section can be very hot and dry and is quite exposed, so watch for storms. Along the way you'll find great views looking back at the Never Summer Mountains.

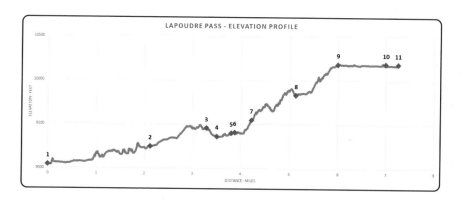

You'll eventually see a cabin on your left. (**#10**) This is a ranger station that is occasionally occupied. You can end your hike here or continue on the dirt road on the right side of the Grand Ditch. Follow it for another 0.3 miles until you see a little white building over the Grand Ditch. Here you'll turn right and follow an old dirt road for a couple hundred feet. The rushing stream to your left is yet another diversion project taking the waters from Specimen Mountain eastward. Before the road begins to climb uphill, down at the base of the road you'll see a sign on your right, declaring the headwaters of the mighty Colorado River. (**#11**) This powerful river begins here in this quiet, marshy meadow.

STRENUOUS HIKES

THE GRAND DITCH AT WAYPOINT #9

64 – THUNDER LAKE

Overview

Hike along a gentle path by the side of North Saint Vrain Creek as it makes its way through the deep forests of Wild Basin. You'll pass by Calypso Cascades and Ouzel Falls before heading deep into Wild Basin, away from the crowds. When you reach Thunder Lake and see the little ranger cabin, you'll feel like moving in, as the views from here are truly inspirational.

The Stats

Distance Round Trip: 13.3 miles
Difficulty Rating: 275
Hiking Time: 8 hours and 50 minutes
Time to Go: anytime
Season: mid-June through October
Primary Ecosystems: montane and subalpine
Views: forest and stream views, a large cascade, a waterfall ending at a dramatic mountain lake
Possible Wildlife: forest animals

Trail Conditions: The first portion of trail is wide and relatively smooth but later is pretty rocky, like most trails.
Reminder: Parking fills quickly, so arrive early. This is a long hike, so be sure to have a water filter with you.
Elevation Start: 8,500'
Highest Point: 10,689'
Total Elevation Gain: 2,844'
Trailhead: This hike begins at the Wild Basin Trailhead; see page 130 for details.

Waypoints

1. Wild Basin Trailhead	0.0	8,500'
2. Campsite Trail junction	1.3	8,886'
3. Calypso Cascades	1.8	9,139'
4. Ouzel Falls	2.7	9,382'
5. Bluebird Lake Trail junction	3.1	9,396'
6. Left after bridge	3.4	9,483'
7. Lion Lake junction	4.7	10,065'
8. Waterfall view	5.5	10,413'
9. Thunder Lake	6.6	10,594'

Hike Description

The first portion of this hike is up to Calypso Cascades. This is described in detail on page 222. You can then follow the Ouzel Falls hike on page 120. In summary, follow the Wild Basin Trail up past

Calypso Cascades (#3) and on up to Ouzel Falls. (#4) There are no confusing intersections to worry about along this stretch, as there is just one main trail to follow.

From Ouzel Falls, head across the bridge. The trail will turn to the east and head up to a point where there is a large rock slab. Here you can get a glimpse over the Wild Basin valley. The trail takes a sharp left and heads downhill. After a couple of switchbacks it winds its way through some very large boulders. The trail then hugs the side of a large rock wall on your left. This section is generally cool and moist; you'll probably even find moss growing here. The trail continues on relatively flat and then it passes the junction for the Bluebird Lake Trail; this hike is described in detail on page 404. (#5) Continue straight along this delightful and quiet section of trail until it crosses the North Saint Vrain Creek.

At the top of the hill after the bridge, take a sharp left turn to continue on toward Thunder Lake. (#6) The next half a mile has very little elevation gain and is quite enjoyable as it quietly leads you westward. If you pay attention, there is one point where you might get a glimpse of Mount Alice straight in front of you. At nearly four miles the flat trail comes to an end as it begins its upward climb. In not too long you'll come across an overlook on your left where you get a good view out to the south of Meadow Mountain and Saint Vrain Mountain, and to the west you can see Copeland Mountain. In about half a mile you'll cross a small stream. This is a good place to filter water and fill up your water bottle, as there isn't another for a while. Just a minute later the trail passes the Lion Lakes junction. (#7) That trail climbs very steeply upward for nearly two miles. You'll skip that pain and continue straight ahead to Thunder Lake.

The trail continues to gently climb, making another switchback.

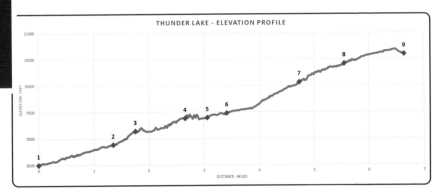

STRENUOUS HIKES

MOUNT ALICE AND THUNDER LAKE

Shortly after this you'll catch glimpses of the peaks ahead and you'll notice that the trees are changing. There are now more limber pine here and signs of getting closer to the alpine zone. At about five and a half miles you'll hear a more distinct roar off to your left. There is an opening in the trees up near an area of boulders. (**#8**) You can look across the valley at a very large and elegant waterfall in the distance.

In less than half a mile the trail crosses a rushing stream, then begins to level out and winds gently through the trees. You'll notice marshes off to your left and a meadow off to your right. Keep your eyes open for moose around here. You'll then cross the final stream. From here it won't be long. In a few minutes you'll reach an intersection with a trail that leads to the Thunder Lake campsites (wilderness camping permit required). Here you'll turn left and head downhill, descending about 90' in elevation. After passing the horse corral, the forest will part and you'll be rewarded with a stunning view. The jagged peaks of Tanima and Mount Alice tower over a log ranger cabin with Thunder Lake just off to its left. (**#9**) These days the ranger cabin is only used occasionally. If there is no one there, there's a nice bench out front where you can sit and take shelter from the weather. If you follow the trail down along the north side of the lake, there are a few places where you can get down close to the lake; just be sure to stay on the trail or rocks to protect the meadows and wildflowers.

65 – THE BOULDERFIELD

Overview

This is a longer hike, mostly above tree line, which takes you high up onto Longs Peak. The Boulderfield is the end of the official trail and as far as you can go while still being just a hike. The views on the way up are terrific and the scene as you approach the Boulderfield is awe-inspiring.

The Stats

Distance Round Trip: 11.6 miles

Difficulty Rating: 278

Hiking Time: 7 hours and 45 minutes

Time to Go: early morning

Season: June until first snow

Primary Ecosystems: subalpine to alpine

Views: stunning views of the sheer east face of Longs Peak as well as views down over Colorado's Front Range

Possible Wildlife: forest animals during the first two miles and then you may see ptarmigan, pikas, marmots, and elk

Trail Conditions: The trail is very much uphill. Above tree line expect a rocky and sandy trail with many large rock steps. The last section is over rocks and boulders.

Reminder: Most of this trail is completely exposed and so should not be hiked if there is a potential of thunderstorms. It is best hiked early in the morning. Carefully check weather conditions.

Elevation Start: 9,400'

Highest Point: 12,720'

Total Elevation Gain: 3,318'

Trailhead: This hike begins at the Longs Peak Trailhead; see page page 122 for details.

Waypoints

1. Longs Peak Trailhead	0.0	9,400'
2. Left at Eugenia Mine junction	0.5	9,682'
3. Alpine Brook switchback	0.9	9,932'
4. Lightning Bridge	2.0	10,584'
5. Joe Mills Junction	2.6	10,951'
6. Right at Chasm Junction	3.4	11,539'
7. Granite Pass	4.4	12,077'
8. Dramatic view of Longs Peak	5.2	12,451'
9. Boulderfield	5.8	12,720'

Hike Description

The first section of this hike up to Chasm Junction is described in detail in the Chasm Lake hike on page 354. In summary, follow the

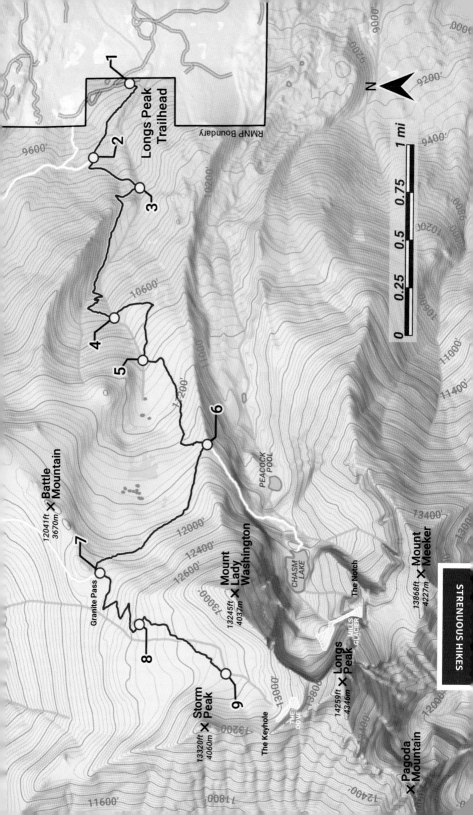

STRENUOUS HIKES

N

0   0.25   0.5   0.75   1 mi

Longs Peak
Trailhead

RMNP Boundary

1
2
3
4
5
6
7
8
9

Battle
Mountain
12041ft
3670m ✕

Granite Pass

Mount Lady
Washington
13245ft
4037m ✕

Storm
Peak
13320ft
4060m ✕

PEACOCK
POOL

CHASM
LAKE

The Notch

MILLS
GLACIER

The Keyhole

THE
DOVE

Longs Peak
14259ft
4346m ✕

Mount
Meeker
13868ft
4227m ✕

Pagoda
Mountain ✕

Longs Peak Trail through deep forest for just over two miles to reach tree line, then continue above tree line up the many stone steps to reach Chasm Junction. (#6)

At Chasm Junction you'll take a sharp right turn and head toward the north. The trail climbs steadily along the east side of Mount Lady Washington with many rock steps. You'll see in the distance ahead of you several very large rock piles. These are up at Granite Pass. As you approach them the trail becomes a bit more steep and rocky. Off to the right of these rock piles you'll see Battle Mountain, and farther off to the east you'll see Twin Sisters Peaks. Eventually, the trail will level out beside these rock piles and you'll have reached Granite Pass. (#7) Here you'll notice a trail heading off to your right. This is the North Longs Peak Trail, which leads down to Glacier Gorge. It is a considerably longer trail than the one you've just done.

Continue straight ahead up to the northwest. Notice the incredible rockwork that the trail crew has done here to protect the tundra from the thousands of footsteps that pass this way. The trail climbs up the side of the hill and makes numerous switchbacks. As it does, the scene out to the north opens up, giving you great views of the Mummy Range, Stones Peak, and Glacier Basin. You might even be able to see Bierstadt Lake in the trees below. After the fifth switchback, Longs Peak appears to tower over the area. (#8) This is one of the most dramatic views in Rocky in my opinion; on a summer morning when the flowers are blooming it's even more incredible. Shortly after this the trail levels out and you get your first view of the Boulderfield. You'll quickly see why it was given that name.

Continue following the trail as it winds back and forth and grows ever rockier. At times it can be difficult to follow; just be sure to stay

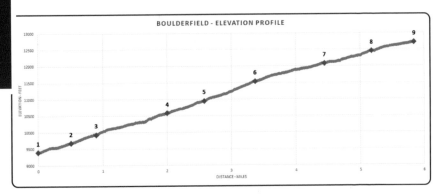

LONGS PEAK FROM WAYPOINT #8

off of the vegetation. There are occasional historic rock cairns to help guide you. Along this stretch you'll encounter a small stream. In the early summer the entire trail sometimes becomes a stream, so wear waterproof boots. Some sections of the stream are just deep enough to filter water; using a filter with a hose will give you better access to the water under the rocks. This is your only option until you get back down below the trees, so filter water now if you think you might need it before you get back down.

Before you arrive in the heart of the Boulderfield, it transitions from trail to boulder hopping. This gives you a little taste of what it is like if you were to continue up to the Keyhole. After a bit of boulder hopping, the trail does resume and then arrives at a sign beside a small wooden structure in this moonscape environment. This is the end of the official trail. (**#9**) Here you'll find a series of camping spots (wilderness camping permit required) in between rock piles meant to hold back the wind. The Boulderfield is a crazy place that gives you a real sense of the harshness of life at this elevation.

If you are continuing on to the summit of Longs Peak, turn to page 462.

66 – BLUEBIRD LAKE

Overview

Experience the full variety of the Wild Basin area. You'll walk through deep forest, past Calypso Cascades and Ouzel Falls. You'll then climb up through the site of a large forest fire, where life is coming back. Then you'll head through a bit of rough and marshy terrain. Later you'll walk through meadows, scramble up rocks, climb up a snowfield, and arrive at Bluebird Lake right at tree line and surrounded by imposing peaks.

The Stats

Distance Round Trip: 12.7 miles	**Trail Conditions:** average trail conditions until the Ouzel Lake Trail junction, then rough trail conditions
Difficulty Rating: 281	
Hiking Time: 8 hours and 30 minutes	**Reminder:** Don't be in the open burn area if storms are threatening. Also, be aware that moose are very active in the area around Ouzel Lake.
Time to Go: early morning	
Season: mid-June through October	
Primary Ecosystems: montane to subalpine	**Elevation Start:** 8,500′
	Highest Point: 10,983′
Views: streams, cascades, waterfall, tree line lake	**Total Elevation Gain:** 3,105′
	Trailhead: This hike begins at the Wild Basin Trailhead; see page 130 for details.
Possible Wildlife: forest animals, moose, elk	

Waypoints

1. Wild Basin Trailhead	0.0	8,500′
2. Calypso Cascades	1.8	9,139′
3. Ouzel Falls	2.7	9,382′
4. Left onto Bluebird Lake Trail	3.1	9,403′
5. Right at Ouzel Lake junction	4.5	9,978′
6. Log bridge	5.9	10,638′
7. Bluebird Lake	6.4	10,983′

Hike Description

The first portion of this hike is up to Calypso Cascades. This is described in detail on page 222. You can then follow the Ouzel

STRENUOUS HIKES

Meadow
Mountain
11634ft
3546m ×

N

Wild Basin
Trailhead

1

Copeland Falls

2

Calypso Cascades

FINCH
LAKE

3

Ouzel Falls

4

SANDBEACH
LAKE

5

OUZEL
LAKE

THUNDER
LAKE

6

7

Copeland
Mountain
13176ft
4013m ×

BLUEBIRD
LAKE

Tanima
Peak
12434ft
3790m ×

MOOMAW
GLACIER

Ouzel
Peak ×

Ogalalla ×
13081ft
Cony Pass

0   0.5   1   1.5   2 mi

Falls hike on page 258. It continues on the Ouzel Lake hike on page 350. In summary, follow the main Wild Basin Trail up past Calypso Cascades (**#2**) and Ouzel Falls. (**#3**) Turn left at the Bluebird Lake Trail junction, which is at about three miles. (**#4**) Then follow the trail up through the large burn area until you arrive at the Ouzel Lake junction at about 4.5 miles. (**#5**)

From the junction with the Ouzel Lake Trail, take the trail on the right and head toward Bluebird Lake. From here the trail is much narrower and less developed than what you've experienced so far. During this next stretch it will wind through willows, over logs, cross several muddy stretches, and be very rough and rocky. This is also the stretch where you are most likely to run into moose, so keep your eyes wide open and give them plenty of space.

At around five miles patches of forest begin to return and then eventually you find yourself back in the trees. Here the trail conditions improve. You'll soon cross a couple of streams and then the trail will turn to the right and begin to climb again. In about a quarter of a mile the trees give way to a flower-filled meadow that has a small seasonal waterfall off to your right. In a short while the trail climbs a small hill and then heads through a rock field with great views of Ouzel Peak.

In another short while you'll reach a log bridge over a rushing stream coming down from Bluebird Lake. (**#6**) If you look upstream you can see it cascading down the rocks. Soon after the bridge, the trail begins to climb quite steeply. You'll have to pay close attention in order to follow the trail, as you'll occasionally be crossing bare rock and in some places you may even need to use your hands to help you climb up steep sections. When you get a chance, look off to your south and notice the stream beautifully cascading down the rugged rocks. It's coming from Junco Lake.

STRENUOUS HIKES

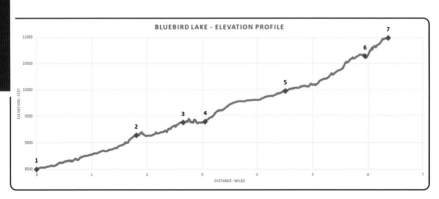

At the top of the steepest section, you get a little reprieve. The trail continues to climb but not quite as steeply. You'll still be climbing over rock and winding your way around krumholz. Then the trail will lead you to a grassy area between two rock walls. This area often has a large snowfield that you'll have to cross even into late summer. Poles are recommended to help you keep your balance. Be aware that this snowfield can be quite slippery. You may want to kick your toes into it to get a foothold.

At the top of the snowfield, you have only to walk a short distance before Bluebird Lake comes into view. Follow the trail down a short ways and enjoy a great overlook of Bluebird Lake nestled between Copeland Mountain on the south, Ouzel Peak to the southwest, and majestic Mahana Peak to the north. (#7) For many years this lake was dammed to serve as a water reservoir for cities along the Front Range, but this was all removed following the failure of the dam at Lawn Lake.

STRENUOUS HIKES

OUZEL PEAK OVER BLUEBIRD OUTLET

67 – BIGHORN FLATS

Overview

This hike is simply delightful as you stroll through the heart of Rocky over the open tundra with amazing views all around. After climbing Flattop Mountain, the rest of the hike is fairly gentle. The Bighorn Flats section of the hike isn't about reaching a particular destination but about experiencing the airiness and peacefulness of being on top of the world.

The Stats

Distance Round Trip: 12.9 miles

Difficulty Rating: 301

Hiking Time: 8 hours and 35 minutes

Time to Go: early morning to avoid afternoon storms

Season: mid-June until first snow

Primary Ecosystems: subalpine and alpine

Views: grand views over much of Rocky Mountain National Park with gorgeous rolling tundra

Possible Wildlife: forest animals, marmots, pikas, elk, white-tailed ptarmigan

Trail Conditions: The trail is easy to follow. It is rocky and sandy above tree line.

Reminder: This is a highly exposed trail and there is no quick way down, so only attempt when there is no threat of bad weather. September and October might be best. There is no water on this hike, so bring enough. Please stay on the trail and off of the vegetation!

Elevation Start: 9,475′

Highest Point: 12,326′

Total Elevation Gain: 3,490′

Trailhead: This hike begins at the Bear Lake Trailhead; see page 110 for details.

Waypoints

1. Bear Lake Trailhead	0.0	9,475′
2. Left onto Flattop Mountain Trail	1.0	9,968′
3. Dream Lake Overlook	1.6	10,491′
4. Rest Rock	2.4	10,982′
5. Emerald Lake Overlook	2.9	11,358′
6. Horse tie-up	3.9	12,163′
7. Flattop summit	4.2	12,326′
8. North Inlet Junction	4.5	12,218′
9. Ptarmigan Point	5.2	12,243′
10. Eureka Ditch	6.5	11,906′

N

Bear Lake
Trailhead

BEAR
LAKE

9800'

9400'

Alberta Falls

10000'

THE
LOCH

10200'

DREAM
LAKE

LAKE
HAIYAHA

EMERALD
LAKE

10600'

11000'

11400'

11600'

12000'

LAKE
HELENE

ODESSA
LAKE

Notchtop
Mountain ×
11929ft
3636m

Flattop
Mountain ⊗
12326ft
3757m

Hallett
Peak ×
12720ft
3877m

Otis
Peak ×
12483ft
3805m

12400'

12200'

12200'

11600'

11400'

PTARMIGAN
LAKE

12200'

11200'

10800'

10600'

10200'

10400'

STRENUOUS HIKES

0   0.25   0.5   0.75   1 mi

The first portion of this hike is up to the top of Flattop Mountain, as is described on page 362. In summary, you'll follow the Fern Lake Trail from Bear Lake (#1) up to the junction with the Flattop Trail. (#2) Turn left here and this trail will lead you up to tree line and then into the alpine zone, eventually leading you to the summit of Flattop Mountain. (#7)

From the top of Flattop Mountain continue on the trail, which now becomes the Tonahutu Creek Trail. It leads to the northwest and soon heads downhill. At 4.5 miles you'll reach the intersection with the North Inlet Trail. (#8) That trail is the quickest way to Grand Lake and not where you are headed, so continue past the junction. Don't follow the old trail that continues straight, but instead follow the main well-defined gravel trail that leads off to the right. In about 0.1 miles this trail will lead you up to the edge of a cliff. Here you can look down and see a number of lakes far below. On the left is Odessa Lake, then Lake Helene below and in front of you, and behind it is the larger Two Rivers Lake. It is an impressive viewpoint you don't want to miss.

The trail climbs up Ptarmigan Point, and as you climb you'll see Snowdrift Peak off to your left. (#9) This section of trail is often lined with wildflowers during late June and early July. From the top you can look out to the southwest and see Shadow Mountain Lake and some of Grand Lake. From here the trail winds gently through the tundra as it slowly descends across the Bighorn Flats. This large area seems like an ideal environment for bighorn sheep, but in all my years I have yet to see one up here. Ahead of you is the main part

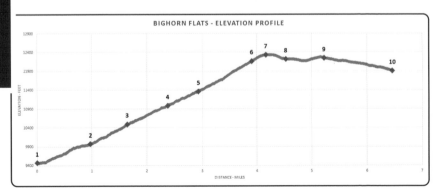

SNOWDRIFT PEAK FROM BIGHORN FLATS

of the hike. There is no dramatic destination, just a delightful stroll through this beautiful tundra area.

If you decide to stop and take a break up here, look for a boulder that is right on the trail to rest upon rather than walking onto the delicate tundra grasses to reach a rest spot. The Bighorn Flats is a precious area that we need to protect from our wandering feet. As you are up here keep your eyes open for white-tailed ptarmigan, the smallest bird in the grouse family. They generally rely on camouflage for safety.

After a long, flat section the trail begins to gradually descend. You'll begin to encounter large historic rock cairns marking the path that have been there for many decades. Off to your left you'll notice a snowfield that generally stays for much of the year. Feel free to rock hop over to it and take a slide. As you continue on you'll see the Tonahutu Valley and the Haynach Lakes area begin to appear. The trail slowly makes its way down there. You can feel free to go as far down the trail as you feel like, but you will have to climb back up again. I generally stop at 6.5 miles at the Eureka Ditch, which you will see as just a small trench on your right, that has been dug into the tundra. (**#10**) It was built to capture water headed to the west and instead send it down to the east side of the mountain. It was dismantled in 1995. From here the trail begins to descend more steeply. Get a good view of the valley ahead and then turn around to enjoy a very different and equally wonderful perspective on your way back.

68 – HAYNACH LAKES

Overview

This hike takes you from the Kawuneeche Valley through the woods and then alongside the edge of Big Meadows. From here the trail continues up the Tonahutu Valley, passing Granite Falls. Along the way it crosses several large burn areas from a fire in 2013. At the junction with the Haynach Trail, you'll climb steeply upward, eventually arriving at beautiful tarns and lakes surrounded by high mountains.

The Stats

Distance Round Trip: 16.3 miles

Difficulty Rating: 309

Hiking Time: 10 hours and 55 minutes

Time to Go: early morning

Season: mid-June through October

Primary Ecosystems: montane and subalpine

Views: forest, meadows, waterfall, alpine lakes

Possible Wildlife: forest animals, moose, elk, three-toed woodpeckers

Trail Conditions: average

Reminder: Much of this hike is through moose territory, so stay alert; also, don't be at the lakes if there is a likelihood of lightning.

Elevation Start: 8,794′

Highest Point: 11,115′

Total Elevation Gain: 2,924′

Trailhead: This hike begins at the Green Mountain Trailhead; see page 120 for details.

Waypoints

1. Green Mountain Trailhead	0.0	8,794′
2. Left onto Tonahutu Trail	1.8	9,402′
3. Right at Onahu Trail junction	2.3	9,467′
4. Granite Falls	5.0	9,834′
5. Large burn area	5.5	9,968′
6. Left onto Haynach Trail	6.7	10,349′
7. Last of the Haynach Lakes	8.2	11,098′

Hike Description

The first half of this hike is described in detail in the Granite Falls hike on page 122. In summary, you'll follow the Green Mountain Trail (**#1**) until you reach the junction with the Tonahutu Trail. (**#2**)

STRENUOUS HIKES

Green Mountain Trailhead

TRAIL RIDGE ROAD (US HWY 34)

Green Mtn.
10282ft
3134m

Nakai Peak
11916ft
3632m

HAYNACH LAKES

Sprague Mountain
12697ft
3870m

Snowdrift Peak
12205ft
3720m

N

0   0.5   1   1.5   2 mi

Turn left and follow the trail around the meadow. On the north end of the meadow, the trail will follow Tonahutu Creek until you reach Granite Falls at around five miles.(#4)

Following Granite Falls the trail makes a short, steep climb and then levels out. It crosses a bridge and heads along the edge of a large beautiful meadow. It doesn't last long and soon you are back in the woods climbing again. The trail levels out once more, and the next thing you know you're surprised to find the forest suddenly end. Here you enter a very large burn area, significantly larger than the last one you passed through. (#5)

For nearly half a mile the trail will wind up and down through this area. Because the trees have no needles, you are quite exposed to the elements, and it can get very hot and dry in here. Be sure you have enough water with you. As you pass through, pay attention to the great variety of life that is returning. Also, look for the many animals that are making themselves at home here, from the three-toed wood-peckers to moose and elk.

You'll exit the burn area into a meadow where you'll get your first good look at the Continental Divide. On the other side of the meadow, you'll enter into the forest and begin to ascend along the side of a steep slope. Here you'll notice that the forest is opening both above you and below you, with an increasing amount of growth on the forest floor. The large spruce trees here feel almost regal along this stretch.

You'll know you are getting close to the turn for Haynach when you cross a long log bridge. The stream here is coming down from Haynach Lakes and cascades joyfully down the hillside and under the bridge. Just about a quarter of a mile farther you'll see a junction sign for Haynach Lakes on your left-hand side. (#6) Turn left at this junction.

STRENUOUS HIKES

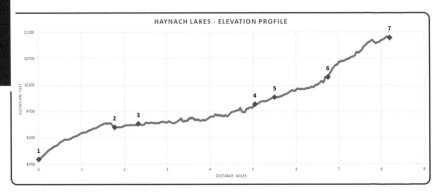

The trail here seems to go straight up. It is nearly a fifty-degree slope, one of the steepest sections of trail you'll find in the park. The first six hundred feet are the most difficult and then the trail becomes a little less cruel. As it begins to level out, the forest continues to open up, with hints of meadow here and there. The trail is at times a bit rough with tree roots, rocks, and mud, but the scenery makes up for it. At about 7.5 miles the trees give way to a large meadow. The trail will cross through part of it, and this section can be a bit wet and muddy, so be prepared.

After the meadow, the trail reaches another steep section along a gorgeous flower-lined stream. This section is about a third of a mile long and feels challenging, but don't give up yet, as you are getting close. At the top of the hill, you'll descend a short ways and then reach the first of the Haynach Lakes on your left. Try to admire them from the trail to protect the delicate meadow area. From here it is just a quarter of a mile to the last and largest of the Haynach Lakes. As you arrive, the trail fades away into the meadow and you'll feel like building a cabin right here. (#7) As you enjoy this special place, be on the lookout for afternoon storms, as this is not a good place to be during any potential electrical activity.

STRENUOUS HIKES

ONE OF THE FIRST LAKES

STRENUOUS HIKES

END OF THE TRAIL

STRENUOUS HIKES

69 – CRYSTAL LAKES

Overview

This hike is a continuation of the Lawn Lake hike. It takes you higher up into the tundra to a series of three lakes that lie right below the jagged north face of Fairchild Mountain. The trail is not very well maintained and is a bit of a climb, but it is a wonderfully dramatic and yet peaceful location. From the start at Lawn Lake to the destination at Crystal Lake, you pass through all three ecosystems of the park.

The Stats

Distance Round Trip: 15.0 miles

Difficulty Rating: 311

Hiking Time: 10 hours

Time to Go: early morning

Season: July until first snow

Primary Ecosystems: montane, sub-alpine, alpine

Views: deep forest followed by open tundra and alpine lakes surrounded by tall mountains

Possible Wildlife: forest animals and then pikas, marmots, elk, ptarmigan

Trail Conditions: From Lawn Lake onward, this trail is not well maintained. At times it is quite muddy, goes through streams, and through thick willows that cover the trail.

Reminder: This upper portion of the hike is through open tundra; do not attempt if there is any chance of storms.

Elevation Start: 8,540'

Highest Point: 11,553'

Total Elevation Gain: 3,219'

Trailhead: This hike begins at the Lawn Lake Trailhead; see page 122 for details.

Waypoints

1. Lawn Lake Trailhead	0.0	8,540'
2. Roaring River overlook	0.9	9,021'
3. Ypsilon Lake Trail junction	1.3	9,218'
4. First switchbacks	2.1	9,487'
5. Stream access	4.3	10,298'
6. Last switchbacks	4.5	10,423'
7. Black Canyon junction	5.5	10,832'
8. Lawn Lake	6.1	11,007'
9. Tree line	6.7	11,124'
10. Left onto Crystal Lakes Trail	7.0	11,422'
11. Crystal Lake	7.5	11,525'

The first portion of this hike is up to Lawn Lake as is described in detail on page 342. In summary, you'll follow the Lawn Lake Trail (**#1**) for just over six miles to Lawn Lake. (**#8**) There are no confusing intersections on this trail.

From Lawn Lake continue northwest on the main trail out through the flower-filled meadows toward the distant peaks. After a relatively gentle start, the trail turns upward and into the trees. The trail can be a little rough here and then it comes back out into an open meadow. During the spring through early July, this section can get quite muddy, and you may even encounter snow well into July on some sections, but at this time of year you will also find meadows filled with wildflowers: bluebells, Indian paintbrush, columbine, daisies, buttercups, etc.

As the trail reaches the end of Lawn Lake, be sure to take a look backward and notice Longs Peak with its block-shaped top looking down on the lake. In just a minute you'll hear the roar of the water cascading down the rocks from Crystal Lakes. You'll soon find the trail heading right through a number of small streams and more mud. Some areas of the trail will be overrun by very thick willows and you'll have to push your way through them, some being taller than most people. Since this section of trail is not often maintained, you may also find fallen trees or other obstacles to overcome.

At about 6.7 miles you'll reach the last of the trees. (**#9**) Do not go beyond this point if there is any sign of potential storms. From here this narrow trail ascends quite steeply through the tundra. On the way you'll see a number of streams and cascades by the trail or just off in the distance a little ways. The scenery here is pretty wonderful,

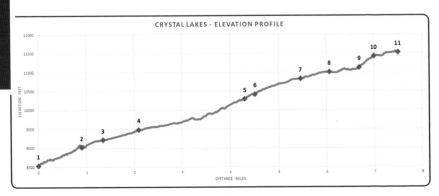

though the trail itself is rather rough. Be sure to stay on the trail, hard though it may be, in order to protect the delicate tundra.

In a short ways you'll reach a junction. (#10) Here you'll turn to the left, as the other trail leads up to the saddle between Fairchild Mountain and Hagues Peak. Our trail will descend a short ways and then cross a wide stream. There isn't a bridge, so you will have to rock hop to get across. The trail then makes a steep but short climb uphill, which leads you to a lovely meadow and the first little pond. Continue across the outlet to find the rest of the trail, which will lead you up to the second lake. The trail continues along the eastern end of this lake and leads you up to the main lake. This section of trail can be a little difficult to follow, as vegetation occasionally hides it. The trail ends at the boulders beside Crystal Lake. (#11) Here you can climb up and enjoy the view. This lake sits right at the base of the cliffs of Fairchild Mountain, creating a dramatic scene. This is a great place to picnic and spend a while.

STRENUOUS HIKES

POND BEFORE LITTLE CRYSTAL LAKE

70 – BEAR LAKE TO GRAND LAKE
(North Inlet)

Overview

Take a journey across Rocky Mountain National Park, experiencing all three of the park's ecosystems. You'll start at Bear Lake and climb Flattop Mountain. From there you'll cross an expanse of open tundra before descending to the North Inlet valley. You'll then follow the North Inlet Creek through deep forest to the western edge of the park at Grand Lake. This route is the shortest way from Bear Lake to Grand Lake.

The Stats

Distance One Way: 16.8 miles

Difficulty Rating: 330

Hiking Time: 11 hours and 10 minutes

Time to Go: early morning to avoid afternoon storms

Season: mid-July until first snow

Primary Ecosystems: montane, sub-alpine, and alpine

Views: grand views over much of Rocky Mountain National Park, followed by deep forest and stream views

Possible Wildlife: forest animals, marmots, pikas, elk

Trail Conditions: typical rocky trail with several very steep switchbacks on the descent

Reminder: Ask a ranger about trail conditions, as one section may be impassible until mid-July. Be off the tundra before storms arrive. Bring plenty of food and water, as this is a long hike. This is a one-way hike; you'll need to have a ride waiting for you on the other side.

Elevation Start: 9,475'

Highest Point: 12,326'

Total Elevation Gain: 3,246' (4,186' elevation loss)

Trailhead: This hike begins at the Bear Lake Trailhead; see page 110 for details. It ends at the North Inlet Trailhead; see page 124 for details.

Waypoints

1. Bear Lake Trailhead	0.0	9,475'
2. Left onto Flattop Mountain Trail	1.0	9,964'
3. Dream Lake Overlook	1.6	10,491'
4. Emerald Lake Overlook	2.9	11,358'
5. Flattop summit	4.2	12,326'
6. Left onto North Inlet Trail	4.5	12,218'
7. Hallett Creek crossing	8.0	10,629'
8. North Inlet Junction	9.7	9,595'

STRENUOUS HIKES

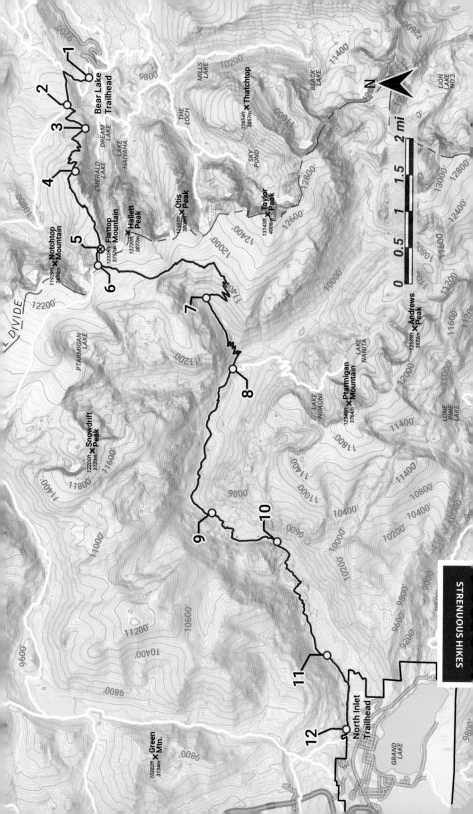

9. Big Pool	**12.1**	**9,060'**
10. Cascade Falls	13.5	8,803'
11. Summerland Park Cabin	**15.8**	**8,507'**
12. North Inlet Trailhead	16.8	8,520'

Hike Description

The first part of this hike is described in detail in the hike up Flattop Mountain, page 362. In summary, you'll follow the Fern Lake Trail from Bear Lake to the junction with the Flattop Mountain Trail. (**#2**) You'll turn left here and follow the trail up through the trees and then up across alpine terrain until you arrive at the summit of Flattop Mountain. (**#5**)

From Flattop Mountain continue down the trail for about 0.2 miles and you'll reach the intersection with the North Inlet Trail. (**#6**) Turn left here and follow it. This trail will lead you all the way to Grand Lake. It is a wide and gentle trail heading to the south, lined by large historic stone cairns along both sides of the path. Slowly the trail slopes downward. You'll be walking on the backside of Hallett Peak, which is off to your left.

In about three-quarters of a mile you'll see a deep, forested valley appear in front of you. This is where you will eventually head, but first the trail is going to travel around to the far side of this valley, as there are too many cliffs on its north side. As you cross the eastern edge of the valley, look left to see the summit of Otis Peak. Be aware that this area of trail gets a bit rocky and has some areas where willows are attempting to take over the trail.

When you reach the far side of the valley, you'll cross a stream. This is typically where you might first encounter snow in the early

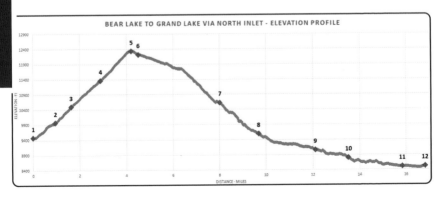

STRENUOUS HIKES

NORTH INLET TRAIL AFTER WAYPOINT #8

summer. If you do encounter a snowfield here, don't attempt to go any farther, since the snowbanks farther down the trail are along very steep sections and are extremely dangerous. They usually melt by the second week of July. Check with a ranger for trail conditions if you plan to attempt the trail before then.

From here to Hallett Creek the trails drops over one thousand feet. It begins this descent by traveling rather precariously along the edge of this very steep slope. You'll then hike seven switchbacks on your way down to the valley below. After that last switchback the trail finally heads back into the trees. You'll cross several small streams before arriving at the bridge over Hallett Creek. (#7)

The rest of this journey is detailed on page 458 as Part 3 of the Western Loop. In summary, you'll follow this trail through the forest all the way to the North Inlet Trailhead. (#12) From there it is just a half-mile walk down the dirt road into town.

71 – BEAR LAKE TO GRAND LAKE
(Tonahutu)

Overview

Take the scenic route from Bear Lake to Grand Lake and experience the heart of Rocky Mountain National Park. This hike will take you up Flattop Mountain, out across the beautiful Bighorn Flats, down through the Tonahutu valley, past Granite Falls and Big Meadows to the Tonahutu Trailhead, which is only half a mile from downtown Grand Lake.

The Stats

Distance One Way: 17.8 miles

Difficulty Rating: 337

Hiking Time: 11 hours and 55 minutes

Time to Go: early morning to avoid afternoon storms

Season: mid-June until first snow

Primary Ecosystems: montane, sub-alpine, alpine

Views: grand views over much of Rocky Mountain National Park, followed by deep forest and stream views

Possible Wildlife: forest animals, marmots, pikas, elk, ptarmigan

Trail Conditions: This is a typical rocky trail, with some large steps and on the final few miles there are many exposed tree roots.

Reminder: A significant section of this hike is above tree line; leave early and turn around if there is any sign of an approaching storm. Bring plenty of water, as there is none above tree line.

Elevation Start: 9,475'

Highest Point: 12,326'

Total Elevation Gain: 3,176' (4,087' elevation loss)

Trailhead: This hike begins at the Bear Lake Trailhead; see page 110 for details. It ends at the Tonahutu Trailhead; see page 127 for details.

Waypoints

1. Bear Lake Trailhead	0.0	9,475'
2. Left onto Flattop Mountain Trail	1.0	9,964'
3. Dream Lake Overlook	1.6	10,491'
4. Emerald Lake Overlook	2.9	11,358'
5. Flattop summit	4.2	12,326'
6. North Inlet Trail	4.5	12,218'
7. Eureka Ditch	6.5	11,906'
8. Boulder field rest stop	8.3	10,601'
9. Haynach Lakes Trail junction	8.7	10,349'

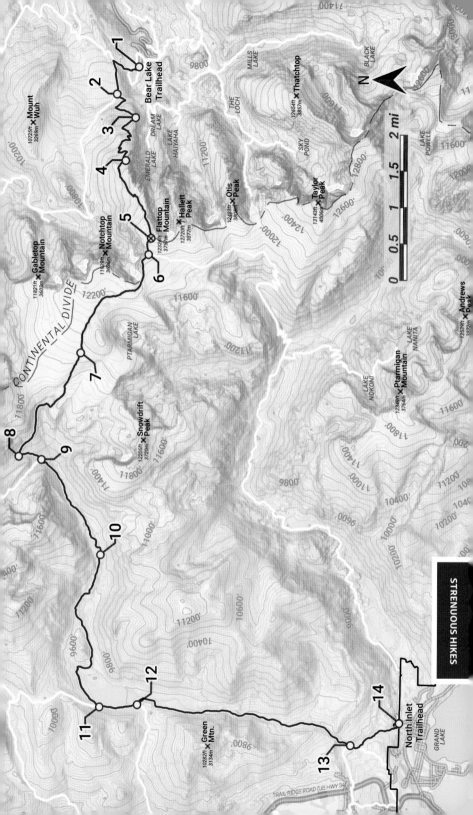

STRENUOUS HIKES

N

1

2

3

4

5

6

7

8

9

10

11

12

13

14

Bear Lake
Trailhead

North Inlet
Trailhead

CONTINENTAL DIVIDE

10725ft ×Mount
3265m   Wuh

11821ft ×Gabletop
3601m   Mountain

11429ft ×Notchtop
3486m   Mountain

12324ft Flattop
3750m   Mountain

12720ft ×Hallett
3877m   Peak

12483ft ×Otis
3804m   Peak

13143ft ×Taylor
4006m   Peak

1265ft ×Thatchtop
3857m

12200ft ×Snowdrift
3720m   Peak

12349ft ×Ptarmigan
3764m   Mountain

10282ft ×Green
3134m   Mtn.

12539ft ×Andrews
3972m   Peak

BLACK
LAKE

MILLS
LAKE

THE
LOCH

SKY
POND

LAKE
POWELL

LAKE
HAIYAHA

DREAM
LAKE

EMERALD
LAKE

PTARMIGAN
LAKE

LAKE
NANITA

LAKE
NOKONI

GRAND
LAKE

TRAIL RIDGE ROAD (US HWY 34)

0   0.5   1   1.5   2 mi

10. Granite Falls	10.4	9,834'
11. Onahu Trail junction	13.1	9,467'
12. Green Mountain junction	13.6	9,402'
13. Kawuneeche Visitor Center junction	17.0	8,806'
14. Tonahutu Trailhead	17.8	8,552'

Hike Description

The first part of this hike is described in detail in the hike up Flattop Mountain, page 362. The next section of the hike from Flattop Mountain to the Eureka Ditch is then described in the Bighorn Flats hike on page 408. In summary, you'll follow the Fern Lake Trail from Bear Lake (#1) up to the junction with the Flattop Mountain Trail. (#2) Turn left here and this trail will lead you up to tree line and then into the alpine zone, eventually leading you to the summit of Flattop Mountain. (#5) Continue on the trail as it leads you out across the tundra until you reach the Eureka Ditch at about 6.5 miles, which is where the trail begins to descend more steeply. (#7)

From the Eureka Ditch continue to follow the trail downhill. It gradually becomes steeper, with a few sections that are less steep. Enjoy these wide-open views because before long you will be back in deep forest. In just over a mile from the Eureka Ditch, you'll cross over a small creek; this is the beginning of Tonahutu Creek, which will be your guide the rest of the way. After this, it isn't long until you enter the trees, followed by a boulder field. At the bottom of this boulder field there is a nice spot to have a rest and filter water to fill your water bottle. (#8)

The trail here soon enters darker woods as it heads downward. You'll next pass the junction for the Haynach Lakes area (#9),

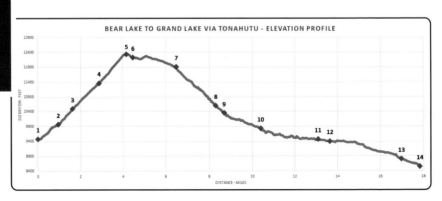

followed by a delightful stream crossing. In just a short ways you'll **429**
cross a meadow and then enter a burn area from the 2013 Big
Meadows Fire. This is a hot and dry area but also fascinating as you
notice the wide variety of life that is returning.

At the end of the burn area it isn't far to Granite Falls. (**#10**) Be
sure to take a break here and spend a little time at the base of this
gorgeous fifty-foot cascade. Then continue on, passing through more
burn area, alongside lush meadows, and eventually reaching the edge
of Big Meadows, which stretches to the south for over a mile and a
half. The trail then heads along its western edge, passing a junction
with the Onahu Trail (**#11**), followed by two old buildings that were
part of an early homestead. Along this entire stretch it is common to
encounter moose, so be on the lookout. You'll then reach the Green
Mountain Trail junction. (**#12**) Some people choose to turn right
here and get picked up at the Green Mountain Trailhead, saving
themselves 2.5 miles. But for the full walk into Grand Lake, continue
straight at this intersection.

From here the trail heads a little more into the woods, with occasional visits to the edge of Big Meadows. This last section of trail
is generally very quiet and peaceful with very few people. It heads
through thick forest but always with the sound of the nearby Tonahutu Creek. Occasionally you'll pass beside small meadows where
you might catch elk, moose, or deer grazing. This section of trail is
more sheltered from the sun, which can make it quite enjoyable on a
hot day. Eventually you reach a junction for the Kawuneeche Visitor
Center. (**#13**) To reach Grand Lake continue straight ahead. In just
under a mile after traveling this very smooth and gentle section of
trail, you arrive at the Tonahutu Creek Trailhead. (**#14**) If you are
headed to the town of Grand Lake, it is only 0.5 miles from here.
Continue down the dirt road to the highway, cross to the other side,
and you'll find a path leading you into town.

TRAIL TO THE TONAHUTU VALLEY NEAR WAYPOINT #7

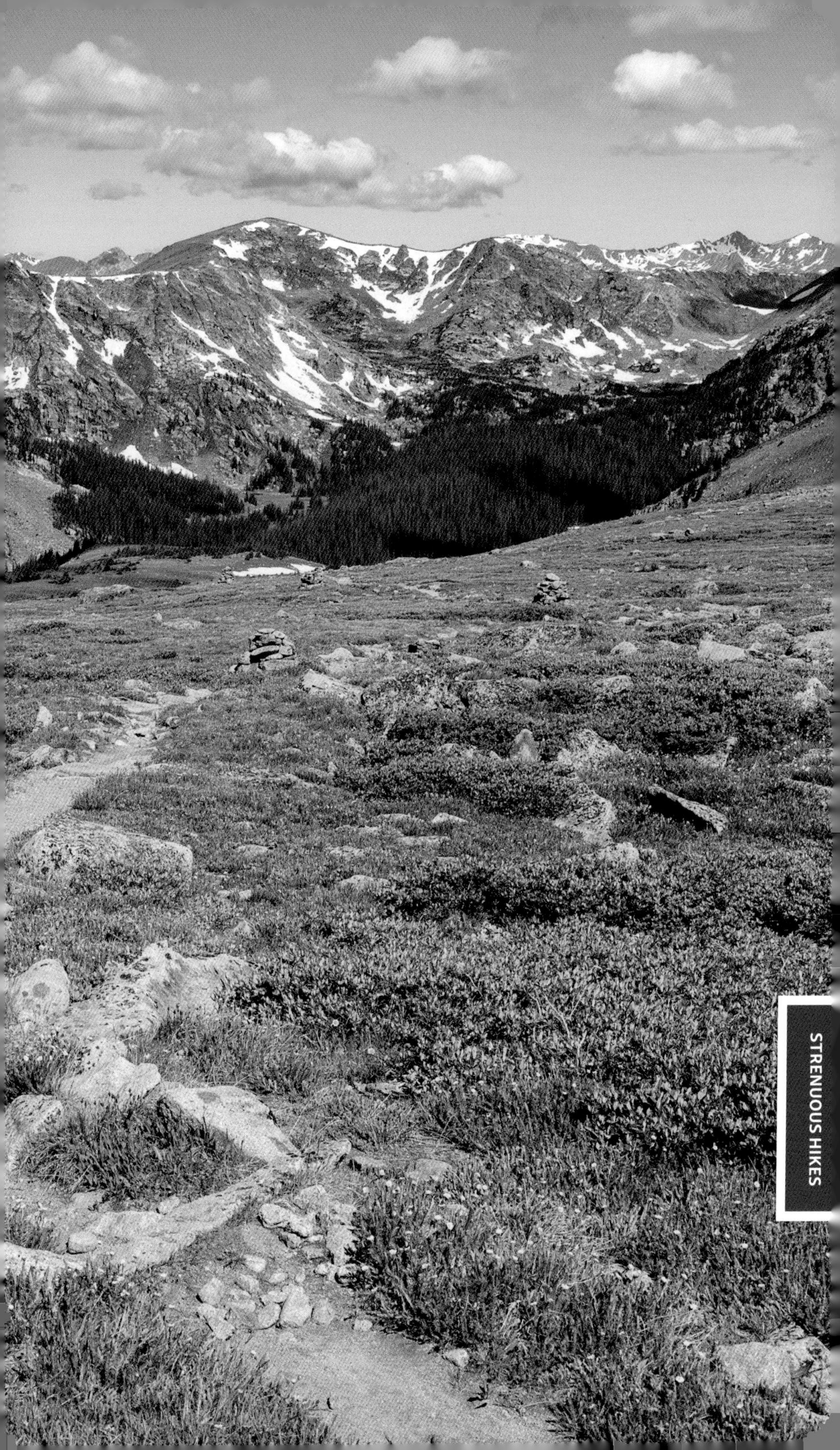

72 – LOST LAKE

Overview

This is a longer hike that is typically done as part of a backpacking trip, but for the very fit it can be done as one long day trip. The trail leads you along the North Fork of the Big Thompson River starting just east of the town of Glen Haven. It takes you through deep forest and open meadows all the way to its start at Lost Lake. This is a trail for those who love longer hikes through quiet forests, with only the sound of an accompanying stream.

The Stats

Distance Round Trip: 18.6 miles

Difficulty Rating: 351

Hiking Time: 12 hours and 25 minutes

Time to Go: early start if doing this in a day

Season: mid-June until first snow

Primary Ecosystems: montane and subalpine

Views: forests, streams, meadows, a mountain lake

Possible Wildlife: forest animals

Trail Conditions: This long trail is pretty average, much of it sandy, as well as a few wet and muddy areas.

Reminder: This is a very long trail, so be sure to start early, bring plenty of food, head lamps, and a way to filter water.

Elevation Start: 7,789'

Highest Point: 10,768'

Total Elevation Gain: 3,307'

Trailhead: This hike begins at the Dunraven Trailhead; see page 116 for details.

Waypoints

1. Dunraven Trailhead	0.0	7,789'
2. Cheley Camp	1.3	7,804'
3. Left on dirt road	1.5	7,893'
4. Dunraven Glade	2.7	8,200'
5. RMNP boundary	4.3	8,909'
6. North Boundary Trail junction	5.1	9,254'
7. Stormy Peaks junction	7.3	10,131'
8. Lost Meadow	8.0	10,408'
9. Lost Lake	9.3	10,730'

Hike Description

This hike begins in Roosevelt National Forest, and much of the first half of the hike is through Comanche Peaks Wilderness. Be

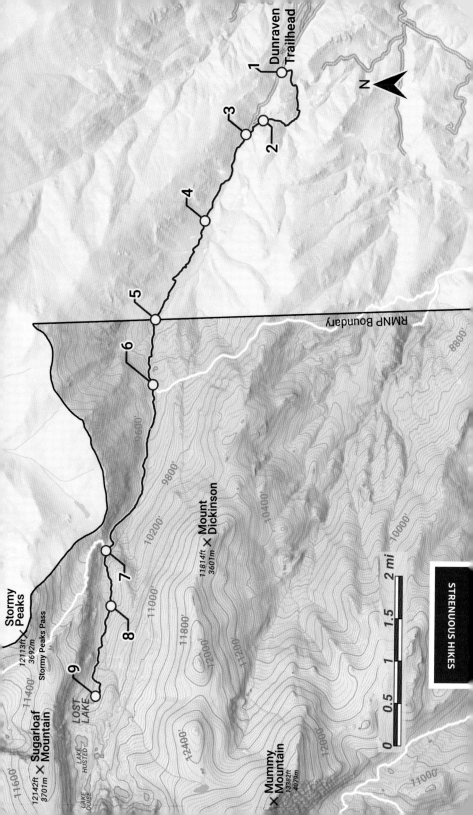

Dunraven Trailhead

Stormy Peaks

Sugarloaf Mountain
12142ft
3701m

12113ft
3692m

Stormy Peaks Pass

LOST LAKE

LAKE HUSTED

LAKE LOUISE

Mount Dickinson
11814ft
3601m

Mummy Mountain
13382ft
4079m

RMNP Boundary

N

STRENUOUS HIKES

0   0.5   1   1.5   2 mi

aware that the first few miles of trail are heavily used by horses, so stay aware and give them the right-of-way. Also, take note that the flood of 2013 destroyed much of the first few miles of the trail, especially areas close to the stream, so large areas of trail have been rebuilt. Some new sections have been built quite a ways from the stream, so it may not exactly match older maps, though the maps in this book are up-to-date.

The trail begins (#1) by heading directly south and soon begins a fairly steep descent of about 160 feet down to the edge of the North Fork of the Big Thompson River. You'll then follow this stream all the way up to Lost Lake. During this first section you'll be right next to it, and at just over half a mile you'll cross a bridge to the other side. In another half a mile the trail will cross the property of one of the Cheley camps. (#2) Check it out online to see how it is a life-changing place for many. As you reach the end of the camp, the trail will cross back over to the other side of the river and then connect with a dirt road. (#3) Turn left here. This is part of an old road that used to run all the way back to Dunraven Glade where there was a small settlement. This road soon turns back into a trail. It then begins to climb up the side of the hill on the right, as the old route was washed away. At just under three miles the forest opens at Dunraven Glade. (#4) This is a wonderful meadow dotted with ponderosa pines and filled with the sound of the rushing stream; it would be a great destination by itself and ideal for a picnic. The trail continues climbing above the meadow and soon returns into the trees, traveling first through a lodgepole pine forest and then through a varied forest while becoming increasingly rockier on the way.

At 4.3 miles the trail leaves Comanche Peaks Wilderness and

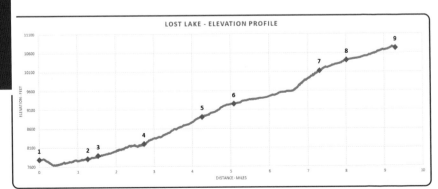

Roosevelt National Forest and enters Rocky Mountain National Park. (#5) In a few tenths of a mile the trail begins to level out and stays pretty gentle now for almost two miles. At a little over five miles you'll reach a junction with the North Boundary Trail. (#6) That trail leads down to the Cow Creek Trail but it is a long, rough trail with very few views. This is a good place to take a short break. If you need to filter some additional water, you can find it just a short ways down the North Boundary Trail. Then continue westward. At around 5.5 miles you'll enter a meadow with a sign saying Halfway. Don't be discouraged; you've hiked more than halfway there, but you are only halfway in terms of elevation gain. While you are here you'll get your first glimpse of the mountains ahead. Then in about half a mile you'll pass my favorite name for a campsite, "Happily Lost."

At around 6.5 miles you'll begin a more significant climb with about 600' of elevation gain over the next mile. Just take it slow and steady. Here the forest is transitioning from montane to subalpine. See if you can notice it. Before you get to the top, you'll reach the junction for the Stormy Peaks Trail. (#7) This is a nice detour if you have time, but be aware that the trail is one of the steepest in the park. At the intersection, you'll want to turn left. Before long you'll reach the top of the hill, and things will level out. There are still a few small hills to be climbed, but the worst is behind you.

At eight miles you reach my favorite part of this hike. The forest opens at Lost Meadows and you get a great view of the trail leading right toward the towering peaks in the distance. (#8) Soon you're back in the forest, and this section can be quite muddy, especially in early summer, so be prepared to get mud on your boots. This is also moose territory, so keep your eyes open. After climbing a few small hills and other wet sections, you'll pass by the first of the campsite trails for Lost Lake. You'll turn left here and cross the log bridge. You're almost there now. Follow the trail past the next campsite and at the sign for campsite #2, turn right and follow the trail down to the lake. (#9) Here you'll find a large lake with Sugarloaf Mountain high above it. If you walk around to the outlet stream off to your right, you'll get a great view of Rowe Peak and its smaller companions.

STRENUOUS HIKES

STRENUOUS HIKES

HAPPY HIKERS IN LOST MEADOWS · WAYPOINT 48

73 – LAKE NANITA

Overview

This hike leads you from Grand Lake up the North Inlet valley and then climbs from there up to two gorgeous lakes in the heart of Rocky Mountain National Park. While it can be done in a day by those who are very fit and fully acclimated to the elevation, most people who visit the park do this as a side trip while backpacking on the North Inlet.

The Stats

Distance Round Trip: 20.5 miles

Difficulty Rating: 389

Hiking Time: 13 hours and 40 minutes

Time to Go: early morning

Season: July until first snow

Primary Ecosystems: montane and subalpine

Views: meadows, marshland, and forest

Possible Wildlife: marmots, moose, and forest animals

Trail Conditions: Most of this trail is through deep forest. At times the trail is rough, but always very clear. There can be snow near the top into mid-July.

Reminder: This is a very long hike. Bring adequate food, a water filter, first aid, and a tracking device if possible. Leave very early if you plan to do this in one day.

Elevation Start: 8,520′

Highest Point: 11,077′

Total Elevation Gain: 3,690′

Trailhead: This hike begins at the North Inlet Trailhead just outside of Grand Lake; see page 124 for details.

Waypoints

1. North Inlet Trailhead	0.0	8,520′
2. Summerland Park Cabin	1.1	8,507′
3. Cascade Falls	3.4	8,814′
4. Big Pool	4.6	9,057′
5. Shallow lake	5.8	9,239′
6. Right at North Inlet Junction	7.1	9,607′
7. Lake Nokoni	9.3	10,774′
8. Lake Nanita	10.2	10,792′

Hike Description

The first part of this hike is described in the Summerland Park hike on page 129 and is then continued on the Cascade Falls hike

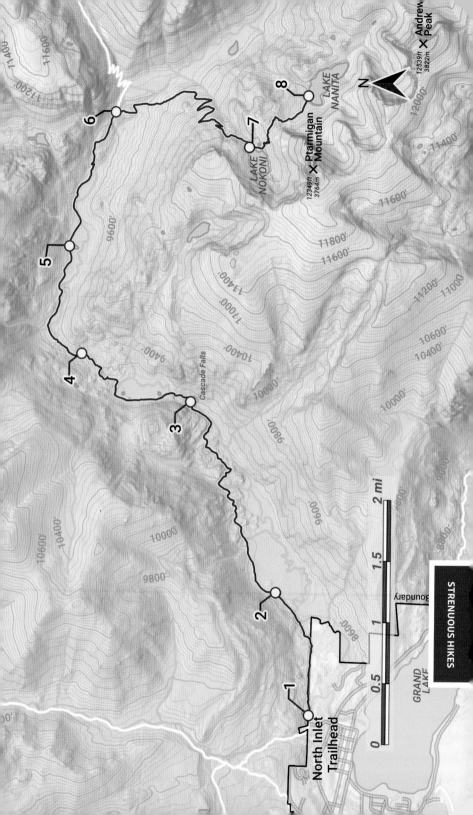

STRENUOUS HIKES

× Andrew Peak
12539ft
3822m

× Ptarmigan Mountain
12349ft
3764m

LAKE NANITA

8

7

LAKE NOKONI

6

5

Cascade Falls

4

3

2

1

North Inlet Trailhead

GRAND LAKE

Boundary

0   0.5   1   1.5   2 mi

N

on page 262. In summary, you'll follow the North Inlet Trail (**#1**) first through the meadows of Summerland Park (**#2**) and then climb up through the forest until you reach Cascade Falls (**#3**) at 3.4 miles.

Just a short ways past Cascade Falls you will pass a horse tie-up and then immediately after that you'll pass the junction for the horse bypass. The trail then comes alongside the river, following it for a short ways. This is a wonderful part of the hike. The trail then turns into the woods. As it does so, look off to your right and you'll see a marshy meadow that stretches on for some distance. You may run into moose in this area. Be aware that they are sometimes in the forest on the left side of the trail. On the morning I'm recording this there is a mule deer peacefully grazing in the silence of the meadow.

After the meadow, you'll cross two bridges over streams coming down from the side of Mount Patterson. The trail rejoins the North Inlet along a rocky bank. This is a good place to take a break and filter water for your water bottle. Just before five miles you'll pass an area of deeper water on the creek known as Big Pool. (**#4**) This is a popular area with some anglers. About half a mile later you'll cross another stream, this one coming down from the side of Snowdrift Peak.

At about 5.6 miles you'll notice another meadow on the right-hand side of the trail, then you'll walk through one of my favorite forested sections of trail. This is where I shot the cover for my book *Whispers in the Wilderness.* Just after this you'll notice a large shallow lake on your right, surrounded by marshy meadow. (**#5**) As you continue on you'll cross two bridges across Ptarmigan Creek. Notice all the fallen trees here from an intense windstorm, which occurred in early 2017. The trail then begins to climb more significantly, making a couple of switchbacks. Just under half a mile later you'll arrive at North Inlet Junction. (**#6**) The sign is on the right but it is not obvious. If you are tired it is possible to miss it, so keep your eyes open after the switchbacks.

At the junction, turn right and head down the trail and then down the rocky stairs. In 0.2 miles you'll reach a large bridge crossing the North Inlet. This is a great place to stop and have a break. If you need to filter water, you can find a good spot just a little ways farther up the trail. From here the trail begins its steep upward climb, heading primarily south for quite some ways. At about 8.5 miles you'll reach

STRENUOUS HIKES

the first turn to your right. This takes you into the woods and across   **441**
a small stream, followed by a left turn.

Now the trail begins climbing again. You'll make six switchbacks
and then the views begin to open. You'll notice a great deal of rockwork done to build this trail, including a section of trail that was
carved into the granite. From here the trail climbs less steeply and you
soon arrive at beautiful Lake Nokoni tucked in at the base of Ptarmigan Mountain. (#7) This place is spectacular enough that it would be
a worthy destination, but there's more to see ahead, so onward!

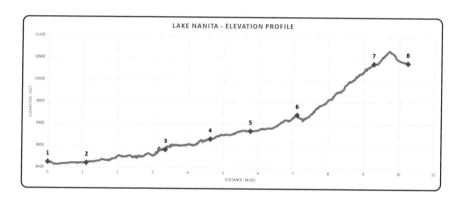

This next section often has snow in early summer. Be prepared
to either walk on the snow or on rocks to get around it. Some years
it simply isn't passable until mid-July. The trail climbs very steeply,
making six shorter switchbacks on its upward climb. Then it climbs
some more. Just before ten miles, the trail reaches the highest point
and begins a steep descent. At the bottom you'll arrive at a large
flower-filled meadow that will join you on a gentle walk to the lake.
(#8) Once you arrive at the lake's edge, you will enjoy one of my
favorite views in Rocky Mountain National Park. Filter some water,
soak in the beauty of this place, and then get ready to return, as you're
only halfway and it will probably take you as long to get down as it
took you to hike up.

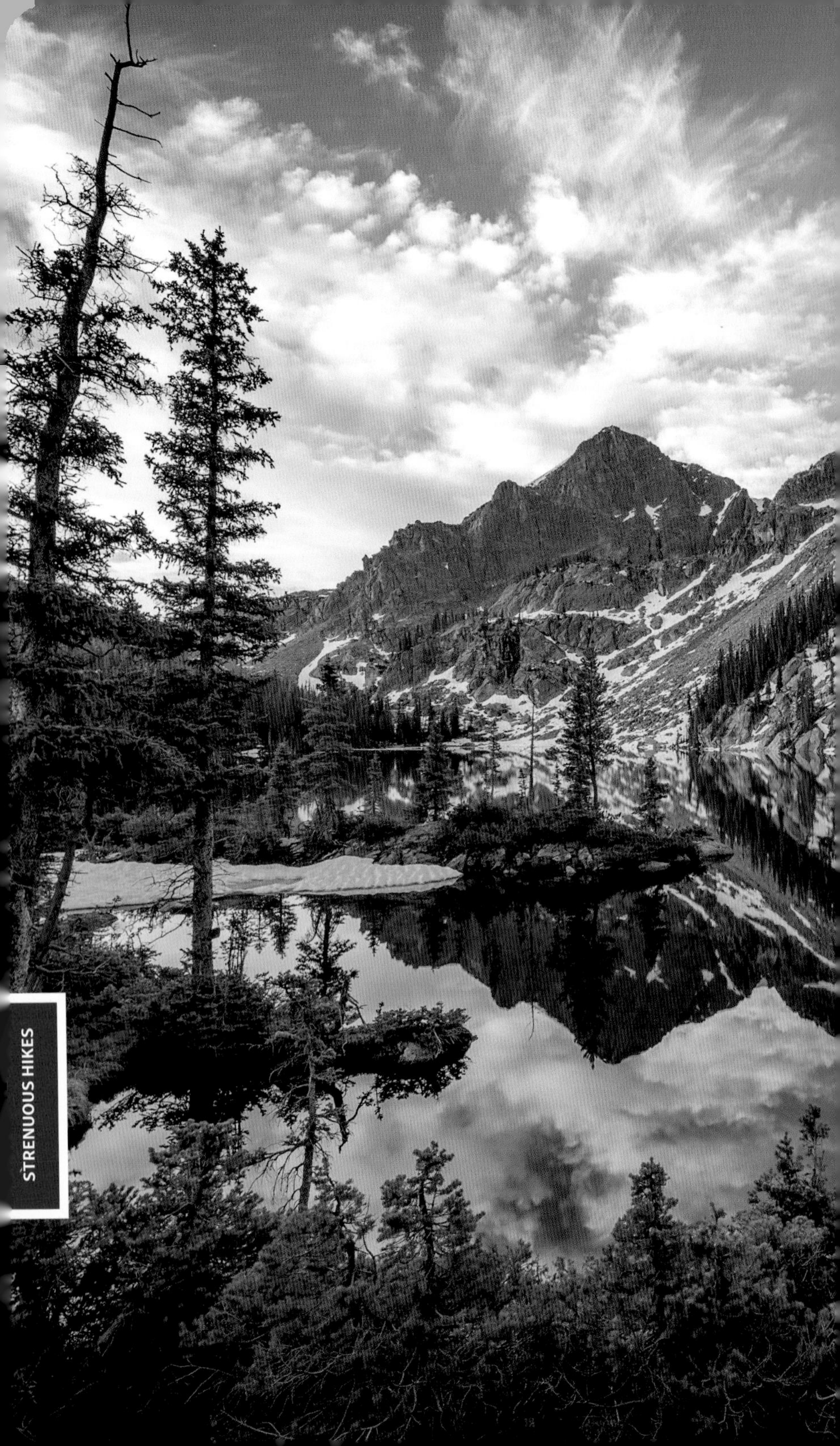

ANDREWS PEAK AND LAKE NANITA

74 – WESTERN LOOP

Overview

This loop hike is one of the classic hikes of Rocky Mountain National Park, giving you a chance to experience the full variety of the park's ecosystems as you hike through montane, subalpine, and alpine zones. Most people complete this hike over a period of three or more days, though there are a few who do it as a very long day hike. This section of trail is also part of the Continental Divide Trail.

The Stats

Distance: 25.8 miles

Difficulty Rating: 476

Hiking Time: 17 hours and 5 minutes

Time to Go: be in tundra during early morning or late evening

Season: July until first snow

Primary Ecosystems: montane, sub-alpine, and alpine

Views: forest, tundra, marsh, meadows

Possible Wildlife: forest animals, moose, elk, deer, marmots, and ptarmigan

Trail Conditions: vary greatly

Reminder: This is a significant hike, normally done in three days. You want to be fully acclimated before you attempt it to avoid altitude sickness. See the elevation portion of the safety chapter at the beginning of this book for more information.

Elevation Start: 8,552'

Highest Point: 12,273'

Total Elevation Gain: 4,411' (4,443' elevation loss)

Trailhead: This hike begins at the Tona-hutu Trailhead (see page 127 for details) and ends just a few hundred feet away at the North Inlet Trailhead, page 124.

Waypoints

1. Tonahutu Trailhead	0.0	8,552'
2. Haynach Lakes Trail junction	9.2	10,349'
3. Hallett Creek crossing	16.7	10,635'
4. North Inlet Trailhead	25.7	8,520'

Hike Description

Because this hike is quite long and is generally done in three segments, I've divided this hike into those segments. On the first day, hikers generally try to make it to a campsite near tree line. The next morning they make an early start, climb up above the trees, cross through the tundra, and then get back down to a campsite in the trees before the afternoon

storms arrive. The third day they make the remainder of the hike to the trailhead.

There is no clear consensus on whether hiking the route clockwise or counterclockwise is best. Because the climb is a little more gentle when hiked in a clockwise route, this is how I've chosen to write about it. If you do it in the opposite direction, you'll just need to read these segments in reverse order.

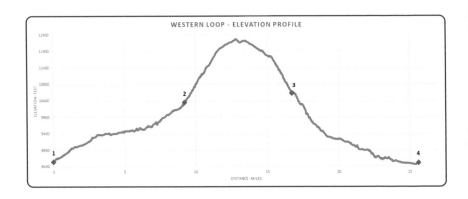

APPROACHING THE HIGHEST POINT

BACKPACKING NEAR WAYPOINT #2

74A – WESTERN LOOP – PART 1
(Tonahutu to Haynach Lakes Junction)

Overview

This first portion of the Western Loop follows Tonahutu Creek. It first leads through deep forest, alongside the aptly named Big Meadows where you are likely to see moose, and then up the Tonahutu valley, past graceful Granite Falls, and then through several large burn areas from a large forest fire before arriving at the Haynach Lakes Junction.

The Stats

Distance One Way: 9.2 miles

Difficulty Rating: 195

Hiking Time: 6 hours and 10 minutes

Time to Go: anytime

Season: mid-June through October

Primary Ecosystems: montane and subalpine

Views: forest, meadows, and streams

Possible Wildlife: moose and forest animals

Trail Conditions: better than average

Reminder: Keep your eyes open, as this is prime moose territory.

Elevation Start: 8,552'

Highest Point: 10,349'

Total Elevation Gain: 2,055'

Trailhead: This hike begins at the Tonahutu Trailhead; see page 127 for details.

Waypoints

1. Tonahutu Trailhead	0.0	8,552'
2. Kawuneeche Visitor Center junction	0.9	8,804'
3. Big Meadows	3.2	9,363'
4. Green Mountain junction	4.2	9,403'
5. Right at Onahu Trail junction	4.8	9,467'
6. First burn area	6.4	9,551'
7. Granite Falls	7.5	9,834'
8. Large burn area	8.0	9,968'
9. Haynach Lakes Trail junction	9.2	10,349'

Hike Description

The Tonahutu Creek Trail starts on the north side of the industrial building. (**#1**) That's the last building you'll see for quite a while, as the

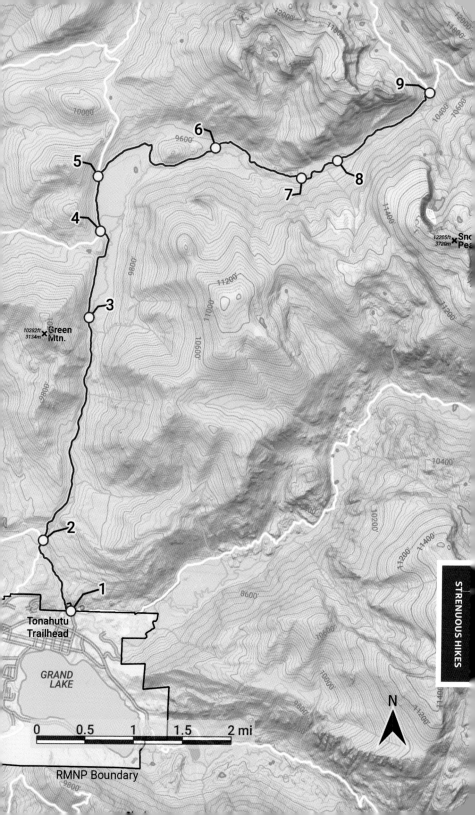

9

12000

11800

11600

11800

10000

9600

6

5

4

3

10282ft
3134m **×** Green
Mtn.

9800

2

1

Tonahutu
Trailhead

GRAND
LAKE

9800

7

12205ft
3720m **×** Sno
Pea

8

11400

11200

11200

10400

10600

10200

11200

11400

11200

11400

10400

10600

11000

11200

9800

11200

9800

11400

11200

8600

10800

10600

9800

STRENUOUS HIKES

0   0.5   1   1.5   2 mi

N

RMNP Boundary

trail heads into the woods. In just a minute after starting you'll come alongside Tonahutu Creek, which will be your guide all the way to the tundra. The trail on this first stretch is wide, gentle, and very smooth. At just under a mile the forest becomes very thick lodgepole pine, and here you'll pass your first junction. This one leads to the Grand Lake Lodge. Continue straight on and in about a minute you'll pass a second junction, which leads to the Kawuneeche Visitor Center. (**#2**)

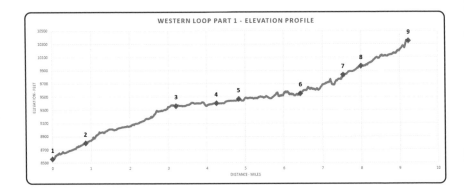

After crossing the creek at Harbison Ditch, you'll begin your first climb. It isn't very long and the trail levels out again. This section of forest is wonderful, though it can get muddy. At about 1.9 miles you'll see the first meadow off to your left. Soon there's one on your right, followed by another short climb. Then just after three miles you get your first view of Big Meadows stretching out to the north. (**#3**) At four miles you'll find a perfect little picnic spot overlooking the meadow. It even has logs cut and set out to provide excellent seating. Then just a short ways farther you reach the Green Mountain Trail junction. (**#4**)

The next sections are described in detail on first the Granite Falls hike (page 320) and then on the Haynach Lakes hike (page 412). To get accurate mileage while using those other hikes, simply add 2.5 miles to their mileage or use the waypoints listed above. In summary, you'll continue straight on the trail along the western edge of Big Meadows. It will turn to the north (**#6**) and lead you up the Tonahutu Creek valley, leading you through a burn area (**#7**), past Granite Falls (**#8**), and then through another burn area before eventually arriving at the Haynach Lakes junction. (**#9**)

STRENUOUS HIKES

THROUGH THE BURN AREA NEAR WAYPOINT #8

74B – WESTERN LOOP – PART 2
(Haynach Lakes junction to Hallett Creek)

Overview

This is the highlight of the Western Loop Trail, as it takes you high up into the tundra, along the edge of the Continental Divide. You'll have views of expansive tundra, high peaks, and a view over large areas of Rocky Mountain National Park.

The Stats

Distance One Way: 7.7 miles

Difficulty Rating: 174

Hiking Time: 5 hours and 5 minutes

Time to Go: early morning

Season: July through October

Primary Ecosystem: alpine

Views: expansive tundra and peak views

Possible Wildlife: elk, ptarmigan, marmots, pikas

Trail Conditions: sandy trails with rocky stairs

Reminder: This hike is highly exposed; there is nowhere to take shelter if a storm moves in. Avoid if there is a likelihood of thunderstorms. Also, remember not to walk on the tundra, only on the trail or rocks. Lastly, ask the park service about dangerous snowfields on the North Inlet if traveling before mid-July.

Elevation Start: 10,349'

Highest Point: 12,273'

Total Elevation Gain: 1,976' (1,690' elevation loss)

Waypoints

1. Haynach Lakes Trail junction	9.2	10,349'
2. Boulderfield rest stop	9.6	10,601'
3. Tree line	10.2	11,037'
4. Eureka Ditch	11.6	11,906'
5. High point (Ptarmigan Point)	13.0	12,273'
6. Right onto North Inlet Trail	13.6	12,223'
7. Stream crossing	15.5	11,675'
8. Hallett Creek crossing	16.9	10,635'

Hike Description

This section of hike should not be done during a thunderstorm. Checking the forecast, watching the skies, and leaving early can help you avoid them and stay safe.

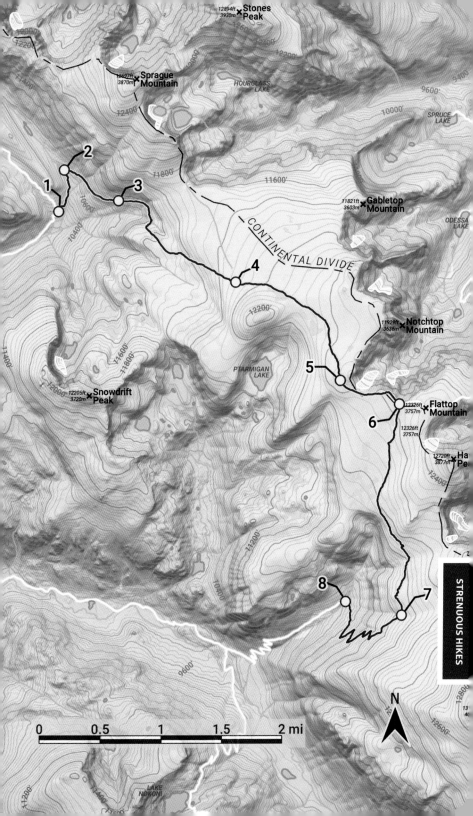

12894ft
3930m ✕ Stones
Peak

12497ft
3870m ✕ Sprague
Mountain

HOURGLASS
LAKE

10000'

SPRUCE
LAKE

9600'

9400'

11821ft
3603m ✕ Gabletop
Mountain

ODESSA
LAKE

2

1

3

11800'

CONTINENTAL DIVIDE

11600'

4

12200'

11929ft
3636m ✕ Notchtop
Mountain

12205ft
3720m ✕ Snowdrift
Peak

PTARMIGAN
LAKE

5

6

12326ft
3757m ✕ Flattop
Mountain

12326ft
3757m

12720ft
3877m ✕ Ha
Pe

8

7

STRENUOUS HIKES

0   0.5   1   1.5   2 mi

N

LAKE
NOKONI

From the Haynach Lakes junction continue east. (**#1**) It climbs fairly steeply through dark forest. You can hear streams off to the right. The trail briefly comes alongside a stream coming down from Sprague Glacier. Just another couple minutes up the trail, you'll reach a Boulderfield with a stream running through it and a sign warning you about the dangers above tree line. (**#2**) This is a good spot to filter water and fill up your water bottles before heading above tree line.

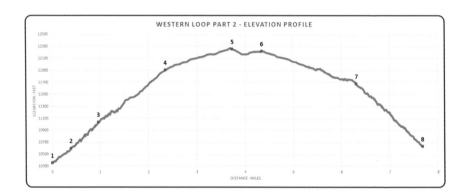

As you pass through the Boulderfield the trail is a bit rough and rocky. Occasionally there is a stream running down it. Soon, though, you'll head into the trees and the trail will be much smoother but unfortunately much more steep. This is actually the steepest section of the Tonahutu Trail. At just over ten miles the trail emerges from the trees and you enter the alpine world. (**#3**) The trail gets quite narrow and sandy with a steep drop on your right; hiking poles might be helpful here. Notice the abundant stonecrop blooming on the left side of the trail. As the trail climbs up along the side of the hill, you'll pass through one more small section of trees and then cross a small stream. This stream is the very beginning of Tonahutu Creek and is the last you will see of this faithful guide. You'll then make your way around a rock outcrop; be sure to look off to your right to see where you've come from.

As you climb the many stone stairs that have been so carefully built, you'll notice the four- to five-feet-tall historic rock cairns that guide your way. When you notice the trail leveling off, you are approaching the Eureka Ditch. (#4) This was built to redirect water to the city of Loveland but was dismantled in 1995. From here the trail is much more gentle and enjoyable as it winds through the tundra. You can read about this section in more detail on the Bighorn Flats hike (page 115).

At just over twelve miles the trail will crest a small ridge and open up views ahead of you. To your left will be a big pile of rocks, which is the summit of Knobtop Mountain.

At 13.0 miles you'll reach the highest point of the hike on the side of Ptarmigan Point. (#5) From here you can see down to Shadow Mountain Lake, part of Grand Lake. To the south you can see the block summit of Longs Peak and the rounded Hallett Peak, as well as many other views and peaks. You'll then head down the hill and in half a mile you'll get a great view down to your left of Odessa Lake, Lake Helene, and Two Rivers Lake.

In just a tenth of a mile from that view you'll reach the North Inlet Trail Junction. (#6) Turn right here and walk along this level path between very tall historic rock cairns that guide you into the distance. Slowly the trail slopes downward and after a while you'll see a valley appear in front of you. The trail is going to travel around the far side of this valley and then descend into it. To your left you'll be passing Hallett Peak, then when you are on the edge of the valley you'll have Otis Peak off to your left. This area gets a bit rocky and has some areas where willows are attempting to take over the trail. At the far side of the valley, you'll cross a stream. (#7) This is typically where you might first encounter snow in the early summer. If you do, turn around because the later snowfields are quite dangerous.

From here to Hallett Creek the trails drops over one thousand feet. It begins this descent by traveling rather precariously along the edge of this very steep slope. You'll then hike seven switchbacks on your way down to the valley below. After that last switchback the trail finally heads back into the trees. You'll cross several small streams before arriving at the bridge over Hallett Creek. (#8)

NORTH INLET TRAIL AFTER WAYPOINT #6

74C – WESTERN LOOP – PART 3
(Hallett Creek to North Inlet Trailhead)

Overview

This is the third segment of the Western Loop. It takes you from Hallett Creek, which is just below tree line, along the North Inlet Creek through deep forest, past numerous cascades, past Granite Falls, and then through the meadows of Summerland Park, down to the edge of the town of Grand Lake. It is a really enjoyable walk through the forest.

The Stats

Distance One Way: 8.9 miles

Difficulty Rating: 82

Hiking Time: 5 hours and 55 minutes

Time to Go: anytime

Season: June through October

Primary Ecosystems: subalpine and montane

Views: forest, streams, waterfall, and meadow

Possible Wildlife: forest animals and moose

Trail Conditions: average

Reminder: This is a long downhill hike; hiking poles can help protect your knees and ankles.

Elevation Start: 10,635'

Highest Point: 10,682'

Total Elevation Gain: 380' (2,495' elevation loss)

Waypoints

1. Hallett Creek crossing	16.9	10,635'
2. North Inlet Junction	18.7	9,595'
3. Shallow lake	20.0	9,237'
4. Big Pool	21.2	9,047'
5. Cascade Falls	22.5	8,793'
6. Summerland Park Cabin	24.6	8,507'
7. North Inlet Trailhead	25.8	8,520'

Hike Description

After crossing the bridge at Hallett Creek, continue down the trail. (#1) At first it may be a bit muddy, but soon the trail dries up and broadens as it heads westward. In a few minutes you'll hear the roar of Hallett Creek off to your left in the meadow. At this point the

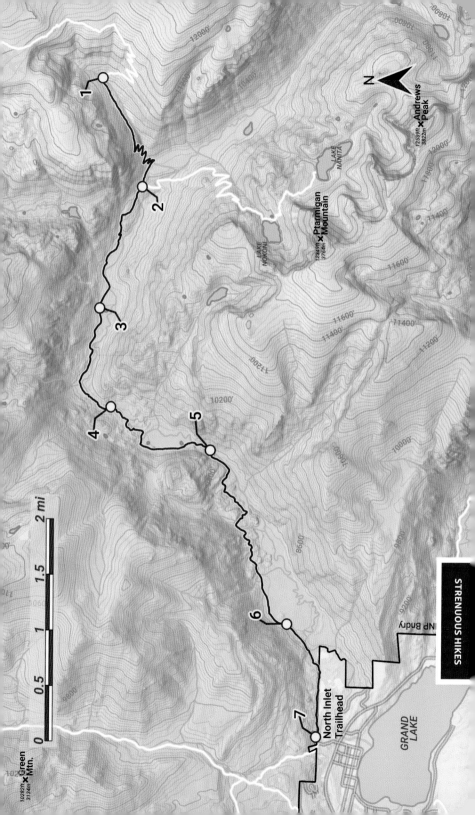

STRENUOUS HIKES

Green Mtn.
10282ft ×
3134m

Andrews
12539ft ×Peak
3822m

2 mi
1.5
1
0.5
0

1

2

3

4

5

6

7

North Inlet
Trailhead

RNP Bndry

GRAND
LAKE

LAKE
NANITA

Ptarmigan
×Mountain
12349ft
3764m

LAKE
NOKONI

N

rocky trail is sloping downward and aiming directly toward Ptarmigan Mountain. Soon the views over the valley to your left open and you get terrific views out toward Andrews Peak.

Just before eighteen miles you'll reach the start of a series of switchbacks. Over the next 0.7 miles you'll drop about six hundred feet with a total of ten switchbacks. At switchback number six there is a good place to take a break next to a series of cascades.

About a quarter mile after the last switchback, you'll pass the North Inlet Junction, which leads up to lakes Nokoni and Nanita (page 115). (**#2**) Continue straight past the junction and in half a mile you'll descend a few more switchbacks. About a third of a mile later you'll cross two log bridges over Ptarmigan Creek.

The trail comes alongside a large meadow on your left, and in a bit you'll see a shallow lake off to your left. (**#3**) This is a popular place with wildlife, so keep your eyes open. You'll pass through a beautiful section of forested trail, particularly when looking behind you.

The trail comes alongside the river a couple of times, with places to sit and enjoy the roaring waters. Then you'll pass by an area called Big Pool, where there is a fairly deep section of the stream where the waters seem to take a brief pause before continuing their journey to Grand Lake. (**#4**)

Just over a mile later you'll reach Cascade Falls. (**#5**) It is a bit of a scramble down to the falls but is a refreshing place to take a break. At this point you will probably see a significant increase in hikers, as you're not too far from your destination.

Two miles later the trail comes out from the woods alongside the Summerland Park cabin. (**#6**) From here the trail transitions to a dirt road and heads through the meadows of Summerland Park. You'll

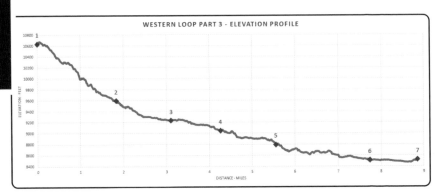

WESTERN LOOP PART 3 - ELEVATION PROFILE

VIEW OF ANDREWS PEAK AFTER WAYPOINT #1

soon find North Inlet Creek on your left, taking a much more casual and peaceful journey than it has so far.

This last stretch is quite exposed and can be very hot, so be sure to drink. You'll see a fence on your left that serves as the border for a horse meadow. There are occasionally horses out there to greet you. When the fence comes to an end, the road climbs upward through the trees and after a couple of turns it arrives at the North Inlet Trailhead, about four hundred feet from where your journey on the Western Loop began. (#7)

75 – LONGS PEAK (Keyhole Route)

Overview

Longs Peak is the highest summit in Rocky Mountain National Park, reaching a height of 14,259'. It can be seen from all over northern Colorado and beckons to those within its view to come and climb it. Yet this mountain is no walk in the park. **This is a serious and dangerous climb.** The journey to the summit of Longs Peak begins with a steep six-mile hike to the Boulderfield. At this point the trail ends and it transitions from a hike to a scramble. About half a mile later it becomes a serious climb that should only be attempted by those who are fully prepared and have ideal weather conditions. During this climb you'll hug the side of the mountain as you skirt over narrow ledges with drops of over one thousand feet.

While the climb to the summit isn't very long in terms of distance, it generally takes people as long to get to the summit and back down to the Boulderfield as it took them to get to the Boulderfield from the trailhead. For most people this is four to five hours. Factor this into your calculation of how much time you will need to get to the summit and back down below tree line to beat the afternoon thunderstorms. The lack of anywhere to take shelter from lightning makes it vitally important that you heed getting back down below tree line before storms arrive.

The Stats

Distance Round Trip: 14.1 miles

Difficulty Rating: not rated

Travel Time: 10–15 hours

Time to Go: 1:00–3:00 a.m. (It is necessary to leave so early to be back below tree line before thunderstorms arrive.)

Season: mid-July to mid-September

Primary Ecosystem: alpine

Terrain: The first two miles are through forest, followed by four miles of tundra. You then pass through a large Boulderfield. The remainder of the journey is on cliff edges and up a steep gully of loose rock.

Views: As you wrap around the peak, you'll experience views in every direction. This is the highest point between central Colorado and the Arctic Circle.

Trail Conditions: From the Boulderfield onward *it is not a hike, but a serious climb*. While there are some markers, there is no trail. The route crosses enormous sheer vertical rock faces with falling rocks. There are narrow ledges, loose rock, and steep cliffs. It requires scrambling and good route finding. A fall along here could be fatal.

Reminder: This route is a serious climb and is not for those with a fear of heights. It is highly exposed and should not be attempted if there is a potential for bad weather or when there is still

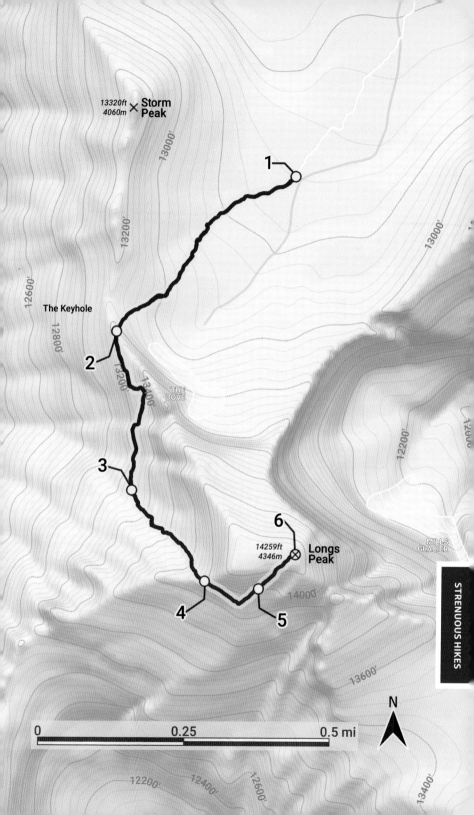

13320ft
4060m × Storm
Peak

1

13000'

13200'

12600'

The Keyhole

12800'

2

13200'

13400'

THE
DOVE

3

6

14259ft
4346m ⊗ Longs
Peak

4

5

12200'

MILLS
GLACIER

14000'

13600'

STRENUOUS HIKES

0   0.25   0.5 mi

N

12200'   12400'   12600'   13400'

any snow or ice on the route. Don't get summit fever, and be willing to turn around at any time. If you have any symptoms of altitude sickness, turn around. A helmet is recommended to protect against falling rock. Bring plenty of food and water. Don't forget: the summit is only halfway!

Elevation Start: 9,400'

Highest Point: 14,259'

Total RT Gain: 5,415'

Trailhead: This route begins at the Longs Peak Trailhead; see page 122 for details.

Waypoints

1. The Boulderfield	5.8	12,720'
2. The Keyhole	6.3	13,218'
3. The Trough – bottom	6.6	13,277'
4. The Trough – top	6.8	13,966'
5. Bottom of the Homestretch	6.9	14,041'
6. Longs Peak summit	7.0	14,259'

Hike Description

The first section of this trip is described in detail in the first portion of the Chasm Lake hike on page 354. From Chasm Junction the hike continues up to the Boulderfield. This is described on page 115. In summary, you'll hike from the Longs Peak Trailhead up to Chasm Junction above tree line. You'll then turn right and follow the trail up through the open tundra past Granite Junction, up to the Boulderfield at 12,700' above sea level.

The trail ends at the Boulderfield and from here onward it is a much more serious trek. Before I continue to describe it I strongly recommend that you visit: www.HikingRocky.com/longs. Here you will find more in-depth details about this route, known as the Keyhole Route, as well as current conditions. You want to be certain you know what you are getting into before attempting this, as it is not like anything else in this guide. In fact, we debated whether to include the summit of Longs Peak because of the danger it poses.

You'll generally want to be at the Boulderfield by sunrise to give you the best chance of getting back down into the forest before storms develop. (**#1**) From the Boulderfield look to the west-south-west toward the low point on the horizon. There you will see an unusual rock formation, a hole cut through part of the rock. That is the Keyhole, your next destination. There is no set trail. I find it

STRENUOUS HIKES

THE KEYHOLE AND AGNES VAILLE SHELTER

easiest to head to the right first and then wind around to the left. You'll be walking over boulders most of the way. Though it is only half a mile, it may take you thirty to sixty minutes. The last stretch up to the Keyhole is very steep and will require the use of hands and feet. (#2) When you get near the top you'll notice the Agnes Vaille Shelter, which was built to honor her after she died following a winter summit of Longs Peak in 1925. This shelter provides protection from the wind but no protection from lightning.

LONGS PEAK AND ROUTE FROM WAYPOINT #2 - #4

As you pass through the Keyhole (sometimes known as the "Blowhole" by locals for the way the wind often howls through here) the world drops away on the other side, and you'll be looking over Black, Frozen, Italy, and Green lakes far below. Look to your left and you'll see a painted bull's-eye on the rock. These will be your guides to the summit. Failure to follow these could have serious consequences. Follow the bull's-eyes for the safest route. Sometimes they will lead you upward and sometimes downward, so scan until you can find the next one before moving. This first section after the Keyhole is called the Ledges. Travel across a series of very narrow ledges along a cliff edge. Carefully climb a constricted slot-like section with two iron bars drilled into the rock. Continue upward toward the high point along the Ledges section. Then follow a gradually descending traverse to the base of the Trough. Take note of the Ledges/Trough junction, as some climbers have difficulty locating this point while on the descent.

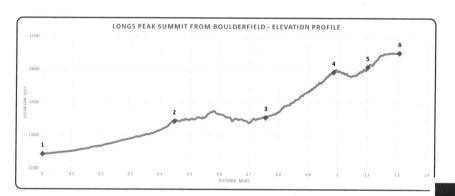

LONGS PEAK SUMMIT FROM BOULDERFIELD - ELEVATION PROFILE

When you arrive at the Trough you will know it. (**#3**) It is a very steep gully filled with loose rock that stretches up for quite a long ways. People near the top of it will appear smaller than ants. It is highly recommended that you wear a helmet here, as there may be falling rock. Be sure to climb carefully to avoid knocking rocks down on others. Continue to watch for the bull's-eyes to lead you the best way up this challenging section. When you reach the top of the Trough, there is a short but very steep rock to be climbed. (**#4**) I estimate it is

APPROACHING WAYPOINT #3

about fifteen feet high. Once you scale this you arrive at the start of the Narrows.

The Narrows crosses a sheer vertical rock face on a narrow ledge. Take your time and pay attention to where you put your hands and feet. A series of boulders and natural handholds in the rock wall will assist you on this constricted ledge. After you pass the Narrows, the bull's-eyes will lead you upward to the northeast where you will eventually reach the Homestretch. (#5)

The Homestretch is a polished granite slab that guards the summit. This section requires scrambling with your hands and feet. It is very steep and is often slowgoing, especially on the way down. Be sure to avoid any snow or ice, which can be found on this ledge throughout the summer. Although many options exist, the bull's-eyes will generally provide you with the best route to the summit.

As you crest the top of the Homestretch you'll find yourself on a very large and relatively flat but rocky field. If it wasn't for all the rocks it would make a great football field. Head straight ahead toward the highest boulders. This is the official summit of Long Peak. (#6) Just beyond is a stomach-turning view of Chasm Lake far below.

Remember that once you've reached the summit, you are halfway on your journey. Take a moment to have a snack and catch your breath. From up here you have a good vantage point to look around; be aware of any forming storms in the distance. Even if you don't see a sign of developing storms, be sure to be off the summit early in the day, as they can form very quickly. I've been up there on a clear morning and had a major thunderstorm develop from nothing within an hour. I was pelted with intense hail and had lightning crashing all around. It's very scary and dangerous. You're not only a target for lightning but the rocks can get very slippery as well. This greatly increases the difficulty and the time required to descend. Whether or not the weather is cooperating, remember to use great caution and stick to the route, following the bull's-eyes. Most accidents occur on the way down.

STRENUOUS HIKES

NAVIGATING THE LEDGES AFTER WAYPOINT #4

LOOKING DOWN THE TROUGH FROM JUST BELOW WAYPOINT #4

DEFINITIONS

Alpine: This is the zone that begins around 11,500 feet. It covers the top third of the park. Here the average temperature is not warm enough to support trees.

Cairns: A man-made pile of rocks that designates the location of the trail. While there are numerous historic rock cairns, making new cairns is not allowed in national parks.

Ecosystem: A community of both living and nonliving things that have developed a complex intertwined relationship. There are three distinct ecosystems in Rocky Mountain National Park: montane, subalpine, and alpine.

Krumholz: German word for "crooked wood" used to describe the small deformed trees you'll find around tree line. The deformity comes from the harsh conditions. Many of these trees can be hundreds of years old.

Montane: The montane zone is the lowest ecosystem of Rocky Mountain National Park, beginning at about 7,000 feet and extending up to about 9,000 feet.

Postholing: Breaking through a hard layer of snow and sinking up to the knee or waist because the hiker forgot to wear snowshoes or skis. This can be the most miserable way to hike in the Park and it also ruins the trail for others.

Saddle: A saddle is the lowest point between two connected mountains.

Scrambling: This is when the hike requires the use of your hands for additional stabilization. Normally scrambling involves climbing up a steep section of rocks but not so steep that you require ropes and a harness.

Scree: This term is used to refer to large piles of rocks at the base of a cliff or a mountain; generally scree is used to refer to small unstable rocks that will often slide with each step.

Subalpine: The subalpine zone is the middle ecosystem in Rocky Mountain National Park and is a transitional zone between the thick forests of the montane ecosystem and the treeless alpine zone. It begins at about 9,000 feet and extends up to about 11,500 feet.

Switchback: Instead of heading straight up a mountain, most trails conquer the steepest sections by zigzagging up a slope, making the climb gentler. Switchbacks generally make a nearly 180-degree turn.

Tarns: These are small bodies of water found throughout the mountains. Technically it refers to ponds carved out by glaciers, but the term is often used more broadly. It comes from the Old Norse word *tjörn*, which simply means "pond."

Talus: This term is used to refer to large piles of rocks at the base of a cliff or mountain; generally these are larger rocks that are often semi-stable.

Trailhead: The starting point for a hike. Normally this will have a parking lot for vehicles and a sign designating the start of the trail.

Tree line: The transition point between forest and open tundra. Above this area it is too cold for trees to grow. Here you will find smaller dwarf trees that are just managing to survive.

Tundra: Areas where the average temperature is too cold for trees to grow. In Rocky Mountain National Park that area begins between 11,000 feet and 11,500 feet. Generally tundra is used to refer to the areas above tree line that appear grassy, though they are actually not typical grass but special plants that have adapted to the extreme temperatures and winds.

Undergrowth: The plants that grow beneath the trees in a forest.

ADDITIONAL RESOURCES

I f you would like to learn more about Rocky Mountain National Park there are many great books available. Here is a short list of some you may find helpful. Many of these can be found in the bookstores in the park itself.

Human History

- *Rocky Mountain National Park: A History* by C. W. Buchholtz. This is a very enjoyable and easy-to-read book on the history of the area, beginning with the earliest-known humans to have traveled through here, up to the modern era. The book is filled with fascinating stories that will keep you reading.
- *Rocky Mountain National Park Pictorial History* by Kenneth Jessen. This is a great book of old photos of the national park, giving you an idea of how things have changed. It shows many buildings that once existed in the park such as Old Forest Inn, Eugenia Mine, Stead's Ranch, etc., as well as the early days of Old Fall River Road and Trail Ridge Road.
- *Rocky Mountain National Park: The First 100 Years* by Mary Taylor Young
- *My Pioneer Life: The Memoirs of an Estes Park Frontiersman* by Abner E. Sprague
- *Mountain Valley Journals: Sketches of Moraine Park and Estes Park Through Time* – Rocky Mountain Conservancy

Natural History

- *Rocky Mountain National Park Natural History Handbook* by John C. Emerick. Learn about the geological formation of the park, its various ecosystems, wildlife, and plant life. It's filled with beautiful color photos and detailed diagrams.

- *Mammals: Wild & Watchable Wildlife* – Rocky Mountain Conservancy
- *Wildlife Viewing of the Rocky Mountains* – Rocky Mountain Conservancy
- *Alpine Wildflowers of the Rocky Mountains* by Beatrice E. Willard and Michael Smithson
- *Geology Along Trail Ridge Road: A Self-Guided Tour for Motorists* by Omer B. Raup

INDEX

QUICK STATS

Destination	Trailhead	Distance One Way	Elevation Gain 1 Way	Elevation Loss 1 Way	Starting Elevation	Destination Elevation	Highest Point	Page
Adams Falls	East Inlet	0.3	92	36	8,400	8,426	8,475	175
Alberta Falls	Bear Lake	0.9	166	230	9,475	9,394	9,475	188
Alberta Falls	Glacier Gorge	0.8	233	14	9,175	9,394	9,394	188
Alluvial Fan Bridge	East Alluvial Fan	0.2	110	64	8,576	8,613	8,651	154
Alluvial Fan Bridge	West Alluvial Fan	0.2	28	0	8,585	8,613	8,613	154
Alluvial Fan Hike	West Alluvial Fan	0.4	101	110	8,585	8,576	8,651	154
Alpine Ridge Hike	Alpine Visitor Center	0.3	209	0	11,796	12,005	12,005	210
Alpine Visitor Center	Milner Pass	4.0	1,209	163	10,750	11,796	10,750	210
Arch Rocks	Fern Lake	1.2	158	75	8,155	8,238	8,238	197
Balanced Rock	Lumpy Ridge	3.9	1,371	468	7,840	8,744	8,847	310
Bear Lake	Fern Lake	8.5	2,655	1,225	8,155	9,475	10,700	292
Bear Lake	North Inlet	16.8	4,186	3,246	8,520	9,475	12,326	422
Bear Lake	Park & Ride	3.6	290	1,131	8,635	9,475	9,765	200
Bear Lake	Tonahutu	17.8	4,087	3,176	8,552	9,475	12,326	426
Bear Lake Loop	Bear Lake	0.6	71	71	9,475	-	9,522	146
Beaver Boardwalk Hike	Beaver Boardwalk	0.1	0	10	9,146	9,136	9,146	133
Bierstadt Lake (NW Access)	Bear Lake	2.0	290	332	9,475	9,435	9,765	200
Bierstadt Lake (NW Access)	Bierstadt Lake	1.7	605	29	8,850	9,435	9,454	238
Bierstadt Lake (NW Access)	Park & Ride	1.6	782	0	8,635	9,435	9,435	200
Big Meadows	Green Mountain	1.7	678	73	8,794	9,403	9,475	284
Big Meadows Loop	Green Mountain	7.3	1,325	1,325	8,794	-	9,922	284
Big Pool	North Inlet	4.6	835	308	8,520	9,047	9,047	438
Bighorn Flats Hike	Bear Lake	6.5	2,968	522	9,475	11,906	12,326	408

Destination	Trailhead	Distance One Way	Elevation Gain 1 Way	Elevation Loss 1 Way	Starting Elevation	Destination Elevation	Highest Point	Page
Black Canyon Trail Hike	Lumpy Ridge	2.0	385	262	7,840	7,963	7,963	230
Black Lake	Bear Lake	4.8	1,415	279	9,475	10,611	10,611	302
Black Lake	Glacier Gorge	4.7	1,499	63	9,175	10,611	10,611	302
Bluebird Lake	Wild Basin	6.4	2,794	311	8,500	10,983	10,983	404
Boulderfield	Longs Peak	5.8	3,318	0	9,400	12,720	12,720	400
Bridal Veil Falls	Lumpy Ridge	6.3	1,891	927	7,840	8,822	8,847	376
Calypso Cascades	Wild Basin	1.8	639	0	8,500	9,139	9,139	222
Cascade Falls	Bear Lake	13.5	2,913	3,523	9,475	8,803	12,326	422
Cascade Falls	North Inlet	3.4	574	280	8,520	8,814	8,861	262
Chasm Falls	Chasm Falls Parking	0.1	0	48	9,091	9,043	9,091	160
Chasm Falls	West Alluvial Fan	2.3	560	48	8,583	9,043	9,091	162
Chasm Junction	Longs Peak	3.3	2,133	0	9,400	11,533	11,533	354
Chasm Lake	Longs Peak	4.2	2,566	80	9,400	11,797	11,806	354
Chasm Meadow	Longs Peak	3.8	2,290	80	9,400	11,530	11,610	354
Chipmunk Lake	Lawn Lake	3.9	2,204	64	8,540	10,680	10,744	346
Colorado River Source	Colorado River	7.3	1,797	613	9,010	10,184	10,194	390
Confusion Junction	Finch Lake	2.3	1140	0	8,470	9,610	9,610	330
Confusion Junction	Finch Lake	2.3	1,218	0	8,476	9,610	9,610	330
Copeland Falls	Wild Basin	0.3	76	0	8,500	8,576	8,576	222
Coyote Valley Hike	Coyote Valley	0.6	12	30	8,834	8,816	8,834	142
Crystal Lake	Lawn Lake	7.5	3,130	117	8,540	11,525	11,553	418
Cub Lake	Cub Lake	2.4	699	103	8,080	8,671	8,676	246
Cub Lake Loop	Cub Lake	6.1	674	674	8,080	-	8,751	254
Das Boot	Lumpy Ridge	1.3	740	25	7,840	8,555	8,555	242
Deer Mountain	Deer Mountain	3.1	1,243	167	8,930	10,006	10,006	276
Dream Lake	Bear Lake	1.1	474	29	9,475	9,920	9,921	205
Dream Lake Overlook	Bear Lake	1.6	1,004	0	9,475	10,479	10,479	362
Dunraven Glade	Dunraven	2.7	556	145	7,789	8,200	8,200	432
East Meadow	East Inlet	0.6	137	53	8,400	8,498	8,501	175
East Meadow Overlook	East Inlet	1.3	241	66	8,400	9,878	8,575	338
Eastern Ute Hike	Ute Crossing	6.2	318	3,288	11,438	8,437	11,659	298
Emerald Lake	Bear Lake	1.7	771	135	9,475	10,111	10,132	226
Emerald Lake Overlook	Bear Lake	2.9	1,873	0	9,475	11,348	11,348	362
Estes Cone	Lily Lake	3.7	2,220	141	8,931	11,010	11,010	358

Destination	Trailhead	Distance One Way	Elevation Gain 1 Way	Elevation Loss 1 Way	Starting Elevation	Destination Elevation	Highest Point	Page
Estes Cone	Longs Peak	3.2	1,793	183	9,400	11,010	11,010	326
Estes Park Overlook	Lumpy Ridge	0.9	558	0	7,840	8,398	8,398	242
Eugenia Mine	Longs Peak	1.4	459	28	9,400	9,841	9,859	326
Eureka Ditch	Bear Lake	6.5	2,968	522	9,475	11,906	12,326	408
Fern Falls	Fern Lake	2.6	779	110	8,155	8,824	8,824	288
Fern Lake	Bear Lake	5.0	1,341	1,231	9,475	9,527	10,700	292
Fern Lake	Fern Lake	3.7	1,482	110	8,155	9,527	9,527	288
Finch Lake	Finch Lake	4.3	1,954	250	8,470	9,925	10,119	330
Flattop Mountain	Bear Lake	4.2	2,866	0	9,475	12,326	12,326	362
Flattop Mountain	North Inlet	11.6	3,246	380	8,520	12,326	12,326	422
Flattop Mountain	Tonahutu	13.6	4,087	310	8,552	12,326	12,326	426
Forest Canyon Overlook	Forest Canyon Parking	0.1	14	26	11,699	11,654	11,654	163
Gem Lake	Lumpy Ridge	1.7	1,029	25	7,840	8,844	8,844	242
Glacier Gorge Junction	Bear Lake	2.1	565	240	9,475	9,786	9,810	250
Glacier Gorge Junction	Glacier Gorge	2.0	659	24	9,175	9,786	9,810	250
Grand Lake (North Inlet TH)	Bear Lake	16.8	3,246	4,186	9,475	8,520	12,326	422
Grand Lake (Tonahutu TH)	Bear Lake	17.8	3,176	4,087	9,475	8,552	12,326	426
Grand Lake Overlook	East Inlet	3.0	869	102	8,400	9,167	9,167	338
Granite Falls	Bear Lake	10.4	2,866	2,492	9,475	9,834	12,326	426
Granite Falls	Green Mountain	5.0	1,298	258	8,794	9,834	9,834	320
Granite Falls	Tonahutu	7.5	1,540	258	8,552	9,834	9,834	320
Granite Pass	Longs Peak	4.4	2,677	0	9,400	12,077	12,077	400
Hallett Creek Crossing	Bear Lake	8.0	2,866	1,697	9,475	10,629	12,326	422
Hallett Creek Crossing	North Inlet	8.9	2,495	380	8,520	10,629	10,682	422
Hallett Creek Crossing	Tonahutu	16.7	3,979	1,898	8,552	10,629	12,273	444
Haynach Junction	Bear Lake	8.7	2,873	1,977	9,475	10,349	12,326	426
Haynach Junction	Green Mountain	6.7	1,813	258	8,794	10,349	10,349	412
Haynach Junction	Tonahutu	9.2	2,055	258	8,552	10,349	10,349	448
Haynach Lakes	Bear Lake	10.2	3,639	1,994	9,475	11,098	11,115	426
Haynach Lakes	Green Mountain	8.2	2,614	310	8,794	11,098	11,115	412
Haynach Lakes	Tonahutu	10.7	2,856	310	8,552	11,098	11,115	448

Destination	Trailhead	Distance One Way	Elevation Gain 1 Way	Elevation Loss 1 Way	Starting Elevation	Destination Elevation	Highest Point	Page
Hidden Valley Loop	Hidden Valley	0.4	76	76	9,412	-	9,479	165
Holzwarth Ranch	Holzwarth Historic Site	0.5	28	28	8,911	8,912	8,912	150
Homestretch	Longs Peak	6.9	4,641	278	9,400	14,041	14,041	462
Jewel Lake	Bear Lake	3.1	739	256	9,475	9,954	9,958	302
Jewel Lake	Glacier Gorge	3.0	818	40	9,175	9,954	9,958	302
Keyhole	Longs Peak	6.3	3,818	0	9,400	13,218	13,218	462
Lake Haiyaha	Bear Lake	2.0	920	170	9,475	10,220	10,265	270
Lake Haiyaha Loop	Bear Lake	5.3	1,370	1,370	9,475	-	10,265	270
Lake Haiyaha via Alberta Falls	Glacier Gorge	3.2	1,299	259	9,175	10,220	10,220	270
Lake Irene	Lake Irene Parking	0.1	0	30	10,664	10,634	10,664	168
Lake Irene Overlook	Lake Irene Parking	0.4	0	110	10,664	10,554	10,664	168
Lake Nanita	Bear Lake	12.8	4,511	3,132	9,475	10,792	11,077	422
Lake Nanita	North Inlet	10.2	2,981	709	8,520	10,792	11,077	438
Lake Nokoni	Bear Lake	11.9	4,208	2,821	9,475	10,774	10,774	422
Lake Nokoni	North Inlet	9.3	2,678	424	8,520	10,774	10,774	438
Lake of Glass	Bear Lake	4.3	1,567	230	9,475	10,812	10,812	314
Lake of Glass	Glacier Gorge	3.9	1,661	24	9,175	10,812	10,812	314
Lake Verna	East Inlet	6.6	2,043	216	8,400	10,227	10,266	382
La Poudre Pass Ranger Station	Colorado River	7.0	1,797	613	9,010	10,184	10,194	390
Lawn Lake	Lawn Lake	6.1	2,535	65	8,540	11,007	11,010	342
Lightning Bridge	Longs Peak	1.9	1,177	0	9,400	10,577	10,577	354
Lily Lake Loop	Lily Lake	0.8	17	17	8,931	-	8,942	134
Lily Ridge Loop	Lily Lake	1.3	189	189	8,931	-	9,114	184
Little Yellowstone	Colorado River	4.6	1,160	501	9,010	9,660	9,727	390
Loch (The)	Bear Lake	2.9	962	240	9,475	10,197	10,197	266
Loch (The)	Glacier Gorge	2.8	1,046	24	9,175	10,197	10,197	266
Lone Pine Lake	East Inlet	5.0	1,608	164	8,400	9,844	9,844	338
Longs Peak	Longs Peak	7.0	5,137	278	9,400	14,259	14,259	462
Lost Lake	Dunraven	9.3	3,124	183	7,789	10,730	10,768	432
Lost Meadow	Dunraven	8.0	2,764	145	7,789	10,408	10,408	432
Lulu City	Colorado River	3.5	796	434	9,010	9,363	9,492	280
Lumpy Loop	Lumpy Ridge	10.7	2,604	2,604	7,840	-	9,122	376
Mills Lake	Bear Lake	2.8	727	245	9,475	9,957	9,962	250
Mills Lake	Glacier Gorge	2.7	816	29	9,175	9,957	9,962	250
Mirror Lake	Corral Creek	6.3	1,535	536	10,034	11,028	11,033	372
Moore Park	Longs Peak	1.7	487	164	9,400	9,706	9,859	326

Destination	Trailhead	Distance One Way	Elevation Gain 1 Way	Elevation Loss 1 Way	Starting Elevation	Destination Elevation	Highest Point	Page
North Inlet / Tonahutu Junction	Bear Lake	4.5	2,866	108	9,475	12,223	12,326	408
North Inlet / Tonahutu Junction	Tonahutu	13.6	4,031	310	8,552	12,223	12,273	426
North Inlet Junction	North Inlet	7.1	1,383	308	8,520	9,595	9,595	422
North Inlet Junction	Tonahutu	18.7	4,103	3,060	8,552	9,595	12,273	444
North Inlet Junction	Bear Lake	9.7	2,938	2,803	9,475	9,595	12,326	422
North Inlet TH (Grand Lake)	Bear Lake	16.8	3,246	4,186	9,475	8,520	12,326	422
Nymph Lake	Bear Lake	0.5	231	0	9,475	9,706	9,706	205
Odessa Hike	Bear Lake	8.5	1,358	2,677	9,475	-	10,700	292
Odessa Lake	Bear Lake	4.2	1341	791	9,475	9,967	10,700	292
Odessa Lake	Fern Lake	4.3	1,923	110	8,155	9,967	9,967	288
Ouzel Falls	Wild Basin	2.7	125	130	8,500	9,382	9,387	258
Ouzel Lake	Wild Basin	5	1,833	308	8,500	10,025	10,025	350
Park & Ride	Bear Lake	3.6	290	1,131	9,475	8,635	9,765	200
Pear Lake	Finch Lake	6.3	2,396	294	8,470	10,594	10,605	386
Pool (The)	Bear Lake	6.9	1,225	2,381	9,475	8,319	10,700	292
Pool (The)	Cub Lake	3.5	674	434	8,080	8,317	8,751	254
Pool (The)	Fern Lake	1.7	270	110	8,155	8,319	8,350	197
Rest Rock	Bear Lake	2.4	1,508	0	9,475	10,983	10,983	362
Ribbon Falls	Bear Lake	4.7	1,336	289	9,475	10,522	10,522	302
Ribbon Falls	Glacier Gorge	4.6	1,420	73	9,175	10,522	10,522	302
Sandbeach Lake	Sandbeach Lake	4.3	2,027	30	8,316	10,313	10,343	334
Shadow Mountain Dam (Direct)	East Shore	2.6	260	289	8,440	8,379	8,500	234
Shipler Cabins	Colorado River	2.1	494	278	9,010	9,247	9,282	280
Sky Pond	Bear Lake	4.3	1,652	240	9,475	10,887	10,887	314
Sky Pond	Glacier Gorge	4.2	1,726	24	9,175	10,877	10,877	314
Sprague Lake Loop	Sprague Lake Parking	0.8	34	34	8,701	-	8,721	138
Storm Pass	Lily Lake	3.1	1,451	141	8,931	10,241	10,241	358
Storm Pass	Longs Peak	2.6	1,019	183	9,400	10,236	10,236	326
Summerland Park Cabin	North Inlet	1.2	38	51	8,520	8,507	8,507	192
Summerland Park Hike	North Inlet	1.6	107	51	8,520	8,576	8,576	192
Thunder Lake	Wild Basin	6.6	2,469	375	8,500	10,594	10,689	396
Timber Lake	Timber Lake	5	2,256	222	9,054	11,088	11,091	368
Timberline Falls	Bear Lake	4.2	1,505	240	9,475	10,740	10,740	314
Timberline Falls	Glacier Gorge	3.8	1,589	24	9,175	10,740	10,740	314
Timberline Pass	Upper Beaver Meadows	4.3	3,182	66	8,345	11,461	11,461	298

Destination	Trailhead	Distance One Way	Elevation Gain 1 Way	Elevation Loss 1 Way	Starting Elevation	Destination Elevation	Highest Point	Page
Timberline Pass	Ute Crossing	1.9	252	198	11,438	11,461	11,659	218
Toll Memorial	Rock Cut	0.6	176	0	12,110	12,286	12,286	180
Tombstone Ridge Hike	Ute Crossing	1.9	252	198	11,438	11,461	11,659	218
Tonahutu TH (Grand Lake)	Bear Lake	17.8	3,176	4,087	9,475	8,552	12,326	426
Trough (The)	Longs Peak	6.6	3,957	179	9,400	13,277	13,374	462
Tundra Communities Hike	Rock Cut	0.6	176	0	12,110	12,286	12,286	180
Twin Sisters Saddle	Twin Sisters	3.1	2,178	34	9,206	11,350	11,350	306
Upper Beaver Meadows	Ute Crossing	6.2	306	3,276	11,438	8,437	11,659	298
Upper Beaver Meadows Loop	Upper Beaver Meadows	1.1	108	108	8,345	-	8,544	171
Ute Meadow	Upper Beaver Meadows	2.9	1,189	66	8,345	9,534	9,534	298
Ute Meadow	Ute Crossing	3.3	252	2,125	11,438	9,534	11,659	298
Western Loop	Tonahutu	25.8	4,311	4,343	8,552	8,520	12,273	444
Western Ute Hike	Alpine Visitor Center	4	163	1,209	11,796	10,750	11,796	214
Ypsilon Lake	Lawn Lake	4.3	2,255	238	8,540	10,559	10,744	346

ABOUT THE AUTHOR

Erik Stensland was born in Minnesota in 1968 but moved many times before he was 18. His first real memories are from the mountains outside of Helena, Montana, where at ages 5 and 6 he would spend his days hiking through the forest, exploring miles of mountain terrain around his house. Everywhere he moved he was drawn to the natural world, spending his days creating his own secret trails up to the top of nearby hills or climbing a tree to get a better view. His junior high and high school years were spent cycling throughout the countryside where he could enjoy quiet and beautiful views. Throughout Erik's life, the beauty of nature has called to him.

After college Erik moved overseas, living in Austria, Bulgaria, Albania, and Kosovo. He met his wife, Joanna, in Austria and they spent over a decade working with the Albanian people, doing everything from creating an ecotourism program, teaching English, assisting local artists, starting a refugee agency, helping local churches meet the needs of their society, and many other projects.

After suffering severe burnout, Erik and Joanna moved to Colorado in 2004. Erik became a landscape photographer in the hope that this might be a way to heal in the silence of the wilderness. While it has involved more office work than he ever imagined, he's still managed to explore nearly every corner of Rocky Mountain National Park, hiking every trail, most of them more times than he can count.

In 2007 Erik opened his gallery in Estes Park. Since then Erik has become one of the primary photographers focusing on Rocky Mountain National Park. He's published numerous books, opened other gallery and display locations, and contributes to various local and national publications.

Erik tends to avoid the spotlight and can most often be found heading in the opposite direction of the crowds, looking for quiet trails that lead into places of beauty and silence.

PHOTO BY CHRISTOPHER AMUNDSON

OTHER BOOKS BY ERIK STENSLAND

I f you enjoyed this book, you might enjoy some others by Erik Stensland. These can all be purchased through the bookstores in and around Rocky Mountain National Park, through the Rocky Trail Press website, or whever books are sold.

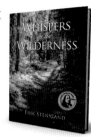

Whispers in the Wilderness explores the longing that many of us have for the natural world and suggests that it is the trailhead for a journey to wholeness. Through short daily reflections on the natural world paired with gorgeous photographs from Rocky Mountain National Park, author and photographer Erik Stensland encourages us to go deeper within ourselves and discover the healing that nature is offering. – Winner of four national awards!

Wild Light is a large hardcover book that celebrates the beauty of Rocky. It was ten years in the making, covering every region, ecosystem, and season through stunning photographs and beautiful prose. If you love Rocky Mountain National Park, you'll want this gorgeous book on your coffee table.

The Landscape Photographer's Guide to Photographing Rocky Mountain National Park – Are you planning a visit to Rocky Mountain National Park? Do you want to take stunning photos of this incredible landscape? Then you will want to get a copy of this one-of-a-kind book telling you where to go and when to be there. In it you'll learn lots of helpful insights that you would only gain by having lived here yourself.

Memories of Rocky Mountain National Park
– Relive your visit to Rocky Mountain National
Park, one of America's most loved national parks,
with this attractive paperback photo book. This
book is a great memory of your visit and is also
a great gift for friends or family who love Rocky
Mountain National Park.

Yearly Calendars – With our scenic calendars, you can enjoy a
year-long journey through the heart of Rocky Mountain National
Park. You'll experience rarely seen views from one of America's
favorite national parks. From tranquil snow-covered forests to the
flower-carpeted meadows of summer, celebrate the beauty of our
natural world.

Available at **RockyTrailPress.com**

or wherever books are sold.

GALLERY INFO

If you visit Estes Park, Colorado, make sure you pay a visit to my gallery, "Images of RMNP". Here you will find a large number of fine-art photographs that are perfect for your home or office. We also have books, cards, calendars, and much more. We're located at 203 Park Lane, Estes Park, CO.

If you are on the west side of Rocky you can visit my gallery space inside Studio 8369 at 1117 Grand Avenue, Grand Lake, CO.

You can also visit us online at: **ImagesofRMNP.com** or follow us on the main social networking sites.

NATURE FIRST

The Alliance for Responsible Nature Photography

Be Part of the Solution

Throughout the world we are seeing a growing impact on our world's wild and natural lands. The reasons behind this are complex, but some of the factors include:

- The popularity of social media and ease of sharing photos and location information online
- A significant rise in the popularity of photography
- Sharp increases in the number of visitors to public lands and wild places
- Lack of widespread knowledge of basic stewardship practices and outdoor ethics.

As a result of these factors and others, we have reached a point at which both visitors and photographers are causing extensive and negative impacts on the natural world. Many photographers are trampling wild lands, ignoring regulations, damaging sensitive areas, interrupting and

diminishing the experiences of other users, disturbing wildlife, and inviting (implicitly or explicitly) the public to do the same.

Photographers were once leaders in protecting our world's wild places and so to see the nature photography community contributing to the destruction of these places is deeply disturbing. In 2017 a group of passionate nature photographers gathered in Ridgway, Colorado to try and find a way to change this trend. The result of their effort was a set of best practices that could reduce their impact and help the photo community regain their role as ambassadors for nature.

Seven principles were crafted to help guide both professional and recreational photographers in sustainable, minimal impact practices. These principles were designed to promote awareness of potenital impact and at the same time be flexible enough to apply to varying situations across the globe. While seemingly simple, these principles can make a significant difference to the natural world.

Visit the Nature First website to read about these principles in more detail.

PRINCIPLES:

 1. Prioritize the well-being of nature over photography.

 2. Educate yourself about the places you photograph.

 3. Reflect on the possible impact of your actions.

 4. Use discretion if sharing locations.

 5. Know and follow rules and regulations.

 6. Always follow Leave No Trace principles and strive to leave places better than you found them.

 7. Actively promote and educate others about these principles.

Join the movement...take the pledge:
https://NatureFirstPhotography.org

Love Rocky Mountain National Park?

If you have walked the **Lily Lake Trail,** explored the **Fall River Visitor Center** or introduced a child to nature through the park's **Junior Ranger** program, you know our work. We are thousands of dedicated, passionate members and donors working tirelessly to meet the unmet needs of Rocky Mountain National Park and other public lands partners.

Public Lands Partner

The Rocky Mountain Conservancy is a vibrant, growing organization with an active core membership of nearly 3,000 individuals and families, and an additional 14,000+ contributors, including individuals, corporations, local businesses and foundations. These park aficianodos support Rocky Mountain National Park through through their donations and memberships to the Conservancy.

How we work

The Conservancy operates Nature Stores at Rocky Mountain National Park and other public lands in Colorado and Wyoming. In addition to providing visitor services, educational publications and mementos, these stores provide funds that support the interpretive programs at the sites where they are located. Profits from these earned income activities also underwrite Conservancy operations and mission-driven programs ensuring that a greater share of philanthropic donations directly fund projects in and around Rocky Mountain National Park.

Signature programs and projects:

- Land Protection
- Historic Preservation
- Trail Improvement
- Next Generation Fund
- Conservation Corps
- Field Institute
- Publications
- Membership

Learn more at RMConservancy.org

ROCKY MOUNTAIN CONSERVANCY

Rocky Mountain Conservancy Programs

Rocky Mountain National Park Fund
Since 1985, the Conservancy has raised more than $20 million for more than fifty projects in Rocky Mountain National Park, from trail improvements and land protection to Junior Ranger and other youth programs.

Conservancy Conservation Corps
The Conservation Corps provides a unique service-learning experience for college students interested in natural resource conservation. For eleven weeks, crews work in Rocky Mountain National Park and national forests building and maintaining trails, restoring native habitat and learning from expert researchers and staff.

RMNP License Plates
Spearheading and managing this license plate program has proven to be a winner! More than 6,500 plates have been claimed to date, with 100% of the $30 donations earmarked for park projects.

Field Institute programs
Through half-day, day-long and multi-day classes and tours, park visitors can explore a wide range of topics through outdoor educational adventures and tours in the park, including hiking and skill-building, photography, art, natural history and cultural history.

Retail and Publications
Since 1931, the Conservancy has provided park-related educational products and publications to serve visitors andsupport the park's educational mission.

ROCKY MOUNTAIN CONSERVANCY